INTRODUCTION TO EDUCATIONAL GERONTOLOGY

Edited by

RONALD H. SHERRON
Virginia Commonwealth University

D. BARRY LUMSDEN
North Texas State University

With a Foreword by

ROSALIND K. LORING
President, Adult Education Association of the U.S.A.

HEMISPHERE PUBLISHING CORPORATION

Washington   London

To my parents and children, Gina and Danny (DBL)

To all of us who are certainly aging (RHS)

Hemisphere Publishing Corporation
1025 Vermont Avenue, N.W., Washington, D.C. 20005

1 2 3 4 5 6 7 8 9 0   L I L I   7 8 3 2 1 0 9 8

Library of Congress Cataloging in Publication Data
Main entry under title:

Introduction to educational gerontology.

Includes bibliographies and indexes.
1. Gerontology—Studies and teaching—United States.
2. Education of the aged.   I. Sherron, Ronald H.
II. Lumsden, D. Barry.
HQ1064.U5I59   362.6′042′0715   78-13292
ISBN 0-89116-101-5

Printed in the United States of America

CONTENTS

FOREWORD

In our fast-moving, constantly changing, youth-oriented nation, our society is aging. A greater proportion of people today than ever before in the history of this country are living past middle age. Dramatic medical breakthroughs have extended the ordinary life-span by 20 years. At the turn of the century, 1 in every 25 residents of the United States was over 65. Today, the ratio is nearly 1 in 10. By the year 2000, it will be 1 in 9. Future senior citizens will make up an even more significant portion of this country's human resources. This aging society, now and into the next century, can become our problem or our pride.

It is true that many of our aged are hampered by poverty, physical disability, or other afflictions; so they cannot survive without substantial direct help. But the vast majority, through education and human services assistance, can enhance their own capacities for adjustment and independent living and need not be daunted by the problems of aging.

Mature citizens of this generation have revamped and relearned lifestyles through several major wars, a devastating depression, the fear of possible nuclear annihilation, upheavals of social values, dislocations of family, job mobility, and the stresses both economic and psychological of this swift-moving time. Added to these major changes have been the necessity to combat the negative aspects of aging, the dangers of human obsolescence, the alienation of the aging parent in today's disrupted family, the loss of esteem brought on by forced retirement, serial employment, the shifting nature and values of life trends, and the midlife crises that occur so frequently between the ages of 35 and 55.

Adult educators have put forth intensive efforts to alert the community on campus and off, as well as their own faculties and administrators, to deal with our aging population in a positive, upbeat manner. Through education they have shown that the midlife and later years can become a growing, expanding, fulfilling venture instead of a depressing, downhill road.

As the issues of aging have become more clearly defined and our analysis more sophisticated, innovative educators have been quick to sense the need to overhaul our learning systems to accommodate older students throughout the nation who are returning in increasingly greater numbers to some type of educational experience. This new surge of adult students toward our campuses and community centers, combined with the new seeking of reeducation to improve the quality of life, is a milestone in our more positive attitudes toward maturity.

Only a few years back, 1957 in Los Angeles, I planned a conference to discuss the problems of the aged and aging in our learning programs. That program was a fiasco, a conference to which nobody came. Our educators, our community leaders, and our government officials were concerned only with our under 30 society. The word "gerontology" was distantly heard. Age and the study of it were disdained, it seemed.

It has taken prodding and recruiting with repeated attempts at communication to bring to the attention of our higher institutions of learning, of our federal government, and even of our professionals in the field of human services that there is a vital group of people in our social structure who are no longer young, who are deserving of attention, and who are still ascending, not declining. Considering the number of older adults in our society and the sweeping benefits learning can bring to this group, current efforts have fallen sadly short of the adult educators' goals.

Yet there are promising beginnings in every agency offering human services, both public and private. They are opening up existing programs for older people, making it easier for them by tailoring the programs to this new audience. As national concern grows and essential human services are better provided by health, welfare, transportation, nutrition, housing, and other agencies, new opportunities for education and learning are created. The recent federal legislation delaying enforced retirement is one more step toward recognizing the potential of our aging citizenry.

Although what happens after midlife is the responsibility of the individual, learning and the opportunities education has to offer provide the pathway toward maintaining vitality and the process of growth. Adult educators for the past decade have advocated reeducation of our older citizens, whether it be in the realm of job retraining, the pursuit of new second careers, or the renewal of aspirations via new hobbies and adult games. By regrooming of both mental and physical capacities, rehabilitation of the life force occurs for more satisfying later years. All of this can come about only through understanding, research, study, exploration, and intercommunication between the practitioners and their target clientele. Gerontologists have blazed the trail to entice and enrich the lives and minds of our older citizens, but they have also encouraged more education for the educators and social service workers, and for those professionals engaged in all branches of human services.

If we believe that 20 million older Americans can solve their problems and expand their personal lives primarily through their own efforts, then mobilizing the information contained in this volume has a deep central purpose. The editors, Ronald H. Sherron and D. Barry Lumsden—adult educators and researchers in the field of gerontology—have fashioned this highly relevant, sensitive subject matter and covered its many facets in this important introductory book. They bring it to the forefront at a time when the aging adult has, at last, been singled out as a subject of national concern.

The genesis of this volume began at the First National Conference on Educational Gerontology in Virginia Beach, Virginia in June 1976. This highly successful meeting, where adult educators could articulate, explore, and exchange information on problems and philosophy, survival needs, and methods of enriching the lifestyle of our older citizens, met with such enthusiastic response that the editors decided to publish, under one cover, the papers presented there. Then, with additional studies recruited from adult educators from colleges and universities across the nation, the book was developed to its present form.

The Adult Education Association of the U.S.A. is pleased to cosponsor this publication. As an organization, we have been much involved in the study of the best ways to provide education for older citizens, and we think this is a significant addition to the literature of the field.

Rosalind K. Loring
President, Adult Education Association of the U.S.A.
October 1977

PREFACE

Educational gerontology is a dynamic, fast-growing, new branch of social gerontology. No longer can the educational needs and interests of older adults go unattended. Around the world today, public and private agencies and institutions are becoming increasingly aware of their responsibilities, both delegated and voluntary, to provide learning opportunities for and about the aged.

The major purpose of this book is to provide a general overview of the program development process and an in-depth treatment of essential program factors involved in planning, implementing, managing, and evaluating educational programs for the aging. This book is designed to serve as an introductory text for first courses in educational gerontology and as an initial orientation for administrators, counselors, and other practitioners responsible for planning and conducting educational programs for and about the elderly.

It is our sincere hope that this new volume will excite its readers as much as its preparation did its contributors and editors. It is also our hope that in some significant way this book will further contribute to the establishment of educational gerontology as a legitimate and academically respectable branch of social gerontology.

Ronald H. Sherron
D. Barry Lumsden

1

TOWARD A DEFINITION OF EDUCATIONAL GERONTOLOGY

DAVID A. PETERSON

University of Nebraska at Omaha

Educational gerontology is one of the most recent additions to the growing list of terms that are beginning to form the categories and subcategories of the field of study and practice related to the processes of human aging. Like such terms as *social gerontology, industrial gerontology,* and *psychogerontology,* the adjective *educational* is used to denote a restricted set of perspectives and activities that has come into prominence of late and that offers both academic and professional opportunities. As both interest in the interrelated stages of human development and action to improve the quality of life for older people have become widespread, educational institutions and methods have gained a significant place.

Technological developments often lead to social problems. The problems typically go unrecognized or ignored until they reach crisis proportions. The plight of the aged in this country has recently flashed across the public consciousness as one of these social problems. Their difficulties with income maintenance in retirement, transportation inadequacies, impingement of crime on their personal freedom, deterioration of their health, and access to medical services, as well as their difficulties with housing, leisure, family, and dependency, have led to this recognition. Government and voluntary programs, hurriedly established to ameliorate the worst of these maladies, are generally remedial efforts focusing only on short-term measures and restricted to contemporary problems that plague the current cohort. Little of a preventive nature has been undertaken.

Educational programs, on the other hand, provide an exception to the typical approach. They have been developed in a manner that addresses current needs but that incorporates the potential for longer term solutions to problems. They affirm the positive nature of humans at whatever age by drawing upon the potential that resides within each individual so that growth and development may result. This focus upon the potential of each individual offers hope for both the long and the short run. Howard McClusky, an educator whose life and writings attest to this viewpoint, summarizes this position as follows:

When we turn to education we find a more optimistic domain. In fact, education is itself essentially an affirmative enterprise. For instance, education for older persons is based on the assumption that it will lead to something better in the lives of those participating. It also proceeds on the collateral assumption that older persons are capable of a constructive response to educational stimulation. Thus, because of its faith in the learning ability of older persons and, because of its confidence in the improvement that results from learning, education, in contrast with other areas in the field of aging, can be invested with a climate of optimism which is highly attractive to those who may be involved in its operation. (McClusky, 1973)

In seeking the unique contribution that education can make to the field of gerontology, we immediately reach the heart of the matter—that the last of life is populated by more than problems and decline. The final stages of life are an opportunity for integration or summing up, for seeking the meanings that have been avoided or postponed. Education can be a means of facilitating this reflection and insight. It can offer an understanding of the contemporary changes in the social order and a mechanism of adjustment to those changes. It deals with social problems but provides a way to transcend them. Education, then, is a viable approach to problems in the fields of aging and gerontology. In this chapter, the history of this development is outlined and the parameters, activities, problems, and future of these affirmative undertakings are described.

THE ANTECEDENTS OF
EDUCATIONAL GERONTOLOGY

Educational activities in the field of aging, like many programmatic interventions that have resulted from the perceived needs of others, have been viewed somewhat differently by various observers and commentators. Probably the first institutional use of the term *educational gerontology* was at the University of Michigan where a graduate program of instruction bearing that name was established within the School of Education in 1970. This was undertaken as a cooperative endeavor of the School and the Institute of Gerontology and has continued to enroll many students. Use of the term quickly spread beyond Michigan and doubtless was spontaneously generated in several locations at approximately the same time. This occurrence reflected the substantial interest and burgeoning activity in this area, which has needed only modest effort to move toward an organized interface between the fields of gerontology and education.

Only recently has an awareness of the unique problems and potential of people in the later stages of life occurred. The twentieth century is the first time in history that the size of the older population and the extent of retirement from fulltime work have become important. Previously, the preponderance of individuals worked throughout their life, so the roles they carried and the services they required necessitated little change in social or family functioning as they grew old. During the past few decades, however, the situation has been drastically altered. Family disintegration, retirement economics, and the extension of life have vastly multiplied the size and the deprivation of this older group. A cursory review of the genesis of these developments will provide some understanding of the forces that have caused these changes to occur and have attracted the interest of many professional groups. Educators, as one of these potential service groups, have finally begun to accept the role that is available to them in assisting older people.

The growth of the social problem and the educational opportunity that is referred to as retirement was facilitated by five major events that occurred within the Western world. Atchley (1976) describes these events as: (1) the development of an economic surplus and the acceptance of the concept of property in agrarian society, (2) the increase in productivity resulting from industrialization, (3) the lengthening of the life-span through improved public health and sanitation, (4) the redistribution of wealth that accompanied the rise of labor unions and government, and (5) the decline of the concept of craftsmanship and the meaning of work. Each of these events built upon the preceding ones in a manner that allowed the development of the leisure period we call retirement.

To leave the labor force during the later years of life, it was first necessary for sufficient economic surpluses to be available. Because most people made their living from the land, these surpluses originated with the development of improved agricultural processes and the expansion of farming into the fertile Great Plains. Land became a valuable asset, and older people typically retained ownership of the arable acreage after they had relinquished the labor to their children. Thus, they were assured of a continuing income during their later years.

Industrialization modified the family agrarian system and created a drastically increased economic surplus. Expanded use of water, coal, and electrical power fostered the creation of massive productive complexes that created cities, drawing younger people away from the family and the rural environment. Although life seemed better in the urban areas, as people retired they discovered that they had few economic resources to replace the lost wages.

A portion of the increased national resources were directed toward improved understanding of communicable disease and the control of the most feared child killers. Increased hygiene, disease prevention, and improved health care extended the life expectancy of younger people; as a result, there was a massive increase in the number of individuals surviving until adulthood. Obviously, this allowed the growth of the older population that we have experienced during the past 75 years.

Realignment of wealth from agriculture to corporate boardrooms changed the relationship of the average citizen to financial resources in later life. No longer able to rely on income from the land, the workers found that labor union and government support were necessary to wrest from big business a share of the riches created by our abundant natural resources and technological ingenuity. Pensions and government retirement benefits provided a measure of security in later life so that the typical wage earner left the work force by the age of 65.

The final event was the decline of the craft form of production, which gave workers a feeling of satisfaction and achievement as it provided a source of income. As mass production and specialization of labor occurred, the workers found that their contributions to the final product were totally indistinguishable. Their commitment to the task suffered as they lost the satisfaction that accompanied precise workmanship. Increasingly, employees were deprived of part of the meaning of life as the earning of income was separated from the satisfaction of craftsmanship. Work consequently became a drudgery that many chose to leave, at the first opportunity, for retirement or unemployment.

These technological and social developments have fundamentally modified the position older people hold in the contemporary United States. Rather than being the conservators of property and wealth, they have been forced to rely upon the generosity of employers or the largess of federal programs to meet economic needs. No longer perceived as the repositories of the wisdom and knowledge of the culture, they have been relegated to the category of retired people who formerly were productive citizens. Instead of being the purveyors of the culture and the educators of the young, they have found their skills outmoded and their experience sought only for oral histories of the old days.

Development of Interest in Aging

The development of the field of gerontology over the past 25 years has brought a glimmer of change to this depressing situation. In addition to noting the afflictions of our older citizens, some academic and professional groups have emphasized the potential that lies within the older generations and have attempted to formulate methodologies for tapping that underdeveloped resource. In particular, people whose major professional commitment is channeled through institutions of education have begun to recognize that the values of study, learning, and intellectual growth are not restricted exclusively to the young but have relevance to persons of every age. This awareness appears to be most pronounced at the fringes of educational development, e.g., in the areas of adult, continuing, and community education. Professionals in these fields are constantly challenged to meet the learning needs of adult, mid-career, employed, or retired individuals, i.e., of the nontraditional student.

A small but dynamic field of educational practice has developed during this century that concentrates on the education of mature individuals. This field, generally termed *adult,* or *continuing, education,* was initiated in response to the need for citizenship education of the masses of immigrants who entered this country during the early years of the twentieth century. These activities soon expanded to include literacy education of those who had not had the opportunity of formal schooling. A variety of programmatic and organizational developments followed: family education by the Cooperative Extension Service; religious education by churches and synagogues; retraining of workers by business and industry; credit courses given by extension programs through off-campus, correspondence, and media formats; and a diversity of noncredit education for individuals who had family, employment, personal, or financial limitations to fulltime student status.

Although the literature describing these developments makes appropriate mention of the need for and the value of education at every stage of life, most of the programming was, in reality, designed for and appropriate to younger and middle-aged adults (Smith, Aker, & Kidd, 1970). Awareness of the value of education for people already retired increased during the 1950s (see Hunter, 1974). Educational programs designed for older people were initiated in several locations, and development at the national level was significantly facilitated by the publication of Donahue's (1955) pioneering book, *Education for Later Maturity,* which provided both a theoretical and a practical description of educational programs for older people. It is sobering to review the large number of programs Donahue's book describes and to realize that many of the innovative activities of today were operating 20 years ago.

The number of educational experiences available to older adults has continued to grow, although the 1950s and the 1970s have been the times of greatest development. The 1971 White House Conference on Aging provided a substantial impetus in this direction by raising the nation's awareness of older people; it was especially influential in the educational area because a large number of its recommendations related the value of education to the various categories of needs examined by the delegates (*Toward a National Policy,* 1973). Education for older people subsequently gained a legitimacy it had not previously attained, and this has led to the expansion of existing programs and the initiation of literally hundreds of new undertakings during the past five years.

This expansion was doubtless facilitated by a new receptivity of educational institutions to serving new groups of clientele. Institutions of higher education are realizing that preadulthood education no longer suffices to equip the individual for all the personal or vocational adjustments that will occur over the life-span. Educational services need to be made available to nondegree, part-time students in order for them to succeed in this rapidly changing society (Hesburgh, Miller, & Wharton, 1973). Education has become such a necessary and integral part of life for most Americans that this is now being called a "learning society," one in which continued education through the life-span is, not only a privilege, but a right (Cross, 1974). This development has come at a time when the traditional clientele of higher education (18–22 year olds) is declining both in absolute numbers and in the proportion enrolling in college. Reduced matriculation of young adults has forced public and private educational institutions to recognize another clientele, the mature and even the older adult, as the most receptive audience for the expansion of educational programming. Thus, through happenstance, the needs of older people and the needs of educational institutions conveniently mesh and may be predicted to lead toward the development of a significant symbiotic relationship in the years just ahead.

Concurrent with these developments, agencies offering social and health services to older people have realized that these services will succeed only if the most rigorous and intensive planning accompanies their development. This will be achieved through the preparation and employment of highly skilled professionals who understand the uniqueness of the older clientele. Unfortunately, professionals with this background are rare, so most services are delivered by those who must learn and serve simultaneously. The outcome has been a record of less-than-complete success, which has somewhat reduced the enthusiasm both of funding agencies and of the clientele served.

In an attempt to remedy this situation, institutions of higher education have created undergraduate, graduate, and continuing education endeavors designed to prepare professionals for planning, administration, and delivery of services. These gerontology education efforts vary considerably from one institution to another but typically include close working relationships with service agencies in order to provide field experience and job opportunities for their students. Higher education's response to this need for knowledgeable personnel is another indication of institutional willingness to adjust to protect its own existence. By initiating new instructional areas to appeal to new clientele, higher education can both be responsive to real needs and bolster its vulnerable position in the years ahead.

Thus, the birth of educational gerontology has occurred at a time when the number and proportion of the current population over 65 has increased; when there are significant concerns about the quality of life of older people in the United States; when the realization of the potential that lies within this group has become widespread; when the need for additional, expanded services for older people is recognized; and when the value of personnel educated in gerontology has gained acceptance. Educational gerontology is a fragmented, unorganized, and very youthful response to these developments, but a response that has shown such vigor and promise that it is appropriate to begin to examine more closely its definition, purpose, and extent.

Terminology

Gerontology is a young field that has experienced spectacular growth over the past two decades. The field has generated a nomenclature that is not always precise and that frequently contributes to misunderstanding and confusion. This occurs when terms such as *aging* and *aged* are used interchangeably and when concepts such as *field of aging* are accorded varying connotations. To reduce misunderstanding within this chapter at least, seven of these terms are briefly defined here.

Aging is a word that has many meanings applied to it; here it is used to refer to the physical, psychological, and social processes of growing older that begin at conception and continue until death. *Aged,* on the other hand, is used to refer to that group of people who are already very old, say beyond 75 or 80 years of age—that group often referred to as the "old-old." *Older people* refers to all people who are retirement age (typically 65) or above.

The *field of aging* is a phrase that receives substantial use. Here, it refers to that group of personnel and agencies that offers human services to older people and that comprises the advocacy system for this older group. Educational institutions may provide a direct service to older people and, consequently, be part of the field of aging. A *gerontologist,* however, may or may not be a part of that field. Gerontologists are faculty or staff of institutions of higher education (or related organizations) who are primarily involved in instruction or conducting research. They are expected to have special knowledge about the processes of aging and/or about planning and executing service programs for older people. They may conduct *training* which is an instructional activity designed to develop a skill or to prepare individuals for specific occupational roles, or *education,* which is a broader approach and provides understandings and knowledge over a wider range of topics. *Gerontology Education,* then, is the process of instructing professionals and paraprofessionals who are expected to gain employment in the field of aging. It is not typically geared to training individuals for roles in specific agencies or services.

A review of the literature of continuing education and gerontology has uncovered no definitions of the parameters of the field. Consequently, the following definition is proposed as a starting point for future discussions on the topic. *Educational gerontology* may be defined as the study and practice of instructional endeavors for and about aged and aging individuals. It can be viewed as having three distinct, although interrelated, aspects: (1) educational endeavors designed for people who are middle aged and older, (2) educational endeavors for a general or specific public about aging and older people, and (3) educational preparation of people who are working or intend to be employed in service to older people in professional or paraprofessional capacities. These three aspects include those undertakings that are most central yet most descriptive of the field. Although some writers might opt to exclude the second or third aspect, both aspects do appear to be intimately interrelated and most difficult to exclude when one considers the role of education in the field of aging. Thus, educational gerontology is an attempt to interface the process and institutions of education with the knowledge and need of human aging so that the quality of life of older citizens can be improved. By its very nature, education is a preventive, anticipatory mechanism; consequently, educational gerontology includes concern for the successful aging of each of us, young or old.

EDUCATION FOR OLDER PEOPLE

Educational gerontology has developed from relatively new fields—adult education and social gerontology. The interface of these two fields is of recent origin, so it is not surprising that the confluence has less precision than might be desired. Like the proverbial elephant, the field is described differently by various observers. A review of the literature of continuing education, for instance, indicates that educational gerontology is an extension of adult education into the later stages of life. Lifelong education, as it is now called, has gained widespread attention (Curtis & Wartgow, 1972; Ecklund, 1969; Havighurst, 1970; Hesburgh et al., 1973; Houle, 1974; Huberman, 1974) and is currently being encouraged by many educational institutions.

A review of the literature on education for older people reveals a predominant emphasis on programmatic reports of projects that are typically unique to a particular environment and whose success or failure is measured in the number of participants and their expressed satisfaction with the educational endeavor (Anonymous, 1968; Donahue, 1954; Easter, 1974; Helling & Bauer, 1972; Kauffman & Luby, 1974; Mason, 1970; Pattison, 1973; Scott, 1974; Uphaus, 1971). The projects described are diverse but generally adhere to the format of adult education—informal, noncredit, short-series courses that attempt to keep pressure and anxiety to a minimum (Hixson, 1969; Norton, 1970; Scott, 1974). Many instructional activities appear to vary from one year to the next, depending upon the instructor and the participants. Some are difficult to distinguish from recreation programs, and most emphasize social participation and enjoyment and downplay intellectual rigor. In several locations, substantial catalogs of courses have been developed; these often appear to be the product of one charismatic coordinator rather than to flow from the establishment of some instructional model or curricular innovation that has engendered clientele support.

The content of the programs varies from one sponsor to another, but often focuses upon expressive outcomes—ones that are expected to have some intrinsic meaning to the individuals and that are not likely to require deferred gratification (Londoner, 1971). Many organizations have attempted to determine the wants of the people involved and have developed instructional programs of an instrumental nature, i.e., designed to overcome problem areas or have value outside the educational setting (Hiemstra, 1972).

Sponsorship of these educational activities is widely dispersed. Literally hundreds of institutions of higher education have become heavily involved in the past few years, as a recent survey indicates (Association for Gerontology in Higher Education, 1976). Community and junior colleges, as well as public schools with a community education emphasis have been especially responsive to this developing interest. Many of these institutions have created educational programs exclusively for older people; others have offered tuition discounts or waivers as an inducement for older people to enroll in their regular course offerings (Academy for Educational Development, 1974; DeCrow, n.d.; Hendrickson & Barnes, 1964; Korim, 1974; Myran, Huber, & Sweeney, 1971). Although these activities are still the exception and provide a sense of great pride to the local institution, they are becoming increasingly more common as the interest of this new clientele is recognized.

Voluntary associations, government-funded projects, and community agencies have also taken the lead in many areas in developing programs with appeal for that portion of the older population that they serve. Churches, YM-YWCAs, senior centers, area agencies on aging, community action programs, nutrition projects, Cooperative Extension, libraries, senior councils, and associations of older people offer numerous education experiences to retirees and to those who are approaching old age. This plethora of sponsors injects such diversity into the level, format, and focus of the programs as to make any generalization on the quality of instruction extremely difficult.

Older People
as Educational Participants

Historically, older people have not been conspicuous consumers of educational services. In fact, they have been significantly underrepresented participants in instructional offerings of educational and community institutions. A 1969 study by the U.S. Bureau of the Census (Okes, 1971) indicated that 11% of the population over 17 years of age who were not full-time students participated in some form of organized, adult education activity annually. There was, however, an inverse relationship between age and educational participation, i.e., the older the person, the less likely the involvement in organized education. For people over age 65, only 1.6% participated (Okes, 1971). Other studies have shown a similar low level of participation (Johnstone & Rivera, 1965). The causes of this phenomenon were not explored in these studies.

Other researchers have suggested that the statistics on educational participation significantly understate the amount of learning done by older people. They have shown that adults are more likely to choose individual approaches to learning than to enroll in organized courses of study. Hiemstra's (1975) research indicates that the average older person undertakes at least three self-motivated learning projects, which consume a total of 324 hours annually. This amount of learning involvement is substantially more than was recognized by the Census Bureau or by Johnstone and Rivera. The definitions of education and of learning projects appear to be the variable that causes this discrepancy. By defining participation differently, it is possible to substantially alter the statistics on the mean amount of involvement by the older person.

Purposes of Education
in Later Life

In recent years, numerous forces have combined to encourage greater educational participation by people in the later years. Birren and Woodruff (1973) identified six major reasons for this increased involvement: (1) the changing age structure of society, (2) an increasing educational level (and subsequent interest in education) of aging cohorts, (3) the rapidity of social change, (4) career-pattern changes, (5) the expanding role of women, and (6) the changed attitudes toward education. In addition to these, educational institutions' willingness to attempt nontraditional approaches, their need to recruit alternative student groups to offset declining enrollment, and their desire to relate more closely to the needs of their clientele all have helped them to see older people as a potential audience.

The educational programming for middle-aged and older people that has been developing is based on the premise that adults of every age have some needs that can best be met through an increase in skills and knowledge. Various writers have identified educational needs of people in the later years. Donahue (1952), Ecklund (1969), Frank (1955), and Stanford (1972) have stressed its usefulness in coping with changes in later life; Peterson (1975) and Somers (1966) have suggested the vocational advantages associated with education; Sarvis (1973) and McClusky (1974) have identified the need for education so that older people can continue to contribute to their society. Each of these are real needs; the ability of education to meet them will significantly influence the quality of life of older adults.

Moody (1976), in an insightful article, provides conceptual categorizations of four modal patterns for treatment of the aged. He identifies the characteristics and the basic attitudes of these modal patterns and relates them to the philosophical purposes for which education is provided. In this way, he provides a hierarchy of educational pursuits that can be used to ascertain programmatic appropriateness. His first pattern is titled "rejection and neglect of older people," and he suggests that it has resulted in age segregation, poverty, and neglect. No rationale for education of older people can be identified in this pattern inasmuch as the usefulness of older individuals is foreshortened. The second pattern is titled "social services," and it is typified by transfer payments and community services developed by liberals to make life better for older people. Education, in this case, is provided to further leisure-time pursuits, to keep people busy, and to entertain those who have extensive time to fill. *Participation* is the third pattern; it includes second careers and social advocacy designed to increase the social integration of older people. Educational endeavors would include consciousness raising, the provision of advocacy skills, and retraining for continued work roles. Moody suggests that *self-actualization* is the fourth pattern and that is accompanied by psychological growth, self-transcendence, and ego integrity. Education for this pattern would be the means of encouraging self-understanding and insight, probably drawing heavily from the content of the humanities. It is his suggestion that educators providing programs for older people need to examine more closely the purposes they have for these activities in order to assure themselves that they are not perpetuating modal patterns that are inappropriate and outmoded.

Preparation for Retirement

One area of education for older people that reveals more consistency and growth than others is that of preparation for retirement. It has been developed by businesses, associations of retirees, labor unions, and educational institutions, and it shows considerable planning and some evaluation (Fillenbaum, 1971; Hunter, 1974; Kalt & Kohn, 1975; Kasschau, 1974; Kauffman, 1970; Kelleher & Quirk, 1974; Manion, 1974; Morkert, 1974; Monk, 1972).

Major surveys of retirement preparation programs in industry have revealed that many of the larger corporations do offer some type of planning program but that these typically are limited to the economic aspects of retirement (Bankers Trust Co., 1970; Francke, 1962; Pyron, 1969; Pyron & Manion, 1970). Programs sponsored by the labor unions appear to have the same limitation and do not include much content on the issues of social integration, family reorientation, physical change, psychological adjustment, and securing meaning from life (Clague, Palli, & Kramer, 1971; Greene, Pyron, & Manion, 1969; O'Rourke & Freedman, 1972).

University programs have typically been more comprehensive than those of companies and unions, and they have had more rigorous evaluation attached to them (Bolton, 1976; Charles, 1971; Greene et al., 1969; Hunter, 1968; Simpson, Back, & McKinney, 1966). However, even these endeavors have not lent themselves to replicable evaluation because the program methodology often involves a series of lectures by content experts who doubtless vary in quality, preparation, and instructional capabilities. In order to minimize this instructor variance, other approaches to retirement preparation are needed that can provide the consistency required. One approach to this problem is the set of educational materials, titled "Planning and the Third Age," that has been designed and evaluated by the University of Nebraska at Omaha Gerontology Program. Although continuing evaluation is under way, Bolton's (1976) report of seven pilot programs indicates the consistency and positive results of the methods and materials.

Research on Learning and Intelligence

Universities have indirectly encouraged the development of education for older people through extensive research on the continuing ability of people to learn regardless of their age (Arenberg, 1973; Baltes & Labouvie, 1973; Bromley, 1974; Palmore, 1970). An outmoded but still prevalent stereotype holds that older people are incapable of learning or changing their behavior and that time so increases the inflexibility of individuals as to render educational undertakings useless. Until this misconception could be overcome, there was little support for the development of educational programs for pre- or postretirees. The research on learning, memory, and intelligence, then, played a key role in clearing the way for current developments.

The changes that occur in intelligence over the life-span have been extensively studied. Early research suggested a substantial decline in IQ with increasing age. Recent studies have indicated that it is more appropriate to view intelligence as being composed of several "intelligences," some of which are more resistent to decline than others. "There is a general classic pattern of aging decline; verbal abilities show relatively little, if any, deficit with advancing age, but psychomotor abilities decline appreciably" (Botwinick, 1973, pp. 184–185). Some IQ subtests are timed and the speed of performance is a crucial variable. In these cases, older people do less well because they are slower in their behaviors. After reviewing the literature of the field, Botwinick concludes, "People of high initial level retain their verbal abilities when old and, while they decline in their preceptual-integrative abilities, the decline is not as great as that of their initially less able age peers" (p. 197).

Laboratory studies on learning of people in various age categories have also provided support for the idea of education for older people. The accumulated data indicate that both learning and performance continue at a high level for many older people. However, efficiency of their learning is not always comparable to that of younger people, and some assistance in modifying learning styles may be necessary. Arenberg and Robertson (1974) conclude their review of the learning literature by indicating that (1) older people can maintain and recall about as much information in their primary memory as can young adults; (2) rapid pacing of learning tasks generally proves to be a handicap to older people; (3) conditions that can increase the use of organizational strategies for handling incoming information improve memory for an older person; (4) learning of material that is contradictory to established habits or preconceived ideas is susceptible to interference, and thus, the learning is more difficult; and (5) retrieval of information from secondary memory is especially difficult for older people.

It is not apparent that the insights that may be drawn from the research on intelligence and learning have been extensively applied in educational programming for older people. This may have resulted from the researchers' hesitancy to suggest specific, usable techniques that are indicated by the findings. It may also be caused by the programmers' lack of familiarity with the extensive work that has been done. Obviously more applications of the findings need to be sought for the improvement of programs (Elias, 1974; Hickey & Spinetta, 1974; Urban & Watson, 1974).

One area in which some application has resulted from the research is in sensory changes that occur with age. Visual and auditory deterioration is normal and may reduce the ability of older individuals to take in the information presented in any educational program. Awareness of this phenomenon is widespread, and supplementary lighting, modification of materials, and amplification systems are quite commonly used. Recently, simulations of these perceptual changes have become available to program planners who wish to gain some depth of insight into the adjustments that older people must make (Shore, 1976).

EDUCATION ABOUT AGING

The second major dimension of the field of educational gerontology involves the general dissemination of knowledge about the processes of human aging and the facilitation of empathy toward those who are old. Because all people who survive sufficiently long will become old, educators have begun to recognize that awareness of the normal (as well as the potentially pathological) aspects of human aging may be useful in preparing for and adjusting to old age. It is anticipated that this awareness can serve the function of increasing the understanding of old age and might lead to improved attitudes and more realistic images of later life. It is hoped that, as more individuals realize their own relationship to old age, more of them will be willing to divert increased resources to the current older cohort so that these individuals may have a better life and also so that they themselves can look forward to a successful retirement.

It is generally accepted that the United States provides an example of a youth culture, one that confers reduced status, roles, and rewards on older people. This current situation is buttressed by widespread attitudes that predispose individuals to ignore or reject their own aging process and to put forth a facade of perpetual youth. These attitudes are evidenced early in life and are likely to continue throughout the entire life-span.

The mass media have not provided any stimulus to change these negative attitudes nor the inaccurate stereotypes that often accompany them. Media presentations of old age generally focus on the human interest aspects rather than on the needs, potential, or contributions of older people. The media have a particular role that they can play in the change of attitudes, yet current presentations, such as Johnny Carson's older lady sketches, do not assist in the improvement of attitudes. There is not, as yet, good data on the prevalence and influence of these forces because research on the media is only beginning to examine the roles older people play.

To assess the image of the elderly that is presented in the media, several content analyses have been undertaken. Northcott (1975), in an examination of older people on prime-time television, reported that senior citizens comprised only 1.5% of the role portrayals. He concluded that older people tended to be seen in contrast to a competent adult male and/or an attractive, young, adult female, rather than as individuals able to rely upon themselves.

In a brief review of television programming between 1969 and 1971, Aronoff (1974) found that only 4.9% of the characters were old. He concluded that aging in prime-time drama was associated with evil, failure, and unhappiness. "In a world of generally positive portrayals and happy endings, only 40 percent of the older male and even fewer female characters are seen as successful, happy, and good" (p. 87). Petersen's (1973) data do not support this negative conclusion. She reported that nearly 13% of the people appearing on prime-time television were over age 65 and over half of the role portrayals were favorable. She concluded that visibility of older people on television was proportionate to their numbers in the United States population and that existing programming projected a favorable image.

Studies of newspaper coverage of aging have been conducted by Evans, Evans, and Peterson (in press) and by Macdonald (1973). Macdonald's study categorized news articles that related to aging in a major midwestern daily newspaper over a three-month period and compared them with similar articles that appeared ten years earlier. His findings suggested that significant progress had not been achieved in attaining a sympathetic and balanced reporting of aging news. Evans and Evans, reporting on a content analysis of five major, metropolitan daily newspapers for the month of January 1975 and on two dailies for that month in 1970 and 1965, confirmed Macdonald's conclusion that no increase in coverage or balance in aging-related articles occurred over the period. They observed that some cities received coverage much superior to that received by others and suggested strategies to increase and improve aging coverage in the press.

Seltzer and Atchley (1971) examined a number of children's books that had been published over the last 100 years and reported that negative attitudes and stereotypes about older people were not as common as had been expected. Peterson and Karnes (1976), in a similar review of adolescent literature, found older women were underrepresented but that positive presentations of older people prevailed.

Although the commercial media have done little to improve attitudes toward the elderly, attempts have been made by agencies, organizations, and educational institutions concerned with the elderly to change attitudes. Even though there is a lack of conclusive data that indicate that attitudes are particularly susceptible to modification by public information, many attempts have nevertheless been made. Evaluation of these programs has typically been limited, and when evaluation is included in the programs, the results have been discouraging (Haskins, 1968; Klapper, 1960; Salcedo, 1973). The poor results are generally either because the message does not reach the intended audience, or because the audience is not at all receptive. Consequently the changes that result from communitywide, public education programs are usually unknown or unreported.

Educational institutions have attempted to overcome these drawbacks and improve attitudes toward older people by raising community awareness through workshops, conferences, classes, and educational television programming (Burdman, 1974; Donahue, 1967; Feltman, 1974; Jacobs, 1970; Jacobs, 1974; Smith and Barker, 1972; Wray, 1970). The number of these undertakings has increased rapidly during the past few years, but reports of the results have been limited to summaries of content and process and have included little indication of effectiveness.

There can be no doubt that substantial changes in the quality of life for older people will depend in large part upon the attitudes and stereotypes the general public holds toward older people. The recent National Council on the Aging (NCOA) national poll on aging confirms the misinformation and negative perceptions that exist (Harris & Associates, 1975). The current hit-and-miss planning is not likely to achieve the desired result. Even though information dissemination will expand, a more comprehensive approach is needed to raise awareness of the needs, to balance the positive and negative aspects of the aging process, and to emphasize the value of contemporary action aimed toward improving life for both current and future older cohorts.

EDUCATION OF PROFESSIONALS
AND PARAPROFESSIONALS

The last decade has witnessed a phenomenal growth in programs of gerontology instruction within institutions of higher education. These programs have provided both preservice education for individuals preparing to enter the field of aging and continuing education for those already holding professional or paraprofessional positions (Beattie, 1974; Birren & Gribbin, 1971; Hudis, 1974; Peterson, Donahue, & Tibbitts, 1972; Weg, 1972, 1973, 1974). Universities established the first of these education programs to prepare doctoral-level researchers in the biological and psychological sciences. More recently, universities have expanded professional instruction at the baccalaureate and master's levels, and community colleges and four-year institutions have initiated instruction in numerous applied areas at the associate and bachelor's level (Atchley & Seltzer, n.d.; Bullock & Bauman, 1974; Johnson, 1974; Schaie, 1974; Sinex, 1974; Thorson, 1973; Tillock, 1974; Wilson, 1974).

This preservice (or career) education has occurred and expanded primarily because of three interrelated developments:

1. For the first time, there is an accumulating body of systematic knowledge about older people and aging that has not been widely disseminated. Awareness of the rapid growth of this knowledge and of its perceived value to personnel in service and planning agencies has resulted in numerous attempts to organize it into courses, workshops, and publications.
2. Programs and services for older people have expanded quickly in most areas of the country. Effective operation requires qualified

personnel, yet there is little information available on which agencies and programs are proving viable and are likely to continue. Staffing requirements and workforce demands are not very clear but are being responded to in generic or temporary manners.

3. Programs and services for older people are demanding special skills and activities that require preparation.

Although these developments are still being analyzed, it is clear that some adjustment in traditional education is necessary. The recency and diversity of these preservice education programs has caused some confusion and conflict over (1) the most appropriate focus of instruction, (2) the purposes of the education, (3) the types of credentials and (4) the structural arrangements created to facilitate and administer these programs.

Focus of Instruction

Much of the current gerontology education has been stimulated by the federal government's attempts to increase the supply of trained workers and to bring the supply into line with the needs of present and developing service programs. As an increasing number and variety of planning and service agencies have developed, inadequate supplies of professionally prepared individuals to staff those agencies has resulted. Although the positions are eventually filled, many of those accepting major responsibilities have inadequate or inappropriate educational backgrounds, little relevant experience, or a lack of necessary skills. Several government agencies have provided financial support to educational institutions willing to develop didactic or clinical instruction; among these agencies are the National Institutes of Health, the Social and Rehabilitation Service, the Veterans Administration, and the Administration on Aging (Office of Management and Budget, 1975).

There has not developed among educational institutions, however, a clear consensus about whether these programs are primarily or solely directed toward meeting the workforce needs of certain federal programs. Many institutions have preferred to provide a cognitive understanding of the processes of aging, a sensitivity to the needs of older people, or affective experiences with retirees rather than to prepare individuals for specific positions in government programs (Donahue, 1967; Hudis, 1974; Seltzer, 1974). Although this appears to be the most appropriate alternative, many institutions continue to identify specific, current workforce shortages as the rationale for their instructional efforts.

Federal agencies encourage the latter approach by specifying workforce relevance as one of the criteria for funding approval (U.S. Department of Health, Education, and Welfare, 1976). Although, future employment projections and generic approaches are able to be incorporated, the focus on quantifiable workforce needs will continue to direct the focus of gerontology

education development so that some of the purposes of this instruction (identified below) will be minimized or ignored.

Purposes of Gerontology Education

The purposes of gerontology education are not explicitly described in the current literature; programs occasionally operate with their underlying instructional aims only hinted at in their accompanying descriptions. It would appear that there is no consensus on the priority or salient purposes for gerontology education, that, instead, programs with different disciplinary foci and at different levels incorporate varying aims. The following goals seem among the most common but are not presented as a definitive or exclusive list of those that guide current educational activity.

1. The purpose of much gerontology education is the provision of an understanding of aging as a natural and multifaceted process that affects all life. Emphasis is typically placed on the distinction between normal and pathological aspects of aging in the physical, psychological, and social areas. The developmental and dynamic aspects of aging and old age are conveyed through cognitive, affective, and experiential instruction, which is assumed to benefit learners by assisting them to better appreciate this aspect of the world of knowledge. In its pure form, the adherents to this purpose would assume that application of this body of knowledge to personal adjustment or service delivery would be the responsibility of the student.

2. A second purpose is the discrediting of inaccurate stereotypes and myths that surround old age and the replacement of these with an understanding of old age in the contemporary United States. The unique characteristics of the current cohort of older people are compared with older people in other cultures and at other times so that the universal nature of aging and the multitude of cultural and temporal variations can be identified.

3. A third purpose, one that is less often expressed but that appears to be present, is the underscoring of the value of the individual regardless of his or her age. In a youth culture, oldness is devalued. The gerontology education programs attempt to counteract this by emphasizing the value of the human life, the natural dignity of old age, and the potential of the later stages of life for older people and society.

4. Another purpose of gerontology education is to improve the quality of life in old age by disseminating knowledge and skills that will be useful in providing service to older people. Understandings of the history and legislation behind existing service programs, of the needs

for programmatic expansion or modification, and of appropriate service strategies are the outcomes of many instructional programs. This knowledge and skill is often accompanied by a commitment to action approaches that will solve the contemporary problems of older people.

5. Some gerontology education endeavors have, as their purpose, the development of knowledge and skill that will be used to expand or disseminate information. Training in these research and teaching areas, although only indirectly related to the lives of contemporary older people, also carries an action orientation in many institutions. Because practice can be improved primarily through research and instruction, preparation of individuals to successfully carry out these roles is badly needed.

6. Finally, much gerontology education has, as its purpose, the supplementation of professional or disciplinary instruction and the focusing of it on the older person. Gerontology education, in this regard, is viewed as a complementary area of study that allows the student to direct professional skills or knowledge toward a specific clientele group—older people. Thus, for example, counselors will learn in what ways their skills can best be utilized in working with older people and in what ways they need to modify traditional approaches. Gerontology education, then, is an attempt to sensitize professionals from several professional fields to the needs of older people and to encourage them to direct their skills toward helping older people.

Credentials

There does not appear at this time to be any clear or developing consensus within the field on the credential that should result from gerontology education. Some institutions offer a number of courses that may be combined in any way students choose; others offer a sequence that may result in a certificate or a specialization in aging. A few colleges and universities make an undergraduate or graduate major available, whereas others offer a degree, such as a master of gerontology.

This diversity makes it extremely difficult for students, gerontologists, and employers to be certain of the level of knowledge or skill that a student who has completed a gerontology education program has attained. In fact, there is no way to tell because the terms used have different meanings in various institutions. In the literature, no real movement can be found toward clarifying this situation by developing some standardization of terms and definitions. Therefore, the following four terms and definitions are suggested inasmuch as they seem consistent with at least some of the current practice:

1. *Gerontology course.* The unit of measure of gerontology instruction is the course. This may vary from one to four or more credit hours

but should have the processes of aging, the condition of older people, or the provision of service to people in the later years as the primary content of the instructional experience.

2. *Gerontology minor.* A minor would be designated as a planned sequence of courses, typically totaling from 12 to 18 hours of credit. This sequence could include credit for clinical or field experience and would usually be taken as an integral part of a degree program. The minor, inasmuch as the term has other denotations in some institutions, could also be referred to as a concentration or a specialization. It may be legitimated by having its receipt indicated on a transcript or by the provision of a certificate of completion.

3. *Gerontology major.* A major in gerontology would consist of an extensive sequence of courses totaling 24 or more hours of credit. Field or clinical work might be included, but gerontology course work would comprise the primary focus of the degree program. Although the diploma received upon graduation might only list a bachelor of arts or a master of science, for example, the transcript would indicate gerontology as the graduation major.

4. *Gerontology degree.* It may be anticipated that some institutions will choose to offer a degree in gerontology. This would involve a major in gerontology as well as appropriate supporting minors and general-education requirements. It would be evidenced by a diploma that would indicate a bachelor of arts in gerontology, a master of gerontology, or some similar designation.

Structural Arrangements

The rapid growth of gerontology education during the past ten years has encouraged many institutions to create an administrative structure that serves as a focal point for all gerontology activity, that facilitates development throughout the institution, that encourages consistency and provides stability to these efforts, and that effectively competes for resources, both within and outside the institution. These administrative or structural arrangements can be categorized into five levels that reflect the authority and autonomy of the units in terms of resources, faculty, students, and curricula.

1. An intradepartmental structure exists when gerontology is part of an established department and its activities are governed by that department. In this case, resources, faculty, students, and curricula are not under the authority of a gerontology faculty but are a function of the host department. Thus gerontology instruction is a component of another department's offerings.

2. An interdepartmental committee is created when activities involve two or more established departments. Typically, this occurs when gerontology is viewed as a multidisciplinary activity and when no

single department has sufficient staff to develop a full program of instruction. Students may be admitted to the interdepartmental program or may remain with a home department; curricula would typically be coordinated by the interdepartmental faculty committee, but faculty members and financial resources would be likely to remain under the control of the participating departments.

3. A center or institute offers a more permanent administrative structure because it has control of some resources and has a permanent staff who are independent of the traditional departments. Students and curricula are likely to be shared with the departments; the institute or center may offer a certificate for completion of a prescribed sequence of courses, and students are admitted to both the department and the center or institute program. Faculty appointments and the legitimacy to teach credit courses typically remain with the departments, however.

4. A department of gerontology would have the authority to teach credit courses, to admit and enroll students, to design course sequences leading to majors or minors, to offer regular faculty appointments, and to have the necessary financial resources to carry out these activities. Few institutions of higher education have developed departments of gerontology to date but have opted instead to establish centers, institutes, or interdepartmental committees to facilitate their educational activities. More colleges and universities are beginning to explore this avenue, however, and the future may see many departments of gerontology.

5. A school or college of gerontology would comprise the final level of structure. The school or college would have the authority to admit students, design curricula, control its own resources, have faculty, as well as offer degrees in gerontology. Only one school of gerontology exists at this time, and it would be surprising if many more were established in the next few years.

CURRENT AND FUTURE TRENDS
OF EDUCATIONAL GERONTOLOGY

Activities that have been initiated under the title of educational gerontology show a great amount of diversity: They have been established by a wide variety of sponsors, have been geographically dispersed, and have included a bewildering array of methodology and content. Consequently, identification of any trends that may be occurring is difficult to undertake and more difficult to support. There are, however, a few consistent developments that can be noted:

1. There has been an amazing amount of growth over the past five years. The 1971 White House Conference on Aging doubtless caused some of

this inasmuch as it involved literally hundreds of thousands of people at local, regional, state, and national meetings. Education emerged as a pervasive interest of the participants of these meetings and as an intervention strategy worthy of consideration in many of the problem areas. Other recent developments have also played a part: the quickening interest of the media in older people, the increased government expenditures on programs for the aged, the declining interest in other social problem fields, the continued growth of the older population, and the increasing militancy of certain groups of senior citizens. Each of these has expanded the awareness of the field and encouraged increased activities by educational and community institutions and agencies.

2. Professionalization of the field is commencing as increased care is devoted to design and implementation of programs and as program planners incorporate sound evaluation into the program process. Evaluative research reports are becoming more common, and this needed development should lead to increased program consistency and quality. As greater knowledge becomes available on the outcomes of the different types of instructional activities, planning for new programs should improve.

3. There does not appear to be any widely accepted leadership being undertaken for the field. There are a number of organizations that have the potential for facilitating communication and encouraging professional development as well as for providing technical assistance to those agencies attempting to initiate programs. These include the Association for Gerontology in Higher Education, the Gerontological Society, the Adult Education Association of the U.S.A., and the American Association of Community and Junior Colleges. None of these seems to have defined educational gerontology as its primary interest. If the field is to develop well in the years ahead, it will be very helpful to have some organization or groups of organizations assume the needed leadership so that communication, planning, funding, and evaluation can be facilitated.

4. Government and foundation funding for activities in the field of educational gerontology are slowly expanding. Interest in education for adults and older people has led a few government agencies such as the Fund for the Improvement of Postsecondary Education, the National Institute of Education, the Administration on Aging, the National Endowment for the Humanities, and the National Institutes of Health to provide some funds for the field. It seems reasonable to expect a continued increase in these resources unless there is a serious retrenchment of government spending for social programs in the years ahead.

5. There appears to be a trend toward upgrading the personnel of many educational programs. The administrators and teachers who staffed the early undertakings in this area had little or no formal preparation in gerontology or adult education. Observation of recently circulated descriptions of job openings reveals an expectation of higher educational requirements and more

academic exposure to the fields of adult education and gerontology. This is a hopeful sign, for improved programming should result from the employment of more qualified personnel.

Although past developments in the field of educational gerontology have been substantial, the future looks especially bright. Both contemporary social trends and the activities within the field incline observers to suggest that there should be increasing interest, support, and clientele for organizations involved in these kinds of activities for the foreseeable future. A few projections on the shape of the future as it relates to educational gerontology conclude this chapter:

1. There will continue to be an increase in the number of older people in this country. As those cohorts who are middle aged today reach the age of retirement, it may be expected that they will have more interest in education than have their predecessors because their level of formal education will be substantially higher. This should provide a larger and more receptive clientele for liberal studies, second-career preparation, and education for coping with the problems that come with the later stages of life.

2. Life-span educational endeavors may be expected to draw larger numbers of participants as the amount of leisure time expands, as more people use reeducation to change careers throughout their lifetime, and as nontraditional approaches to education become more accepted and available. This movement should link easily and well with education for retirees and may be expected to provide the initial experience and positive mind set that will encourage individuals to continue education into the later years of life.

3. Increased accountability in educational programming is likely to occur in the future. As more government dollars are channeled into the community and educational institutions, increased control and oversight by federal agencies is likely to result. Much of the evaluation currently conducted on educational activities is limited to assessments of the happiness of participants and the number of people in attendance. The future is likely to see this evaluation supplemented by more refined measures of outcomes that can be quantified to indicate the results of the programming.

4. It appears that gerontology education is moving to establish a professional field of study that would be accompanied by autonomous degrees, departments, and faculty. This will involve a long process, for institutions of higher education do not lightly establish new degree programs, especially in times of financial stringency. There are, however, sufficient programs already to assess the long-term trend. Whether or not this is the most desired outcome is debatable, but it is not unusual for an interdisciplinary field to develop into an institute or center and finally to become a full-fledged department, thereby gaining acceptance as a professional area.

5. The amount of resources available from outside the agencies and institutions that do the programming may be expected to rise appreciably in the future. As government agencies and foundations become convinced of the

needs of older people and the value of educational programming, they may be expected to direct more of their funding into those institutions and agencies that have a record of achievement in these areas (Peterson, Powell, & Robertson, 1976). Public schools and institutions of higher education are also expected to allocate more of their resources toward this clientele group as legislatures and school boards learn to respect the potential voting power of the older citizens. By using educational interventions, it may be possible to assist older people while avoiding the drawbacks that welfare and social-activist approaches often provoke.

In conclusion, educational gerontology is a new and developing field with all of the enthusiasm, promise, and problems that accompany such development. A complex array of programs have already grown up without the coordination and consistency needed for a cohesive field of endeavor. Even though there is confusion at times, one can only be pleased with the growth that has occurred in recent years because the potential of education for improving the quality of life of older people is beginning to be utilized. Much is yet to be done, but the vigor and vitality of the field currently overshadows its organizational or programmatic weaknesses and leads one to be very hopeful that the future will see consolidation and improvement as well as continued growth.

REFERENCES

Academy for Educational Development. *Never too old to learn.* New York: Author, 1974.

Anonymous. *A time for learning. Harvest Years* (Special issues), June–August, 1968.

Arenberg, D. L. Cognition and aging: Verbal learning, memory, problem solving and aging. In C. Eisdorfer & M. P. Lawton (Eds.), *The psychology of adult development and aging.* Washington, D.C.: American Psychological Association, 1973.

Arenberg, D. L. & Robertson, E. A. The older individual as a learner. In S. M. Grabowski & W. D. Mason (Eds.), *Learning for aging.* Washington, D.C.: Adult Education Association of the U.S.A., 1974; Syracuse: ERIC Clearinghouse on Adult Education.

Aronoff, C. Old age in prime time. *Journal of Communication,* 1974, *24*(4), 86–87.

Association for Gerontology in Higher Education. *National directory of educational programs in gerontology* (1st ed., B. M. Sprouse, Ed.). Washington: Administration on Aging, Office of Human Development, Department of Health, Education and Welfare, 1976.

Atchley, R. C. *The sociology of retirement.* New York: Wiley, 1976.

Atchley, R. C., & Seltzer, M. M. *Developing educational programs in the field of aging.* Oxford, Ohio: Scripps Foundation Gerontology Center, n.d.

Baltes, P. B., & Labouvie, G. V. Adult development of intellectual per-formance: Description, explanation, and modification. In C. Eisdorfer &

M. P. Lawton (Eds.), *The psychology of adult development and aging.* Washington: American Psychological Association, 1973.

Bankers Trust Co. *Study of industrial retirement plans.* New York: Author, 1970.

Beattie, W. M., Jr. Gerontology curricula: Multidisciplinary frameworks, interdisciplinary structures and disciplinary depth. *The Gerontologist,* 1974, *14,* 545–548.

Birren, J. E., & Gribbin, K. Methods of meeting the need for education and research training in the field of aging. In *Research and training in gerontology, a working paper* (U.S. Senate Special Committee on Aging). Washington, D.C.: U.S. Government Printing Office, November, 1971.

Birren, J. E., & Woodruff, D. S. Human development over the life span through education. In P. Baltes & W. Schaie (Eds.), *Life span developmental psychology.* New York: Academic, 1973.

Bolton, C. R. Humanistic instructional strategies and retirement education programming. *The Gerontologist,* 1976, *16,* 550–555.

Botwinick, J. *Aging and behavior.* New York: Springer, 1973.

Bromley, D. B. *The psychology of human aging.* Baltimore: Penguin, 1974.

Bullock, J., & Bauman, J. W., Jr. Gerontology in medical education: An elective program in reserach and training. *The Gerontologist,* 1974, *14,* 319–323.

Burdman, G. D. M. Student and trainee attitudes on aging. *The Gerontologist,* 1974, *14,* 65–68.

Charles, D. C. Effect of participation in a pre-retirement program. *The Gerontologist,* 1971, *11,* 24–28.

Clague, E., Palli, B., & Kramer, L. *The aging worker and the union: Retirement and middle aged and older workers.* New York: Praeger, 1971.

Cross, P. Learning society, *The College Board Review* (No. 91), Spring 1974, pp. 1–ง.

Curtis, D. V., & Wartgow, J. F. *Evaluating nontraditional higher education: A new perspective.* Park Forest South, Ill.: Governor's State University, 1972.

DeCrow, R. *New learning for older Americans: An overview of national effort.* Washington, D.C.: Adult Education Association of the U.S.A., n.d.

Donahue, W. T. Education's role in maintaining the individual's status. *The Annals of the American Academy of Political and Social Science,* January 1952, pp. 115–125.

Donahue, W. T. *The common body of knowledge.* Paper presented at the 20th Annual Conference on Aging, University of Michigan, July 1967.

Donahue, W. T. Grand Rapids learns about the aging. *Adult Leadership,* May 1954, pp. 22–24.

Donahue, W. T. (Ed.). *Education for later maturity.* New York: Whiteside, 1955.

Easter, M. P. Senior power: A case study in education for aging. *Adult Leadership,* September 1974, pp. 81–84.

Ecklund, L. Aging and the field of education. In M. W. Riley, J. W. Riley, Jr., & M. E. Johnson (Eds.), *Aging and society, vol. 2: Aging and the professions.* New York: Russell Sage Foundation, 1969.

Elias, M. F. Symposium—The real world and the ivory tower: Dialectics of professional training, education, and delivery of services to elderly persons. *The Gerontologist,* 1974, *14,* 525–526.

Evans, D., Evans, K., & Peterson, D. A. Recent trends in newspaper coverage of the elderly. *International Journal of Aging and Human Development,* in press.

Feltman, K. *The development and evaluation of a unit of gerontology for secondary school students.* Unpublished doctoral dissertation, University of Michigan, 1974.

Fillenbaum, G. G. Retirement planning programs—At what age, and for whom? *The Gerontologist,* 1971, *11,* 33–36.

Francke, W. H. Preparing workers for retirement. *University of Illinois Bulletin,* 1962, *59,* 26.

Frank, L. K. Education for aging. In W. T. Donahue (Ed.), *Education for later maturity.* New York: Whiteside, 1955.

Greene, M. R., Pyron, H. C., Manion, U. V., & Winkelvoss, H. *Preretirement counseling, retirement adjustment, and the older employee.* Eugene: University of Oregon, Graduate School of Management and Business, 1969.

Harris, L. & Associates. *The myth and reality of aging in America.* Washington, D.C.: National Council on the Aging, 1975.

Haskins, J. B. Evaluation of effects of education and mass communication techniques. *1968 National Safety Congress Transactions,* 1968, *24,* 77–109.

Havighurst, R. J. Changing status and roles during the adult life cycle: Significance for adult education. In H. W. Burns (Ed.), *Sociological backgrounds of adult education.* Chicago: Center for the Study of Liberal Education for Adults, 1964.

Helling, J. F. & Bauer, B. M. Seniors on campus. *Adult Leadership,* December 1972, pp. 203–204.

Hendrickson, A., & Barnes, R. F. *The role of colleges and universities in the education of the aged.* Columbus: The Ohio State University Research Foundation, 1964.

Hesburgh, T. M., Miller, P. A., & Wharton, C. R., Jr. *Patterns of life long learning.* San Francisco: Jossey-Bass, 1973.

Hickey, T., & Spinetta, J. J. Bridging research and application. *The Gerontologist,* 1974, *14,* 526–530.

Hiemstra, R. P. Continuing education for the aged: A survey of needs and interests of older people. *Adult Education,* February 1972, pp. 100–109.

Hiemstra, R. P. *The older adult and learning.* Lincoln: University of Nebraska, 1975. (ERIC Document Reproduction Service No. CE 006 003).

Hixson, L. E. Non-threatening education for older adults. *Adult Leadership,* September 1969, pp. 84–85.

Houle, C. O. The changing goals of education in the perspective of lifelong learning. *International Review of Education,* 1974, *20,* 430–443.

Huberman, M. Looking at adult education from the perspective of adult life cycle. *International Review of Education,* 1974, *20,* 430–445.

Hudis, A. An introductory course in gerontology. *The Gerontologist,* 1974, *14,* 312–315.

Hunter, W. W. *A longitudinal study of preretirement education.* Ann Arbor: University of Michigan, Division of Gerontology, 1968.

Hunter, W. W. Preretirement education and planning. In S. M. Grabowski & Mason, W. D. (Eds.), *Learning for Aging.* Washington, D.C.: Adult Education Association of the U.S.A., 1974; Syracuse: ERIC Clearinghouse on Adult Education.

Jacobs, H. L. Education for aging in the educational system. In H. L. Jacobs, W. D. Mason, & E. Kauffman (Eds.), *Education for aging: A review of recent literature.* Syracuse: ERIC Clearinghouse on Adult Education, 1970.

Jacobs, H. L. Education for aging in the elementary and secondary school system. In S. M. Grabowski, & W. D. Mason (Eds.), *Learning for aging.* Washington, D.C.: Adult Education Association of the U.S.A., 1974; Syracuse: ERIC Clearinghouse on Adult Education.

Johnson, J. R. Response to a view of training within the medical school. *The Gerontologist,* 1974, *14,* 542–544.

Johnstone, J. W. C., & Rivera, R. J. *Volunteers for learning.* Chicago: Aldine, 1965.

Kalt, N. C., & Kohn, M. H. Pre-retirement counseling: Characteristics of program and preferences of retirees. *The Gerontologist,* 1975, *15,* 179–181.

Kassachau, P. L. Reevaluating the need for preretirement education. *Industrial Gerontology,* 1974, *1*(1), 42–59.

Kauffman, E. Retirement. In H. L. Jacobs, W. D. Mason, & E. Kauffman (Eds.), *Education for aging: A review of recent literature.* Syracuse: ERIC Clearinghouse on Adult Education, 1970.

Kauffman, E., & Luby, P. Non-traditional education: Some new approaches to a dynamic culture. In S. M. Grabowski, & W. D. Mason (Eds.), *Learning for aging.* Washington, D.C.: Adult Education Association of the U.S.A., 1974; Syracuse: ERIC Clearinghouse on Adult Education.

Kelleher, C. H., & Quirk, D. A. Preparation for retirement: An annotated bibliography of literature (1965–1974). *Industrial Gerontology,* Summer 1974, 49–73.

Klapper, J. T. *The effects of mass communication.* New York: Free Press, 1960.

Korim, A. S. *Older Americans and community colleges: A guide for program implementation.* Washington, D.C.: American Association of Community and Junior Colleges, 1974.

Londoner, C. A. Survival needs of the aged: Implications for program planning. *Aging and Human Development,* May 1971, pp. 1–11.

Macdonald, R. *Content analysis of perceptions of aging as represented by the news media.* Paper presented at the Gerontological Society Annual Meeting, Miami, November 1973.

Manion, U. V. Issues and trends in preretirement education. *Industrial Gerontology,* Fall 1974, pp. 28–36.

Mason, W. D. Informal programs in education for aging. In H. L. Jacobs, W.

D. Mason, & E. Kauffman (Eds.), *Education for aging: A review of recent literature.* Syracuse: ERIC Clearinghouse on Adult Education, 1970.

McClusky, H. Y. Co-chairman's statement (section on education). In *Toward a national policy on aging* (Final report, Vol. II, 1971 White House Conference on Aging). Washington, D.C.: U.S. Government Printing Office, 1973.

McClusky, H. Y. Education for aging: The scope of the field and perspectives for the future. In S. M. Grabowski, & W. D. Mason (Eds.), *Learning for aging,* Washington, D.C.: Adult Education Association of the U.S.A., 1974; Syracuse: ERIC Clearinghouse for Adult Education.

Monk, A. A social policy framework for pre-retirement planning. *Industrial Gerontology,* Fall 1972, pp. 63–70.

Moody, H. R. Philosophical presuppositions of education for old age. *Educational Gerontology,* 1976, *1,* 1–16.

Morkert, C. E. Pre-retirement education: A community responsibility. *Adult Leadership,* January 1974, pp. 233–235.

Myran, G. A., Huber, R., & Sweeney, S. M. Senior citizen services in community colleges. In *Research and Report Series Number 5.* East Lansing, Mich.: Kellogg Community Service Leadership Program, 1971.

Northcott, H. Too young, too old—Age in the world of television. *The Gerontologist,* 1975, *15,* 184–186.

Norton, P. G. *Consideration of how levels of achievement and anxiety toward education affect older people's participation in adult education programs.* Paper presented at the Adult Education Research Conference, Minneapolis, February 1970. (ERIC Document Reproduction Service No. ED 036 761).

Office of Management and Budget, Executive Office of the President. *Catalogue of federal domestic assistance.* Washington, D. C.: U.S. Government Printing Office, 1975.

Okes, I. E. *Participation in adult education: Initial report* (1969). U.S. Department of Health, Education, and Welfare, National Center for Educational Statistics). Washington, D.C.: U.S. Government Printing Office, 1971.

O'Rourke, J., & Freedman, II. An inter-union pre-retirement training program: Results and commentary. *Industrial Gerontology,* Spring 1972, pp. 49–64.

Palmore, E. (Ed.). *Normal aging.* Durham: Duke University Press, 1970.

Pattison, R. M. Senior citizens renewal action program. *Adult Leadership,* June 1973, pp. 59–60.

Petersen, M. The visibility and image of old people on television. *Journalism Quarterly,* 1973, *50,* 569–573.

Peterson, D. A. Life span education and gerontology. *The Gerontologist,* 1975, *15,* 436–441.

Peterson, D. A., Donahue, W. T., & Tibbitts, C. Faculty seminar in social gerontology: A model for the expansion of gerontological instruction. *Aging and Human Development,* August 1972, pp. 253–260.

Peterson, D. A., & Karnes, E. L. Older people in adolescent literature. *The Gerontologist*, 1976, *16*, 225–231.

Peterson, D. A., Powell, F., & Robertson, L. Aging in America: Toward the year 2000. *The Gerontologist*, 1976, *16*, 264–270.

Pyron, H. C. Preparing employees for retirement. *Personnel Journal*, 1969, *48*, 722–727.

Pyron, H. C. & Manion, U. V. The company, the individual, and the decision to retire. *Industrial Gerontology*, Winter 1970, pp. 1–11.

Salcedo, R. N. Blood and gore on the information campaign trail. *Journal of Extension*, Summer 1973, pp. 9–19.

Sarvis, R. E. *Educational needs of the elderly: Their relationships to educational institutions.* Washington: National Center for Educational Research and Development, 1973. (ERIC Document Reproduction Service No. ED 075 717).

Schaie, K. W. Training of trainers to train trainers. *The Gerontologist*, 1974, *14*, 533–535.

Scott, F. G. Innovative educational opportunities for older persons. *Adult Leadership*, April 1974, pp. 337–343.

Seltzer, M. M. Education in gerontology: An evolutionary analogy. *The Gerontologist*, 1974, *14*, 308–311.

Seltzer, M. M., & Atchley, R. C. The concept of old: Changing attitudes and stereotypes. *The Gerontologist*, 1971, *11*, 226–230.

Shore, H. Designing a training program for understanding sensory losses in aging. *The Gerontologist*, 1976, *16*, 157–165.

Simpson, I. H., Back, K., & McKinney, J. Exposure to information on preparation for, and self-evaluation in retirement. In I. Simpson & J. McKinney (Eds.), *Social aspects of aging.* Durham: Duke University Press, 1966.

Sinex, F. M. A view of training from within the medical school: Attitudes, status, and structure. *The Gerontologist*, 1974, *14*, 538–542.

Smith, B. J., & Barker, H. R. Jr. Influence of a reality orientation training program on the attitudes of trainees toward the elderly. *The Gerontologist*, 1972, *12*, 262–264.

Smith, R. M., Aker, F., & Kidd, J. R. (Eds.). *Handbook of adult education.* New York: Macmillan, 1970.

Somers, G. Retraining the unemployed older worker. In J. Kreps (Ed.), *Technology, manpower, and retirement policy.* Cleveland: World 1966.

Stanford, E. P. Education and aging: New task for education. *Adult Leadership*, February 1972, pp. 281–282.

Thorson, J. A. Training para-professionals in the field of aging. *Adult Leadership*, May 1973, pp. 9–11.

Tillock, E. E. Education of the professional long term health care administrator. In S. M. Grabowski, & W. D. Mason, (Eds.), *Learning for aging.* Washington, D.C.: Adult Education Association of the U.S.A., 1974; Syracuse: ERIC Clearinghouse on Adult Education.

Toward a national policy on aging: Final report of the White House Conference on Aging (Vol. II). Washington, D.C.: U.S. Government Printing Office, 1973.

U.S. Department of Health, Education, and Welfare, Administration on Aging. Announcement of the Administration on Aging Title IV-A Training Program for fiscal 1976. Washington, D.C.: Author, 1976.

Uphaus, R. M. Educating retirees. *Adult Leadership,* May 1971, pp. 17–19.

Urban, H. B., & Watson, W. Response to bridging the gap: Alternative approaches. *The Gerontologist,* 1974, *14,* 530–533.

Weg, R. B. Education for gerontology: Priorities, potentialities, and realities. *The Gerontologist,* 1972, *12,* 257–260.

Weg, R. B. Concepts in education and training for gerontology: New career patterns. *The Gerontologist,* 1973, *13,* 449–452.

Weg, R. B. Response: A view from curricula for gerontology. *The Gerontologist,* 1974, *14,* 549–553.

Wilson, A. J. E. Response to training of trainers. *The Gerontologist,* 1974, *14,* 536–537.

Wray, R. P. Institutions of higher education as a resource for a statewide continuing education program in gerontology. *Adult Leadership,* November 1970, pp. 158–159.

2

EDUCATION AND THE LIFE CYCLE: A PHILOSOPHY OF AGING

HARRY R. MOODY

Hunter College of the
City University of New York

We shall not cease from exploration
And the end of all our exploring
Will be to arrive where we started
And know the place for the first time.

T. S. Eliot

EXPERIENCE

In the art and iconography of cultures the world over, we find a recurrent symbol, a special form of the circular *mandala* called the *Ouroborus,* which depicts a snake eating its own tail. This is an image of the human life cycle: a circle that returns to its origins and completes itself only upon arrival at the starting point. In old age, too, there is a closure, a completion of the life cycle, with an opportunity to "arrive where we started" and "know the place for the first time." With this goal in mind, I would suggest that education of older people should be grounded in life experience: in the history and the life cycle of the learner.

Older people bring to the learning situation a lifetime of personal experience that can be not only their greatest resource but also their greatest stumbling block. The ancient Greeks understood the problem well: the tragic flaw of the dramatic hero serves to remind us that our greatest strength is also our hidden flaw and deepest weakness. So too with the life experience of the older person: experience may lead to wisdom or it may lead to dogmatism. In any event, experience is the unavoidable condition of learning for the older person, and so, as teachers, we ignore it at our peril. I believe that education for older adults will achieve its purpose only when we situate our educational objectives within a conception of the human life cycle as a whole.

Old people have been around a long time, and when they come to subjects like literature or history or psychology, they have already had a wide experience of the phenomenon under study. They are not necessarily knowledgeable about the disciplines we have to offer, but they have another strength. The older person who comes to study these subjects at age 60 or 70 is in many ways much better equipped than the typical 18-year-old college student to appreciate what literature or history or psychology really have to offer us through broadening or deepening our understanding of life. The older person may come to the subject in a deeper way than might have been possible at another point in the life cycle. Too often the learning process of the older adult is examined exclusively from the standpoint of losses: memory, perceptual functions, cognitive deficiencies, and so on. What we need to do is, first, to recognize the special strengths that older people can bring to the classroom, and, second, to use these strengths to enrich the learning experience.

I began with some lines from T. S. Eliot's (1971) poem the *Four Quartets,* a profound meditation on the meaning of time, self, and aging. Among other things, Eliot's poem is a bitter condemnation of the sentimental idea that old age necessarily brings with it wisdom. The poet asks:

> *What was to be the value of the long looked forward to,*
> *Long hoped for calm, the autumnal serenity*
> *And the wisdom of age? Had they deceived us*
> *Or decieved themselves, the quiet-voiced elders,*
> *Bequeathing us merely a receipt for deceit? (p. 26)*

It is the tragic flaw of old age to believe that life experience—the experience of the past—automatically has continued meaning in the present. We have all seen how experience distorts our perception, conditions our responses, and reduces flexibility and ability to learn: we see a thing and we've seen it all before; we know the answer before we have even heard the question. Eliot (1971) writes:

> *There is, it seems to us,*
> *At best, only a limited value*
> *In the knowledge derived from experience.*
> *The knowledge imposes a pattern, and falsifies,*
> *For the pattern is new in every moment*
> *And every moment is a new and shocking*
> *Valuation of all we have been. We are only undeceived*
> *Of that which, deceiving, could no longer harm. (p. 26)*

Every teacher of older people is familiar with the escape maneuvers, defense mechanisms, rigidities, and anxieties that Eliot summarizes in his phrase "the knowledge that imposes a pattern and falsifies." In rigidity, we sense the anguish of old people who feel all too keenly that time has passed them by, that their experience belongs to a world that no longer exists, and that they as people are obsolete and their experience without value or meaning. These people, who often feel "ignorant" because they lack formal educational credentials, are only a mirror image of other old people who glorify the past as a defense mechanism for coping with an uncertain present and a threatening future.

The defense is entirely understandable. The economy and the technological system of our society place decreased importance on life experience and tend to favor skills and knowledge that must be continually updated to avoid obsolescence. Outside the technological sphere, in the domain of customs, values, and family life, old people also find themselves at a disadvantage: their life experience is of less and less value in a world of rapid social change. If old people try to preserve lessons derived from life experience, they are in part simply trying to preserve themselves and their sense of who they are. Yet this very attempt at self-preservation can destroy the possibility for growth and adaptation in the present. As teachers of older adults, we are compelled to understand this predicament because it is our role to facilitate the conversion of life experience from an obstacle, into a source of strength, through education.

Our attitude toward our own past deeply affects the quality of life, whether we hold on to it too dearly or disown it too readily. To *disown the past* means to act as if age makes no difference at all, as if life experience were irrelevant. Don't think about the past too much; be actively engaged in projects and new activities; look to the present and to the future: Such seems to be the advice of Simone de Beauvoir. We often see this approach advocated for older people who return for education in retirement, to discover new hobbies, second careers, or leisure-time activities. Their past, their life experience, is forgotten, by teacher and student alike.

This attitude toward the past is common in America, a country dominated by the image of the future. The past represents what is used up, what is bypassed and rejected. Old people feel it too: how often we meet old people who simply deny that they are old! This, too, is a defense mechanism, a form of denial, that deprives life of its meaning and rejects the irreversibility of the human experience of time. By contrast, consider the older people we know who are emotionally healthy. They have neither the dogmatism that comes from living too much in the past, nor the illusion of an endless present that denies the past and avoids the future. Instead, we find in such people a vivid acceptance of life in the present, a present that includes past and future. Perhaps the deepest definition of successful aging is simply this: to repair the past and prepare for the future by living in the present. To be alive and aware in the present is indeed the key, but this process should not mean avoiding the future—which for all of us is death—but rather, preparing for it in the deepest way possible. It should not mean disowning the past but repairing it instead by extracting from it a kind of insight that allows us to affirm its continued meaning. T. S. Eliot (1971) writes:

> *It seems, as one becomes older*
> *That the past has another pattern, and ceases*
> *to be mere sequence—*
> *We had the experience but missed the meaning,*
> *And approach to the meaning restores the experience*
> *In a different form . . . I have said before*
> *That the past experience revived in the meaning*
> *Is not the experience of one life only*
> *But of many generations . . . (p. 39)*

What would it mean for education in old age to make use of the past, of the learner's life experience? Here is the touchstone: the past ceases to be a mere sequence of events; we elicit from it something of universal significance. "Old men ought to be explorers," says Eliot, but he adds that "the end of all our exploring / will be to arrive where we started / And know the place for the first time." To arrive where we started is to discover in the pattern of life experience a meaning quite different from what it first appeared to be. "The meaning restores the experience in a different form . . . " because the form of education is the universality of knowledge that makes each single human life into a microcosm for all generations. To *repair* the past means to discover in one's own life history something that is timeless. When we study the history of our immigrant forebears, we understand something about all immigrant groups; when old people read *King Lear,* they understand something about the recurrent conflict between parents and adult children. The past is then encompassed in knowledge that is liberating because it is simultaneously both personal and universal. This type of educational experience means neither to be imprisoned by the past nor to disown it, but rather to discover in life experience an unanswered question: the question of *meaning.*

It was Robert Butler who called attention to this point about the value of reminiscence in old age when he described the process of *life review.* In psychodynamic terms, the process of life review constitutes the major developmental task of old age, and it is the fundamental question for any philosophy of aging. Old people looking back at their life experience—just as all of us must, of whatever age, if we are honest with ourselves when we think about our past, about 5 years, 10 years, 50 years ago—cannot help wondering, What did it all mean? What did it amount to? What was the result of all those efforts that seemed so important at the time? This is the universal experience of time and aging that we find expressed in the opening lines of Neihardt's (1961) life story of a Sioux Indian chief, *Black Elk Speaks:*

> *My friend, I am going to tell you the story of my life, as you wish; and if it were only the story of my life I think I would not tell it; for what is one man that he should make much of his winters, even when they bend him like a heavy snow? So many other men have lived and shall live that story, to be grass upon the hills....*
>
> *This, then, is not the tale of a great hunter or of a great warrior, or of a great traveler, although I have made much meat in my time and fought for my people both as boy and man, and have gone far and seen strange lands and men. So also have many others done, and better than I. These things I shall remember by the way, and often they may seem to be the very tale itself, as when I was living them in happiness and sorrow. But now that I can see it all as from a lonely hilltop, I know it was the story of a mighty vision given to a man too weak to use it; of a holy tree that should have flourished in a people's heart with flowers and singing birds, and now is withered; and of a people's dream that died in bloody snow.*
>
> *But if the vision was true and mighty, as I know, it is true and mighty yet; for such things are of the spirit, and it is in the darkness of their eyes that men get lost. (pp. 1, 2)*

The haunting eloquence of this last line expresses our dilemma: "It is in the darkness of their eyes that men get lost." Black Elk, telling the story of his life, sees clearly that the events of his experience—the travels, the adventures, the encounters with people—all of this amounts to nothing at the end. "These things I shall remember by the way, and often they may *seem* to be the very tale itself, as when I was living them in happiness and sorrow." The pattern of the past is not the mere sequence of events, even though it may seem that way as we are living those events. Old age has conveyed to Black Elk the vision to see it all "as from a lonely hilltop." Now he can grasp the pattern of *life as a whole*, and in this process of reviewing his own life, he finds the universality of the human condition. The circle is completed.

Contrast now this autobiography of a wise Indian chief with a work of modern literature such as Samuel Beckett's play *Krapp's Last Tape,* where we find an old man rummaging through tape recordings of intimate thoughts made in previous years. Now, in his old age, he finds the unlabeled tapes scattered through his bedroom. He is unable to put them into any kind of order, and as he listens to them, he cannot even recall what the talks were all about. The tape recordings, our subjective memories of the past, have become a meaningless jumble, like names and faces we can no longer remember. This is the image of old age in the contemporary world: the frightening possibility of total despair, a despair of life that has become meaningless, where time is a mere succession of moments, the future an abyss.

It is this image of the experience of time in old age that Simone de Beauvoir (1972) describes so vividly in *The Coming of Age*:

> *The past is not a peaceful landscape lying there behind me, a country in which I can stroll whenever I please, and which will gradually show me all its secret hills and dales. As I was moving forward, so it was crumbling. Most of the wreckage that can still be seen is colourless, distorted, frozen: its meaning escapes me. Here and there I see occasional pieces whose melancholy beauty enchants me. They do not suffice to populate this emptiness that Chateaubriand calls "the desert of the past." (p. 365)*

Life experience, in and of itself, furnishes us with no intimation of wisdom, only with an appalling recognition of "the desert of the past." As Simone de Beauvoir (1972) describes it, the fate of old age is bleak indeed:

> *A limited future and a frozen past: such is the situation that the elderly have to face up to. In many instances it paralyzes them. All their plans have either been carried out or abandoned, and their life has closed in about itself; nothing requires their presence; they no longer have anything whatsoever to do. (p. 378)*

Samuel Beckett and Simone de Beauvoir portray the existential anguish of the modern world: a complete rejection of the traditional image of old age as a period of wisdom. It is a protest that must be taken seriously. *The Coming of Age* is a profoundly important book, though I believe it will be clear that I disagree with Simone de Beauvoir's conclusions.

If our past is "frozen" wreckage, as Simone de Beauvoir suggests, and if our memories are like scattered tape recordings, then ideed the past becomes a "mere sequence" of events without meaning or purpose. As we look back at our own past, each of us inevitably finds a part of our experience that falls under this description. Our experience *is* puzzling, incomplete, fragmentary; we *do* lack the wholeness, the ego integrity, that is properly associated with the idea of wisom, but this is not the whole story by any means. The past is not finished, is not "frozen," as long as its meaning still escapes me: as long as I recognize in myself the capacity to discover in that past elements of universal significance. It is this sense of discovery that gives the process of life review its true significance and its relationship to continuing education throughout the life cycle.

If we accept this process of life review as being the major developmental task of old age, it must become the starting point for any theory of education that we might evolve. We will need to pay the closest attention to how older people use their life experience in the learning process in order to build on the strengths of experience in old age. As matters stand now, education for older adults tends to follow the pattern of adult education in general: an indiscriminate proliferation of courses based on student interest, guided only by the implicit faith that curiosity and new interests are intrinsically desirable. To date, educators have not been very creative in finding ways to *use* the student's own life experience to enhance the learning process. Many older people would just as soon forget the fact that they are old, and all too often our educational options for them encourage that tendency. We have yet to discover ways of integrating the rich life experience of older people into the classroom, of tying the lessons of experience to the conceptual structure of subject matter, instead of sacrificing one to the other. This observation leads me to my second major point, which concerns the methods of educating older adults, and here I want to focus specifically on the method of *dialogue.*

DIALOGUE

I have said that the unique strength of older people lies in their life experience, which, if we could find a way to unlock it, would unfold remarkable possibilities of growth and understanding. But where to turn for a model to accomplish this? I turn back to the origins of the Western philosophical tradition, to the thought of Plato, and in particular to Plato's (1966) dialogue, the *Meno,* perhaps the earliest treatise on the philosophy of education. This problem addressed by the *Meno*—Is it possible to teach virtue?—turns out to be essential for the education of older adults.

In the dialogue, we find Socrates interrogating a young boy about the principles of geometry. The boy professes to know nothing about geometry: he's never studied the subject, but under Socrates' skillful questioning, he successfully reconstructs a theorem describing the relation between the area of a square and its diagonal sections. The ignorant boy turns out to be not so ignorant as he himself had imagined. He has answered Socrates' questions on his own and yet just a few minutes before he did not "know" the correct answers. Thus, concludes Socrates:

> So a man who does not know has in himself true opinions on a subject without having knowledge.

Meno: *It would appear so.*

Socrates: *At present these opinions, being newly aroused, have a dreamlike quality. But if the same questions are put to him on many occasions and in different ways, you can see that in the end he will have a knowledge on the subject as accurate as anybody's.*

Meno: *Probably.*

Socrates: *This knowledge will not come from teaching but from questioning. He will recover it for himself. (p. 370)*

A whole Platonic epistemology is implicit in this fragment of the dialogue. All of us have opinions arising from our experience of the world. Over and above such opinions stands the realm of systematized knowledge: of science and scholarship. When we consider this realm of systematized knowledge, these opinions derived from life experience are likely to seem but confused, partial renditions of a complex reality. Thus we are inclined to devalue life experience and defer instead to the experts, the scholars, the "people who know" those disciplines that describe the world of our everyday experience. We see this tendency to devalue life experience—and to defer to "the professor"—especially among older people who have been away from school for many years.

Yet, like the slave boy in the *Meno,* all of us possess much more than we realize, and this is especially true for older people whose life experience has given rise to opinions about the world described by formal disciplines such as history or literature or psychology. In our teaching of older people, we need not be so much concerned to convey new knowledge or information as to elicit a new understanding of what is already present in the learners. The model for accomplishing this is given in the structure of the Socratic dialogue itself. Through questions put to the student "on many occasions and in different ways," we discover that the older student "in the end . . . will have a knowledge on the subject as accurate as anybody's."

If life experience is to be the basis for learning in this way, then it demands that we see the role of the teacher differently. In a late dialogue, the *Theaetetus,* Socrates describes his own role as "the midwife of ideas": the man who does not proclaim himself wise but who instead gives birth to wisdom in others through the relentless questioning of the Socratic method. In this view, the teacher's role is neither to accept nor reject altogether the answers given by the pupil. Rather, the answers—the dogmatic conclusions furnished by life experience—are to be turned back upon themselves to discern their premises and thus to expose their limitations. Upon cross-examination, the framework of concepts dissolves into uncertainty *(aporia),* as the pupil recognizes that to have an opinion, even a true opinion, is not the same thing as to have real knowledge. What is the difference? In the *Theaetetus,* Plato proposes the notion that a true opinion becomes knowledge only when it can "give an account of itself." The Greek term here is *logos*—"language, word, concept"—and it is the guiding role of *logos* that determines the validity of the educational enterprise.

There are some important implications here for education with older people. When older adults appear "opinionated," the point is not necessarily to reject the false opinions and certify the true ones. Even if the opinions derived from life experience happen to be true, they are still not yet knowledge. The whole purpose of education is to convert these true opinions into knowledge by revealing their roots in life experience and their connections with a wider context of life. This knowledge is *justified true belief*, or an opinion that can "give an account of itself." As the dialogue unfolds, we realize that knowledge is characterized by qualities of depth, generality, and power to illuminate unforeseen features of the world. Knowledge, in other words, is a leap beyond the empirical facts of a given situation or an individual life history to disclose a wider horizon that may have been missed in the course of life experience but is implicit in it just the same. "We had the experience but missed the meaning," as Eliot puts it.

It is through the process of dialogue that life experience is converted into knowledge. The teacher, like Socrates, points the older people's attention back to their own life experience until "true opinion" is exhibited in its connection to a wider field of facts or beliefs. It is in this sense that knowledge as "justified true belief" serves, not only to justify the conclusions of life experience, but also to explain the experience itself, whenever the teacher of older people is willing to use this life experience in the educational process. For example, consider the case of an older adult who expresses in the classroom a belief that "People are better off trusting their own ethnic group than trusting government officials." The teacher of sociology or political science who treats this opinion with seriousness will urge the student to examine it, to justify it, perhaps to qualify it. If the process of dialogue achieves its goal, the older person ends up by embedding a formerly dogmatic belief in a wider context of social reality. What is more, to justify the belief is also to explain the experiences that gave rise to it: for example, the need for family or ethnic solidarity of immigrant groups facing an alien society. What had previously been a fragmentary opinion becomes generalized and systematized until the student glimpses a larger rhythm of history that served as its background.

Older people cannot enter the classroom simply to receive a ratification of their previous opinions; indeed, one should expect that these opinions will be challenged at the same time that they are taken seriously. To become educated, as Plato realized, is more than to have opinions, even true opinions, about the world. Education, Plato argues in the *Republic*, means to be led out of the shadow world of opinions (whether true or false) and to discover the fundamental ground whereby we can know *why* our opinions are true or false. To have knowledge is to have a justified true belief about the world, and this means to have adequate evidence for holding some beliefs and not others. It does not mean simply to have had certain experiences or even to extract from life experience generalities or regularities: the empiricism of common sense.

This common-sense empiricism is exactly what Socrates describes as the "dreamlike quality" of newly aroused opinions that have yet to be converted into self-conscious knowledge. The danger of a "dreamlike" opinion is that it "imposes a pattern, and falsifies, / for the pattern is new in every moment" (Eliot, 1971, p. 26). By contrast, the Platonic dialogue itself is a return to the origins, a circle that turns back on itself when the older person's life experience itself becomes the basis of learning: "This knowledge will not come from teaching but from questioning. He will recover it for himself."

If older people learn for themselves how to recover knowledge from their own life experiences, then they become both teachers and learners at the same time, and this demand is actually implicit in the fact that Plato did not write treatises, but dialogues. Now, the dialogue form is not a mere literary device but is itself a model for an educational process based on both speaking and listening: Students speak while listening and listen while speaking. In speaking out loud, students listen inwardly and criticize their own opinions instead of simply allowing life experience to voice dogmatic opinions. In listening, students are also inwardly speaking, or actively responding to new ideas presented, not as mere information, but as an evocation of what was already implicit in life experience. True listening includes speaking, includes an active dimension, just as true speaking includes this critical self-consciousness that we might call "thinking out loud," wondering about our opinions, examining ideas in the very act of expressing them.

How can students learn to do this? Not by dogmatic assimilation of new facts or true opinions, but by internalizing the process of dialogue itself, by speaking and listening at the same time. For this reason, Plato describes thinking as "the dialogue of the soul with itself." For older people, thinking means a dialogue between past and present, between the memory of life experience and the structure of the subject matter. Neither element is sacrificed for the other, but both are present, dialectically unified. The past "speaks" through old people but so does the active learning of the moment. To be in dialogue with the past means to be in touch with feelings and opinions, not to subordinate them to the subject matter or to reject them as useless or irrelevant.

This kind of educational experience is immensely difficult to achieve. Everyone, including old people, tends to be dogmatic when speaking from experience. On the other hand, we are all aware of the older person who becomes subservient to "the professor" by casting teachers in the role of people who know all the answers, all the facts. Let us admit as well that many faculty members are comfortable in this superior role. Education based on dialogue means that older people must be *both* teachers and learners, just as those of us who direct the educational process must be both teachers and learners. If we begin to become isolated behind the safety of the subject matter, the discipline, then we too quickly stop listening to the students' own experiences. We are no longer speaking and listening at the same time, but merely speaking—as the professor—while the older people listen to us. As soon as speaking and listening become polarized into the roles of teacher and learner, we become locked in our roles and no longer find a way to legitimize the value of life experience for the classroom. What we really need instead, as Gattegno put it, is "the subordination of teaching to learning."

But can this Socratic model be applied to the education of older adults in our contemporary world? I believe it can and I point to the work of Paulo Freire, the Brazilian educator, whose books, *The Pedagogy of the Oppressed* and *Education for Critical Consciousness,* have much to teach us about education for older adults. Freire's work grew out of his experience in education for literacy among Brazilian peasants. As he worked with these people, he discovered that a persistent block in their learning to read was a deep-seated negative self-image: a feeling that they could not learn, that they were not capable of acquiring the "high culture" of literacy, and that what they did know from their own experience was worthless. The peasants had internalized a negative self-image that systematically devalued their life experience.

There are significant parallels here with the learning situation of older people. In our culture, many older people have internalized a negative self-image that says, "You're too old to learn," or "Your experience is obsolete and worthless." These false messages cannot be overcome simply by putting older people in a classroom and filling them up with new information. Freire, in particular, castigates this "banking model" of the learning process, in which learning is seen as acquiring more and more information, like money saved up in a bank. The point is, rather, that adults, especially older people, already have a lifetime of experience that is rich with meaning if only we could unlock its hidden potential.

The way to do this is not to expose older people to new information, but to initiate what Freire describes as a problem-*posing* education based on themes already implicit in the life experience of the students. This approach is not the same as a problem-solving, technocratic education in which students acquire new skills or analytical methods to solve preestablished problems. Instead, argues Freire, one must *problematize* the entire social, cultural, and historical reality in which we are immersed. To do this, we must identify the *generative themes* that emerge from students' own reality and own life experiences and then, through the process of dialogue, elicit what is universal and significant in those life experiences. Students, in other words, must take responsibility for their own learning processes, not in the absence of a teacher, but in partnerships in which the teacher is a learner as well. Freire insists on the need to free educators from their artificial roles as experts who know all the answers, and at the same time to free the students to be no longer passive objects of education, but rather its essential subjects.

Freire's ideas are of the greatest importance in the education of older people. Like the Brazilian peasants, older people tend to be robbed of their self-worth by being denied a meaningful role in society. The systematic devaluation of life experience leads many to feel that their past is worthless; in Simone de Beauvoir's terms, they face "a limited future and a frozen past." It is no wonder that older people risk dogmatism or despair or else escape it only by disowning the past. Freire's approach of problem-posing education means that we have to "problematize" this situation and challenge the stereotype of old age in our society. In this way, the generative themes implicit in life experience can become the center of the educational process, and older people will no longer be passive learners, but rather, active contributors to their own learning and to society at large.

TRANSCENDENCE

This appraisal of Freire's contribution, however, leaves some important questions unanswered. Freire's methods are in certain respects simply a systematic, philosophical account of effective adult education, or indeed of good education in any setting. Although the idea of generative themes elicited by dialogue gives us a method, it does not provide us with any content for a curriculum. It describes a process or a means of reaching a goal, but it does not tell us what our goal should be. In fairness to Freire, he would probably respond that the goal is simply *praxis,* or "reflective engagement in worldly activities." In the case of oppressed groups, *praxis* takes the form of political struggle and revolutionary consciousness aimed at transforming the world, but it is activity or engagement that remains primary. Is this goal of continuous activity a viable one for older people? It certainly represents one answer to the dilemma of old age in our society, an answer given by Simone de Beauvoir at the conclusion of *The Coming of Age* (1972):

> *The greatest good fortune, even greater than health, for the old person is to have his world still inhabited by projects: then, busy and useful, he escapes both from boredom and from decay. The times in which he lives remain his own, and he is not compelled to adopt the defensive and aggressive forms of behavior that are so often characteristic of the final years. His oldness passes as it were unnoticed. For this to be the case he must have committed himself to undertakings that set time at defiance.... (pp. 492-493)*

For Simone de Beauvoir, the solution to the problem of aging is rooted in an existential philosophy derived from Sartre and Marx and sharing similarities with Freire's concept of *praxis.* It is only the existential project, she tells us, that gives life its meaning, and this requires that older people must avoid turning inward, must transcend their own past by engagement in the present. In contrast to theorists who speak of disengagement from social roles in old age, Simone de Beauvoir insists that it is only through involvement and participation that people remain healthy in old age. But is there not implicit here a subtle rejection of the condition of old age itself? Note the phrase "His oldness passes as it were unnoticed." It seems that for Simone de Beauvoir there are no distinctive strengths or tasks uniquely associated with the condition of age. The answer to the question of what to do in old age is simply "more of the same."

A different point of view is possible, a point of view rooted in a developmental conception of the human life cycle. The great insight of progressive education, from Rousseau to John Dewey, is an insistence that the educational process be adapted to the changing developmental needs of the learner. Progressive education argued that we begin with the psychological growth of the child, not the abstract demands of the subject matter. This means that age is not an accidental, but an intrinsic, part of the learning process. We have not yet found a way to apply this principle to adult education for the very understandable reason that, by the large, we lack a detailed developmental psychology of the adult life cycle. What Freud and Piaget have done for the stages of child development needs to be done for the adult as well. As we look at language, sexuality, moral development, and logical reasoning in the child, we see a growth process tied to norms or developmental tasks mastered over time. Is there something analogous in the developmental process of adulthood and old age? Some psychologists, in particular Carl Jung (1963) and Erik Erikson (1963), have argued that there is.

Jung, for example, observes that the psychological demands of the second half of life are distinctively different from those of the first half. The first half of life is devoted to achieving a stable ego-identity associated with work and family, but the second half of life requires that we divest ourselves of the *persona*—"the mask of adult roles and social performances." The goal of the second half of life is a process of psychological *individuation* or self-realization: returning to our origins to become the total, unified personality symbolized by the archetype of the self: a circle, as in the image of the Ouroborus, a snake swallowing its own tail. In the first half of life, we go outside of ourselves to establish an identity through activity; in the second half, we turn inward to achieve wholeness. Interestingly, Jung warns that the psychopathologies of maturity and old age result from a failure to accept these changing developmental tasks of the life cycle. The aging playboy, the old person who lives in the memory of past glories, the old person who refuses to modify the lessons of past experience: all these represent a failure to live in the present, a failure to transcend the past.

But a developmental process that leads us to transcend the past must be rooted in acceptance of that past. It cannot be an escape or an evasion of the unresolved conflicts of life experience. We cannot disown the past, and this is simply to recognize the immutable law of the return of the repressed: the need to master each developmental stage in sequence, as Erik Erikson (1963) describes it in his chapter "The Eight Ages of Man," in *Childhood and*

Society. For Erikson, the distinctive task of old age is expressed in the polarity of *ego integrity* versus *despair.* Ego integrity means "acceptance of one's one and only life-cycle as something that had to be and that, by necessity, permitted of no substitutions" (p. 268). This sense of self-acceptance means working through the meaning of past experience, as in Butler's notion of life review.

These indications from Jung and Erikson point in their different ways toward a common thread that distinguishes the position of old age from other phases of the life cycle. As Simone de Beauvoir (1972) puts it:

> *In childhood and youth, life is experienced as a continual rise; and in favorable cases—either because of professional advancement or because bringing up one's children is a source of happiness, or because one's standard of living rises, or because of a greater wealth of knowledge—the notion of upward progress may persist in middle age. Then all at once a man discovers that he is no longer going anywhere . . . . There comes a moment when one knows that one is no longer getting ready for anything and one understands that the idea of advancing toward a goal was a delusion. (p. 491)*

In other words, with the arrival of old age, there is a fundamental alteration in the human experience of time, in which the "mirage of the future" disappears and one realizes "one is no longer getting ready for anything." In our future-directed, achievement-oriented culture, this realization can precipitate a tremendous psychological crisis. For the person facing sudden retirement, for example, the crisis may literally be life threatening: What do we live for if time is shrinking and we can no longer believe in the future? Whether we have reached our goals and been perplexed by success, or whether we have discovered that we will never become the person we imagined in youth: in either case, life closes in about itself and demands that the goals of the past be transcended.

The key concept here is *transcendence:* transcendence of the past, transcendence of previous social roles, transcendence of a limited definition of the self. For this reason, Simone de Beauvoir's prescription of "more of the same" (more activity, more projects) simply will not do. If there is to be participation and activity, it will have to be participation with a different qualitative experience of human time, with a recognition of finitude as intrinsic to the human condition. As Gray Panther leader Maggie Kuhn once remarked, the political activity of older people ought to be very different from ordinary interest-group politics. In an age of nuclear weapons, people have been urged to vote for a President who has grandchildren, as if to underscore the fact that our interest in the future does not end with our own life-span. If old people are "the elders of the tribe," then as an interest group, they have the potential of recognizing interests that transcend any single generation. If we educate older people for new roles and activities, it must be based on acceptance of the limitations of time, and it must include the selfless striving of preparation for future generations or creation of conditions for social justice in a world the old people will never live to see. To acknowledge our own finitude and death and still to strive for social change is already recognition of the dimension of transcendence.

Transcendence is acceptance of the past as finished and unfinished at one and the same time. It is a paradoxical attitude of suspended judgment about one's life. To transcend the past means to let go of it, to acknowledge it as finished, not to be repeated, as "the one and only life-cycle," but at the same moment that I am letting go of it, it begins to speak to me; my past speaks and tells of things I did not know before. It is speaking and listening at one and the same time. As the listener, I am in dialogue with my past, neither identified with it nor separate from it. My past is finished, but it is also unfinished because its meaning is never exhausted. It is not frozen, not worthless, but still rich with reflected light that can illuminate the present.

Was this *persona* simply a mask, an accidental covering of the self? Was the past a mere sequence of events without meaning or purpose? If the archetype of the self means completeness, totality, then it means acceptance of the *whole* of myself; it means that nothing can be discarded, nothing rejected as alien or "other" than me. I return to the origins. The value of life experience lies in what I can continually draw from it, as from an inexhaustible well.

Transcendence means overcoming one's previous role and definitions of the self; it means recovering them *in order* to let them go. The enormous value of education in old age lies in the way in which each subject studied can illuminate an aspect of this unrecovered self. For example, the history of the last 40 years allows older people to recognize themselves in the events that shaped their own life histories. The study of psychology or literature allows them to see, objectified, the same forces and conflicts that run through all our lives, to see that the story of the human race is one story. A liberal education is an education that is liberating, that discloses other cultures, other historical epochs, other values, in such a way that we discover, in this "other," our very own selves. Life experience is the starting point because the process of dialogue can begin anywhere and with any person. This educational enterprise is immensely important; it is serious; and above all, it is *difficult.* Perhaps I object to the notion of leisure-time education because it is ultimately demeaning; it seems to suggest that education in old age is not quite serious. The interesting fact is that, from the standpoint of the life cycle, older people have even less "leisure time" than the rest of us: the sense of time is more constricted and choices must be made with this recognition of finitude in mind.

This altered sense of time—the intuition of human finitude—provides the key we have been looking for. It situates the goal of the educational enterprise within the last phase of the life cycle and points to the developmental task defined by Erikson (1963) in the term *ego integrity:* "It is the ego's accrued assurance of its proclivity for order and meaning . . . an experience which conveys some world order and spiritual sense, no matter how early paid for" (p. 268). The continuing assurance of order and meaning demands that life experience be taken as the indispensable contribution and strength of older people. Yet to confront the real meaning of that life experience is to glimpse in experience itself something unsatisfied, something unknown. It is this intuition of the unknown, combined with self-acceptance and transcendence of the past, that stands out in the concluding passage from Jung's (1963) autobiography, *Memories, Dreams, Reflections,* written at age 85, at the very end of his life:

> *I am satisfied with the course my life has taken. It has been bountiful, and has given me a great deal. How could I ever have expected so much? Nothing but unexpected things kept happening to me. Much might have been different if I myself had been different. But it was as it had to be: for all came about because I am as I am . . . I cannot form any final judgment because the phenomenon of life and the phenomenon of man are too vast. The older I have become, the less I have understood or had insight into or known about myself.*

> *I am astonished, disappointed, pleased with myself. I am distressed, depressed, rapturous. I am all these things at once, and cannot add up the sum. . . . There is nothing I am quite sure about. I have no definite convictions—not about anything, really. I know only that I was born and exist, and it seems to me that I have been carried along. I exist on the foundation of something I do not know. In spite of all uncertainties, I feel a solidity underlying all existence and a continuity in my mode of being. (pp. 358–359)*

The fact that there is something incomprehensible or unknown about our life experience need not lead to the despair of *Krapp's Last Tape.* It is precisely *because* we come up against this mystery that we must have *hope.* As Jung puts it: "In spite of all uncertainties, I feel a solidity underlying all existence and a continuity in my mode of being." This is the meaning of Erikson's ego integrity and this is the reason why, in the end, Black Elk and Jung come to a common recognition. As Erikson (1963) says: "A wise Indian, a true gentleman, and a mature peasant share and recognize in one another the final stage of integrity" (p. 269).

Every old person in our classrooms will not be a Black Elk or a Carl Jung, and yet I have always found in conversation with old people, at bottom what each person wishes is to be able to tell his or her own story: to tell the story to himself or to herself and to know the teller of the tale. We all need to tell our stories, and if we bear this burden alone, then this is despair. Each of us wishes to be known and to know ourselves, and when we speak of individuation or ego integrity, this is the immmense task of old age: to know ourselves as a whole, as we really are, in the light of finitude and at the horizon of death.

In this chapter, I have spoken of experience, dialogue, and transcendence: the origin, the way, and the goal. Experience is the indispensable resource; dialogue releases the truth of experience and points toward a transcendence of our previous understanding. Experience, dialogue, transcendence: each phase moves on to the other until the circle completes itself as "we arrive where we started and know the place for the first time." If life experience is an unanswered question, then transcendence means to *live* the question, as Rilke (1963) says:

> *Be patient toward all that is unsolved in your heart and try to love the questions themselves like locked rooms and like books that are written in a very foreign tongue. Do not now seek the answers, which cannot be given you because you would not be able to live them. And the point is, to live everything.* Live *the questions now. Perhaps you will then gradually without noticing it, live along some distant day into the answer. (pp. 34–35)*

An education that teaches us to love the questions themselves will also teach us to tell our own story and, God willing, teach us to bear the burden of our own existence as an infinite labor of perfection. This education alone is worthy of the last stage of life.

REFERENCES

de Beauvoir, S. *The coming of age.* New York: Putnam's, 1972.

Eliot, T. S. *Four quartets.* New York: Harcourt, 1971.

Erikson, E. *Childhood and society* (2nd ed.). New York: Norton, 1963.

Jung, C. G. [*Memories, dreams, reflections*] (A. Jaffe, Ed., and R. Winston and C. Winston, trans.). New York: Pantheon, 1963.

Neihardt, J. G. *Black Elk speaks, being the life story of a holy man of the Oglala Sioux.* Lincoln: University of Nebraska Press, 1961.

Plato, *Meno* (W. K. C. Guthrie, trans.). In E. Hamilton & H. Cairns (Eds.), *The collected dialogues of Plato.* New York: Pantheon, 1966.

Rilke, R. M. *Letters to a young poet* (rev. ed.). New York: Norton, 1963.

3

THE COMMUNITY OF GENERATIONS: A GOAL AND A CONTEXT FOR THE EDUCATION OF PERSONS IN THE LATER YEARS

HOWARD Y. McCLUSKY

University of Michigan

The present is in every age merely the shifting point at which past and present meet, and we can have no quarrel with either. There can be no world without traditions; neither can there be any life without movement . . . .

There is never a moment when the new dawn is not breaking over the earth, and never a moment when the sunset ceases to die. It is well to greet serenely even the first glimmer of the dawn when we see it, not hastening toward it with undue speed, nor leaving the sunset without gratitude for the dying light that was once dawn.

In the moral world we are ourselves the lightbearers, and the cosmic process is in us made flesh. For a brief space it is granted to us, if we will, to enlighten the darkness that surrounds our path . . . . As in the ancient torch race . . . we press forward torch in hand along the course. Soon from behind comes the runner who will outpace us. All our skill lies in giving into his hands the living torch, bright and unflickering, as we ourselves disappear into the future . . . .

Havelock Ellis

Because of the incomplete and provisional state of our knowledge, this chapter is necessarily exploratory in character and makes no pretense of constituting a definitive statement of the field. It is offered here primarily as a means of opening up a new domain of practice and inquiry for the agenda of both the educational gerontologist and the general educator.

THE CONCEPT

The concept of the *community of generations* is an intentional variation on a life-span approach to comprehending the wholeness of life. It is based on the assumption that, although separated by time and experience, each generation nevertheless has a common stake with other generations in relating itself to the wholeness of the life-span of which it is a part. In more operational terms, a community of generations is not a community of "equals" or "similars." It is not an association of persons necessarily similar in performance, ability, social class, or ethnic origin. Moreover, it is not an association of persons necessarily in agreement on substantive matters. On the contrary, it is, to coin a term, a *community of differents,* i.e., an interacting collectivity of people occupying both adjacent and widely separated stages in the progression from the beginning to the end of life. The thesis in this chapter is that this difference is of such a character as to make the achievement of a community of generations a viable possibility. It is this difference that makes an experience of the wholeness of life more comprehensible. It is also this difference that accents the common and compelling need the generations have to learn from one another. Finally it is the celebration of the creative potential of this difference that generates the dynamics for establishing the community of generations as a goal and a context for the education of Persons in the Later Years.

Reservations

Before proceeding with an exegesis of what is essentially an optimistic and developmental view of the potential of instructional processes, we should be prepared to face some of the hard-nosed realities with which any intergenerational effort must contend. In the first place, we must reckon with one of the most pervasive features of human existence—the direction of the flow of responsibility between the generations. In infancy, childhood, and, in our culture, during most of the period of youth, growing individuals are dependent on the generation immediately ahead of them for support and protection. The people of this generation are usually their parents or parent surrogates with whom they necessarily maintain a kind of dependent, or debtor, relationship. This must be so because of the irreversible progression of stages through which people must move in the life cycle. This relationship is, of course, by no means wholly devoid of educational outcomes. For one thing, parents are probably the most important teachers in children's lives. For another, the children, far more than most people admit, are at least implicitly but no less effectively, teachers of their parents. In other words, the family is still the basic educational unit in society. The point, however, is that the dominant-dependent nature of the relationship between the parental generation and the adjacent younger generation can be, and often is, a barrier to productive communication and must be properly handled if its educational potential is to be achieved.

In the second place, in making a case for the idea of the community of generations, we must deal with another feature of the human condition: the facts that, generally speaking, people interact and communicate more readily with their generational peers than they do with people of other generations and that the greater the generational distance, the less the likelihood of communication. One explanation for this point is the fact that the dominant-dependent relationship leads young people to seek the company of their peers in order to achieve a balancing sense of autonomy. This reaching out is especially strong during adolescence, and, as one way of achieving a sense of identity, it accounts in part for the dynamics of the youth culture. A collateral and perhaps more persuasive explanation for a preference for communicating with peers is that people occupying approximately the same stages of life confront, to use Havighurst's terminology, similar *developmental tasks* or *dominant concerns* and therefore have more in common about which to communicate. For example, few experiences produce a greater sense of community among parents than that of being members of a parent-teacher group concerned with the well-being of their children in the same elementary school.

A third major factor responsible for an ideological separation of generations is the outcome of a feature of our educational system—the pervasive practice of segregating the ages in both the curricular and administrative dimensions of educational programs. This practice was consolidated when the school system in the United States adopted the Prussian model of an age-graded organization in which, for example, members of the first grade are 6 years old, members of the second grade are age 7, third grade youngsters are age 8, and so forth. (The growing support for expansion of the ungraded elementary school is a reaction against the rigidities of the prevailing Prussian model.) A plausible case can be made for some grouping according to developmental stages for instructional purposes, especially when we consider the developmental distance between the 6-year-old and the prepubescent 12-year-old or between the pubescent 13-year-old and the 16-year-old. The reason, however, for calling attention in this context to the historic practice of age segregation in the educational system of the United States is that, in proposing the implementation of the concept of the community of generations, we confront a long-established tradition based on the assumption that education occurs more effectively when it is confined to interaction with members of the same generation than when it is designed to encourage communication between the generations. It does not serve the implementation of the community of generations, to romantically ignore some of the tough realities with which any effort at maximizing the potential of intergenerational relations must contend.

Boundaries

The concept of the community of generations could apply to the interrelationships of any combination of generations we might wish to examine, and from an educational standpoint, each combination would present a set of issues and opportunities unique to it as well as the issues and opportunities relevant to the entire life-span. For purposes of this discussion, however, I am concerned mainly, though not exclusively, with the inter-relationships of the generation of childhood and youth with the generation of the later years.

The concept of the community of generations as applied to the educational enterprise has both a procedural and a substantive dimension. Procedurally, it suggests both motivations and strategies whereby the subject matter of instruction may be more effectively internalized. Substantively, it suggests a somewhat innovative approach to the determination of what the subject matter of instruction might be. In both cases, as already indicated, the differences between the positions of the respective generations are regarded, not as a liability, but as a decisive asset in enhancing the influence of educational processes.

THE PROCEDURAL DIMENSION

It is my premise that, if properly arranged, interaction between the generations can be productive for invigorating and broadening the thrust of the teaching-learning process. This premise is based on the fact that each generation occupies a different stage in life-span development and is a product of a somewhat different set of societal forces. I also postulate that these two factors will tend to lead each generation of people to approach an issue or area of subject matter in a way unique to its stance.

Before proceeding further with my argument, I should be careful not to overplay this point. For instance, it can be plausibly argued that a developmental stage (i.e., a stage en route to maturity) and a difference between cohorts would make little difference in approaching such cognitively pure examples of subject matter as mathematics and the physical sciences or perhaps some meticulously objective treatment of the empirical data of history or geography as well. Also, it might be argued that there is often as wide a difference in the viewpoints of members of the same generation as there is between members of different generations. Finally, many issues will, for many people, transcend generational differences. There may be people in both the later and earlier years who feel equally strongly about such problems as protection of the environment, involvement in foreign affairs, or discovery of new sources of energy.

It is sufficient for my case, however, to point out that, for many people, a variation in the stage of life-span development, combined with a difference in the surrounding environment in which successive generations are immersed, can lead to a difference in approaching those aspects of learning for which life-centered experiences possess a unique relevance. If we can accept this hypothesis, we can assemble a substantial volume of psychological theory and research to support it and to explain the dynamics of its operation.

There are several kinds of evidence from the field of psychology that can be employed to account for the dynamics of instruction that differences between the generations might generate. One kind is derived from a study of the operation of *perceptual contrast.* For example, a sound, even of moderate intensity, following a period of prolonged silence, will attract more attention than a sound following a continuous series of sounds; e.g., the bark of a dog or the song of a bird in a silent forest, the crack of a gun fired under the silence of a desert sky. Conversely, a moment of silence abruptly following a period of sustained noise will attract more attention than silence that is merely more of what already exists; e.g., at a noisy sports event the moment of quiet in honor of the memory of a distinguished citizen, the stillness of a night sky at the end of an explosive display of Fourth of July fireworks. Similar results may occur in reaction to contrasts between light and darkness, between movement and rest, and, in more generic perceptual terms (especially important to our argument), between figure and ground.

Another kind of evidence comes from our knowledge of the phenomenon of *homeostasis,* the tendency of the organism to seek to maintain a steady state of equilibrium. If this equilibrium is upset, the organism goes to work to bring about its restoration. For instance, when we are well fed, we are in equilibrium; if we are hungry or starving, our gastronomic system is thrown off balance, and we seek food to regain our preferred state of steadiness. So it is with water when we are thirsty, or rest when we are fatigued, or heat when we are cold, or cold when we are hot. Although our knowledge of homeostasis has been largely physiological in character, many psychologists believe that homeostasis is just as relevant to the understanding of the dynamics of personality as it is to the understanding of bodily conditions. For example, stress, anxiety, fear, or blows to self-esteem upset the steady state of an individual's adjustment; as a consequence a person will strive to remove the source of these threats in order to recover a sense of well-being.

Still another kind of evidence that can be used to explain the dynamics of intergenerational differences may be found in the theory of *cognitive dissonance.* Simplified, this theory holds that if ideas (i.e., cognitions) are perceived by a person as incongruous (i.e., dissonant), that person will employ various strategies to realign the ideas into some state of acceptable, cognitive harmony.

By this time, the reason for making use of the insights that may be derived from psychology should be clear: Diversities of experience and outlook that may result from occupying a different stage in the life-span lend themselves to the use of contrast, disequilibrium, dissonance, and other kinds of inherent or contrived discrepancies as a means for motivating and broadening the processes of instruction. With proper arrangement of the instructional situation, this technique can be accomplished well within the range of acceptable toleration. To paraphrase a well-known cliché, I am simply asserting that the *variety* of intergenerational differences, can be the *spice* of the teaching-learning process. Let me operationalize the argument by illustrating what this point might look like in practice.

First, consider how the reactions of a 10-year-old child, or a 16-year-old youth, or a 25-year-old young adult would compare with the reactions of a 70- or 80-year-old adult upon (1) perceiving a flower, (2) viewing a picture of some historical event, (3) reading a story, (4) solving a problem, or (5) empathizing with some instance of acquisition or loss, or of success or failure.

Second, consider the following questions as topics for a panel discussion in which representatives of the ages indicated are participants: What is best and what is worst about being age 15 or age 25 as opposed to being age 65, or 75, or 85? What is best and worst about being a woman or a man at age 25 and at age 75?

Third, consider what a resourceful teacher could do with Arthur Miller's *Death of a Salesman* in a class where a sizable number of the members has first-hand knowledge what it means to be occupationally frustrated, while others in the class have yet to be employed in a permanent job. Consider what a teacher of political science could do with a course in local government in which some class members have participated in a party caucus or have served on the city council or are veterans of the program of the League of Women Voters, whereas others have yet to vote.

Finally, consider how an intergenerational mix of students affords opportunities for a variety of additional strategies for the stimulation of instruction; e.g., the reversal of intergenerational positions in role playing; the alternation of persons of different generations in observing the processes and content of group discussion; the use of intergenerational teams in planning projects, data collection, and outreach programs of research and community service.

My hypothesis, then, is simply that the combination of differences accommodated by a community of generations would greatly enlarge the scope of procedures available for instruction and, at the same time, result in outcomes ranging from clarification of issues to the production of a creative dialectic.

THE SUBSTANTIVE DIMENSION

In attempting to deal with the substantive dimension of the community of generations, I can make no pretense of offering a definitive statement about such a highly speculative domain. Moreover, I cannot pretend that what

I have to offer is uniformly applicable to all people of all generations. I intend the following points to convey generic and ideal themes in order to indicate the kind of substantive outcomes that may emerge from an involvement of different generations in a common, instructional experience.

I am attempting to formulate an answer to the question What can one generation learn from another generation? More explicitly, What can a Young Person (YP) learn from a Person in the Later Years (PLY) and what can PLYS learn from YPs?

What Persons in the Later Years
Can Learn from Young Persons

First, PLYs can, in the course of interacting educatively with YPs recover some of the idealism they probably had in the earlier years of their own childhood and youth. At the risk of being stereotypical, a case can be made for the fact that, in general, YPs have high expectations, dream dreams, and are idealistic. On the other hand, members of the adult generation are generally prone to trim the aspirations of their youth and to adjust to the frustrating realities with which any implementation of ideals is compelled to contend. Perhaps YPs expect too much, but it is also possible that adults of the middle and later years expect too little. Is it not possible, then, that some exposure to the idealism of youth would stimulate those in the pragmatic, adult years to lift their sights and renew their faith in the vision of a better life? Although it is not inevitable, the probability is great enough to justify a revival of effort.

Second, by associating with YPs in common tasks of learning, PLYs can go far toward renewing a sense of intellectual discovery. In the early stages of life, much of living must necessarily be devoted to processes of discovery. Encountered for the first time, everything is new and must be sampled, tested, and learned. Hence, things, people, events, machines, nature, are all novel to the young and are generally objects of exploration. It would be easy at this point to be naive and forget that much of what, to a YP is frontier must become habitual in order to free him or her for the performance of more mature tasks. As the years pass, however, those objects, people, skills, and procedures necessary for survival become learned so that what was once a matter of discovery becomes a process of maintenance, i.e., sheer performance rather than growth in learning. The law of least effort makes understandable why it is easy for adults to restrict their living to the repetitive performance of procedures already learned and to gradually lose the inclination to break new paths, entertain new thoughts, and explore new frontiers. Again, is it not possible; when and where there are so many new things, facts, technologies, and procedures to be learned as well as a mass of equally exciting and relevant old things not yet learned; that sharing with YPs the challenge of discovery will induce PLYs to achieve a new sense of intellectual adventure? Although it is not inevitable, it certainly seems worth a try.

Third, in working with YPs there is a strong probability that PLYs can rekindle their interest in and achieve an extended sense of a viable future. There comes a time, perhaps about midway in life, when people become aware of the fact that they have a past and aware that the sense of unlimited time that characterized their outlook in the days of youth is giving way to a realization that life is not forever, that time is beginning to run out. It is not surprising, therefore, that when people move into and through the last quarter of life, more and more of their waking hours are absorbed with the increasing volume of the apperceptive past, mixed with a growing awareness of an existential now, together with a sense of a rapidly diminishing future. I use the word *rapidly* here deliberately to reflect the well-nigh universal experience that the longer life lasts, the more rapidly time seems to pass.

In contrast, from the perspective of the life-span, the lives of young people are drastically incomplete. Because of this incompleteness, youth are rich in life expectations. The years stretch out before them in lines of development that they have yet to experience. It is understandable, therefore, that YPs should be activated by a sense of the future so compelling that it dominates their entire outlook on life. It is also understandable that they should devote so much of their effort to anticipating what may lie ahead; for instance, how they will earn a living, the family they hope to establish, or a possible return to education. Recent research (Olmsted, 1976) indicates that even as early as the middle and late teens, YPs are capable of projecting a realistic schedule of major events likely to occur in the full span of their own lives. By associating with young people and by empathetically assisting them to envisage their lives, PLYs could, under favorable circumstances, be more likely to develop an extension of a sense of their own future and achieve the ability to transcend, in part, the perceived limitations of their decreasing life expectancy.

Fourth, by interacting with YPs in educational activities, PLYs would be more likely to maintain a meaningful contact with the stream of societal change. This point goes far toward underscoring the fragility of the status of PLYs in a period in human history when change is so rapid, pervasive, and dominant and promises to become increasingly so in the years ahead.

Let us consider how some of the decisive events in the course of life tend to remove PLYs from the mainstream of change. There is the impact of retirement. When people retire, they automatically lose the day-by-day, face-to-face contact with fellow workers that constituted a major link to the changing world. If they formerly belonged to a labor union or an organization of employees, this association, with its publications and programs of events, tends to weaken. Retirement means, for practical purposes, removal from a part of society, namely the world of work, that perhaps more than any other part reflects the tide of societal change. Then there is the fact that as people gain in years, links with systems of kinship tend to decline; children, formerly a source of communication with the world outside the home, grow up, leave home, and establish their own independence and their own families. Further-more, because of the growing trend toward geographic mobility, brothers and sisters, uncles and aunts, cousins, and other members of the clan are likely to be living in widely scattered locations throughout the country. As a result, PLYs suffer another gradual erosion of ties with the outside world of change. There is also the problem of transportation and the trend toward living in relative isolation that contribute to weakening the bonds of PLYs with the stream of contemporary change as they gain in years.

In contrast, one of the distinctive features of the world of youth is that, by virtue of their unique location in the life-span, YPs are strategically positioned to reflect and transmit the tides of change. To use an analogy from chemistry, YPs are both the litmus paper and the catalyst of societal change. After all, we live in a youth-oriented society, and whatever else they are, YPs are contemporary and live in contemporary culture, and to be contemporary is to keep abreast of change. They absorb the new language, alternatives in life-style, occupations, and recreation like a sponge absorbs water. So, one of the ways in which PLYs can keep up with a rapidly changing society is to maintain a viable contact with YPs, and this can be most meaningfully accomplished by joining them in a community of inquiry.

What Young Persons Can Learn from Persons in the Later Years

Let us now turn to the question of what YPs could, under favorable and appropriate circumstances, learn from PLYs. The answer to this question stems almost wholly from the generic and obvious fact that PLYs have lived longer than YPs. PLYs' advantage as potential instructors is largely due to the advanced position they occupy in the life cycle. In effect, they have had more experience and know more about the wholeness of life. I am not proposing that all PLYs will demonstrate the advantage of their advanced position, nor do I assert that they will all embody the ideal behavior described in the following discussion. I am writing about the ideal expectations and pos-sibilities, some of which some PLYs will be able to approximate, if not achieve.

In the first place, some, possibly many, PLYs in any given instructional setting will have an expertise they can contribute to an educational program, depending, of course, on the level and subject of instruction. In some instances, this expertise may consist of a highly developed skill or craft-manship, the possession of which was much more common 50 years ago than today. In other instances, their expertise may consist of some areas of specialized knowledge, a knowledge that is the product of a lifetime of practice and study. In still other cases, a PLY may possess unusual compe-tence in the management of human relations. These three examples are merely illustrations to which many more could be added. Whatever the nature of the extensive experience of the PLYs, it can be an enormous advantage in working with young people in an educational setting. In fact, it should always be kept in mind that in many situations any number of PLYs may possess a competence in some departments far in excess of that possessed by the instructor of a class. This is another way of saying that probably the only dimension in which an instructor, presumably a younger adult, can be certain of being more competent than a given PLY student, is in the subject matter around which the class is organized. A PLY may express this expertise in various ways: by insightful contributions to a group discussion; by serving as a counselor to younger fellow students; or by serving as a short-term, ad hoc instructor when some topic on the teacher's lesson plan coincides with that expertise.

In the second place, because they have lived longer and have known more of life, with its mixtures of frustration and success, disappointment and fulfillment, PLYs will be in a better position to relate the learning of the classroom to the realities of everyday living. Learning, to them, will not be a thing apart, embalmed in books and libraries and restricted to laboratories and workshops. Learning will, to the PLYs, become a vital part of the exigencies of daily existence. Thus they will demand and be able to contribute relevance to the instruction to a degree that cannot possibly be matched by YPs because of the limitations of experience with which they are compelled to contend. PLYs will be in a much more favorable position to translate theory into practice than YPs, and YPs will in turn be the beneficiaries of this competence.

In the third place, PLYs, as potential instructors of their younger colleagues, will have the advantage of having lived through a most fantastic and turbulent period of history. In consequence, they will possess a perspective on a wide range of human concerns that only a direct encounter with historical events can provide. Take, for example, the history of United States involvement in war. This generation of PLYs will have listened to the recital by their parents or grandparents of stories based on a living participation in our Civil War. Anecdotes and names associated with the battles of Bull Run, Antietam, and Gettysburg and with the surrender at Appomattox will be vivid in the memories of their childhood days. Somewhat later, they or their parents will have taken part, directly or indirectly, in the first worldwide war in the chronicles of the human race. They will have actual photographs or living memories of the battles of the Somme, the retreat to the Marne, the stalemate at Verdun, and the surrender negotiated in the railway car in the forest of Compiègne near Paris. Some will have been there; others will have heard about it from those who were there. Then there was the attack on Pearl Harbor and World War II. This time, some PLYs, but in most cases their children, were caught up in the mobilization of forces. This time the war effort took four years (1941-1945), not one (1917-1918), and the conflict occurred, with new, sophisticated weapons, on three continents and their bordering oceans, rather than just in Western Europe. Since then, there have been the Korean War and the war in Vietnam.

For another example of the historical perspective PLYs can provide, take the very practical, down-to-earth behavior of money. This generation of PLYs will recall when $1 was considered to be a fair wage for a ten-hour day's work. They will also remember the shock causing howls of consternation in the industrial world when Henry Ford advanced the wage rate to $5 a day. Because of these memories, they will have qualms and some reluctance about paying $25 for one hour of the time of a plumber to repair a faucet in the kitchen sink. They will remember what it felt like when the banks were closed during the early days of the depression, and what it was like to be unemployed without insurance or compensation, or what it was like for their own parents and grandparents to face retirement without the support of social security. Some of the current PLYs may wonder why the National Youth Administration (NYA), or the Civilian Conservation Corps (CCC), or an equivalent is not revived in order to check the rise of unemployment among youth.

Communication provides still another example. The PLYs generation will be able to tell about the time when they had to turn a crank at the side of a wooden box to get the attention of the telephone operator instead of being able to dial directly to phone stations in most quarters of the globe, as we can today. They will also be able to tell us about when the radio and television first arrived; what it was like as these twin technologies brought instant news and information into the privacy of their homes from the most distant parts of the world; and how this and the advent of jet airplanes have transformed the image of the world as a potential community, an image, more of fact than of experience and acceptance, with which we have yet to come to terms.

I could continue with an elaboration of the changes that have occurred in the last 65 years or so in transportation, sources of energy, international relations, education, population, food supply, human relations, women's liberation, sexual behavior, civil rights, religious attitudes, family life, etc.; but to do so would only be piling up evidence for the point that by this time should be well established—that this generation of PLYs has had an opportunity to observe and take part in transformations of living that have been massive in scale and dramatic in impact. They are, therefore, living historians of an incredible, recent past, and as such, they are in a position to make an authentic contribution to any learning experience that they might share with YPs and to which the historical dimension is relevant.

Those who have lived through the last amazing and transforming 65 or more years of history will, because of this fact, have much more to offer as potential educators than just a knowledge of historical happenings. They will have achieved a sense of time past and time to come, giving them an outlook that will place issues, problems, and the stream of events in an enduring and stabilizing perspective—a perspective some regard as one of the most valuable outcomes of an educative experience. For instance, they will not necessarily be dismayed when at times everything seems to be going wrong, because they will have known periods like this before and have survived. On the other hand, they will not be unduly swayed by ebullient promises, however attractive, of better things to come, because they have had to retreat from high expectations before and life has continued to be reasonably good. Thus they should be able to help YPs not to panic when the door slams shut or to become too excited when the door blows open.

This attitude could also help YPs to secure a stabilizing grip on the impact of change. Earlier in this discussion, I stressed the point that young people live in a culture of the contemporary and reflect change like a sponge absorbs water. This is obviously a fact, but it is not necessarily a virtue and certainly no cause for celebration, because in extreme forms, being contemporary can border on the pathological. Being an 18-karat contemporary can lead a person to act like a weather vane responding, without the slightest display of autonomy, to every shift in the wind. Being contemporary can mean rushing desperately from passing fad to passing fad, or jumping on every bandwagon that comes in sight without asking where it is going or discovering what it will do after it arrives. This malady is a mild form of neurotic behavior that is not necessarily confined to the younger generation inasmuch as it often strikes adults, especially in mid-life when they suddenly discover that time is running out, whereupon they attempt to secure a new grasp on the meaning of life. It is, however, a kind of malady, an escape into meaningless activity, for which some YPs, in their efforts to be "with it," are especially susceptible.

PLYs, with their perspective, can be a positive force in keeping this drive for the contemporary within constructive bounds and in reminding YPs that change qua change is not necessarily constructive; that much of what appears to be new is simply a return, under a new label, of something that has been around for a long time; and that, in some cases, virtue is more likely to be embodied in something that has stood the test of time, than in something, like a roman candle, that has suddenly caught the attention of people but will soon be lost in the darkness and forgotten. YPs may ask, Is it new? but PLYS may ask the more fundamental questions, Is it important? Will it last? for PLYs will have lived long enough to know that many more start a race than finish it and those who finish are in a better position to know how to get there than those who drop out soon after the bang of the starting gun.

These three broad areas of contributions PLYs can make to the education of young people by no means exhaust the possibilities. To the points already made I could add the role that PLYs could play in helping YPs validate an internalization of enduring values, the pursuit of which gives meaning to life, or to be more operational, I could formulate rec- ommendations that PLYs could submit to YPs looking forward to successful aging in their own later years, but instead I conclude this section of my presentation with an exegesis of what is probably the most important contribution that PLYs can make to the educational development of YPs: helping them to achieve some understanding of the interactive wholeness of the life-span and to see how this understanding can facilitate lifelong development.

To make this point as secure and acceptable as possible, I am prepared to concede that we should not expect people in a world of growing complexity and change to be sufficiently clairvoyant to anticipate with any degree of certainty the paths the future may dictate. Under such circumstances, the wisest strategy is to make the best of every event and task as they appear and to trust that a successful response to their demands will equip people to deal adequately with succeeding demands as they come along. This policy makes good sense for practical, short-run purposes, but it fails to take into account that, whereas society may be changing in unanticipated ways, the critical events, requirements, and turning points of the life cycle are, nevertheless, much more predictable. Because of this fact, individuals can secure a much better grasp on the direction of the years ahead if they are disposed to view the future in the context of the wholeness of lifelong development.

Before we allow ourselves to be carried away by a euphoric acceptance of this point, let us briefly examine some of the trends in contemporary living that stand in the way of its implementation. In a society in which babies are born and the elderly die in hospitals and not at home; in which little children are placed in day-care centers or nursery schools; in which 6-to-12-year-olds are segregated in a six-grade elementary school; in which youth in the 12-to-14 and 14-to-18 age brackets are separated in junior and senior high schools; in which people 18 years of age and older are scattered in community and far-flung four-year colleges; in which more mothers are working at part- and full-time jobs; in which both mothers' and fathers' jobs are usually separated from the home in both function and location; in which grandparents and great-grandparents are usually living alone in single housing units or segregated in housing complexes for "seniors" or in retirement villages often located in distant parts of the country; in such circumstances, how can the society and its people gain an adequate understanding and appreciation of the developmental, life-span wholeness? Obviously, an adequate and realistic answer to this question will require fresh action on many fronts, e.g., community, planning, housing, transportation, kinship system, etc. We are confronting, here, a problem grounded in some of the basic features of modern living and for which an adequate solution will require more than a reordering of the educational enterprise; but properly conceived and properly arranged, educational institutions could go a long way to relieve the situation just described and to recapture some of the sense of life-span wholeness that our fragmenting society is leading us to lose.

In taking this stand, I am not naively proposing that achieving a sense of developmental wholeness will come easily or that its achievement will ever be perfect. I do claim that such an achievement can be approximated and that its approximation should become a goal *deliberately* chosen to give direction to instructional programs. In pursuit of this goal, PLYs would have a unique function to perform and would have an exclusive advantage in doing so.

The uniqueness of their function stems from a point I have stressed before, namely that PLYs have lived longer and experienced more of the totality of life than people who are now young but have yet to experience middle and old age. PLYs, though now old, were once middle aged and young. Thus, because of their apperceptive memory bank, they have the capacity to comprehend much better what life in its wholeness is all about than young people with their lack of experience possibly could.

How would this advantage be expressed? In at least two ways: (1) PLYs could help YPs take a long view of some of the inevitable happenings and turning points they will, in the course of the unfolding years, be compelled to confront, and (2) even more important, PLYs could, through processes of educational exchange and also by serving as models of successful living, assist YPs to view their own later years as a period of progressive development. Thus, they could anticipate their future, not as a plateau followed by an over-the-hill decline, but rather as an ascending spiral with the potential culmination being lifelong fulfillment. To use the formulation of Erikson (1963), YPs could look forward to the middle years as a period for generation and the avoidance of stagnation, and to the later years as a time for the achievement of a sense of ego integrity rather than despair. To borrow from Maslow (1970), YPs could be assisted in perceiving the later years as a time when a person becomes "fully human" and "fully mature," with potentialities "fully realized." Self-actualization would be regarded as a unique and exclusive achievement of PLYs. To quote Maslow (1970):

> *Self-actualization does not occur in young people. In our culture at least, youngsters have not yet achieved identity or autonomy nor have they had time enough to experience an enduring, loyal, post-romantic love relationship, nor have they generally found their calling, the altar upon which to offer themselves. Nor have they worked out their own system of values; nor have they had experience enough (responsibility for others, tragedy, failure, achievement, success) to shed perfectionistic illusions and become realistic; nor have they generally made their peace with death; nor have they learned how to be patient; nor have they learned enough about evil in themselves and others to be compassionate; nor have they had time to become post-ambivalent about parents and elders, power and authority; nor have they generally become knowledgeable and educated enough to open the possibility of becoming wise;*

nor have they generally acquired enough courage to be unpopular, to be unashamed about being openly virtuous, etc. (p. xx)

EXAMPLES

To illustrate the kind of community of generations I have been advocating, I am concerned here with examples of intergenerational projects that are primarily educative in character, although I am not committed to any formal model of instruction. In some instances, the principal learner is a PLY, and the YP is the teacher. In other cases, the direction of exchange is reversed. In still other situations, both YPs and PLYs interact as peers engaged in a common task of learning. I have selected five projects for review. To indicate the range of potential in the field, two projects are located in settings outside the formal school system and three within. In the former category, one project is an innovative venture of the Girl Scouts, and the other is a product of a "rest home." In the latter category, one project takes place at the level of the elementary school, another in a high school, and a third in a college specializing in the baccalaureate degree. I offer none as ideal models, and none embody all of the values I have earlier ascribed to the outcomes of intergenerational education. All are, however, authentic, real-life examples of how YPs and PLYs can get along together in a shared task of inquiry.

Girl Scouts

For a number of years, local Girl Scout troops, as a part of their regular program, have organized projects involving the association of young Scouts with PLYs. These separate efforts became so attractive that the national organization of Girl Scouts, with funds from the Administration on Aging, decided to make this kind of activity a matter of national emphasis and gave it the title Hand-in-hand: Cross-age Interactions (Girl Scouts of the U.S.A., 1975). Some excerpts from the report of the first year of the national project illustrate what actually happens when the young and the PLYs share their interests and contribute their respective talents to activities designed to improve the quality of living for those participating as well as those being served.

Let us begin with a look at the program of the Santiam Girl Scout Council of Salem, Oregon. In Salem, the Scouts collected oral histories from the PLYs, conducted games that both the Scouts and the PLYs could enjoy, and set up an adopted grandparent program designed to foster enduring, one-to-one relationships. The initiative, however, did not always originate with the YPs. For example, one elderly woman, although arthritic and confined to a wheelchair, taught a Scout troop how to knit; at a potluck dinner-concert given by the Scouts' families, a group of senior guests entertained the audience by playing their own brand of recycled instruments and by presenting a skit in which Tiny Tim was the featured character (according to the recorder, everybody "loved it"). Girl Scouts also participate by visiting the elderly in their homes and assisting them with shopping. In cold weather, the older Scouts help PLYs by installing storm windows in their homes. Participation in the Salem project increased 1000% in the first year of its operation.

The Girl Scouts of Lathrup Village, Michigan have organized a day-camp program for the elderly of the area in which the elderly are the campers and the Scouts are the counselors. Activities range from just enjoying the sun and being out in the country to arts and crafts. At the same time, the "campers" ((PLYs) teach the Scouts how to fish and study nature. The Lathrup Village program is not all camping, however. Back home, the Scouts have organized a friendship circle that involves, among other things, the girls telephoning PLYs to offer their services, to learn how they are getting along, or just to talk. As a result, some very close and gratifying relationships have developed.

In Marquette, Michigan the Girl Scout Council is involved with an already established group of PLYs called the Merry Mixers. The two groups are diverse, not only in age, but also in background. The PLYs have spent their entire lives in the Marquette area, whereas members of the Scout troop from Sawyer Air Force Base have lived in such faraway places as Morocco, Germany, and Turkey. This variety in background has turned out to be a great asset in program development. From the PLYs, the Scouts have learned about the past by living history. Crafts are also a source of mutual enjoyment for both the Scouts and the PLYs. Their creations, which are often the product of cooperative effort, are sometimes sold to help cover the costs of the project. From the Scouts, the PLYs receive some much-needed and appreciated services. For example, the girls help partially disabled PLYs with such chores as housecleaning and snow shoveling. They also assist with a hot lunch program that operates out of a school cafeteria. A Cadette troop regularly visits a nursing home, and another troop is helping to locate PLYs who might need health care. As a result, both the PLYs and the young Scouts have been delighted in developing new friendships.

Eureka, Illinois, Rest Home

Let us next examine another kind of program that is outside the formal school system and that is the product of a kind of agency in which we would least expect such a project to occur, namely, a "rest home." The program is the Prairie Crafts workshop, located at the Maple Lawn Homes, a Mennonite rest home in Eureka, Illinois. The project got under way when Ellen Braucht, the Home Extension advisor for Woodford County, received a request from some young homemakers for a workshop on quilt making. Braucht knew that many of the residents of the Maple Lawn Homes were experts in the disappearing skills of quilt making, knitting, crocheting, embroidering, and weaving; she had also observed a growing interest among young homemakers in the creative homemaking skills of the past, so the Prairie Crafts workshop was born. The residents of the Maple Lawn Homes are the instructors and the young homemakers are the students.

Beginning with 50 young homemakers and 12 residents, the project has grown to involve 200 homemakers and 60 residents. There is no charge for instruction. The instructors range in age from 80 to 96; the students are 19 and older. A few young mothers bring their small children to the workshop. This attracts some of the residents who are not involved as instructors, so there is no lack of sitters to take care of the children while their mothers learn how to make quilts. Interest in the project has been high, and soon more quilts were produced than the homemakers could use. As a result, Earl Greaser, the Maple Lawn Homes administrator, arranged to partition off and enclose with glass windows one end of the activity room and named it "Granny's Cupboard." Items in Granny's Cupboard are for sale. According to the latest report, the women of the home have a substantial backlog of orders for their products.

So it happened that a young, alert, Home Extension advisor brought together the skills of a group of women 80 to 96 years of age—skills that are the product of another era—with the needs of a group of young women interested in improving the culture of their own homes. As a result, friendships developed, interests expanded, over 60 elderly women got a new lease on life, and—for a substantial number of young families in the area of Eureka, Illinois—traditional American crafts were preserved to be enjoyed and passed on to future generations.

Fairhaven College—The Bridge Project

To introduce the second category of examples of intergenerational education, we now turn to Bellingham, Washington, the location of Fairhaven College, which for the past few years has been experimenting with the inclusion of a number of people over 60 years of age in the student body. Called the Bridge Project, it attempts to overcome the differences in understanding that presumably exist between the generations. The project began modestly in October, 1973. When the PLYs first arrived on the campus, they and the students were a little wary of each other, but uncertainty soon disappeared. The students found that they could continue to live the way they had been living and that the older people were not apostles of yesteryear seeking to reform them. The older people were relieved to find the students friendly and polite and respectful of their attitudes and viewpoints.

The older people were attracted to the Fairhaven campus by the prospect of classes, concerts, films, plays, lectures and recreation ranging from billiards to mountaineering. In addition some felt that from their own store of knowledge and experience they could contribute to the understanding and awareness of younger people. For others, the greatest appeal was sitting across the tables from youthful faces. And a few thought that at Fairhaven they might be able to satisfy their curiosity about hippies.

The pre-retirement occupations of the Bridgers vary considerably: businessmen, farmers, secretaries, teachers, a meat inspector, a college dean, a military officer, a postman. According to answers given to two questions on their applications, however, occupation had no bearing on their attitude toward age. When asked if they considered themselves old, they all without exception answered no. When asked which period of life they considered the most satisfying they all had difficulty singling out any one particular span of years.

Approximately half of all the participants in the Bridge Project hold Bachelor's degrees, but for the others the Bridge is their first experience with college.

The relaxed atmosphere at Fairhaven, the working and learning together and the "feeling of belonging" that it begets is an integral part of the functioning of the Bridge Project. Perhaps as a result of it the Bridgers have taken the initiative in involving themselves in campus life. One woman organized an arts and crafts fair; another together with a student set up a seminar on tutoring and wrote a tutoring manual for para-professionals. Another Bridger taught an accredited course entitled "Perspective on Aging."

Fairhaven history professor Michael Burnett looks at the Bridge Project from the point of view of his own classroom. "The older people tend to be more anecdotal than analytical in their approach to subject matter! This can slow things down, but it does amplify and does provide more humanity to a class. The Bridger in the classroom has a stabilizing effect; he takes the long view. When students become pessimistic after analyzing a situation, the older person can say 'That's not new. I remember that happening before.' They provide a continuity that students don't get any other way."

The students regard the Bridge Project as good for Fairhaven and good for them personally. Some mention that the Bridgers have given them a broader perspective of themselves, that they have been helped by knowing that these older people have gone through some of the same experiences that they are now going through. Others no longer think of people over the age of sixty as conservative and hard-of-hearing. Says one young man, "Now when I see old people on the bus, I'm more comfortable and ready to talk to them. I feel I might have something in common with them."

The Bridgers too regard their participation in the project as a valuable learning experience. For some the most important learning is academic; for others it is one of personal relationships. Connie Miller, a retired medical secretary leans toward the latter persuasion. "So many of us" she says, "were so busy living day to day during the years of raising a family we had little time for cultural activities. Those of us who worked saw the same people steadily for the last twenty years. At Fairhaven we meet a new group of people; we don't live in the past. We have a chance to grow. I think when we leave here we will be prepared to continue to broaden our acquaintances and to be more understanding of young people and young ideas." (Davis, 1975, pp. 8-9)

Mildred Henry, of the Center for Research and Development in Higher Education at the University of California at Berkeley, has conducted an evaluation of the Bridge Project (in Davis, 1975). In her report, she writes that "Young people are looking for a dependable philosophy to live by and . . . the Bridgers as a whole seem to have a special philosophy for living." She concludes, "The Bridge Project might well be considered highly significant because it is working amazingly well. Certainly it is providing a needed, lively, healthful option to the usual options available in our country to individuals of retirement age."

Brighton High School, Boston, Massachusetts

If we had been in the Allston-Brighton area of Boston on Thursday, October 19, 1972 and had looked at the local newspaper of that date, we would have seen the headline of an article, "This Year, History Takes a New Start at Brighton High School" (Kelsrud, 1972). Had we been in Boston on November 2, 1972, two weeks later, we would have seen a similar headline in the *Boston Globe:* "Young Learning about Age in Brighton Class" (Kriceland, 1972). These headlines refer to an intergenerational venture in education in which high school students join PLYs in reliving recent, twentieth-century history. The project started with the organization of a small group of PLYs who wished to examine the possibility of bringing their real-life experiences into a high school setting. According to the coordinator of the project, Edith Stein ("Elders, High Schoolers," 1974):

About fifteen older people said they were willing to try it and decided on subjects and methods during an eight week orientation period. . . .
As a part of the training procedure, tape recorders were used to enable them to listen to and criticize themselves, improve their diction and presentation.

Only twelve students signed up originally for the opening class. . . . But opening day brought forty students for the class. We were overwhelmed.

The first class meeting was devoted to getting acquainted. In the next meeting, on entertainment in the twenties, a retired vaudeville performer drew on her experience to describe the world of entertainment before television. In the third meeting, devoted to the history of organized labor in the thirties, a labor organizer, now retired, but active in the early thirties, outlined the status of the labor movement at that time. The topics of the remaining meetings were: "The Boston Police Strike of 1919," "The Big Depression," "Social Changes in Our City," "What Do Older People Do Now?" and "Does It Have Any Value in Your Life?" As Stein said ("Elder, High Schoolers," 1974):

> *By the third class, students had to be turned away. This was just a beginning.... We know new ventures are frightening, but we now know they are worth the effort, building a new role for elders which says—"You are important, your experiences give new meaning to all our lives in the community."*

> *The elders now see themselves as pioneers of a new venture which is effecting their lives daily in many ways. They have been called on by Harvard Divinity School to help in a seminar geared to sensitivity training for students who would be ministering to elders. They have appeared on television shows which they and the students have planned and worked on together.*

> *Their entrance into the mainstream of community life by going into the high school with a program of their own design has significantly altered the community. Students at the high school never will look at the elders as they did previously.*

As a postscript to the preceding description of the Brighton high school project, Stein (1975) indicates that a very important clue to the success of the project is the eight-week orientation period in which those PLYs taking part were carefully trained for reentry. Stein warns that if anyone intends to replicate the Brighton project, "The most important aspect is the preparation of the elders for entry into the public schools." She continues, "If the persons who are invited to come and tell the history of the 20th century through their own life experience are limited to those who can do so easily and well—the whole idea is void! The main thing is to refresh and encourage those who are now depleted by the segregation of aging."

The Teaching-Learning Community, Ann Arbor, Michigan

For our last illustration, let us return to the Great Lakes region of the Midwest and learn how "grandpersons" are participating in an authentic

Teaching-Learning Community sponsored by the Ann Arbor, Michigan public school system. "Grandpersons" is the name given to 120 older volunteers currently involved in programs in seventeen of Ann Arbor's public schools.

In one recent three-month period, 246 separate projects were completed under grandperson guidance; they involved fine arts, graphics, crafts, woodworking, carpentry, photography, filmmaking, pottery, weaving, rug-hooking, music, movement, reading, story-telling, environmental arts such as gardening, flower arranging and plant care, and even the forgotten art of lace making.

The volunteers are average older citizens simply using the skills of a lifetime in a new environment, the schools. They come from single dwellings, public housing, retirement and nursing homes. They range in age from 60 to 87, are multiethnic, of every social background and occupation, and become a part of T-LC simply by saying "yes" when invited.

According to Dr. Harry Howard, superintendent of the school system doing the inviting, "Children learning from grandparents, and grandparents thriving on such a relationship may be 'innovative' in the formal educational sense of the word. However, the concepts embodied in T-LC are virtually timeless. Almost by definition, it had to work."

Project Director Carol Tice started it all five years ago by transporting three senior volunteers from school to school in her own car. She now has a project staff of five, a number of aides, and a substantial Title III grant to develop and evaluate T-LC concepts.

Tice says, "When Ralph Waldo Emerson wrote 'Youth is everywhere in place, but age requires fit surroundings,' he was not looking forward to the time when the aged would be expected to live in isolated ghettos with no further social function. 'Fit surroundings' for grandpersons simply means organizing time and space to accommodate their individual interests and needs.

"One of these needs is certainly the need to contribute, to be seen as givers of an important human and historical connection. T-LC creates that type of 'fit surrounding' for older citizens in the public schools."

Whether a retired furniture maker is developing balsa wood models, or a retired photographer is helping kids produce great shots of Ann Arbor's latest yellow fire truck; whether patchwork pillows are being made of authentic Early American designs, or the creation of puppets leads to the writing of scripts and the performance of grandpersons 'on stage', all of these activities have one thing in common: Grandpersons are seen as individuals with important skills to offer.

Each school "setting" is individually fine-tuned to a grandperson's skills, interests, energy level and mobility. The classroom teacher takes the initiative for inviting senior citizen participation, and then, through friendly informal conversations, discovers the range of activities that can be undertaken. The age and size of the student group, as well as the contact frequency, are adjusted to suit the senior volunteer.

As project activities commence, some senior volunteers sit quietly and let the children come to them. Others take the initiative for organizing students around an activity. Most T-LC grandpersons participate once or twice per week, for half day sessions.

T-LC has shown that grandpersons can be plugged into the public schools with important benefits to all concerned. In comprehensive tests by Project Evaluator Dr. James Doyle, an amazing statistic has resulted: 98 percent of participating schoolchildren respond enthusiastically to "their" grandpersons. They express opinions ranging from "Grandpersons are funner people" to the hope that "T-LC can go on forever" and "be on a daily basis."

Observers also have noted that grandpersons often spontaneously effect "cures" on hyperactive children, resulting in calmer, more receptive learning; and that the health of active T-LC participants improves and their medical needs decline. One older volunteer who could barely move across the room to a chair one year ago now arrives from her nursing home pushing the chair of another volunteer.

Whether grandpersons help to make rugs, rediscover lacemaking, or give form to a child's fanciful design, they are an important part of the neighborhood family that schools can build. Teaching and learning thrive where kinship and community are shared with grandperson volunteers (Mehta, 1976, pp. 60–61).[1]

THE MEANING OF THE EXAMPLES

What do the projects I have presented in the preceding section tell us about the organization and operation of programs of intergenerational education? First, in all of the above examples, and in every other instance (not reported here) with which I am acquainted, the initiative for the intergenerational venture did not originate with the PLYs but with the agency or institution involved. This is not surprising. PLYs have no affiliations, no precedence, and no power base that would enable them to walk in the front door of an organization or school without invitation and offer their services

---

[1] Reprinted from *NRTA Journal.* Copyright 1976 by The National Retired Teachers Association.

with the expectation that they would be accepted. Because of this fact and the reticence with which PLYs usually perceive their roles as volunteers, the organization taking the initiative must go out of its way to make them feel welcome and make certain that the conditions for involvement are as favorable as possible.

Second, in all the cases reported above (and in all others, I examined), there was an initial feeling of what might be called "autistic anxiety" among the participants at both ends of the age scale. Working closely with people widely separated in ages was, for both the YPs and the PLYs, a new experience, so new that they had little background for anticipating how to behave, what to say, or what the results would be. As a consequence, members of both generations approached their involvement with a mixture of curiosity and anxiety. This fact itself tells us a great deal about the attitudes that the generations usually hold toward each other. Typically, the generations coexist in a state of mutual toleration with little experience in meaningful and sustained interaction. This means that an educational community of generations will not just happen or arise spontaneously out of existing instructional programs; it will come into existence only by the sustained and careful preparation of arrangements in which both the young and the PLYs will feel at home.

Third, once the ice is broken, the introductions are completed, and the members of each generation have had an opportunity to feel out and sample the behavior of the other, anxiety quickly subsides and gives way to feelings of genuine delight and appreciation among each generation for the presence of the other one. This reaction was common to all the cases reported. It was due not merely to the relief that usually follows a discovery that the cause of an initial anxiety is not as malign as imagined; it was due also to the fact that members of each generation discovered an intrinsic and authentic interest in the activity that brought them together. The implication of the related facts that, when the generations learn to work together, (1) anxiety subsides and (2) interest increases, is that people expecting to set up projects of intergenerational education should have confidence in the potential of the positive motivation that cooperation between the generations will ultimately produce, because *once they try it, they will like it.*

Fourth, the programs I have reported on above were good education for the young as well as for the PLYs. That is, in order to accommodate the needs and make use of the talents of PLYs and make sure that they are engaged in a rewarding experience, it is not necessary to compromise the educational quality of the programs for YPs. In fact, all those in a position to know agreed that the programs generated by the projects were not only educationally superior, but probably better than comparable programs involving only a single (usually young) generation. In other words, the instruction of YPs was not watered down or sacrificed in order to involve and entertain the PLYs. The programs produced quality experiences for the PLYs as well. Thus both generations were rewarded with superior instruction as a result of working effectively together.

CONCLUSION

At this point, I return to the opening paragraph of this chapter. As I cautioned the reader there, information about the field of intergenerational education is incomplete and extremely limited. This limitation may be attributed to the facts that (1) relatively few systematic and sustained efforts have been made to integrate any combination of generations in a collaborative approach to learning, and (2) the few efforts that have been made have occurred so recently that there has been very little time in which to prepare a report of their activities. As a result, it is not yet possible to definitively delineate a full-blown implementation of the idea of the community of generations. Many questions of practice remain to be answered, and many issues of policy remain to be resolved. Despite the sketchiness of the information, however, I believe that enough has already been accomplished to establish the feasibility and importance of my thesis and to support the proposition that the concept of an intergenerational community of inquiry holds great promise for the instruction of people at all stages of the life cycle.

For all practical purposes, the generations usually have little educational commerce with one another. The best that can be said of their relationship is that the generations coexist in a state of mutual toleration. Typically, they walk different paths, which often diverge but rarely converge. It is my premise that this lack of meaningful interaction constitutes a grave loss for both individuals and society. I concede that there are probably some subjects that can best be studied and issues that can best be resolved in instructional situations in which the learners are similar rather than diverse in generational status, but I believe that there are many areas of inquiry in which a mixture of generations could lead to a superior level of educational performance.

In decision making and problem solving, for instance, it is quite possible that YPs would be more likely to suggest innovative solutions, whereas more mature people would be better at evaluating suggestions and anticipating the consequences of their adoption. Similarly, the young might be better at divergent thinking, whereas mature people might be better at convergent thinking. Or take the process of relating time past (history) to time to come (future). Presumably, PLYs are the historians, whereas YPs are the futurologists. Is it possible that PLYs can be taught to extrapolate from their knowledge of history in order more explicitly to anticipate the future, while YPs can be taught to search history more imaginatively for the antecedents of their predictions? Would these respective approaches lead to a higher level of educational performance if they were done interactively rather than separately? I think so. In fact, I believe that the application of an intergenerational approach to education would open an entirely new domain of research theory and practice for the agenda of both the educational gerontologist and the general educator.

According to one of the cardinal principles of gestalt psychology: The whole is more than the sum of the parts. To conclude, I summarize the thesis of this chapter by paraphrasing this well-known principle: The wholeness of intergenerational relations will give rise to more significant educational outcomes than the random collection of coexisting generational parts. We shall see!

REFERENCES

Brahce, C. I. Art bridges the age gap. *Innovator,* 1975, 7(2), pp. 1; 3–5.

Davis, C. C. Fairhaven's senior freshman. *American Education,* 1975, *11*,(4), 6–10.

Elders, high schoolers, join in Bay State teaching program. *Aging,* March–April 1974, p. 17.

Erikson, E. H. *Childhood and society.* (2 ed.). New York: Norton, 1963.

Girl Scouts of the U.S.A. *Hand-in-hand: Cross-age interactions.* New York: 1975, p. 40.

Havighurst, R. J. *Developmental tasks and education.* New York: McKay, 1974.

Kelsrud, P. This year history takes a new start at Brighton High School. *Allston-Brighton Citizen* (Item B), October 19, 1972.

Kriceland, P. F. Young learning about age in Brighton class. *Boston Globe,* November 2, 1972.

Maslow, A. H. *Motivation and personality* (2nd ed.). New York: Harper and Row, 1970.

Mead, M. *Culture and commitment: A study of the generation gap.* Garden City, N.Y.: Doubleday, 1970. p. 91.

Mehta, M. How to be a grandperson. *NRTA Journal,* July–August 1976, pp. 59–69.

Olmsted, M. *The influence of a unit of instruction in gerontology on the attitudes, knowledge and perceptions of high school students of the aging process, the aged and their own aging.* Unpublished doctoral dissertation, University of Michigan, 1976.

Sokoloff, J. Generations exchange gifts at Brighton High. *Allston-Brighton Chronicle-Citizen,* November 9, 1972.

Stein, E. Personal communication, September, 1975.

4

INSTRUMENTAL AND EXPRESSIVE EDUCATION: A BASIS FOR NEEDS ASSESSMENT AND PLANNING

CARROLL A. LONDONER

Virginia Commonwealth University

During the course of the last half decade, the author has both followed with interest and contributed to the development of the concepts of *instrumental* and *expressive orientations* as a means for assessing the educational needs of people throughout the life-span. Through the research and discussion of a number of authors, a considerable body of knowledge has been developed that relates instrumental and expressive classifications to program planning. The existing literature, on program planning in general, and on the processes of assessing needs specifically, lacks, however, a sound, theoretical framework that program-planning practitioners can use. Much of the literature simply provides techniques and procedures for assessing interests and needs, with limited thought having been given to the theoretical basis underlying stated or unstated assumptions.

For some time, the author has been interested, as an academician, in education for persons in their later years (PLYs) and, as a practitioner, for the planning of such activities. Consequently, when the opportunity arose to develop an article on educational programs for older adults, the search for a theoretical framework for needs assessment led the author to the earlier work of R. J. Havighurst (1964, 1969), who had used the terms *instrumental* and *expressive educational activity* in a sociological framework. In researching the sources of these terms, the author was led back to the work of Talcott Parsons (1964), a leading sociologist of the structural-functional school of analysis, whose major contribution has been the development of a systems analysis approach to the study of social structures. Parsons developed an exhaustive set of categories for analyzing all levels of social systems and centered it around the major conceptualization of an *action frame of reference* and the ways individuals and collectivities of individuals interacted with each other in their various social situations.

Among other things, Parsons devised a system for classifying the gratifications people receive when participating in activities as they strive to attain their various goals or objectives. Some activities yield immediate gratification simply by participation in them; Parsons termed these *expressive orientations*. Other activities provided gratification at a later date, upon completion of some desired, future goal; these he termed *instrumental orientations*. These sociological terms were employed in the author's (Londoner, 1971) subsequent article. There he proposed the adoption of these terms as a theoretical construct for identifying and assessing the needs of older adults, and he argued that instrumental educational activities should be given priority over expressive activities because they provide needed coping and growth competencies for meeting the challenges of the later years.

From that initial, substantive, theoretical framework, R. Hiemstra (1972, 1973) developed and/or contributed to several survey research studies that examined the educational preferences of older, retired people in light of the expressive and instrumental categorizations. Such studies have provided gerontological planners with information concerning whether elderly people would indicate preferences for instrumental or expressive forms of educational activities. Hiemstra (1976) found that, for the most part, the older people sampled preferred instrumental over expressive educational activities. These findings support the author's thesis that instrumental adult educational activities for older people provide the competencies essential for survival and growth in relation to their social environment.

Such findings have received criticism based on the use of the two terms as the theoretical framework for needs assessment. Whereas the criticism may be justified on the basis of the simplicity of the either/or dichotomy, as opposed to newer theoretical frameworks, there is the suggestion that some of the critics, lacking a sociological orientation, misunderstood the meanings of the terms as they were proposed by Parsons, from his action frame of reference to social system analyses. It is the author's intent in this chapter to further clarify these terms and to add an additional dimension to the framework, thus providing a more detailed theory for educational needs assessment, especially as it relates to PLYs. The author presents below a motivation-participation model based on a social-psychological, *needs → social system → goal gratification construct*; then a review of the literature on the reserach on instrumental-expressive orientations; and finally, a needs assessment model to aid gerontological planners in developing educational programs.

A SOCIOLOGICAL, THEORETICAL FRAMEWORK

At the outset, readers must discipline themselves to think in the sociologist's thought patterns, employing ideas and clusters of ideas quite differently from psychologists and educators. Sociologists are less interested in individuals as solitary, biological-psychological organisms, than in analyzing them in relation to their patterns of actions and interactions within many levels and structures of social situations. Individual actions (behaviors) are of interest solely because they reveal *orientational* and *relational* ways people habitually organize or structure their activities to achieve personal and collective *motivational goals.* Sociologically, the focus of interest is always that of an action frame of reference; which is a theoretical and analytical approach stressing the interaction of individuals with others as they manifest their values, roles, and goals in specific situations. Social action theory emphasizes the importance of subjective meanings as people interact within specific situations, but the subjective meanings are analyzed in terms of individuals' internalized values and their expectations of the reactions of others in various social relationships.

Parsons's (1964) rationale for using a social action frame of reference is best summed up in his own definition of the phrase, *system of action:*

> *A system of action . . . is a system of the relations of organisms in interdependence with each other and with non-social objects in the environment or situation. It is in order to keep this system distinct from the organism as a physio-chemical system that we prefer, instead of referring to the "behavior of the organism", to speak of the "action of the actor" and instead of using the term environment, to speak of the situation of the action.*[1]

The social system, then, is a focus of interest for sociology. Parsons (1964) best articulated this frame of reference by saying that:

> *a social system consists in a plurality of individual actors interacting with each other in a situation which has at least a physical or environmental aspect, actors who are motivated in terms of a tendency to the "optimization of gratification" and whose relation to their situations including each other, is defined and mediated in terms of culturally structured and shared symbols.*[2]

Paramount for us is the notion of the "optimization of gratification" evaluated by each individual actor. Individual actors can maximize their gratifications through the development of a system of self-expectations related to their own needs and goals and through the possibility of achieving these gratifications by interacting with others in various social-system situations.

In every action and interaction within *action situations* there are a variety of alternative actions available to individuals. These alternatives cause

---

[1] From *The Social System* by Talcott Parsons. New York: The Free Press, 1964, p. 545. Copyright © 1951 by Talcott Parsons. Reprinted by permission.
[2] Ibid., pp. 5–6.

dilemmas because people must weigh the cost of postponing the immediate gratification in lieu of some future, anticipated goal that might provide an even greater sense of gratification once the goal is achieved.

In the social action frame of reference, the *goal-directedness* of a person's actions is paramount because it indicates a future state of affairs the individual is motivationally commited to actively achieving. Accordingly, motivation, in general, is understood as goal-seeking behavior. Extrinsic motivation is motivation based on an expectation of indirect fulfillment of the actor's desires, because the task undertaken to achieve the goal has no inherent gratification for the actor but is perceived as instrumental in attaining the desired objective. Intrinsic motivation is based on an expectation of direct and immediate gratification of the actor's desires, because the motivation stems directly from the task undertaken and is inherent in the task itself. All this is to say that it is imperative to know the *temporality* of the goals (i.e., *when* the gratification is to be actualized) in order to analyze the underlying motive actions of the individual in the action situation.

This clearly implies that the goal, end, or objective toward which an actor is striving is the place to begin analysis of the motivational interactions of people in social settings. Moroever, from a social-system action perspective, it is imperative to examine these desirable ends or goals as they are related to the activities of which they are functions and not to confuse them with subjective psychological interpretations.

It is at the point involving goal analysis that Parsons (1964) raises the issue of instrumental and expressive action orientations as they relate to the temporal achievement of goals and the subsequent gratification or satisfactions that are the consequences of goal attainment. Parsons summarizes it best by saying:

> *Action may be oriented to the achievement of a goal which is an anticipated future state of affairs, the attainment of which is felt to promise gratification: a state of affairs which will not come about without the intervention of the actor in the course of the event. Such instrumental or goal-orientation introduces an element of discipline, the renunciation of certain immediately potential gratifications. . . . Such immediate gratifications are renounced in the interests of the pro- spectively larger gains to be derived from the attainment of the goals, an attainment which is felt to be contingent on fulfillment of certain conditions at intermediate stages of the process.*[3]

Accordingly, instrumental action orientation presupposes the givenness of a goal and therefore requires a self-evaluation or prioritization of

[3] From *The Social System* by Talcott Parsons. New York: The Free Press, 1964, p. 48. Copyright © 1951 by Talcott Parsons. Reprinted by permission.

gratificational desires; it requires knowledge of the conditions necessary to attain the goal despite the desire for immediate emotional gratification, which is understood as the desire to take advantage of the immediately available gratificational opportunities in the meantime, even though they could interfere with the attainment of the desired future goal. Hence, individuals find themselves in the dilemma of choosing between goals, the actions necessary to achieve them, and the further choice of the temporality of actualizing the desired gratifications through goal achievement.

The expressive action orientation is obviously related to an immediate time dimension in which the actor organizes the flow of gratification to a present-time orientation; that is, the actor participates in some activity where goal gratification is immediately available; so that it might be said that "doing" the activity is itself its own emotional reward. Again, the notion that individuals evaluate or prioritize desires comes into focus because they do not postpone gratification for some future-oriented goal, but rather, choose the *cathetic*, or positive, emotional response to the activity at hand.

It is apparently from these statements by Parsons that Havighurst (1969) developed his ideas concerning the action orientations of people engaged in educational activities. He stressed the idea that instrumental educational activities were those in which the goal of the learning lay beyond the immediate activity, whereas expressive educational activities were activities largely participated in for their own sake and in which the gratification is immediately experienced by the individual.

A Psychosocial Interpretation of Adult, Participative Behavior

The following discussion is a preliminary attempt, based on the ideas of instrumental and expressive action orientations and goal gratifications, to explain, in part, what motivates adults to participate in educational programs. Readers are cautioned to remember that there are many ways of "explaining" behavior, and this is merely one way of interpreting the many behavioral patterns we observe daily.

Life may be perceived as a *temporal* line (Figure 1) extending from our past; through our present, daily behaviors; and into the future. What we see and experience in daily (present-time) living is human behaviors. Mentally, we tend to cluster these daily behaviors together into meaningful explanations and to suggest that one has "needs" that cause the behaviors to occur. Continued examination of these needs that trigger daily behaviors reveals that people

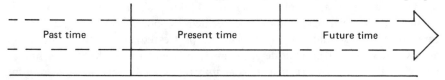

FIGURE 1   Life conceived as a temporal line.

strive to achieve future goals that will gratify their needs. Meeting needs by achieving one's goals usually causes a change in daily behaviors. Thus, it can be said that daily behaviors are modified, in light of the goals we have achieved or strive to achieve, because the goals tend to meet our needs.

An example familiar to the majority of graduate students illustrates what has been said. If social scientists were to study the participation and motivation patterns of graduate students, they might make objective, anecdotal comments as follows: Graduate students exhibit a variety of behaviors in daily (present-time) activities that can be clustered together, logically. One can see graduate students making appointments to see their counselors to plan their graduate programs of courses. These students then go through the enrollment process (often a tedious and frustrating experience); show up for the classes, which are often held at night to accommodate those students who must continue full-time employment to pay for their school expenses; and undergo the weekly readings, periodic examinations, and occasional class reports and term papers in order to receive an acceptable grade for the class.

Social scientists see these complex clusters of graduate-student behaviors repeated daily in the lives of many students and surmise that these students apparently have some needs they are trying to fulfill. When students are interviewed, it is learned that these students are meeting the educational requirements for a given graduate program in order to obtain an advanced academic degree; that is, these students have *educational needs* (the successful completion of all required courses) that triggered the various graduate-student behaviors observed by social scientists in the present time. Further interviews reveal that students want (or need) the advanced degree for professional growth or to enter into another profession. Thus they have participated in graduate school to achieve some future goal that will satisfy their professional needs.

In the psychosocial literature, this description of the motivational patterns of educational participation is referred to as a *needs → social system → goal gratification,* hypothetical construct. It is important to understand the meaning and the logical implications of the term *hypothetical construct,* especially in relation to the notion that life may be likened to a temporal line stretching from the past, through the present, and into the future. Hypothetical constructs are imaginary, underlying factors that social scientists postulate to account for the behaviors they observe in present-time activities. In reality (*real* time), these factors do not exist; they are merely the products of a scientist's imagination to aid in thinking about the behavior being studied. These imaginary factors are termed hypothetical constructs to indicate that they should not be considered or treated as real-time objects or events. They should be considered as abstract elements of theories of human behavior; that is, they are perceived as inferred, causal phenomena accounting for behavior observed in daily living.

All of us are familiar with hypothetical constructs and use them in our daily conversations. Words such as *intelligence, motivation, psychological set, needs,* and *inhibitions* are examples of hypothetical constructs used to explain present-time behaviors. Regrettably, too many people treat hypothetical constructs as if they were real events or objects. One obvious example is the hypothetical construct termed *needs.* Many students of the applied behavioral sciences have adopted Abraham Maslow's (1954) hierarchy of needs as a way of explaining human behavior. They speak freely of people having safety, love, self-esteem, and self-actualization needs—almost as if they were concrete realities—but they are not. They are inferred, underlying, causal factors that Maslow postulated to explain present, real-time behaviors he observed as a psychologist. It is impossible to dissect someone and find a "love" or a "self-esteem" need as one might find a concrete, internal organ such as the liver or heart. These needs simply do not exist as concrete objects for scientific study.

Because the human mind seemingly desires to superimpose logical order and create explanations of behavior, endless psychosocial systems of thought have been developed to explain why we do what we do. These postulated systems of thought are the imaginary, hypothetical constructs we rely on to explain observable human behavior. The proposed *needs →social system →goal gratification* model for educational participation suggested here is also a system of thought to explain human behavior and, therefore, relies on hypothetical constructs. In essence, the model suggests that people have needs that trigger clusters of present-time behaviors; that these present-time behaviors are designed to achieve goal gratification; and that when the goals are achieved, we conclude that people have met their needs.

As simple as this model appears at first reading, when it is combined with Parsons's instrumental-expressive action orientations, it becomes a fairly complex paradigm for explaining why we do what we do. In Figure 2, several new elements are added to the temporal past, present, and future line of Figure 1. *Human behaviors exhibited within social systems* is placed in the present, or real-time, portion of the figure. *Needs* is located in the past portion of the figure and is subtitled "Inferred causal states or conditions." *Goals* is lodged in the future portion of the figure and is subtitled "Inferred gratifications."

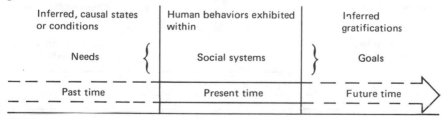

FIGURE 2 The temporal lifeline integrated with the needs → social system → goal gratification model of participation.

The figure should be read in the following manner: The only realities people are capable of observing occur in the present, or real time. These observables are the human behaviors one sees as people act and interact within society's various social systems. Because of the inclination to confer meaning on observed behaviors, we intellectually cluster them into meaningful patterns and infer their causes. Reflective reasoning suggests that these causes are unobservable needs that initiate participatory behaviors within various social systems. These unobservable needs are the intellectual, imaginary factors we have created to confer meaning on the observed behaviors. These needs are placed in the past portion of Figure 2 to indicate that they occur before present-time behaviors and hence may be the inferred, causal linkages to the observed behaviors. As hypothetical constructs, needs may be thought of as the stimuli in stimulus-response chains of events. They act as the initiators of participatory behaviors within social systems. Remember, though, that needs are fabricated from our own, logical thought processes and postulated as the presumed, initiatory stimuli of the participatory behavior.

Goals are lodged in the future portion of Figure 2, showing that they are as-yet-unachieved expectations. Their subtitle, inferred gratifications, implies that their fulfillment (through interaction in social systems) will gratify someone by meeting his or her needs, which are also inferred factors. Goals, like needs, are products of our minds. From all the range of existing possibilities, one postulates an unachieved, yet anticipated, event and reasons that present behaviors are future oriented. The tendency to invest observed behavior with meaning permits meaningful clustering to form goal-seeking patterns of future-oriented, desirable states of affairs. Accordingly, we are likely to say a person is *motivated* (a hypothetical construct) to achieve some goal by participating and interacting with others in social systems. When the goal is achieved, one receives goal gratification, thus satisfying the needs that triggered the observed, participatory behaviors within social systems.

In Figure 3, new elements have once again been added to the model. The needs and goals portions of the model are divided into *instrumentally* and

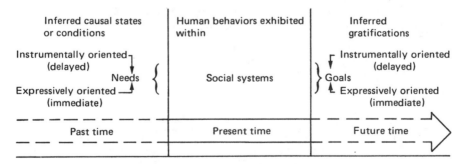

FIGURE 3 Needs → social system → goal gratification model of participation further delineated by instrumental and expressive action orientations.

expressively oriented needs and *instrumentally* and *expressively oriented goals.* We are now in a better position to relate the fully developed model to Parsons's idea of instrumental and expressive action orientations of actors motivated to optimize and actualize their goal gratifications.

The graduate-student example used earlier helps to illustrate the full model as displayed in Figure 3. The reader will recall the social scientist observing graduate-student participation behavior to obtain an advanced degree. Possessing the degree permits either entrance to a higher level professional position or to a new career. The social scientist deduces that the students were motivated by instrumentally oriented goals; that is, he or she perceives graduate students' interactions within an educational system to be oriented toward achieving an anticipated future state of affairs. Clearly, the students had to discipline themselves to delay, and possibly renounce, more immediate gratifications in the interest of the larger gains derived from possessing the degree.

The social scientist then postulates a hypothetical construct termed *instrumentally oriented needs* to account for the observed behaviors of graduate students. Instrumentally oriented needs are meaningful, however, only when they are linked with their instrumentally oriented *goals* and the subsequent gratifications. In other words, the researcher had to have some idea of what the students were anticipating in the future in order to suggest what their needs were.

Suppose, however, the investigator also interviewed some students enrolled in the same graduate courses and found that these students were not degree oriented. They participate just because they enjoy the intellectual stimulation of the graduate course itself. Their goal gratification is immediately available by their class participation. Their goals, the immediate gratification from the learning itself, should be classified as *expressively oriented goals.* Put another way, the learning activities yield immediate gratification simply by participating in them.

Again, the social scientist may postulate another, underlying, hypothetical construct, termed *expressively oriented needs,* to account for the observed behaviors of these particular students. These needs do not exist, of course, in real time; they are, however, envisioned as the imaginary, inferred factors that initiate participatory behavior within courses because of the immediate gratification derived from the participation. These expressively oriented needs are meaningful, however, only when they are linked closely with the person's expressively oriented goals. Thus, needs and goals must be linked together logically for the participatory behaviors of people in educational social systems to be understood.

It should be clear to the reader by now that establishing a functional theory for needs assessment is a difficult matter. Perhaps that is why so little has been done in this area. The natural desire of the busy educational gerontologist for a cookbook, show-me-how-to-do-it approach is a desire for an easy out. Why spend valuable time with so heavy a theoretical orientation? The clear answer is that a good deal of current needs assessment and subsequent programming is erratic and often fails to attract the target audience; or worse, the clients attend a few sessions and then drop out because the program does not "meet their needs." It is this unevenness in assessing needs and the subsequent drop-out phenomenon that require a functional, theoretical approach to needs assessment.

To summarize the chapter to this point, the author has shown that Parsons's instrumental-expressive action orientations within social systems is a useful, theoretical construct for explaining how goal gratifications are optimized by individual and collective actions. Furthermore, he has shown that a needs → social system → goal gratification participation model, based on the theoretical constructs of instrumental-expressive need and goal orientations, offers one explanation for why people behave as they do. Now it is necessary to show the logical interrelatedness of Parsons's and the model's theoretical constructs.

Three Underlying Assumptions of Parsons and the Paradigm

First, both Parsons's and the model's constructs rest on the assumption of a forced choice among alternative, competing choices, each of which attracts the individual actor. The actor is in a dilemma because he or she can not do all things at once. To resolve the dilemma, the actor must decide when to optimize gratifications by achieving either immediate or long-range goals.

Resolving the dilemma is, for the actor, a *choice-point:* that point at which the actor motivationally makes a total commitment to achieving immediate and/or future goals. The choice-point is of ultimate concern to educational gerontologists, for here the actor fully commits psychosocial energies and resources to optimize goal gratifications. Here, too, the educational gerontologist sees the actor opt for either immediate (expressive) or delayed (instrumental) goal gratifications by participating in various kinds of educational activities.

Second, both Parsons's and the participation model's constructs require educational gerontologists to shift from a solely *front-end analysis* (i.e., only examining individual and group needs) to the simultaneous process of looking at goals (those ultimate choices for optimizing personal gratifications) and needs. If educational gerontologists can determine what the PLY is committed to achieving, they will discover the kinds of educational activities PLYs will consistently attend. In some respects, this theoretical approach could be termed *goal assessment for educational gerontologists;* such terminology, however, obscures the strategy by which both goals and needs are examined simultaneously for educational planning.

Third, in an earlier work, the author (Londoner, 1971) mentioned that educational gerontologists relied too heavily on perceived, expressive needs of

PLYs and not enough on instrumental needs. This chapter sharpens that distinction by emphasizing that the instrumental goals of the aged must be analyzed first, before comments about either instrumental or expressive needs are postulated. A large portion of today's PLYs live on fixed incomes. As costs increase, limited incomes purchase less services and personal, daily-living requirements. PLYs are committed to preserving psychological and physical health and well-being as well as to maintaining satisfactory social adjustments. In short, many PLYs have survival goals uppermost in mind to help them resolve daily coping problems.

Many PLYs are committed to surviving and will be more likely to respond to activities designed to meet these survival needs/goals than to recreational and/or liberal educational pursuits. Their basic goals are instrumental (i.e., surviving and coping in a less-than-hospitable culture); and consequently, their needs are instrumental, because they are committed to instrumental, survival goals. Many daily activities are classified as survival patterns of behavior because these activities optimize the goals of PLYs, namely, coping meaningfully with life in the best way possible.

REVIEW OF SELECTED LITERATURE

The author is mindful that numerous studies, especially at the doctoral dissertation level, are in progress. This review[4] is not exhaustive, but rather, attempts to show the variety of ways these ideas have been applied to date. Considerable research has been completed since the seminal thinking of Havighurst (1964) and the author (Londoner, 1971). Hiemstra (1972) completed a study that was the first empirical testing of instrumental and expressive categories of learning. In that study, 86 retired people, participating in senior-citizen center activities or living in residential centers for the aged, responded to a questionnaire that contained 12 instrumental activities (competency areas designed for effective mastery of old-age challenges) and 44 expressive activities (experiences designed to increase a person's enjoyment of life). A significantly higher preference for instrumental activities was elicited as compared to preferences given for expressive activities. The instrumental type of learning activities included such course titles as "Stretching Your Retirement Dollar," "Wills and Estate Planning," "Nutrition and the Aging Process," and "Medical Care in the Retirement Years." Expressive examples included such titles as "Art Appreciation," "Nature Photography," "The Archaeology of Mexico," "Three Black Authors," and "Introduction to Crafts."

Hiemstra (1973) also reported an examination of the above course

[4]The author is sincerely grateful to Professor Hiemstra, who compiled and wrote this literature review and developed the "Data Collection Matrix for Educational Program Planning" (Figure 4). His encouragement to develop this chapter, based on our earlier endeavors, has led to a sharpening of the author's own theoretical position.

preferences in terms of various biographical and demographic characteristics. Exploratory null hypotheses of no differences in the types of preferences according to nominal categorizations for various characteristics were utilized. No significant differences were found in terms of age, sex, or urban versus rural categories. Significance testing did reveal, however, that white-collar workers were less likely than blue-collar workers, and college graduates were less likely than noncollege graduates, to report instrumental course preferences.

Whatley (1974) examined the instrumental and expressive dichotomy by asking (through a questionnaire) gerontologists, adult educators, and people 60 years of age or older to give their perceptions regarding the potential selection of learning activities by older people. She found general consensus among the three groups, with older people making fewer instrumental selections than the adult educators or gerontologists. She further examined the preference made by the older population and found no significant differences for either instrumental or expressive activities when compared by groupings—according to sex, lower versus higher age, urban versus rural residence, and lower versus higher levels of education.

Another study pertaining to instrumental and expressive preferences was conducted by Goodrow (1975). Utilizing a random sample of 268 people over the age of 65, a questionnaire with 16 hypothetical instrumental and 16 hypothetical expressive course titles was administered. He found a significant preference for instrumental learning. A further examination of the data revealed that no significant differences existed between the instrumental and expressive preferences; however, within the instrumental preference category, race, sex, and age groups resulted in significant comparisons.

Burkey (1975) examined 40 course titles (20 instrumental and 20 expressive) by asking 243 older members of a church, all 55 years of age or older, to indicate on a questionnaire their interest toward the learning activities. No differences were found for urban versus rural or small-town categories, lower versus upper age groups, and male versus female classifications. However, people with more than a high school diploma tended to be more expressively oriented in preferences than their counterparts. When categories within each type of learning were examined, older people, younger females, and high school graduates selected significantly more expressively oriented activities. For every demographic characteristic, the composite mean for the number of instrumental preferences was significantly greater than for the number of expressive preferences.

Another study by Hiemstra (1975) utilized an interview approach to examine the preferences of 256 randomly selected people over the age of 54. Selections could be made from 16 expressive and 16 instrumental courses. A significant overall preference for instrumental courses was found. Comparisons according to various demographic or socioeconomic categories revealed that nonwhite, male, rural, and married people made significantly more instrumental preferences than the counterpart groupings. In addition, the same study utilized the methodology initially developed by Tough (1971) to determine the number of learning projects actually carried out in one year by the respondents. After the projects were classified as instrumental or expressive in nature, it was found that a significantly higher number of instrumental projects had been carried out. In a comparison according to the demographic groupings, however, only one significant difference was found: married people carried out more instrumental projects than did single people.

Bauer (1975) examined 685 people, 55 years of age or older, who participated, or had indicated an interest in participating, in the Seniors on Campus program at North Hennepin Community College in Brooklyn Park, Minnesota. The questionnaire survey showed that the respondents preferred expressive types of classes and activities as compared to instrumental types.

One additional study that has centered on the instrumental and expressive scheme was completed by Marcus (1976). Utilizing a multiple-regression analysis on the responses to a questionnaire by 4,000 middle-class participants in educational programs, the author established four determinants of instrumental and expressive participation in educational activities for adults. He found that (1) needs, goals, and time orientation were partial determinants of perceived instrumental ability; (2) age, more than the other factors, affected perceived expressive utility; (3) status and "femaleness" related more to perceived expressive utility than to perceived instrumental utility; and (4) age was the main discriminant. His findings suggest that older people often see expressive utility even in programs classified as instrumental, but that they are not necessarily attracted to mainly expressive activities.

The already considerable research that has been completed on instrumental versus expressive categories of education has by no means provided conclusive evidence by which the educational program planner can develop or conduct ideal learning environments for older people. Dichotomizing educational opportunity into either/or categories has some real drawbacks, as pointed out by DeCrow (no date). However, the apparent preference for instrumental learning opportunities as people grow older and according to specific demographic subgroupings gives some clues for educators to consider. In addition, two fairly broad categories of learning should enable program planners and administrators to establish learning environments that contain both instrumental and expressive opportunities.

A note of caution is in order at this point. Many authorities appear to classify an educational activity as being inherently instrumental or expressive. Havighurst (1969, p. 62), for example, tends to follow this dichotomy of educational opportunities for adults. Such a dichotomy should be resisted however easily educational opportunities intuitively cluster into these classifications. The reason is quite simple; we are analyzing the behaviors of individual actors who seek to optimize goal gratifications. The same educational opportunity can be simultaneously instrumental and expressive; how it is perceived and used by the actors is the crucial point. Is the activity used as an immediate goal gratification (expressive), or in a delayed optimization pattern for some future goal (instrumental)? Continued research and the use of sophisticated, multivariate and regression analyses, it may be hoped, will provide additional insight into the education needs/goals of older people.

NEEDS ASSESSMENT

The assessment of needs as a basis for planning educational programs is not an easy task, nor has an abundance of empirical research on needs assessment as a basis for program planning been carried out. Hiemstra and Long (1974) completed one such study and found that the educational needs perceived by a person were not related to the needs that same person demonstrated through paper-and-pencil testing. A complicating finding was reported by Long (1972) in his study of continuing professional education needs. He found no significant relationship existed between what a panel of experts perceived to be educational needs for a group of professionals and what that same group of professionals perceived to be their own needs.

Assessing needs of individuals or groups of adults is also plagued by the lack of adequate methodologies. The questionnaire survey is relatively in-expensive and fairly easy to administer, but it has severe limitations related to such factors as validity and return rate. The use of advisory councils to determine needs can be time consuming and can require considerable training of the council members. Add to this already complex situation the instru-mental and expressive categorization scheme, and the program-planning process quickly becomes difficult. McMahon (1970) provides some useful discussion of different types of need, and Knowles (1970, 1975) provides some useful descriptions of several needs assessment techniques or devices; both sources will provide some relief from the complexity of the situation.

Figure 4 is offered as a conceptual scheme to assist the program planner in determining needs. Expert advice would include information from such groups or sources as an advisory council, a review of related literature, a panel of judges, the planner's own expertise, or a paid consultant. A perception of need would usually be in the form of information obtainable through a questionnaire, personal interviews, or a panel made up of potential program participants. Needs assessment could be done through demonstration techniques that could include such devices as paper-and-pencil tests, obser-vational data, performance records, and prior evaluation data. Obviously the model will require considerable testing, research, and refinement before the educational program planner can plug into it every programming or needs assessment effort. The model does, however, provide a basis for discussion and experimentation. Following is a brief description of some simulated usage to provide the reader with help in understanding the model.

As one example, the program planner could ask a panel of judges

Needs assessment data: Sources and examples	Type of need
	Instrumental/Expressive

Experts
 	
    Research reports
    Panel of judges
    Interviews
    Advisory councils
    Census data
    Consultants
    National conferences	

Clients
 	
    Interviews
    Survey research
    "Opinionnaires"	

Educational planners
 	
    Observations
    Interviews
    Questionnaires
    Advisory committees	

FIGURE 4 Data collection matrix for educational program planning.

(expert advice) to suggest some preretirement training activities that would be useful in helping a group of factory workers make the transition to retirement during their last two or three years of employment with a company having a policy of mandatory retirement for people reaching age 65. The information obtained from the panel would then need to be sifted through the instrumental and expressive screens so that a mixture of programs could be planned for the employees.

A related example can be described by looking at the client group's perception of needs in the same situation. A questionnaire could be distributed to the group of workers described above to elicit their preferences toward a variety of noncredit learning topics. Such information, when screened through the instrumental and expressive categories and perhaps even compared with some demonstration of needs information, could be utilized to set up some learning experiences that either overlap with or supplement the activities established as a result of the expert advice.

As a final example, an educational planner's observation of the psychosocial environment to establish needs can be utilized. The setting is a nursing home for retired school teachers and the program planner is an interning doctoral student in educational gerontology. The program planner had just finished compiling the results of both personal interviews with residents and a collection of suggestions from the permanent staff, both on the topic of establishing educational and recreational activities. In addition to such information, the intern had observed, over a several-day period, a basic lack of understanding of personal health care related to a fairly confined environment and a general lack of any physical activity. The planner then compiled all of the needs assessment information and, by putting it through both instrumental and expressive screens, was able to develop a comprehensive educational and recreational program.

The model could be made three dimensional, using any number of demographic or socioeconomic characteristics to screen needs or to determine a desired approach for assessing needs (e.g., male versus female, or blue-collar versus white-collar workers). In addition, the program planner could employ such variables as participant preference for the type of learning activity, or could use nominal categories of obstacles or credit versus noncredit preferences as the third-dimension measure.

There are limitations to the model. Implied in the above examples is the suggestion that no one source of information is adequate for program planning. In addition, the author suggests that both instrumental and expressive types of learning activities are necessary. Thus, the program-planning process appears complicated by such factors, in terms of extra time, resources, and analysis requirements. The author anticipates, however, that as such a model and the understanding of instrumental versus expressive categories are both improved, the educational planner will be able to provide learning activities that more broadly meet the needs of older people.

THE EDUCATIONAL PLANNER'S RESPONSIBILITY

What is the program planner's responsibility in facilitating a maximum utilization of available resources and, at the same time, meeting the needs of older people? There is, of course, no simple answer to this question. Most educators providing service to older people want to make the best possible programs or learning activities available within given institutional constraints or resource limitations. In addition, most educators working with adult learners feel comfortable about facilitating input on wants and interests from prospective participants. Nonetheless, as Moody (1976) suggests:

The expectations we bring to an educational experience are regulated and limited by . . . narrowing ideas of what learning is. Institutional inertia reinforces the process until we can conceive of the future only as an expansion or an extension of what we already know.... In the evolving field of education for older adults, this describes exactly the situation at the present time. The alternative is to imagine an educational experience from which students would emerge as different kinds of people, *with a new and enlarged sense of value and deepened understanding of who they are as envisioned in Stage IV. (p. 15)*

Thus, moving educational programming expertise to a "Stage IV" level will require new tools, a stronger theoretical base, and a better understanding of needs and interests of the older adult. The interest in and growing knowledge of instrumental and expressive categories has the potential of contributing to the meeting of such requirements.

REFERENCES

Bauer, B. M. *A model of continuing education for older adults.* Unpublished doctoral dissertation, University of Minnesota, 1975.

Burkey, F. T. *Educational interest of older adult members of the Brethren Church in Ohio.* Unpublished doctoral dissertation, Ohio State University, 1975.

DeCrow, R. *New learning for older Americans: An overview of national effort.* Washington, D.C.: Adult Education Association of the U.S.A.

Goodrow, B. A. The learning needs and interests of the elderly in Knox County, Tennessee (Doctoral dissertation, University of Tennessee, 1974). *Dissertation Abstracts* (University Microfilms No. 75-11, 169).

Havighurst, R. J. Changing status and roles during the adult life cycle: Significance for adult education. In H. Burns (Ed.), *Sociological backgrounds of adult education.* Chicago: Center for the Study of Liberal Education for Adults, 1964.

Havighurst, R. J., Adulthood and old age. In R. L. Ebel (Ed.), *Encyclopedia of educational research,* (4 ed.). New York: Macmillan, 1969.

Hiemstra, R. P. Continuing education for the aged: A survey of needs and interests of older people. *Adult Education,* 1972, *22,* 100–109.

Hiemstra, R. P. Educational planning for older adults: A survey of "expressive" vs. "instrumental" preferences. *International Journal of Aging and Human Development,* 1973, *4,* 147–156.

Hiemstra, R. P. *The older adult and learning.* Lincoln: University of Nebraska, 1975. (ERIC Document Reproduction Service No. CE 006 003).

Hiemstra, R. P., & Long, R. A survey of "felt" versus "real" needs of physical therapists. *Adult Education,* 1974, *24,* 270–279.

Knowles, M. S. *The modern practice of adult education.* New York: Association Press, 1970.

Knowles, M. S. *Self-directed learning: A guide for learners and teachers.* New York: Association Press, 1970.

Londoner, C. A. Survival needs of the aged: Implications for program planning. *International Journal of Aging and Human Development,* 1971, *2,* 113–117.

Long, R. *Continuing education for physical therapists in Nebraska: A survey of current practices and self-expressed needs with recommendations for program development.* Unpublished doctoral dissertation, University of Nebraska, 1972.

Marcus, E. E. *Effects of age, sex, and socioeconomic status on adult education participants' perception of the utility of their participation.* Doctoral dissertation in progress, University of Chicago, and personal communication, April 26, 1976.

Maslow, A. H. *Motivation and personality.* New York: Harper and Row, 1954.

McMahon, E. E. *Needs—of people and their communities—and the adult educator.* Washington, D. C.: Adult Education Association of the U.S.A., 1970.

Moody, H. R. Philosophical presuppositions of education for old age. *Educational Gerontology,* 1976, *1,* 1–16.

Parsons, T. *The social system.* New York: Free Press, 1964.

Tough, A. *The adult's learning projects* (Research in education series, No. 1). Toronto: Ontario Institute for Studies in Education, 1971.

Whatley, L. F. *Expressive and instrumental educational interests of older adults as perceived by adult educators, gerontologists, and older adults.* Unpublished master's thesis, University of Georgia, 1974.

5

CONTEMPORARY APPROACHES TO PLANNING EDUCATIONAL PROGRAMS FOR AGING ADULT LEARNERS

D. BARRY LUMSDEN
North Texas State University

RONALD H. SHERRON
Virginia Commonwealth University

THE MYTH OF EDUCATION AS THE RIGHT OF ALL PEOPLE

There is an educational myth abroad in the United States today, and this myth has it that education is the right of all people of all age groups. According to the *Final Report of the 1971 White House Conference on Aging:* "Education is a basic right for all persons of all age groups. It is continuous and henceforth one of the ways of enabling older people to have a full and meaningful life, and is a means of helping them develop their potential as a resource for the betterment of society" (*Toward a National Policy,* 1972). According to the recent policy statements of the Council of Chief State School Officers (1976):

> *A free public education is everyone's right. It shall not be denied to any person regardless of age.... A wide range of life-long educational opportunities must be made available to all citizens of this nation so that the fundamental rights and responsibilities of free choice may be learned and exercised with regard to each individual's future. (p. 13)*

The council further urged that "legislation be enacted with appropriate funding guaranteeing free public education for all citizens through completion of high school or its equivalent, regardless of age" (p. 2). Why, then, in view of these pronouncements, do we maintain that the notion of education as the right of all people is a myth?

Even in the United States, a country that professes a philosophical commitment to free, universal education, many people question the social and economic soundness of providing educational opportunities for the elderly at public expense (Havighurst, 1976). It is often said that continuing education for the elderly is not likely to make them more economically productive because most of the elderly are unemployed. Using the criterion of the measurable impact of education on the gross national product, many educators and politicians contend that what few educational programs are offered for older adults must be vocational or occupational in nature. It is repeatedly stated that we simply cannot justify the expenditure of public moneys for such leisure-time, expressive learning activities as art appreciation, bridge, and decoupage.

There is an alarming number of educators who seriously doubt that older adults even have educational needs and interests. This belief undoubtedly has its roots in a totally impoverished understanding of Cummings' and Henry's (1961) theory of disengagement. Too many educators hold that it is anomalous for older adults to gradually disengage from life and yet continue to sustain an interest in and a need for continuing education.

There are those educators and public policy makers who concede that older adults do in fact have learning needs and interests, but these educators and policy makers consider these needs and interests to be insignificant and minor when compared with the first-order needs of older adults. For example, if anything is known about Maslow's (1970) hierarchy of needs, we would supposedly understand why educating older adults is less important than feeding them, housing them, and providing them with adequate medical care. According to this way of thinking, not until essential services have been provided can the "frill" of continuing education be added.

It is frequently maintained that whatever educational needs older adults may have, these needs are obviously of an unfelt sort; otherwise, how do we explain the phenomenon of low participation among older adults in those educational programs that are available? For example, according to one source (*Aging in Connecticut,* 1971), even though the university waives tuition for people over age 62, "registration among the elderly is low in the state's schools" (p. 70). Similar reports come from all over the country. Again, it is asked: If older adults are really interested in continuing to learn, why don't they take advantage of what is being done for them? The conventional wisdom has it that their needs are unfelt.

Many educators concede the importance of education for older adults, but defensively argue that planning cannot begin until the needs of our nation's preschoolers, elementary and secondary school youngsters, and college students have been met. After provision for the educational needs of the nation's young has been made, it is contended, funds, if any remain, can be spent on our older citizens. After all, the future of the United States lies with its young people, not with its senior citizens.

In summary, what can be concluded is that the notion of the

desirability of providing for the continuing educational needs of all our citizens is indeed preached, but its implementation is a myth. In reality, what can be said is that education in this country is the right of young people but is a luxury for older adults. A recent long-range planning report of the U.S. Office of Education's Bureau of Occupational and Adult Education stated:

> In this recent legislation [the Education Act of 1974, PL 93-380] the Adult Education Act was extended and appropriations were authorized through FY 1978. The Act includes authorization for the Commissioner to make grants for special projects for the elderly to state and local educational agencies or other public and non-profit agencies for elderly persons with limited English-speaking ability, but no appropriations were authorized and the authority was not extended after June 30, 1975. (U.S. Office of Education, 1975 [italics added])

What, if anything, does this partial catalog of excuses have to do with contemporary approaches to planning educational programs for older adults? It is the opinion of the authors that how we feel and what we believe about things necessarily influence our behavior, which is another way of saying that most contemporary approaches to planning educational programs for older adults are governed by the erroneous beliefs and faulty attitudes reflected in the reasons cited to support the contention that education for all our citizens, regardless of age, is a myth.

CONTEMPORARY PROGRAM–PLANNING APPROACHES

There appear to be at least five different and rather distinct, contemporary planning approaches that are mediated largely by the prevailing cognitive and attitudinal conditions already discussed: (1) avoidance approaches; (2) dilatory approaches; (3) traditional approaches; (4) non-traditional approaches; and (5) the individualized learning resource center approach.

Avoidance Approaches

Without being dogmatic or overly cynical, it is safe to say that the avoidance approach to planning educational programs for older adults is probably the predominant approach today. Perhaps it is even a play on words to talk about an avoidance approach to planning, but psychologists have for years now been discussing avoidance approaches to varying kinds of conflict-producing situations. Very simply stated, avoidance approaches rationalize away the very need to do any educational planning for older adults. Translated into public-policy terms, avoidance approaches leave educational program planning to nongovernmental agencies such as private foundations, religious organizations, and various sorts of philanthropic institutions.

Dilatory Approaches

Dilatory approaches to planning educational programs are essentially procrastinating approaches. As such, dilatory approaches are not qualitatively different from avoidance approaches, especially in terms of social impact. Whereas avoidance approaches tend to rationalize away the very need for educational programming for older adults, dilatory approaches do go at least one step further by acknowledging the real learning interests and needs of older adults. A dilatory approach will, for example, allow for legislation to provide educational opportunities for older adults but at the same time not make allowance for monetary appropriations. It will make allowance for educational programs for older adults, but only after the educational needs of everyone else have been met.

Traditional Approaches

A third approach to planning educational programs for older adults is the most traditional one. Traditional educational planners like to think of themselves as pioneers at the cutting edge of progress. They point with pride to their evening programs, which are held everywhere from their campuses to storefronts to church basements. They tell us of their tuition waivers and point rather boastfully at their curricula, which include virtually everything from noncredit offerings in astronomy to credit courses in advanced zoology. Everything looks just fine until we take a closer look at things and begin to see what these traditional approaches really look like.

Even though older adults might enjoy the advantage of tuition waivers, their actual enrollment in classes and courses is typically on a space-available basis only, which is another way of saying that they may or may not actually be permitted to take courses of their choice. Or older adults may be told that the programs in which they are interested must be self-supporting; that is, a minimum number of people must register for the course and pay a specified fee if the course is to materialize.

Traditional approaches, more often than not, fail to reduce, let alone eliminate, inconveniences and discomforts experienced by the older adults who do participate in continuing education activities. For lack of transportation, educational programs are frequently inaccessible to those who want to participate. Classes are held in facilities and rooms accessible only by flights of stairs. In other words, traditional approaches to planning educational programs say to older adults: Here it is; if you want it, come and get it, but we're not going out of our way to make it available to you. Whatever it is that we do for you will be done within the bureaucratic and academic constraints imposed upon the rest of us by the system.

Nontraditional Approaches

Continuing our progressive ascent up the ladder of betterment, we come to those more refreshing and innovative approaches that we have all come to know as "nontraditional." Interestingly enough, nontraditional approaches to program planning are based squarely upon a number of rather fundamental, and perhaps, even naive assumptions. These assumptions hold that: (1) lifelong learning is important to the continued growth and development of the individual; (2) older adults can in fact continue to learn; (3) older adults do in fact want to continue to learn; and (4) learning is not confined to classrooms where quarter-long or semester-long courses for credit are taught. In other words, nontraditional approaches take it for granted that educational programs exist for the benefit of people and not people for the benefit of educational programs.

The Institutes for Lifetime Learning in Washington, D.C., and Long Beach, California, are among the most outstanding examples in this country of a nontraditional approach to educational programming for older adults. These institutes have been organized and planned by retired people themselves. Presumably, then, the institutes are more sensitive to the needs and interests of older adults. Noncredit courses are offered, typically for an eight-week semester. Classes generally meet once a week for an hour and a half, normally convene in the morning and early afternoon, and are usually held in comfortable lounges and conference classrooms.

Unlike a lot of more traditional institutions, the institutes are not restricted to a particular location insofar as course offerings are concerned. To the contrary, classes are conducted throughout the general, geographic areas in which the institutes themselves are located. Numerous agencies and community organizations with adequate space cosponsor and support institute classes. Synagogues, churches, libraries, banks, community centers, universities, and community colleges offer their facilities. This enables the institutes to go into the community to take courses to the people; it also makes courses accessible to individuals either unable or unwilling to travel to one, possibly remote, location.

The curriculum at the institutes is as varied as the educational interests of the participants. Because the classroom facilities are donated and the program is administered on a local level by older volunteers, the only outstanding instructional expenses are those of the instructors, which range from approximately $5 to $15 a course. For those who wish to study independently, there are courses of home study, for which there are no eligibility requirements. In addition, the institutes offer a radio series of courses that reach literally thousands of listeners throughout the country.

There are weaknesses and drawbacks to nontraditional learning opportunities. Those who consider themselves to be nontraditional change agents are unconsciously, but nonetheless devoutly, traditional. For example, they seem unable to break the habit of continuing to define learning and education in terms of formal courses, teachers, semesters, credits, and the like. They simply do not seem to have the know-how, the desire, or the willingness to jettison some of these traditional and vestigial academic embellishments. Even "model" nontraditional approaches are festooned with the trappings of the institutions so frequently assailed for their inflexibility and lack of innovation.

The Individualized Learning Resource Center Approach

The final type of approach to planning educational programs is the Individualized Learning Resource Center (ILRS) approach. The ILRC is not the only, or even the single best, approach to delivering educational services to older adults. Even though it is essentially a nontraditional approach, its uniqueness qualifies it for special consideration as a distinct planning approach. In response to the unique educational requirements of adults and the failure of more traditional approaches to instruction, the ILRC has emerged in recent years as a powerful, effective, and efficient instructional delivery system (Bullard, 1973; de la Cuesta, 1970; Hinspeter, 1973; Lane & Lewis, 1971; Lumsden, 1976; Peters, 1972; Spanenberg & Smith, 1976; Sullivan, 1974).

Consensus has it that an ILRC is a self-contained learning system in which the individual characteristics of students play a major role in the establishment of objectives and the choice of instructional and learning resources. There also appears to be general agreement that the ILRC makes heavy use of programmed and other types of self-instructional materials and is designed to allow students to pursue their own interests while it fosters independence and creativity. It has evolved from a narrowly conceived, single-concept, programmed-instruction class into the current, programmed, multimedia individualized-learning approach. The modern ILRC:

1. Applies the latest teaching and learning techniques, specifies objectives, assesses learning capacities, provides for individualized and *group* learning experiences, and constantly evaluates the total instructional process for the modification of objectives and methods
2. Utilizes the latest educational technology, i.e., modern, programmed learning systems, audio-visual devices, teaching machines, programmed texts, films, slides, etc.
3. Designs individualized and group programs of instruction for participants and incorporates a variety of innovative experiences, including small-group discussions, field trips, projects, role playing, etc.
4. Allows students to proceed, at their own rate of speed and according to their own attendance schedules, in a nongraded, unstructured approach to learning. Classes do not ordinarily meet at specific times because there are typically no classes per se; rather, group activities

and other kinds of learning experiences are provided to accord with the interests and individual schedules of participants

5. Utilizes learning coordinators and instructional assistants who conduct and manage learning experiences, advise students, and maintain student records
6. Places the major emphasis and responsibility for learning on the student, even though the instructional and counseling staffs do in fact share the responsibility

The ILRC has proven itself to be an effective and efficient means for providing instruction across a broad spectrum of curriculum areas and student populations. Research data and descriptive program statistics indicate the following significant trends:

1. ILRCs are effective vehicles for implementing and facilitating both independent and group study.
2. ILRCs provide the flexibility of scheduling and the variety of instructional procedures necessary for tailoring instruction to the needs of students.
3. ILRCs attract, accommodate, and sustain student participation better than traditional, classroom approaches.
4. ILRCs accomplish stated educational objectives more efficiently than traditional approaches through lower cost per student/hour of instruction and accelerated attainment of projected student goals.

The ILRC provides adult learning experiences that are both horizontally and vertically individualized. Within a single ILRC, different people can be studying completely different subjects; that is, a virtually unlimited number of older adults could be studying, at the same time, everything from art to music to social security. Different people could also all be studying the very same subject but at completely different levels of complexity; for example, many students could be studying mathematics at levels of complexity ranging from simple arithmetic to advanced differential calculus. In addition, instruction is individualized by virtue of the self-pacing nature of self instructional programs. ILRC students can enter and exit the center as they please. While there, they can stay for whatever time they wish. In short, then, the ILRC is an excellent instructional model for assisting older adults to:

1. Learn about and prepare for retirement
2. Earn college credit if desired
3. Adjust, through learning, to new life situations and prepare for new developmental tasks brought about by the continuing processes of aging and maturation
4. Study for self-fulfillment and self-improvement

The obvious and desirable movement toward a greater degree of individualized and personalized learning will require greater utilization of the ILRC concept. Successful use of the center will be largely determined by the degree of congruence between the assumptions behind the center and the sponsoring agency's educational philosophy. Among the basic assumptions of the ILRC are:

1. Planned, sequential learning experiences are more meaningful and effective than random activities.
2. Adults differ in their styles and rates of learning.
3. Multimedia should be an essential component in the design of instruction.
4. Evaluation is basically diagnostic, and the emphasis is on self-evaluation for the primary purpose of improving learning experiences.
5. The teacher is a coordinator and a facilitator of learning as well as a disseminator of information.
6. Learning is a lifelong process and is not to be restricted to any age group.

These basic assumptions should be carefully considered during the initial planning steps of the establishment of an ILRC. Some of the major advantages of the ILRC approach to planning and implementing learning opportunities for older adults are:

1. The learners themselves control the pace of their instruction.
2. Flexible scheduling allows the students to attend at their own convenience and to proceed according to individualized participation patterns.
3. Students are actively involved in the design and conduct of their own learning experiences.
4. Students are provided a virtually unlimited variety of combinations of media formats and curriculum content.
5. The attainment of individual learning goals is practically guaranteed. Properly planned programs preclude failure because the instructional system is essentially nonpunitive. Frequent in-progress monitoring alters the students' curriculum prescriptions, when necessary, and modifies their instructional trajectories at the very first hint of faltering or failure.

Despite these instructional and learning advantages, there are also certain characteristics of the ILRC approach that are potentially problematic. The traditional role of the teacher as a custodian and disseminator of knowledge is drastically altered. The ritualistic meeting of a specified group of people at a specified time is, in most instances, eliminated. So, too, is the closure that comes at the end of terms, quarters, semesters, etc. The ILRC "term" is continuous, with students entering and exiting in a perpetual flow. For all these reasons, it has been proven that ILRC coordinator positions require a new breed of professionals, the basic requirements for which include:

1. An understanding of the principles governing individualized learning
2. The ability to design and manage instruction
3. Knowledge of how to diagnose the individual needs and interests of older learners
4. Adaptability and readiness to adopt new instructional procedures and materials
5. The ability to relate to, and be supportive of, older adults
6. A working knowledge of the principles of counseling and a familiarity with the basics of student evaluation
7. A sincere and evident concern for the needs of older adults and the ability to empathize with their individual problems.

ILRCs can be located almost anywhere. It is not at all unusual to find them situated in church basements, storefronts, libraries, public school classrooms, and mobile classrooms. Insofar as adaptations for use among the elderly are concerned, there is everything to commend the establishment of ILRCs in senior centers, old-age institutions, high-rise apartment complexes, retirement communities, and mobile parks for older people.

A recent report from the National Council on the Aging (1975) identified 4,870 senior centers and clubs that hold weekly meetings for their members. Participants at these centers and clubs indicated that the facility itself, and the opportunity it provided to be with other people, was one of the most compelling reasons for participation. Participants viewed the senior center both as a program of services and activities and as a place to go, to gather for friendship and fellowship, to sit and observe, or just to be near other people. Because older adults yearn for companionship and meaningful activity, the multipurpose senior center provides an ideal facility for the provision of educational opportunities; and the ILRC represents an excellent strategy for personalizing instruction for individuals and groups.

It appears that almost all program planning for older adults is done with a view toward meeting the educational needs of the noninstitutionalized elderly, age 65 and under. Perhaps it is because only a small proportion—fewer than 5% in 1970 (Manard, 1975)—are institutionalized that most of our contemporary educational planning is done for the noninstitutionalized. Nevertheless, national surveys indicate that there are today, in old-age institutions throughout the country, one million elderly adults. Between 1960 and 1970, the numbers of elderly people in old-age institutions increased 105% (Manard, 1975). It is forecast that the numbers will continue to increase through the year 2000. What, if indeed anything, is being done in these old-age institutions to provide continuing educational opportunities? Why cannot ILRCs bring educational opportunities into institutions?

According the 1970 census data, 95% of all people in the United States age 65 and over live in private households (Manard, 1975). Other census data show that 58% of the roughly 20 million people in the United States age 65 and over have no physical activity limitations (Manard, 1975). These data would suggest that, were it not for problems of transportation, money, and fear, a larger proportion of these people would be candidates for participation in learning activities of various sorts, were they available through ILRCs in neighborhood locations.

Another somewhat recent development in housing for the aged is the deluxe, high-rise building in the central city. Frequently, restaurants or central dining rooms are included in the building for use by the residents. Recreational facilities and small shops featuring personal services are usually an integral part of the building complex. These high-rise apartment complexes around the country are ideal locations for ILRCs.

Around the country, most noticeably in Florida, Arizona, and California, so-called retirement communities for the elderly have been developed in the past few years. Many of these retirement communities are virtually self-contained; that is, they include shopping centers, churches, restaurants, recreation facilities, swimming pools, and occasionally medical centers. These retirement communities are also natural settings for the location of ILRCs.

Another concept in housing for the elderly is the mobile-home park. Very often, the management of the park makes provision for the organized social and recreational needs of the residents. These mobile parks around the country are ideal places for setting up ILRCs.

Insofar as specific recommendations for the on-going operation of the ILRC are concerned, the following considerations are of central importance:

1. Because ILRCs may be located almost anywhere, it is obviously important to situate them as close as humanly possible to the older adults to be served. To the extent that ILRCs are located in the immediate vicinity of those for whom the centers are established, the transportation problems many older adults face are overcome.

2. Some older adults who will want to participate in the program activities available through the ILRC will have visual and/or auditory handicaps. For these reasons, preassessment of entering students is essential. ILRC instructional programs more often than not rely heavily upon multimedia learning resources. Students with visual and/or auditory problems are likely to withdraw from the center unless their handicaps are properly diagnosed at the time they enter the center.

3. It is not enough simply to diagnose the learning problems of entering students; provisions must be made to overcome the problems diagnosed. If students have visual problems, they will require eye-

glasses or modifications in the eyeglasses they already have. If they have hearing difficulties, they will need listening aids. The direct or indirect provision of these visual and auditory aids should be available with minimum inconvenience to the students.

4. For those older adults who, for a variety of reasons, simply cannot go to the ILRC, it is strongly recommended that the center coordinate its programs with the programs of other educational institutions in order to extend learning opportunities all the way into the living rooms and bedrooms of the elderly. How? Through local bookmobile programs, through the use of independent instruction offered by the nation's correspondence schools, and by conducting group-learning activities in the homes of the students. Two of the most effective means for extending certain types of learning activities right into the homes of the elderly involve the continued and expanded uses of radio and television.

CONCLUSION

What is needed now in this country is communication with and between local and national politicians, school administrators, and educators about what is necessary to make the nation's educational ideals become realities. The further exploration of new ways and means of adapting current and projected educational programs to the needs of older adults must be rigorously pursued. What is even more important is continuous application of vision and imagination to developing new and bold approaches and structures for extending the educational franchise to all our citizens.

REFERENCES

Aging in Connecticut. Storrs: University of Connecticut, 1971.

Bullard, B. *Centers anyone?* Bloomington, Ind.: Phi Delta Kappa, Inc. 1973.

Council of Chief State School Officers. *Policy statements.* Washington, D.C.: Author, 1976.

Cummings, E., & Henry, W. *Growing old: The process of disengagement.* New York: Basic Books, 1961.

de la Cuesta, L. *Guidelines for adult basic education learning centers.* Newark: New Jersey Department of Education, 1970.

Havighurst, R. J. Education through the adult life span. *Educational Gerontology,* 1976, *1,* 41–51.

Hinspeter, W. L. *Guidelines for the establishment and operation of learning centers.* Fort Monroe, Va.: Department of the Army, Headquarters, U.S. Continental Army Command, 1973.

Lane, C. & Lewis, R. *Guidelines for establishing and operating an adult learning laboratory.* Raleigh: North Carolina State University, 1971.

Lumsden, D. B. *The design and implementation of military learning centers.*

Pensacola: U.S. Naval Defense Activity for Non-Traditional Education Support, 1976.

Manard, B. B. *Old-age institutions.* Lexington, Mass.: D. C. Heath, 1975.

Maslow, A. H. *Motivation and personality.* New York: Harper & Row, 1970.

National Council on the Aging. *Senior centers: A report of senior group programs in America.* Washington, D.C.: Author, 1975.

Peters, J. M. *How to make successful use of the learning laboratory.* Englewood Cliffs: Prentice-Hall, 1972.

Spanenberg, R. W., & Smith, E. A. *Handbook for the design and implementation of a cost effective Air Force learning center.* Lowry Air Force Base, Technical Training Division, 1976.

Sullivan, D. *A survey of the present state-of-the-art in learning center operations.* Lowry Air Force Base, Technical Training Division, 1974.

Toward a national policy on aging: Final report of the 1971 White House Conference on Aging, Vol. 1. Washington, D.C.: U.S. Government Printing Office, 1972.

U.S. Office of Education, Bureau of Occupational and Adult Education. *Long range planning.* Washington, D.C.: Author, June 1975.

6

ALTERNATIVE INSTRUCTIONAL STRATEGIES FOR OLDER LEARNERS

CHRISTOPHER R. BOLTON

University of Nebraska at Omaha

It requires a singularly sensitive instructor to perceive which key opens the door to learning. Most people prefer to use a standard key and when the lock does not turn they see no need for self-reproach but refer to the inadequacy of their pupils.

Belbin and Belbin

The advent of educational gerontology as an emerging field of study and practice has created a fascinating but often perplexing circumstance that educators have only begun to examine. As we explore the potential of education for older adults, we are often faced with both the opportunity and the frustration of reexamining our traditionally held beliefs regarding the educational process. This is especially true in considering the complexities of instructional strategies for older learners. Our brief experience in this teaching-learning process has been given only a cursory treatment in the literature, represents only a modicum of variation in methods, and almost totally lacks even the simplest evaluation research regarding the applicability of the variety of alternative strategies available. Although this may seem hard criticicsm given without opportunity for rebuttal, the intention behind it is to cause us to refrain from practicing tried and potentially *not* true methods without first being assured that our decisions have been made from informed choices.

WHAT WE KNOW ABOUT INSTRUCTION FOR OLDER ADULTS

Available knowledge concerning the instruction of older adults is very meager but at the same time is considerably greater than we may think.

Several writers have cataloged a variety of special problems that older learners face and that have meaning for our choice of instructional strategy. Anderson (1955) cited the heavy reliance older learners place on past experience, as a potential strength in formulating frames of reference, and as a hindrance, when it is manifested as inflexibility. He proposed that older learners are more resistant to risk taking than younger learners and that we should avoid situations that might possibly make older learners appear foolish. Anderson also suggested that, should older learners be unable to derive immediate meaning from the learning experience, competing interests will affect their learning motivation. Belbin and Belbin (1972) expressed these same concerns with the added caution that individual differences among older learners are especially important, "Ageing is the great exaggerator of individual characteristics . . . " (p. 185).

There is little evidence available that clearly specifies the most applicable instructional strategies that should be employed when teaching the elderly. A publication of the Academy for Educational Development (1974) recommended that application of the concepts of *andragogical theory* (a theory of teaching adults) would be useful in teaching the elderly. Geist (1968) suggested several points to be considered in the process, namely: (1) clear presentation, (2) a slower pace than normally employed with younger students, (3) learning by activity, and (4) providing well-spaced pauses to prevent fatigue. Canestrari (1963), in a study of learning, found that when aging people were allowed to pace themselves, their learning performance compared favorably with that of younger subjects. Granick and Friedman (1973), in a review of research on the intellectual functioning of the elderly, concluded that older people have the ability to learn and can benefit from educational programs. Hixson (1969) suggested that the learning environment for older people should be nonthreatening. Several important aspects of a nonthreatening learning climate are: a nonclassroom atmosphere; informal meetings; slower pace; and no homework, grades, tests, examinations, or term papers. The goal of this approach, according to Hixson, is to prevent the students from placing themselves in competitive situations.

Samuel Hand (1973) reminded us to incorporate into our instructional strategies our understanding of the physiological changes that occur in later maturity. Changes in visual acuity and hearing ability dictate that the learning environment be comfortable for older learners. Roger DeCrow (n.d.), however, contended that "In real life learning these intrinsic [physiological] differences are of little consequence" (p. 57). It is his belief that instructional methods that are appropriate for adults are also appropriate for older adults and that there is no need to pursue a "new science of 'geriagogy,' the teaching of older people which is a concept common in Europe" (p. 57). There are those who disagree with DeCrow's position, however. Altman, Smith, and Oppenheimer (1975) believe that "The older adults' unique developmental and physiological stage in the life cycle as well as their isolated status, as imposed by our society, requires that we design a pedagogy and methodology reflective of their distinct time and place in society" (p. 3). It appears as evidenced by van Enckevort's (1971) discussion of the activity of *gerontology*, the theory of *gerontagogics*, and the science of *gerontagology*, that European educators would subscribe to this notion.

One area of intensive research on older learners, conducted in a laboratory setting, is reported by Arenberg and Robertson (1974). Their summary of learning research includes:

1. *Although older learners can maintain and recall about as much information in primary memory as young adults, when the capacity of primary memory is exceeded age deficits emerge.*
2. *Under conditions of fast pacing, whether the presentation rate or the response rate is increased, the older learner is usually handicapped; his performance is especially benefited by self-pacing.*
3. *Some conditions which increase the organization of information into secondary memory improve learning for the older individual.*
4. *Under some conditions, especially those which oppose established habits or preconceived ideas, learning of the older individual is especially susceptible to interference.*
5. *Retrieval of information which includes a substantial search of secondary memory is especially difficult for the older learner. (p. 30)*

It is evident from this summary of older-adult learning reserach that the primary outcomes of the teaching-learning process are the traditionally held cognitive recall variables. Possibly the laboratory studies conducted by learning-theory psychologists have missed the mark when considering often-prescribed goals of education for older learners.

Over the past 25 years a significant number of instructional methods and techniques useful in teaching students of all ages have been developed. Although there has been considerable research conducted to evaluate the viability of these assorted methods and techniques, the results are still inconclusive. When we consider the application of most of these methods and techniques to the instruction of older learners, we find a complete dearth of evidence to support or reject any given method. In lieu of research data, it is therefore necessary to present a representative overview of the types of strategies available and to allow educators the opportunity of informed selection of their choice. It is hoped that as we explore the potential of the alternatives, some evidence of usefulness or lack thereof will be generated and shared for the greater good of the field of educational gerontology and the nonscience of "gerontogogy."

The instructional strategies classification scheme employed here is a result of the writer's understanding of the fundamental differences that exist between instructor–authority-focused and learner–autonomy-focused strategies.

The division of strategies into traditional and alternative categories is derived from a model discussed by Howard Bowen (1975) and modified by the writer. No attempt has been made to generate an all-inclusive encyclopedia of methods and techniques, although the review of the conceptual basis for each strategy covers the current state of the field.

INSTRUCTOR–AUTHORITY–FOCUSED STRATEGY

Concepts

The instructional strategy classified as instructor–authority focused represents most traditional forms of pedagogic instruction. This strategy employs concepts familiar to those of us versed in elementary and secondary educational methods. The principal concepts of the instructor–authority-focused strategy encompass a number of terms that aid in our recognition of associated methods and techniques.

Direction The instructor–authority assumes the control or management of the students learning experiences. The students in turn follow directions explicitly, respond when appropriate and in a mandated fashion, and are otherwise provided all cues to their learning behavior. Incorrect responses to directives result in negative reinforcement, and correct responses are positively reinforced. Often this type of instructional strategy is modeled on Skinnerian behavior-modification techniques, although that model is not always conscientiously followed. The essence of Skinner's theory is carried in the premise: "Behavior is determined by its consequences." We should not, however, carry the SR concept to an extreme, for as Skinner states, "Learning does not occur because behavior has been primed (stimulated); it occurs because behavior, primed or not, is 'reinforced' " (Skinner, 1968).

Prescription The students' learning style is presupposed and generalized to learners' availing themselves of courses of study employing this type of strategy. In a group instructional setting, prescription will usually indicate an attempt to gear the level of teaching toward a presumed middle third of students' learning abilities. The lower third are expected to upgrade their abilities, whereas the upper third are unchallenged. In an individualized instructional setting, the prescription can more accurately reflect the learners' style and abilities. In some more mechanical (technological) methods, only certain levels of ability are preprogrammed, thus only increasing the number of steps in the hierarchy of styles and abilities, not totally individualizing the prescription.

Authority Dependence Whether the source authority is the professor standing before the class or the computer blinking its cathode-ray tube in the learners' faces, the authority resides with the method or technique. The curriculum is prescribed, the pertinent facts are selected, the levels of complexity are predetermined, and the quiz questions and correct answers are selected by the source authority. The learners act as passive receivers tuned only to one wavelength and allowed no alternatives. The source authority relies almost totally on cognitive content as its principal learning resource.

Efficiency Efficiency is assured by the elimination of all but the most necessary inputs from the learners. Even in the instance of the structured-discussion instructional method, discussed later, efficiency is assured through the complete control of the discussion by the instructor. Given the high degree of reliance placed upon the source authority, this strategy is an extremely efficient system, for it directs the input, disregards its processing, and prescribes the output.

Malcolm Knowles (1973) describes an instructor–authority-focused instructional strategy in terms of (1) the conditions of learning, and (2) the skills required of the learners involved. The conditions of learning are:

1. A willingness to be dependent
2. A respect for authority
3. A commitment to learning as a means to an end (e.g., course credit, certificates, degrees, etc.)
4. A competitive relationship with fellow students (for group instruction methods)

The skills are the ability to:

1. Listen uncritically
2. Retain information
3. Take notes
4. Predict exam questions

Although the instructor–authority-focused strategy is often maligned by proponents of the learner–autonomy-focused strategy, we must keep in mind that many, probably most, older learners have little, if any, educational experience with other than strictly pedagogical methods. For many older learners the reliance on a source authority is the only possible means of acquiring the insights they require from a learning experience. This is not to suggest that older learners cannot learn new tricks, or, in this case, alternative modes of instruction. Depending on the nature of the subject matter to be taught, however, we might find that older learners, embarking on what may be their first attempt at formal education in 40 or 50 years, may derive more benefit from an experience that is consistent with their long-held frame of reference regarding educational practices.

Methods

The division of instructional methods and techniques into traditional and alternative categories is useful because it brings out the fact that we have placed considerable reliance on traditional methods in our development of instructional strategies for older learners. Although these methods have a place in older adults' learning experiences, there are a number of alternative methods that may also prove beneficial, and their consideration will markedly increase our options in instructional design.

Traditional Methods   There are undoubtedly methods appropriate to the traditional category that are not described here; no attempt has been made to prepare an extensive listing. The methods listed, however, are both representative and illustrative of the traditional category of instructor–authority-focused instructional strategies and should make the range of possibilities clear.

Lecture   The most popular, the most criticized, and the oldest instructional method is the lecture. Whether characterized in terms of Mark Hopkins' "two-on-a-log" or the modern "tele-lecture," the lecture method remains a mainstay of educational practice. The lecture method, along with its companion, the traditional discussion method, has long been a source of study and research. Gayles (1966), in a review of research on comparisons of these two methods, concluded that neither the lecture nor the discussion method is "better" than the other. There is evidence, however, to suggest that the lecture is superior in assuring immediate recall, whereas the discussion method leads to better problem solving and promotes more favorable student attitudes toward the subject matter (Bane, 1925; Barnard, 1942; Casey & Weaver, 1956; Dawson, 1956; Nolan, 1974; Thompson, 1974; Wooley, 1974).

The lecture method consists of an instructor presenting facts, concepts, and principles regarding the chosen topic. More than likely, the chosen topic is selected by the instructor and is part of a series of lectures comprising a course, workshop, or institute. The primary function of the lecture is the transmittal of factual information to students; interaction between instructor and students or among students is minimized and restricted to direct questioning about the topic at hand. The principal instructional outcome for the lecture is the retention of facts by the students; effectiveness of the lecture is measured by students demonstrating content recall, usually on paper-and-pencil multiple-choice tests.

Structured Discussion   In contrast to the lecture, the structured-discussion method allows greater latitude in student–instructor interaction. This method is still highly authority focused, with the instructor clearly directing the discussion of the prescribed topic. Usually the content of the discussion is expected to be derived either from previous class lectures or from assigned reading. Students' personal opinions or personal experiences are not permitted to become the content of a structured discussion. As in the case of the lecture method, the structured-discussion method presents a viable and, for older learners, familiar classroom experience that should not be overlooked in our instructional designs for older adults.

Directed, Independent Study and Directed Readings   More individualized, but nevertheless traditional, are the *directed independent study* and the *directed readings* methods. Both of these are used extensively in post-graduate education programs and represent a viable individualized approach for instructors wishing to adhere to traditional methods. The directed, independent study method employs a one-to-one, instructor–learner relationship. The instructor prescribes the learning tasks for the learner on the basis of the instructor's conceptualization of the topic subject matter. This method relies on the instructor to assume a highly directive role and to indicate the source authorities the learner is to employ to meet the course requirements: A directed reading is similar to a directed, independent study but is usually restricted to instructor-prescribed readings.

Other Traditional Methods This strategy also includes television instruction, video-taped lectures and discussions, recordings, slide and tape presentations, and motion pictures.

Alternative Methods As will be readily noticed, all of the alternative instructor–authority-focused instructional methods described in this section are individualized approaches. Cross (1976) describes the evolution of this current trend toward individualization as the coming of the *instructional revolution.* Cross predicts that "once we have reached our goal of education for *all,* we will turn our attention to providing education for *each*" (p. 2). The current proliferation of new, innovative, and usually individualized, instructional methods suggests that Cross's prediction is well on the way to realization. Another discussant of revolutions in education, Robert Ruskin (1974), states:

> *The fifth revolution is an extremely recent phenomenon. Some of the instructional techniques that fall into this category include: the Personalized System of Instruction, Computer Assisted Instruction, the Audio-Tutorial System, Individually Prescribed Instruction, and Programmed Instruction. Most of these techniques have originated within the past two decades, with the lion's share of their development taking place in the last 5 to 10 years. (p. 2)*

The Personalized System of Instruction Developed by F. S. Keller and J. G. Sherman in the mid-1960s, the personalized system of instruction (PSI) represents one of the most recent individualized instruction methods. PSI is an instructor–authority-focused strategy because it derives its fundamental theory orientation from Skinnerian learning concepts. As described by Ruskin (1974), there are five basic characteristics of the PSI.

1. Behavioral objectives constitute the principal means of describing the goals of a learning experience in which written materials serve as the fundamental means of communication between instructor and learners. Reading guides, prepared by the instructor, direct each learner in the prescribed course of study.
2. The amount of content materials for a course of study is

predetermined by the instructor and divided into equivalent sub-divisions making up "units" of the course. Learners are expected to demonstrate "mastery" of each unit before proceeding to the next. Tests on a given unit are repeated by each learner until the "threshold level of mastery" is achieved.

3. The PSI is self-pacing. Individual learners are allowed to move through a course of study as rapidly or as slowly as they choose provided they master each unit prior to moving to the next. The time constraints of the traditional semester or alternative school-year units (e.g., trimester) are thus ignored, allowing learners the opportunity to have somewhat greater control over the logistics of their educational experience.

4. Lectures and demonstrations presented by the instructor become vehicles for the motivation of learners rather than the source authority for the course of study. This is made possible by the fact that instructors are free to present "more interesting" aspects of the subject during a lecture because they are not required to present the crucial content of the course in their lectures.

5. "The fifth and possibly most important feature in the Personalized System of Instruction is the reliance on undergraduate students to serve as peer-tutors" (p. 13). The stated objective of peer tutoring is to allow learners who have recently completed the course to tutor learners presently involved in that same course. The advantage, according to Ruskin, is that

A peer-proctor system works effectively because the proctors, being undergraduates who have only recently mastered the material, can communicate subtleties of the course content to other students in a way that is readily understandable. This communication is not always in evidence when a highly educated professor tried to discuss course content with an undergraduate. (p. 13)

PSI for Older Learners? For older adults seeking educational experiences to aid them in pursuing a second career, such as real estate, which requires a relatively structured curriculum, the PSI appears to present a highly promising alternative to traditional courses. The ability to attend a lecture whenever one chooses would allow older learners to fit the learning experience into their potentially irregular schedule, and self-pacing would provide older learners the time necessary to master the subject no matter how rusty their learning abilities might have become. PSI allows the economy of resources so necessary in adult education programs because it uses standardized study guides and written materials and provides the flexibility of time so essential for older learners. We should be experimenting with PSI for our older learners and cataloging data on its usefulness as a method of instruction for older adults.

Programmed-Instruction Modules A unit of instruction also based upon Skinnerian learning theory, the programmed instruction module is, unlike the PSI, a self-contained, individualized unit that is only a part of a total instructional program. There are seven essential parts of a programmed module as described by Musgrave (1975):

1. *Rationale.* A statement justifying the inclusion of a particular module in a specific course; written in a clear, precise manner to convey to the learner the importance and relevance of the goals and objectives of the module.
2. *Prerequisites.* A clear and explicit statement of those concepts and facts essential for commencing construction of a module.
3. *Objectives.* A clear, concise statement of the observable behavior or performance outcomes necessary for successful completion of a module; includes both the performance criteria (the nature of the concepts, facts, etc., to be learned) and the level of performance.
4. *Preassessment.* A pretest conducted to determine learner readiness for a particular module, or to detect learner need to complete a preparatory module first.
5. *Enabling Activities.* Self-instructional and programmed books or media by the use of which a student can independently complete activities and fulfill the performance objectives. The preparation of enabling activities is a very time-consuming process requiring a high degree of sophisticated skill. Educators not prepared to engage in the preparation of a programmed instruction module should investigate the many already available for purchase.
6. *Postassessment.* A posttest employed to measure the learner's mastery of the module performance objectives; successful performance allows the learner to move to another project; unsuccessful performance requires the learner to repeat the module or undergo remediation.
7. *Remediation.* An explicit part of the programmed-instruction module, it contains a detailed explanation of what the learner must do upon failure to satisfactorily complete the postassessment. Upon the completion of remediation, the learner reattempts the posttest, presumably with greater assurance of success.

Programmed-Instruction Modules for Older Learners? As in the case of the PSI, programmed modules seem to be a promising alternative to traditional methods in the instructor–authority-focused strategy, but a caution is warranted. As has been stated previously, older adults generally bring a certain reluctance to new learning experiences that could inhibit their persistence and performance. Of primary concern is test shyness, because testing is an essential part of programmed modules. This does not mean that we should reject this method, however; we should be capable of redesigning preassessment and postassessment measures to make them nonthreatening to older learners. Once this hurdle is mastered, the programmed-instruction module should allow us to offer older learners a wide variety of individualized educational experiences that are both economical of personnel and space and educationally effective.

Computer-assisted Instruction A computer system is the means of presenting individualized instructional material to a number of learners simultaneously as they sit before individual computer consoles in the computer-assisted instruction (CAI) method. The computer is used to communicate the subject material to the students in much the same way the PSI employs written materials and the programmed modules employ enabling activities. In CAI, however, the instructional plan developed by an instructor or curriculum specialist is completely carried out in interaction between the learners and the computer. It should be noted that CAI differs from computer-managed instruction (CMI); CAI uses the computer as a surrogate teacher wheras CMI employs the computer in monitoring learner achievement, prescribing, and reporting learner progress. CAI, through its use of highly complex and sophisticated computer programs, represents the most adaptable, and therefore most individualized, method of the instructor-authority–focused strategy. The computer program allows for a vast variety of alternative branch programs that permit learners to follow the branches most suited to their learning style and ability. The CAI requires mastery of one level of learning within a given topic before the learners proceed to the next, just as in PSI and programmed modules. Because the computer program and the computer hardware complexities permit the instructional designer to break down a learning unit or module into minute parts, the learners progress by mastering small bits of learning, gradually accumulating the level of performance necessary to complete a learning unit.

Computer-assisted Instruction for Older Learners? CAI is a possible alternative instructional method for older learners, although the expensive computer terminals, software programs, and computer rental will prevent CAI from being a commonly employed approach. Possibly those educators in community colleges, universities, or governmental agencies presently using CAI will find that certain CAI systems will be suitable for older adults. We must keep in mind, however, that most older adults have never had the opportunity to use computer consoles and would have to be thoroughly oriented to the complexities of CAI in order to remove whatever apprehension they might have in using and understanding computer equipment and processes. Educators having access to CAI programs should encourage the use of the computer in extending the learning alternatives available to older learners. We should not be deterred by the previous caveat about the apprehension older adults experience in nontraditional instructional settings because we also keep in mind that students in general have displayed a high degree of adaptability to innovative instructional methods (Hodgkinson, 1975).

Conclusions

This review of traditional and alternative methods of the instructor-authority-focused instructional strategy represents only an introduction to the many types of instructional methods and techniques available to educational gerontologists involved in the design of educational programs and activities for older learners. Given our fundamental understanding of the learning styles and abilities of older adults, we will be well advised to incorporate the methods of this strategy into future educational programming efforts. We will need to explore the feasibility of adopting alternative, individualized methods to respond to the increasingly diverse educational needs of older learners even though we remain confident of the important role traditional methods have played and will continue to play in creating effective learning experiences for older adults. An instructor-authority-focused strategy will represent the only acceptable means by which many older learners can learn, and we must commit ourselves to implementing a variety of these methods to the greatest advantage of our students. We must also begin generating useful evaluation research data to gain a clearer understanding of the utility of instructor-authority-focused methods for teaching older adults.

LEARNER–AUTONOMY–FOCUSED STRATEGY

Concepts

While the instructor-authority strategy can be readily and regularly conceptually classified, the learner–autonomy strategy includes methods that employ a broad range of diverse concepts, none of which is necessarily typical of all methods included within the strategy. A case in point that readily clarifies this difference is the contrast in goals of learner-autonomy-focused methods that stress either affective learning, cognitive learning, or a combined affective and cognitive outcome. Probably the best approach to elaborating the varied conceptual bases of the learner-autonomy-focused strategy is to define the most frequently used concepts and allow the reader the opportunity to refer to these definitions as the discussion of methods progresses.

A fundamental conceptual mechanism associated with the learner-autonomy strategy is the notion of *andragogy,* as clarified by Malcolm Knowles (1971, 1973, 1975). The term *andragogy,* according to Knowles, is dervied from the Greek words *aner* meaning "the man" and *agogus* meaning "leader of"; thus *andragogy* literally means "the art and science of teaching adults." Knowles (1973) cites four main assumptions upon which andragogical theory is based.

1. *Changes in Self-concept.* "The assumption is that as a person grows and matures his self-concept moves from one of total dependency (as

in the reality of the infant) to one of increasing self-directedness" (p. 45).

2. *The Role of Experience.* "This assumption is that as an individual matures he accumulates an expanding reservoir of experience that causes him to become an increasingly rich resource for learning, and at the same time provides him with a broadening base to which to relate new learnings. Accordingly, in the technology of andragogy there is a decreasing emphasis on the transmitted techniques of traditional teaching and increasing emphasis on experiential techniques which tap the experience of the learners and involve them in analyzing their experience" (pp. 45–46).

3. *Readiness to Learn.* "This assumption is that as an individual matures, his readiness to learn is decreasingly the product of his biological development and academic pressure and is increasingly the product of the developmental tasks required for the performance of his evolving social roles" (p. 46).

4. *Orientation to Learning.* "This assumption is that children have been conditioned to have a subject-centered orientation to most learning, whereas adults tend to have a problem-centered orientation to learning" (p. 47).

Affective education, humanistic education, and *confluent education* are concepts that have only recently been developing meaning for educators. These educational concepts have been roughly drawn together into what Borton (1970) feels is a new field that he defines as a "new direction in education stemming from the cooperation of psychologists and educators and balancing the traditional emphasis on skills and cognitive information with an explicit attention to the important areas of feelings, values, and interpersonal behavior" (p. 135). Brown (1971) provides definitions of the concepts *confluent* and *affective:*

> Confluent education *is the term for the integration or flowing together of the* affective *and* cognitive *elements in individual and group learning—sometimes called humanistic or psychological education.* Affective *refers to the feeling or emotional aspect of experience and learning. How a child or adult feels about wanting to learn, how he feels as he learns, and what he feels after he has learned are included in the affective domain. (pp. 3-4)*

Although most of the effort toward implementing affective, humanistic, and confluent teaching practices has been conducted with younger students in special learning projects (Borton, 1970; Brown, 1971; Weinstein & Fantini, 1970), there have been numerous, related, human-potential–movement training and educational programs for adults throughout the past 30 years (Beene, Bradford, Gibb, & Lippitt, 1975).

There are basically four concepts that are generally applied in the learner–autonomy-focused instructional strategy.

Nondirectiveness Rogers (1969) affords us with the best example of non-directiveness in his analysis of traditional teaching:

> *Teaching, in my estimation, is a vastly overrated function. Having made such a statement, I scurry to the dictionary to see if I really mean what I say. Teaching means: "to instruct." Personally, I am not much interested in instructing another in what he should know or think. "To impart knowledge or skill." My reaction is, why not be more efficient, using a book or programmed learning? "To make to know." Here, my hackles rise. I have no wish to make anyone know something. "To show, guide, direct." As I see it, too many people have been shown, guided, directed. So I come to the conclusion that I do mean what I said. Teaching is, for me, a relatively unimportant and vastly overvalued activity. (p. 103)*

Rogers goes on to describe the process of *facilitation of learning*, which is essentially a process by which a facilitator shows concern for the climate of the learning experience, acts as a guide to learning resources, becomes a participant in the learning process, and focuses the educational experience on those purposes that have meaning for the learner.

Process Centering Borton (1970) defines processing as: *a way of doing* that has form and structure, a way of operating, a purposive behavior. Processes allow us to connect the information we receive to new responses—actions, feelings, dreams, thoughts" (p. 76). Process-centered instruction focuses primarily on learners becoming progressively more sophisticated in the process activity of learning. Described another way, a focus on process is a focus on practice in organizing the information imparted in the learning experience in the manner most useful to the learner. Borton concludes that "the purpose of education is to produce people who have developed a conscious grasp of the processes through which they themselves grow. A curriculum with that goal educates man in his own humanity, in his power to change his life by changing the processes he uses to form himself" (p. 91).

Learner Discovery The methods of this strategy place a heavy emphasis on *learner discovery*, with the instructor facilitating the process and guiding learners to the resources required to accomplish the learning goal. Often, the heuristic nature of the learner–autonomy strategy leads to a trial-and-error situation that invites considerable criticism from proponents of the more efficient, instructor–authority-focused strategy. Although sometimes inefficient, this heuristic element is often felt to produce more meaningful learning experiences for the learner, and it can contribute to learners' analyzing and extending their abilities to solve problems through individual and group inquiry (Gilstrap & Martin, 1975).

Proaction Knowles (1973) contends that traditional pedagogy conditions learners to respond reactively to stimuli from teachers and that we must help adults to learn other proactive ways of learning, "for in adult life, learning will take place for the most part only if the learner takes the initiative; teachers are not as omnipresent" (p. 172). A proactive strategy, for Knowles, would include the following required conditions:

a. *Intellectual curiosity*
b. *Spirit of inquiry*
c. *Knowledge of resources available*
d. *Healthy skepticism toward authority*
e. *Criteria for testing reliability and validity*
f. *Commitment to learning as a developmental process (p. 174)*

The learning skills Knowles (1973) suggests as a requirement for proactive strategies are ability to:

a. Formulate questions answerable by data
b. Identify data available in printed materials (e.g., by table of contents, index)
c. Scan quickly
d. Test data against criteria of reliability and validity
e. Analyze data to produce answers to questions

Methods

Learner–autonomy-focused instructional methods have a long and varied history beginning in 1946 at a state workshop on intergroup relations at the State Teachers College in New Britain, Connecticut, under the leadership of Kurt Lewin, Kenneth Benne, Leland Bradford, and Ronald Lippitt (Benne, Bradford, Gibb, & Lippitt, 1975). Growing out of this first effort in laboratory education was the National Training Laboratory in Group Development, renamed in the mid-1950s and recognized by the initials NTL (for National Training Laboratories) and located in Bethel, Maine. Since these early experiences of the personal development movement, there has been a wide proliferation of similar organizations in this country and in many foreign countries. Most renowned among these offshoots of the NTL are the Esalen Institute in California and Tavistock in England.

Laboratory Method The principal instructional method developed for use by the NTL and related organizations devoted to personal and organizational growth and change is the laboratory method. As Kenneth Benne (1975) describes it: "Perhaps most fundamentally, the method is a way by which people are helped to learn how to learn for themselves. It stands for experiential learning" (p. 25). The original intent of the laboratory method was to focus on adult learners and the unique educational needs of adults. "The founders of the first laboratory were thus concerned about unmet learning and growth needs in the various organized associations of adult life, not just in formal education. They saw failure in meeting these needs as a dangerous condition in contemporary life" (Beene, 1975, pp. 38–39). Conceptually the laboratory method employs several previously mentioned concepts, including:

1. *A Way of Learning.* Experiential learning through responsible participation by learners in a group setting—the hallmark of the laboratory method—determines what they need to learn, invents or creates ways by which to achieve learning goals, and assumes responsibility for managing the learning environment.
2. *Process as Content.* "The innovators of laboratory methods in education thus emphasized understanding and skill in methods of instituting the conditions and processes of experiential learning in various associations and relationships of life as an important outcome of education" (Beene 1975, p. 27).
3. *A Way of Planned Change.* Training is designed to aid participants in developing skills for changing the quality and character of the social environment in which they function.
4. *A Process of Cooperative Action Research.* The innovators of the laboratory method believed there is a gap between practitioners of fundamental research in the social sciences and "groups who are suffering the effects of debilitating and dehumanizing social conditions and who are struggling, often ineffectually, to meliorate these conditions" (p. 30). Action research allows learners the opportunity to validate empirically derived theories of human functioning and interaction for their personal use through trial in a nonthreatening learning environment.
5. *A Process of Knowledge Utilization.* This is essentially an extension of action research, to facilitate the utilization of research-tested social and behavioral knowledge in an action setting.
6. *A Way of Resocialization and Reenculturation.* "Human organisms become persons and selves as they enter into membership in various associations and, in the process, internalize, make their own, the language, the standards, the thought-ways, value-ways, and behavior-ways, which prevail as a way of life in these associations" (Beene, 1975, pp. 35–36). The laboratory method is intended to be a means by which individuals are aided in developing abilities in independent thinking and action, thus allowing for personal, tradition-free control over the processes of continuing socialization.

self-planned learning experience, Tough (1971) provides a list of the preparatory steps in planning self-learning.

1. Describing what knowledge and skill is needed to learn
2. Deciding the activities, methods, resources, or equipment for learning
3. Deciding where to learn
4. Setting specific deadlines or intermediate targets
5. Deciding when to begin a learning episode
6. Deciding the pace at which to proceed during a learning episode
7. Estimating the current level of one's knowledge and skill, or one's progress in gaining the desired knowledge and skill
8. Detecting any factor that has been blocking or hindering one's learning, or discovering inefficient aspects of the current procedures
9. Obtaining the desires resources or equipment, or reaching the desired place or resource
10. Preparing or adapting a room (or certain resources, furniture, or equipment) for learning, or arranging certain other physical conditions in preparation for learning
11. Saving or obtaining the money necessary for the use of certain human or nonhuman resources—perhaps for buying a book, renting equipment, or paying for lessons
12. Finding time for the learning
13. Taking certain steps to increase the motivation for certain learning episodes

Self-directed and Self-planned Learning for Older Learners? It appears, on the surface at least, that self-directed learning represents one of the most viable instructional methods available for working with older learners. The high degree of learner autonomy in this approach is useful to the educator in its efficiency of time and is effective for the learner in its freedom from the constraints of fixed-time-and-place instructional methods. Hiemstra (1975) found that, from a sample of 214 older learners age 55 years and older, the number of learning projects averaged 3.3 per person per year and that these people spent an average of 324.5 hours on learning projects per year. "Although the majority of the respondents carried out fewer than four projects and spent fewer than 300 hours in learning, many people are engaged in considerable learning each year" (p. 55) Hiemstra affords us an excellent example of one learning project reported in his research: "One 86 year old gentleman in Lincoln [Nebraska] spent nearly 600 hours last year learning how to grow an organic garden. His activities included attending meetings, reading books, watching ETV programs on gardening, attending gardening meetings, and talking with other gardeners" (p. 55). This example clearly shows the variety of resources a self-directed learner can employ in a learning project. What is needed in operationalizing this method is to insure that older learners understand the practical steps involved in preparation. To facilitate their learning process they require reassurance when desired or needed. The potential for peer-group facilitation of learning projects would further enhance the older learner's autonomy. Innovative techniques, such as a learning exchange, can free older adults from reliance on the often costly mechanisms of present-day educational institutions.

Education for Transiting A third methodological approach to instruction in the learner–autonomy-focused strategy is derived from the work of the Brazilian educator Paulo Freire and is termed *education for transiting.* Freire's approach to adult education developed through his work in South America, where he attempted to assist illiterates in overcoming the oppression of stereotypes and tradition through a process of *conscientization.* As Farmer (1972) describes the methodology, "Freire's approach to adult education is designed to assist persons to transit from one way of perceiving reality to a more adequate way; from a state of oppression to a state of increased personal freedom" (p. 1). Although education for transiting may be more appropriately classified as an educational philosophy, the approach is founded in Freire's method of dialogue with the learner and in assumptions regarding how an oppressed learner goes about achieving a reformulated self-image essential to conscientization. Freire's approach, closely allied with previously discussed humanistic methods, places greatest stress on the capacity of learners to change and thus free themselves from deterministic forms of existence, and the ability of learners to critically analyze, demythologize, and decode the way they perceive themselves in relation to the world they live in.

Education for transiting places heavy emphasis on assessment of needs from the learners' role perspective rather than from the educator's role perspective. In other words, needs are *not prescribed* from the intellectual orientation of the educator, but determined through the self perception and role perspective of the learners.

Farmer (1972) describes five characteristics of education for transiting useful in understanding the completely learner–autonomy-focused nature of this method:

1. The learning experience starts with identification of reality as perceived by the learners.
2. The learning experience is oriented to reflection and action on the part of the learners in relation to their common problem or concern.
3. The learning focuses on real problems for which there are no predetermined answers and frequently only proximate solutions. It is exploratory, research, or development oriented.
4. The teaching method relies heavily on dialogue between students and teachers, students and students, and between both teachers and students and the world.

5. Both teaching and learning are engaged in through existential involvement on the part of both teachers and learners.

It should readily become clear that education for transiting is not a method for every educational circumstance. As a method, it is entirely learner centered to the extent that the instructor–facilitator acts only as a catalytic agent for the proactive growth of the learner. *Praxis,* the process of acting upon, of practicing the solutions for a problem or concern, is a fundamental part of this method. Again, we refer to Farmer (1972) for suggestions as to when education for transiting is most appropriate:

1. Motivation on the part of the learner is lacking
2. Prescriptive forms of educational programming have failed
3. Individuals or groups of individuals, as a result of social, psychological, or economic concerns, feel oppressed or powerless
4. People are faced with life situations resulting from personal, vocational, social, or cultural changes
5. "Higher order problems for which there are no solutions are being addressed educationally"
6. The primary focus of the educational activity is on learner-developmental tasks

Critics of Freire, among them Boston (1972), suggest that education for transiting is too radical an approach and borders on education as a means to political anarchy. For many critics, the pedagogy of the oppressed is too one sided, too subversive, too revolutionary, too existential, to be adopted by our sophisticated, highly developed educational systems (Foy, 1971; Friedenberg, 1971; Harman, 1971; Knudson, 1971). For Boston (1972) the method is too critical. "A number of people who have worked on the Freire model are beginning to discover that Freire's methods make it possible to be critical about nearly everything—except those methods themselves" (p. 89), certainly a criticism that should not be overlooked.

For many adult educators, the highly unstructured, free-form, learner-centered nature of this approach will be sufficiently disconcerting to produce an extreme avoidance response. Jack London (1972) counters this reactive, entrenched response by suggesting that our current adult education establishment should be more open to change: "Asked to characterize American adult education in one sentence, I would say this field is led by some very conservative educators. It appears few controversial issues posing a threat to the status quo are welcomed in its programs" (p. 22).

Education for Transiting, Conscientization, for Older Learners? Certainly the first question regarding the applicability of education for transiting for older learners is: Are older adults, the elderly, oppressed? The following quotations from several well-known educators will help us to better answer this question.

Wilma Donahue (1955):

Literally millions of older people are striving to learn their positions in the community and to find new roles for themselves, hundreds of thousands of families are concerned about responsibilities for parents. The large majority of middle-aged are looking forward to their later years with apprehension; and we are all threatened with a psychologically, economically, and medically dependent older population that is capable of engulfing our social organization. (p. vii)

Lawrence Frank (1955):

Many older persons living today are unhappy and bewildered. Some are bitter and resentful. For the most part they feel isolated and neglected, often useless and unwanted, no longer able or permitted to work. Nor are they capable of finding a way of living that will bring any real sense of satisfaction and fulfillment. (p. 1)

David Peterson (1974):

At least half the persons in the older population must be viewed as under-educated, and nearly three million are categorized as functionally illiterate. (p. 45)

Harry Moody (1976):

We shun and fear old people because, symbolically, they represent our own fate; in their despair, it is really our own that we fear. This intrapsychic process of repression, of unconscious dread and denial, is recapitulated and "writ large" even in the very social institutions and mechanisms that modern life evolves to "deal with" the problem of aging: the enforced segregation of the nursing home and the "gold coast" retirement communities. (pp. 3-4)

From these examples we should be able to reasonably conclude that, to an extent greater than is generally accepted, older adults do represent, both to the general population and to themselves, an oppressed segment of present-day society. Whether a pedagogy for the oppressed, education for transiting, or conscientization will represent a viable alternative instructional strategy for older learners is yet to be seen. We are probably correct in assuming a need for more care and consideration in adopting this method than previously discussed methods due to the critical nature of its approach. We cannot, however, fail to recognize that many of the problems and concerns the elderly encounter are directly related to their assigned status as old, useless retirees. We will need to assume a more proactive approach in creating educationally related personal growth experiences oriented toward higher critical consciousness if we are to become true facilitators for older learners. It seems important to at least allow older adults the opportunity to experience education for transiting even if the only outcome of such a trial is their rejection of the method. This writer, for one, is not predicting such an outcome; he is convinced that older adults do truly represent an oppressed people and that the pedagogy for the oppressed may very well represent that quality of critical consciousness essential for the abolition of elder oppression.

Conclusions

Does the learner–autonomy-focused instructional strategy have a place in educational gerontology? There are some among our ranks who would content that it does, namely Altman, Smith, and Oppenheimer (1975); Bolton (1976); Moody (1976); Morrison (1976); and Wolf and Wolf (1976). Although our experience with humanistic, affective, confluent methods is seriously limited, there is the growing concern among instructional planners for older learners that we have lost sight of the uniqueness of education for aging. Moody (1976) states: "Older people must experience a kind of 'consciousness raising' that allows them to adopt a positive attitude toward their situation and to take steps to change it. They need help in shedding the self-hatred caused by stereotypes and the prevailing attitudes of society at large" (p. 8). The argument is continued by Rubin (1975):

> We are obliged to remember . . . that we are living in a dark time when man is increasingly to be confronted with painfully difficult choices. These choices involve not the comparatively easy options of the past regarding "right against right"–questions, in short, having to do with priorities among competing passions." (p. 183)

Rubin's point, although focused on younger learners, certainly holds true for older learners, possibly holding even more true for those in later maturity. It is probably sufficient to say that the learner–autonomy-focused instructional strategy is increasingly gaining in its credibility with the educational community. Humanistic methods cannot be overlooked as a viable alternative in our instructional designs, nor can they be given carte blanche acceptance without verifying data on their educational impact. As in the case of the other methods and techniques discussed here, we must empirically determine their value before we accept or reject *any* of them.

REFERENCES

Academy for Educational Development. *Never too old to learn.* New York: Author, 1974.

Altman, L., Smith, D.C., & Oppenheimer, P. W. *Education and the older adult* (Mimeo). New York: New York City Community College, Institute of Study for Older Adults, 1975.

Anderson, J. E. Teaching and learning. In W. T. Donahue, (Ed.), *Education for later maturity.* New York: Whiteside, 1955.

Arenberg, D. L., & Robertson, E. A. The older individual as a learner. In S. M. Grabowski & W. D. Mason (Eds.), *Learning for aging.* Washington, D.C.: Adult Education Association of the U.S.A., 1974; Syracuse: ERIC Clearinghouse on Adult Education.

Bane, C. L. The lecture vs. the class-discussion method of teaching. *School and Society,* 1925, *21,* 300–302.

Barnard, J. D. The lecture-demonstration vs. the problem-solving method of teaching a college science course. *Science Education,* 1942, *26,* 121–132.

Beene, K. D. Conceptual and moral foundations of laboratory method. In K. D. Beene, L. P. Bradford, J. R. Gibb, & R. O. Lippitt (Eds.), *The laboratory method of changing and learning.* Palo Alto: Science and Behavior, 1975.

Beene, K. D., Bradford, L. P., Gibb, J. R., & Lippitt, R. O. (Eds.). *The laboratory method of changing and learning.* Palo Alto: Science and Behavior, 1975.

Belbin, E., & Belbin, R. M. *Problems in adult retraining.* London: Heinemann, 1972.

Bolton, C. R. Humanistic instructional strategies and retirement education programming. *The Gerontologist,* December, 1976, *16*(6), 550–555.

Borton, T. *Reach, touch, and teach.* New York: McGraw-Hill, 1970.

Boston, B. O. Paulo Freire: Notes of a loving critic. In S. M. Grabowski (Ed.), *Paulo Freire: A revolutionary dilemma for the adult educator.* Syracuse University, Publications in Continuing Education, 1972, pp. 83–92. (ERIC Clearinghouse on Adult Education.)

Bowen, H. R. Teaching and learning: 2000 A.D. In C. T. Stuart & T. R. Harvey (Eds.), *Strategies for significant survival.* San Francisco: Jossey-Bass, 1975.

Bradford, L. P. Creating a learning environment. In K. D. Beene, L. P. Bradford, J. R. Gibb, & R. O. Lippitt (Eds.), *The laboratory method of changing and learning.* Palo Alto: Science and Behavior, 1975, pp. 111–138.

Brown, G. I. *Human teaching for human learning: An introduction to confluent education.* New York: Viking, 1971.

Canestrari, R. E. Paced and self-paced learning in young and elderly adults. *Journal of Gerontology,* 1963, *18,* 165–168.

Casey, J. E., & Weaver, B. E. An evaluation of lecture method and small group method of teaching in terms of knowledge of content, teacher attitude, and social status. *Journal of the Colorado-Wyoming Academy of Science,* 1956, *4,* 54.

Cross, K. P. *The instructional revolution.* Paper presented at the annual meeting of the American Association for Higher Education, March 8, 1976.

Dawson, M. D. Lectures versus problem-solving in elementary soil sections. *Science Education,* 1956, *40,* 394–404.

DeCrow, R. *New learning for older Americans: An overview of national effort.* Washington, D.C.: Adult Educational Association of the U.S.A., n.d.

Donahue, W. T. (Ed.). *Education for later maturity.* New York: Whiteside, 1955.

Farmer, J. A., Jr. Adult education for transiting. In S. M. Grabowski (Ed.), *Paulo Freire: A revolutionary dilemma for the adult educator.* Syracuse University, Publications in Continuing Education, 1972. (ERIC Clearinghouse on Adult Education.)

Foy, R. Review of pedagogy of the oppressed. *Educational Studies,* 1971, *2*(3/4), 92–93.

Frank, L. K. Education for aging. In W. T. Donahue (Ed.), *Education for later maturity.* New York: Whiteside, 1955.

Freire, P. *Education for critical consciousness.* New York: Seabury, 1973.

Friedenberg, E. Review of pedagogy of the oppressed, *Comparative Education Review,* 1971, *15*(3), 378–380.

Gayles, A. R. Lecture vs. discussion. *Improving College and University Teaching,* 1966, *14*(2), 95–99.

Geist, H. *The psychological aspects of the aging process.* St. Louis: Green, 1968.

Gilstrap, R. L., & Martin, W. R. *Current strategies for teachers.* Pacific Palisades, Calif: Goodyear, 1975.

Granick, S., & Friedman, A. S. Educational experience and the maintenance of intellectual functioning by the aged: An overview. In L. Jarvik, C. Eisdorfer, & J. Blum (Eds.), *Intellectual functioning in adults.* New York: Springer, 1973.

Hand, S. What it means to teach older adults. In A. Hendrickson (Ed.), *A manual on planning educational programs for older adults.* Tallahassee: Flordia State University, Department of Adult Education, 1973.

Harman, D. Methodology for revolution. *Saturday Review,* June 19, 1971, pp. 54–55.

Hiemstra, P. *The older adult and learning.* Lincoln: University of Nebraska, 1975. (ERIC Document Reproduction Service No. CE 006 003)

Hixson, L. E. Non-threatening education for older adults. *Adult Leadership,* September 1969, pp. 84–85.

Hodgkinson, H. L. Evaluation to improve performance. In D. W. Vermilye (Ed.), *Learner-centered reform—Current issues in higher education.* San Francisco: Jossey-Bass, 1975, pp. 116–125.

Knowles, M. S. *The modern practice of adult education.* New York: Association Press, 1971.

Knowles, M. S. *The adult learner: A neglected species.* Houston: Gulf, 1973.

Knowles, M. S. *Self-directed learning: A guide for learners and teachers.* New York: Association Press, 1975.

Knudson, R. Review of pedagogy of the oppressed. *Library Journal,* 1971, *96,* 1261.

London, J. Reflections upon the relevance of Paulo Freire for American adult education. In S. M. Grabowski (Ed.), *Paulo Freire: A revolutionary dilemma for the adult educator.* Syracuse University, Publications in Continuing Education 1972. (ERIC Clearinghouse on Adult Education)

McClusky, H. Y. Education for aging: The scope of the field and perspectives for the future. In S. M. Grabowski & W. D. Mason (Eds.), *Learning for aging.* Washington, D.C.: Adult Education Association of the U.S.A., 1974, pp. 324–355.

Moody, H. R. Philosophical presuppositions of education for old age. *Educational Gerontology* 1976, *1*, 1–16.

Morrison, M. H. A human relations approach to problem solving. *The Gerontologist,* 1976, *16*(2), 185–186.

Musgrave, G. R. *Individualized instruction.* Boston: Allyn & Bacon, 1975.

Nolan, J. D. Are lectures necessary? *Science Education,* 1974, *4*, 253–256.

Peterson, D. A. The role of gerontology in adult education. In S. M. Grabowski & W. D. Mason (Eds.), *Learning for aging.* Washington, D.C.: Adult Education Association of the U.S.A., 1974, pp. 41–60.

Rogers, C. *Freedom to learn: A view of what education might become.* Columbus, Ohio: Merrill, 1969.

Rubin, L. J. Affective education: Fact and fancy. In H. Talmage (Ed.), *Systems of individualized education.* Berkeley. McCutchan, 1975.

Ruskin, R. S. *The personalized system of instruction: An educational alternative.* Washington, D.C.: American Association for Higher Education, 1974.

Skinner, B. F., *The Technology of Teaching,* New York: Appleton-Century-Crofts, 1968.

Thompson, R. Legitimate lecturing. *Improving college and university teaching,* 1974, *22*(3), 163–164.

Tough, A. *The adult's learning projects* (Research in Education Series, No. 1). Toronto: Ontario Institute for Studies in Education, 1971.

van Enckevort, G. *Andragology: A new science* (mimeo). Amersfoort, Nederlands: Nederlands Centrum Voor Volksontwikkeling, April 1971. Also published in: *Journal of Adult Education in Ireland.*

Weinstein, G., & Fantini, M. D. *Toward humanistic education: A curriculum of affect.* New York: Praeger, 1970.

Wolf, B., & Wolf, V. A look at preretirement planning in the laboratory method. *Adult Leadership,* February 1976. pp. 206–8, 213–14.

Wooley, J. Improving the lecture. *Improving College and University Teaching,* 1974, *22*(3), 183–185.

7

FEDERAL POLICY IN EDUCATION FOR OLDER ADULTS

E. PERCIL STANFORD
San Diego State University

ANTONIA DOLAR
North Day Care Senior Planning Council

No societal institution is more a part of our democratic system than education; yet the amount of criticism surrounding public education is growing. The major criticism is that the educational system is anachronistic due to its failure to keep pace with a rapidly changing society and an advancing technology. Educators and social scientists have identified sources of ferment that challenge all aspects of this society, from national policies to individual responses.

The past decade has been accompanied by an increasing awareness of the effects of advanced technology upon society. This single factor, interacting upon several others, creates a situation that requires immediate attention. Advanced technology results in increased leisure and simultaneously contributes to the complexity of society. This new constellation of forces requires innovative institutional and political responses. Education is closely related to each of these factors. It is required to maintain or expand technology; it is required to function within a complex society; and it is desired by those with increased leisure. The concept of continuous, or lifelong, learning is receiving widespread endorsement as one solution to the problems facing society.

As the demands made upon the educational system to solve the dilemmas of a complex society increase, policies that regulate the educational system must be altered to accommodate the new developments. In the past, demands have been placed upon the educational system by the poor, ethnic groups, the handicapped, and the unemployed. Federal and state policies have broadened to encompass those demands. Presently, another group is placing demands upon the educational system—the elderly. Federal response to this group's demands is still evolving.

As demographers project increased numbers of older adults in this nation during the next decade, an interest has arisen in developing or expanding programs and services that will be required by this population. Stimulated by the White House Conferences on Aging (1961, 1971) and by the enactment of the Older Americans Act (Administration on Aging, 1974), a variety of disciplines have focused on the contributions of their particular fields to the older adult. Thus, professionals in the field of adult education (acknowledged since 1926, with the creation of the American Association of Adult Education, see Morris, 1971, p. 49) are expanding their concerns to include the specific needs of the older adult population. The value of education for this target population is categorized succinctly by McClusky (Grabowski & Mason, 1974) according to the various needs it fulfills:

1. Coping Needs. To acquire skills such as reading, writing, and computation that are required for functioning in society
2. Expressive Needs. To engage in activities that are enjoyable and meaningful
3. Contributive Needs. To engage in activities that are beneficial to others
4. Influence Needs. To engage in activities that result in maintaining control over one's environment
5. Transcendence Needs. To engage in activities that result in continued self-development

It is apparent from a review of these needs that education for the older adult does not fulfill one need that it ostensibly fills for the younger adult population: the need for employment or a career. In fact, of the 15 million adults enrolled in adult education programs nationwide, 56.1% indicated that their motivation was vocationally based (National Center for Education Statistics, 1969, p. 23). Although the number of older adults engaged in educational programs is only 400,000 (or 2% of the total), 76% state that their participation stems from a general desire to learn (Harris & Associates, 1975, pp. 106–109), compared with 14.2% for the younger adult population (National Center for Education Statistics, 1969, p. 23).

Education for the older adult is not the same as education for the adult population in general inasmuch as learning is motivated by different forces for the two groups. It is acknowledged that the older adult population does not currently have ample opportunity to pursue vocational goals and that, were this fact altered, the motivation for education of the older adult population might alter as well. It, is, however, precisely *because* education for older adults is not vocationally or economically rewarding that federal legislation has been negligible in this regard.

The recommendations of the education section of the 1971 White House Conference on Aging state that "Education is a basic right of all age groups. It is continuous and henceforth is one of the ways of enabling older people to achieve a full meaningful life. It is also a means for helping them develop their potential as a resource for the betterment of society." Still, despite this statement and the eloquent arguments of educators who are proponents of lifelong learning, the federal government has not espoused the concept of education as a means of attaining personal well-being or meaning. A historical review of federal legislation in education for the older adult must begin with legislation enacted for higher education and adults in general, because legislation in education for older adults is a relatively new development.

HISTORY OF FEDERAL LEGISLATION IN ADULT EDUCATION

Office of Education

The current placement of the Office of Education within the Department of Health, Education, and Welfare (HEW) took place in 1953 concurrent with the establishment of that department. Initially, the Office of Education was housed in the Department of the Interior (1869). It was transferred to the Federal Security Agency, the precursor of HEW, in 1939 (Superintendent of Documents, 1975). In 1972, the Education Amendments expanded the Office of Education by creating both the Education Division and the National Institute of Education, with responsibility, respectively, for coordination and supervision and for leadership and research. Figure 1, a diagram of the current structure of the Office of Education, indicates that the location of the adult education programs (which include programs for the older adult) are attached to divisions of occupation or work, a significant factor in understanding the development of federal policies in education for the older adult.

Legislation for Adult Education

Historically, federal legislation concerned itself initially with support for the physical needs of schools and universities and expanded to include assistance for students, support for teachers, and finally to provide support to institutions of higher education and to develop state programs. Until this decade, educational programs established by the federal government have emphasized the acquisition of practical skills and knowledge that were consistent with national labor-force needs or otherwise in support of national priorities (increased food production, defense, technology, etc.). An exception has been federal legislation for education for the handicapped.

The first legislative programs for higher education was established in 1862. The Morrill Act provided for the release of federal lands to the states

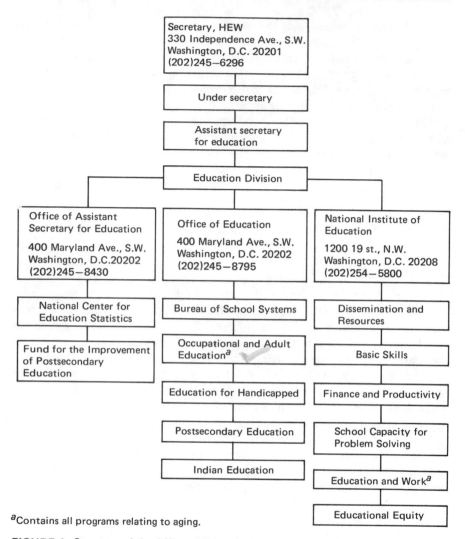

ᵃContains all programs relating to aging.

FIGURE 1 Structure of the Office of Education.

for the establishment of agricultural and mechanical schools. Land grant colleges, as they are still known today, illustrate an early commitment to provide practical education that would benefit the nation directly; in this case with expanded knowledge in agricultural methods or mechanical expertise that would result in increased food production (Superintendent of Documents, 1974, p. 436). In 1914, the Cooperative Extension was created by another legislative action directed toward "acquainting families with information, services, and skills helpful in the creation of a sound and stable life" (Superintendent of Documents, 1974, p. 443). The U.S. Department of Agriculture, authorized by the Smith-Lever Act, administers this program which emphasizes practical knowledge provided to rural communities through a unique system using county agents. The Smith-Hughes Act of 1917 was the original Vocational Education Act; it provided for the promotion of vocational education in agriculture, the trades, and the industries. The provisions of this act included training for teachers within the various vocational fields (Superintendent of Documents, 1974, p. 517). Legislation from the period of 1917 to 1950 focused on education for specific target groups, such as the physically handicapped and the veterans. Adult education as a general target of federal legislation was nonexistent.

The next developmental phase of education for adults included federal support for teachers, which insured that national goals would be attained by creating an entire cadre of professionals skilled in the sciences, technology, and research. The National Science Foundation Act of 1950 provides for the "progress of science, advancement of national health, prosperity and welfare, and the securement of national defense" (Superintendent of Documents, 1974, p. 682). The realization of these goals is the responsibility of the National Science Foundation through its activity of funding research programs and providing scholarships and fellowships to professionals for their advancement.

The National Defense Education Act, enacted in 1958, illustrates again the concern of the federal government with personnel development and the expansion of disciplines that would foster the nation's goals at that time. This act provides for the strengthening of the national defense and for encouragement and assistance "in the expansion and improvement of educational programs to meet critical national needs; and for other purposes" (Superintendent of Documents, 1974, pp. 546–547), which include teacher fellowships and training programs. The National Defense Education Act was the first piece of legislation that provided direct aid to students. This new venture on the part of Congress was accompanied by incertitude and led to the inclusion of the following statement in that legislation: "The Congress reaffirms the principle and declares that the States and local communities have and must retain control over and primary responsibility for public education. The national interest requires, however, that the Federal government give assistance to education for programs which are important to our defense (Superintendent of Documents, 1974, p. 547). This piece of legislation was the precursor of other federal actions that establish national priorities for education.

RECENT FEDERAL LEGISLATION IN EDUCATION

There are two major legislative acts that have had direct bearing on educational programs for adults: the Adult Basic Education Act of 1964 and the Higher Education Act of 1965. These pieces of educational legislation were enacted at a time when a panoply of programs was being created to address national priorities focused on illiteracy, poverty, and unemployment. During this time, educational programs and educational institutions were funded to redress those ills by providing education, conducting research, engaging in training of professionals and paraprofessionals, and creating community schools for the involvement of all possible segments of society.

Education for the older adult was first isolated as a priority as a result of the 1973 Amendments to the Older Americans Act, but the two programs authorized for this target population (Section 310 of the Adult Basic Education Act and Title I of the Higher Education Act) have not been funded to date. There has been no federal legislation for education for the older adult exclusive of the Older Americans Act. Therefore, educators and gerontologists desiring to establish educational programs for the older adult must seek federal funds that are aimed at either: (1) the adult or the higher education population in general, or (2) a specific population of which some elderly are a part, e.g., the handicapped, the institutionalized, veterans.

The Adult Basic Education Act

Not until 1964, in the Economic Opportunity Act, Title II, Part B (the Adult Basic Education Act), did federal legislation specifically mention adult education as an independent entity. The Adult Basic Education Act provided funds to assist adults (then defined as those 18 years of age and over, now as those 16 and over) in overcoming language difficulties and developing reading, writing, and computational skills. Although the act was administered by the Office of Education, it was not until 1966 that fiscal control was transferred from the Office of Economic Opportunity into the Office of Education, thus placing the entire program within that agency. This act, amended in 1966, 1968, 1970, 1972, and 1974, provides the only comprehensive legislation to date on education for the adult. Briefly, the development of the act is as follows:

1966
1. Authorized grants to states for the expansion of educational programs in preparation for occupational training and for more profitable employment so that people might become more productive and responsible citizens
2. Appropriated funds for experimental demonstration and research projects
3. Established the National Advisory Committee on Adult Education that advised, coordinated, and eliminated duplication of programs and reviewed effectiveness of current programs

1968
Revised state allotments and included nonprofit agencies as eligible for adult education grants

1970
1. Revised state allotments

2. Specified that special emphasis must be made within state plans for adult basic education programs
3. Renamed the National Advisory Committee the National Advisory Council on Adult Education (NACAE) and enlarged the membership to 15

1972
Added a new section entitled Improvement of Educational Opportunities for the Adult Indians

1974
1. Defined and introduced community school programs
2. Amended state plans to include: coordination and cooperation with labor-force and occupational education programs; provision for bilingual education programs; inclusion of institutionalized people within adult education programs
3. Established a 15% limit on demonstration projects and teacher training programs at the state level
4. Established the Clearinghouse on Adult Education
5. Established state advisory councils to assist in planning and evaluating adult education programs
6. Authorized special projects for the non-English-speaking elderly to provide them with the necessary language skills to function in society[1] (Congressional Research Service, 1975, pp. 1–30)

The title of the legislation is misleading, as the term *adult* is applied to anyone 16 years of age or over. According to the National Advisory Council on Adult Education, there are currently $54\frac{1}{3}$ million adults in need of adult basic education, but the total older adult population over 65 in this country comprises less than *half* of the target population established by NACAE. Furthermore, only 13.8 million older adults are estimated as requiring the basic type of education provided by this legislation (Administration on Aging, 1974).

Although the Adult Basic Education Act focuses on all adults, it is narrow in that its primary goal is provision of rudimentary skills that result in employment. Only 16% of the elderly are currently in the labor force and they comprise 3.4% of the entire United States labor force. It is fair to assume that those older workers currently employed already have the basic functional educational skills provided by the act, inasmuch as national statistics indicate a larger proportion of high school graduates remain in the labor force relative to non-high school graduates (National Advisory Council on Adult Education, 1974a, p. 5).

The Higher Education Act

The Higher Education Act of 1965 provided funds to institutions for a variety of programs ranging from direct student aid to construction of academic facilities. This legislation contains 12 titles and has been admended in 1966,

---

[1] This has not been funded.

1967, 1968, 1972, and 1974. A summary of the provisions contained within the titles is as follows:

Title I: Community Service and Continuing Education Programs
1. Based on the Cooperative Extension Act; intended to provide grants to institutions to test and demonstrate solutions to urban and community problems (1965)
2. Established the National Advisory Council on Extension and Continuing Education (1965)
3. Authorized national and regional demonstration projects, stemming from technological, sociological, or environmental problems (1972)
4. Authorized special programs and projects relating to problems of the elderly (result of the 1973 amendments to the Older Americans Act; has not been funded)

Title II: College Library Assistance and Library Training Research
1. Authorized funds to institutions to expand library resources and engage in cooperative library programs with other institutions (1965)
2. Authorized training programs for library personnel and also research and demonstration projects (1965)
3. Authorized funds for Library of Congress to acquire resources (1965)

Title III: Strengthening Developing Institutions
1. Authorized funds for assistance to accredited institutions of higher education to strengthen academic quality through:
   a. Faculty and student exchange
   b. Faculty and administrative development programs
   c. Introduction of new curricula
   d. Cooperative education programs
   e. Joint use of facilities (1972)
2. Established the Advisory Council on Developing Institutions (1972)

Title IV: Student Assistance
1. Established a variety of grant programs for students enrolled in higher education, including: Basic Educational Opportunity Grants, Supplemental Education Opportunity Grants, Grants to States for Student Incentives, Special Programs for Disadvantaged Students, Grants to Institutions, Grants to Veterans, and cost-of-education payments
2. Provided for federal, state, and private low-interest, insured, student loans; established terms, definitions, and regulations for federally insured loans (1965)
3. Work Study Programs provided legislation aimed at low-income students (1965)
4. Cooperative Education Program, authorized funds to institutions to plan,

develop, and implement programs that combined employment and academic instruction (1968)
5. Direct Loans to Students (1972)

Title V: Educational Professions Development
1. Authorized funds to improve the quality of teaching, assess personnel needs in education, recruit promising educators, and devise stimulating personnel training programs for educators (1967)
2. Established the National Advisory Council on Education Professions Development (1967)
3. Established the Teacher Corps Program (1967)
4. Provided grants to states for recruitment of educational personnel (1967)
5. Provided fellowships for educators and related personnel (1967)
6. Improving training of personnel in programs other than higher education (1967)
7. Provided training of personnel in higher education (1967)
8. Provided training for vocational education personnel (1968)

Title VI: Financial Assistance for the Improvement of Undergraduate Instruction.
Authorized funds for developing and improving undergraduate degree programs (1965)

Title VII: Construction of Academic Facilities
Expended Funds for the Construction of academic facilities in specific areas (1972)

Title VIII: Networks of Knowledge
Authorized expenditures for educational institutions to develop cooperative agreements for the purpose of sharing facilities, technology, and other resources (1968)

Title IX: Financial Assistance for the Improvement of Graduate Instruction
Expended funds to develop professional and graduate degree programs (1972)

Title X: Community Colleges and Occupational Education
1. Authorized expenditures for the development of community colleges and the creation of state advisory councils on community colleges and occupational education; established the National Advisory Council on Vocational Education (1972)
2. Established the Bureau of Occupational and Adult Education in the Office of Education (1972)

Title XI: Law School Clinical Experience
Provided for student field-experience programs within law schools (1968)

Title XII: General Provisions of the Act

The 1972 Amendments of the Higher Education Act established the post-secondary education commissions and authorized expenditures for statewide planning for postsecondary education so that, "all persons within a State who desire, and who can benefit from, Postsecondary Education may have an opportunity to do so."

The Higher Education Act is much broader in its scope than the Adult Basic Education Act, affording a greater opportunity for programs directly or indirectly (as in training for instruction in gerontology) benefiting the elderly to be developed within one of the 12 titles. As with the Adult Basic Education Act, the one segment relating specifically to the older adults resulted from the Older Americans Act, and similarly, this section has not been funded. Unlike the Adult Basic Education Act, the Higher Education Act does not specify one target population for all programs emanating from it, thereby increasing the possibility for older adults to qualify under one of the many programs authorized by the legislation.

Despite the range of programs resulting from the Higher Education Act, there are few that aid older adults directly by enabling them to participate in educational programs. The majority of the programs can be used to train instructors in gerontology, acquire books about aging, or otherwise assist in expanding knowledge *about* aging. Legislation in education for older adults, as a defined target population, is still a woefully neglected area.

OLDER AMERICANS ACT

The Older Americans Act (OAA) is unique in that it transcends functional boundaries in addressing the needs of a single target population: the elderly (Hudson, 1973). Enacted in 1965, this legislation was to provide a comprehensive network of programs for its constituents via ten objectives and five titles. It was amended in 1967, 1969, 1972, 1973, 1974, and 1975. Education was implied in the original act in an objective that stated that the elderly should have, "pursuit of meaningful activity within the widest range of civic, cultural, and recreational opportunities" (Administration on Aging, 1974, p. 2).

It was not until 1973, however, that education was specifically mentioned for the older adult as an objective within the amendments: "Make available comprehensive programs which include a full range of health, education, and social services to our older citizens who need them" (Administration on Aging, 1974, p. 3). Again, in Section 302 of Title III, *continuing education* was defined as a valid social service within the Older Americans Act (Administration on Aging, 1974, p. 14). Title III, Section 308, Model Projects, emphasizes educational opportunities for the older adult as a priority.

The 1973 Amendments of the Older Americans Act, as stated earlier, amended two pieces of educational legislation (Title I of the Higher Education Act and Section 310 of the Adult Basic Education Act) among others. One other important addition to the Older Americans Act of 1973 was the inclusion of a new Section 203 under Title II, Federal Agency Cooperation. This section mandated cooperation and coordination with the Administration on Aging (AOA) on the part of any federal agency planning or implementing a program "substantially related to this Act" (Administration on Aging, 1974, p. 6). As explained by Hudson (1973), the Federal Agency Cooperation section was one of several attempts at consolidation of programs for client groups with similar needs. In this case, it was a sweeping consolidation and coordination of the needs of the older adult within any program established by the federal government pertaining to housing, health, transporation, nutrition, education, income, or any other goals established by the Older Americans Act.

This action simply reflected other developments of consolidation resulting in the general and special revenue-sharing acts legislated during the Nixon administration. In each case, functional programs were consolidated, eliminating specific target groups defined by federal legislation. This was a marked departure from previous federal legislation that defined both target populations and program objectives. To date, the Older Americans Act remains a unique blend of consolidation and coordination within all federal programs that include mandated priorities (*see* the 1975 Amendments to the OAA) for specific programs for older adults.

It is interesting to review the legislation passed subsequent to the Federal Agency Cooperation section of the 1973 Amendments to the Older Americans Act. The later special revenue-sharing legislation such as the Comprehensive Employment Training Act (CETA), the Urban Mass Transporation Act (UMTA), the Housing and Community and Development Act, the Health Services Act, and Title XX of the Social Security Act, *all* have specific references to the older adult. Before equating these legislative actions with increased benefits for the older adult, however, it is vital that two facts be established:

1. These special revenue-sharing programs do not constitute a new source of funds, but rather a regrouping of existing funds.
2. In none of the programs are specific funds allotted for the elderly. Generally, the older adults are one of several priority groups vying for the same funds. The main issue then becomes one of equitable distribution of funds among several priority groups.

Of the special revenue-sharing acts mentioned above, the potential increased benefits to the elderly are contained within:

UTMA. Requires that any *new* projects implemented with federal funds must be accessible to older adults and handicapped people

Title XX. Requires that of five priority programs, three must serve the elderly population; legislation does not specify an amount of funding for each program

Housing and Community Development Act (Title VII). Requires that in federally subsidized housing, 40% of the units are to be reserved for senior citizens

The legislation that has received the greatest amount of attention and study to date is the State and Local Fiscal Assistance Act of 1972 (general revenue sharing). This legislation lists eight priority categories of expenditure, one of which is social services for the poor and the elderly. All decisions for expenditure are made locally, thus enabling a community to determine its own priorities within the general guidelines established by the legislation.

Nationally, there has been .2% spent on the elderly from general revenue-sharing funds.[2] Of course, individual states and communities expend more than the national average. In California, a total of 1.3% of general revenue-sharing funds has been expended for the elderly (from 1972 to 1975), and a total of $5,874,329 has been expended from the general funds of cities and counties (Dolar & Male, 1975, p. 7). Despite this high percentage, California, with the largest number of elderly in the nation, does not spend an equitable amount of its funds for their welfare (Dolar & Male, 1975).

Given the disparate goals contained within the Older Americans Act, coupled with the fact that funds for the two categorical legislative acts in education have not been appropriated, federal policy regarding education for the older adult is clear: there is no comprehensive federal policy addressing the educational needs of the older adults. Educational programs for the elderly will have to be funded via the Older Americans Act or via that existing legislation in education which does not exclude the elderly as a target population.

Table 1 lists some federal programs that can be used to fund educational projects for the elderly or educational programs in gerontology. The National Advisory Council on Extension and Continuing Education (1973, pp. 93–98) isolated 203 distinct programs that provided continuing education (many were in-service training programs for staff of federal agencies); the National Advisory Council on Adult Education (1972), pp. 18–83) isolated 53 programs focusing on adult education and training. An attempt to determine the

[2] From a letter to Representative Claude Pepper of Florida from the General Accounting Office, April 25, 1974.

TABLE 1 Federal Programs Supporting Education for Older Adults

Program	Authorization Legislation	Provisions	Administrative Agency
	Vocational Education Act, 1968 Amendments; transferred funds of this act to the Vocational Education Amendments of 1968	Provides for the promotion of vocational education and cooperation with states to provide for vocational education and the preparation of teachers of vocational education—did not specify post-secondary age	Office of Education 400 Maryland Ave., S.W. Washington, D.C. 20202
	Title XX of the Social Security Act, 1935, amended 1974	Provides federal funds to operate and establish social service programs related to five goals: 1. Economic self-support 2. Achievement of self-sufficiency 3. prevention of neglect and abuse 4. Elimination of inappropriate institutional care 5. Provision of appropriate institutional care Three of the five services must be directed toward the elderly, although education is not mentioned specifically; it may be a component of the service delivery system	Administered locally

TABLE 1 Federal Programs Supporting Education for Older Adults (*Continued*)

Program	Authorization Legislation	Provisions	Administrative Agency
	State and Local Fiscal Assistance Act, 1972 (general revenue sharing)	Provides as one of its eight priority categories social services for the poor and the aged (to date .2% spent nationally on the aged)	Administered locally
	Higher Education Act, 1965, as amended by Older Americans Act, 1973 (education programs to resolve problems of the elderly in Title I)	Provides federal support to institutions of higher education to plan, develop, and implement programs that utilize resources of higher education to solve specific problems of the elderly (program never funded)	Office of Education
Adult Education: Appalachian Regional Development Program	Appalachian Regional Development Act, 1965, as amended	Supplements to federal adult education programs, administered through U.S. Office of Education	Appalachian Regional Commission 1666 Connecticut Ave., N.W. Washington, D.C. 20008
Library Grants for Adult Basic and Continuing Education	Appalachian Regional Development Act, 1965	Supplements to federal library grants provisions specifically for adult basic and continuing education	Appalachian Regional Commission

Program	Legislation	Description	Administered by
CETA—Incorporates Manpower Program, OEO	Economic Opportunity Act, 1964, as amended	Provides skill training for purpose of increasing employment	Administered locally
Cooperative Extension	Adult Basic Education Act, Smith-Lever Act, as amended	Provides out-of-school, applied education in agriculture and consumer education	Federal Extension Service U.S. Dept. Agriculture South Building 14 & Independence, S.W. Washington, D.C. 20250
Project Transition, Department of Defense		Provides counseling, training, and education to servicemen retiring or completing military duty	Directorate for Educational Programs and Management Training Department of Defense Pentagon
Educational Renewal	Adult Basic and Continuing Education Act, Title VII; Elementary and Second Education Act; Education Professions Development Act, Section 309; Adult Education Act, Section 222; Economic Opportunity Act; and Sections 402 and 412 of the General Broadcasting Provisions Act	Provides for National Priorities Adult Special Projects, Adult Education; Teacher Education, Adult Education; Adult and Continuing Education, Broadcast Facilities	Office of Education
Adult Education: Grants to States	Adult Education Act, Title III	Provides for basic education programs developed at state level for adults functioning at or below eighth-grade level	Division of Adult Education Bureau of Adult, Vocational and Technical Education Office of Education

TABLE 1 Federal Programs Supporting Education for Older Adults (*Continued*)

Program	Authorization Legislation	Provisions	Administrative Agency
Adult Education: Special Projects	Adult Education Act, Title III, Section 309	Provides for innovative programs for teacher training, adult basic education, and adminis- trative systems to boost state adult programs; target population: adults 16+ with less than twelfth-grade level education	Division of Adult Education Bureau of Adult, Vocational and Technical Education Office of Education
Adult Education: Teacher Education	Adult Education Act, Title II, Section 309, as amended	Provides training for personnel involved or preparing to work in adult education; trainees targeted are low-income residents and Vietnam vets	Division of Adult Education Bureau of Adult, Vocational and Technical Education Office of Education
Dissemination of Educational Information: Educational Renewal Policy Research Centers and National Institute of Education	General Education Provisions Act, Sections 402 and 412, as amended	Provides information to state and local educators on technical literature and innovative programs and pro- vides a rational planning base	National Institute of Education 1200 19 St., N.W. Washington, DC 20208
Adult and Continuing Education: Public Library Services	Library Service and Construction Act, as amended	Provides grants to states for development, extension, and promotion of public library services and services to special institutionalized target populations and the physically handicapped	Division of Library Programs Office of Education,

Library Resources	Adult Basic Education Act, Section 909, as amended	Provides support for community learning-center demonstrations targeted for low-income and ethnic populations	Division of Library Programs Office of Education
Adult and Continuing Education: Library Resources Broadcast Facilities and Educational Technology Demonstrations	Section 402 and 412 of the General Education Provisions Act	Provides grants for establishment, expansion, and improvement of broadcasting facilities for educational TV and demonstrations utilizing technology to deliver educational services	Division of Library Programs Office of Education
Vocational Education: Basic Grants to States for Adult Education	Vocational Education Amendments of 1968, Title I, Part E	Provides grants to states to conduct vocational education programs; includes construction ancillary services, and demonstration and experimental program funding	Division of Adult Education Bureau of Adult, Vocational and Technical Education Office of Education
Vocational Education: Adult Consumer and Homemaking	Vocational Education Amendments of 1968, Title I; Office of Education and Related Agencies Appropriations Act, 1972	Provides funds to states to conduct training programs in homemaking skills; targeted for economically depressed areas	Division of Adult Education Bureau of Adult, Vocational and Technical Education Office of Education
Vocational Education: Adult Students with Special Needs	Vocational Education Amendments of 1968, Title I; Office of Education and Related Agencies Appropriations Act, 1972	Provides funds to states to develop special programs for disadvantaged	Division of Adult Education Bureau of Adult, Vocational and Technical Education Office of Education

TABLE 1 Federal Programs Supporting Education for Older Adults (*Continued*)

Program	Authorization Legislation	Provisions	Administrative Agency
Adult Basic and Extension	Migration and Refugee Assistance Act, 1962; Older Americans Act as amended; Vocational Rehabilitation Act	Provides: 1. Rehabilitation training: Community college institutional support, adult basic and extension 2. Rehabilitation training: Community college student support 3. Community service training: short-term institutional support 4. Aging training: Institutional support 5. Rehabilitation training: Voluntary organizational and student institutional support 6. Rehabilitation training: Hospitals, institutional, and student support	Division of Training Social and Rehabilitation Services Administration 330 C St., S.W. Washington, D.C. 20201
ACTION, including SCORE, RSVP, Foster Grandparents, Vista	Domestic Volunteer Services Act of 1973	Provides federal funds for programs utilizing older people; minimal training or educational component	ACTION 806 Connecticut Ave., N.W. Washington, D.C. 20525

Program	Authorizing Legislation	Description	Contact
Indian Adult Education and Community Development	Snyder Act, as amended	Provides adult basic education	Adult Education/Community Development Staff Bureau of Indian Affairs Washington, D.C. 20240
Indian Adult Vocational Training	Indian Adult Vocational Training Act	Provides vocational and skills training for adult Indians 18+ years	Adult Education/Community Development Staff Bureau of Indian Affairs
Indian Agricultural Extension	Indian Adult Vocational Training Act	Provides federal funds to state universities' extension programs to improve family and living conditions for Indians	Adult Education/Community Development Staff Bureau of Indian Affairs
Indian on Job Training	Snyder Act, as amended; Indian Adult Vocational Training Act, as amended	Provides federal funds for creation of jobs and incomes for Indians	Division of Industrial and Tourism Development Bureau of Indian Affairs
Inmate Education, Federal Prison System	Department of Justice Appropriation Act, 1972	Provides elementary and secondary education programs to inmates	Bureau of Prisons U.S. Dept. of Justice Washington, D.C. 20202
Operation Mainstream	EOC Opportunities Act, 1964	Provides funds for poor adults in rural areas; includes basic educational training	Office of Program Management Manpower Development U.S. Dept. of Labor Washington, D.C. 20212
Veterans Assistance Centers	Veterans Educational and Training Amendment Act, 1970	Provides funds to provide one-stop service, counseling, and training of recently discharged veterans; targeted for educationally deprived or environmentally deprived servicemen	Veterans Administration Vermont & H, N.W. Washington, D.C. 20402

TABLE 1 Federal Programs Supporting Education for Older Adults (*Continued*)

Program	Authorization Legislation	Provisions	Administrative Agency
	Older Americans Act, Title III	Provides funds for model projects administered and demonstrated via state offices on aging and the AOA	Administration on Aging 400 Donohoe Building Washington, D.C. 20201
	Older Americans Act, Title IV	Provides training funds for short- and long-term training to establish programs in gerontology	Administration on Aging
	Older Americans Act, Title VII	Provides nutrition-program supportive services including education	Administration on Aging
Veterans Wives, Widows, and Adult Dependents (18+)	Veterans Educational and Training Amendment Act, Armed Forces Education Act	Provides funds for the specified target group for the purpose of continuing their education	Veterans Administration
Vocational Rehabilitation for Veterans	Veterans Educational and Training Amendment Act, 1970	Provides funds for education, training, and rehabilitation of veterans and servicemen with a service-connected disability	Veterans Administration

Adult education programs offered in a variety of departments:
OEO, Agriculture, Defense, HEW/Social and Rehabilitation Services, Housing and Urban Development, Interior, Justice, Labor, ACTION, Veterans Administration

degree of funds made available for the elderly through a sampling of these general programs was made. Table 2 indicates the extent of successful acquisition of educational funds for the older adult. The majority of funds available for educational programs for the older adult and in gerontology stems from the Older Americans Act, not from other general education legislation.

What ramifications does this fact have in the interpretation of federal policy regarding education for older adults? There are several premises that must be clearly established before addressing this question.

TABLE 2 Number of Education Projects for Older Adults Actually Funded under Federal Programs

Program titles	Total number of educational projects specifically for older adults
1. Fund for the Improvement of Postsecondary Education, 1973–1976	8[b]
2. Community Service and Continuing Education, 1974–1975 (Special Projects)	4[c]
3. National Institute of Education	0
4. Special Services for Disadvantaged Students in Institutional and Higher Education	0
5. Curriculum Development, Division of Vocational Education Research	0
6. Training, Education for the Handicapped	0
7. State Agency Cooperation (Special Projects)[a]	0
8. Educational Personnel Development[a]	0
9. Older Americans Act, Title II, Model Projects, 1974–1975	18

Note. The figures included on this chart were gathered from an informal telephone survey. In several instances, comprehensive data was not available and the number of programs were estimates. It is clear, however, from this sketchy survey that AOA expends the majority of federal funds for education of older adults. Yet, data from Community Service and Continuing Education indicate that developments among the states in this area are expanding.

[a]These programs are being eliminated or combined in other legislation.

[b]Includes projects carried over beyond one year.

[c]Represents national projects; there were a substantial number of programs funded by individual states: 1974–59 projects in 33 states, 1975–77 projects in 35 states.

1. There is no federal policy on education for older adults exclusive of the Older Americans Act.
2. There is no explicit federal policy on adult education except for an operational one.
3. There is an increasing tendency toward federal consolidation of functional programs across population groups (e.g., general and special revenue sharing) resulting in the establishment of local priorities for utilization of funds.
4. The elderly do not receive an equitable share of funds in programs for which they are not a priority group.
5. Historically, federal legislation in education has focused on education resulting in occupational advancement.

CONCLUSION

The existing federal policy regarding education for older adults is the result of a nonpolicy in comprehensive education for the nation. Were there a commitment to the value of education for purposes other than employment, there would be no difficulty in funding educational programs for the elderly. Altering the conventions of a nation is no easy task; yet data presented here indicate that the elderly, through the Older Americans Act, have affected both state and federal policy, albeit faintly, to the extent that the elderly are mentioned within legislation.

Educators seeking to remedy the existing situations have two alternatives for action, advocating special educational programs for the older adult or advocating comprehensive educational programs to broaden the current federal emphasis on education for occupation. Positive and negative aspects are inherent in each approach. Still, to be effective, strategies must be based in reality. The historical and current events described here indicate that the federal government is committed to consolidation of programs within functions, not for target populations, and that the federal policy is to place the burden of selecting priority groups to receive services upon the states and localities.

It would seem that an effort that combined strengthening state support for education for older adults with that of garnering existing federal funds for educational programs for the elderly would be the wisest at this time. The ideal situation for the nation—the expansion of education to include general self-development and well-being for all age groups throughout their lives—should not be forgotten. In fact, older adults could, were their efforts successful, provide the impetus for altering the current, narrow concept of education, thus rendering a service to all age groups. Their efforts and those of their advocates in the past have demonstrated that federal policy can be affected.

REFERENCES

Academy for Educational Development. *Never too old to learn.* New York: Author, 1974.

Administration on Aging. *Older Americans Act Of 1965 and other related acts.* Washington, D.C.: U.S. Government Printing Office, 1974.

Adult Education Division. *Adventure in human development: Fact sheet.* Washington, D.C.: U.S. Government Printing Office, 1976.

Carnegie Corporation. *Diversity by design: The Committee on Non-traditional Study.* San Francisco: Jossey-Bass, 1973.

Congressional Research Service. *Adult Education Act: Legislative history— 1964-1974.* Washington, D.C.: Author, 1975.

Congressional Research Service. *Federal programs and benefits assisting the elderly.* Washington, D.C.: Author, 1975.

Dolar, A., & Male, M. *Utilization of revenue sharing funds for the elderly in California.* Sacramento: California Commission on the Aging, 1975.

Estes, C. L., Shaw, M., & Stunkel, E. *Developments and trends in aging.* Sacramento: California Commission on the Aging, no date.

Grabowski, S., & Mason, W. D. (Eds.). *Learning for aging.* Washington, D.C.: Adult Education Association of the U.S.A., 1974; Syracuse: ERIC Clearinghouse on Adult Education.

Harris, L., & Associates. *The myths and realities of aging in America.* Washington, D.C.: National Council on the Aging, 1975.

Hudson, R. B. *History of the older Americans Act.* Paper presented at the annual meeting of the American Political Science Association, 1973.

Morris, R. (Ed.). *Encyclopedia of social work*, (Vol. I). New York: National Association of Social Workers, 1971.

National Advisory Council on Adult Education. *Annual report.* Washington, D.C.: Author, 1972, 1973, 1974a, 1975a.

National Advisory Council on Adult Education. *A target population in adult education.* Washington, D.C.: Author, 1974b.

National Advisory Council on Adult Education. *1975 recommendations.* Washington, D.C.: Author, 1975b.

National Advisory Council on Extension and Continuing Education. *Annual report.* Washington, D.C.: Author, 1973.

National Center for Education Statistics. *Participation in adult education: Final Report.* Washington, D.C.: U.S. Government Printing Office, 1969.

National Commission on the Financing of Postsecondary Education. *Financing postsecondary education in the United States.* Washington, D.C.: U.S. Government Printing Office, December, 1973.

Superintendent of Documents, U.S. Government Printing Office. *A compilation of federal education laws.* Washington, D.C.: Author, 1974.

Superintendent of Documents, U.S. Government Printing Office. *U.S. Government manual, 1975-76.* Washington, D.C.: Author, 1975.

Walmsley, G. M. *Education and training in aging.* Salt Lake City: Rocky Mountain Gerontology Center, 1975.

8

EVALUATION OF EDUCATIONAL PROGRAMS IN SOCIAL GERONTOLOGY

THOMAS A. RICH

University of South Florida

Several recent reviews of evaluation in education point to both the need for and the problems of application of current methodologies (Phi Delta Kappa National Study Committee on Evaluation, 1971; Perloff, Perloff, & Sussna, 1976). In Perloff et al. (1976), some of the anxieties and resistances to evaluation as well as some of the technical problems are discussed. They point out that

> *Since program evaluation is still clearly in its infancy as a field of study and is yet to achieve the cohesion and the tautness expected in the multidiscipline field let alone a unitary discipline, it would be presumptuous, prodigal and even disruptive to wrap up the field in a neat package, pontificating upon its past and prescribing its future. (p. 587)*

Pfeiffer (1972) also pointed out that it is well known that it is difficult to evaluate training programs in medical schools, nursing schools, or other types of institutions; but he indicates a need for evaluation to be made. In other references, the lack of funding for evaluation is also cited as a frequent problem. In the literature examined, evaluations of educational programs, such as educational gerontology, are more noted for discussions of the difficulties involved than of workable methods.

In this chapter, I undertake a discussion of goals and objectives, as these are the primary basis for setting up an evaluation schema. Who sets these goals and what the priorities become is a topic of concern. Research necessary for understanding the background of existing programs, consumer needs, and projections of needs is an integral part of goal and objective setting. Descriptions of target populations, specific objectives for measurement, implementation steps, methods of measurement, methods of feedback to existing and new programs, and evaluation of the product of the programs are also a part of the present concern. My recommendations are very basic, but they represent a beginning.

GROWTH PROBLEMS:
ACADEMIC AND FEDERAL ISSUES

Examination and development of evaluative procedures in gerontological education and training programs go beyond academic exercises in accountability and have serious implications for the survival of the field. With some important exceptions, as noted in Kushner and Bunch (1967), today's education and training programs are the offspring of the Older Americans Act of 1965, which created the Administration on Aging. To a lesser extent, the National Institute of Child Health and Human Development has also influenced program development. The national recognition of the increasing magnitude of the problems of older people, both in numbers and in substantive issues to be dealt with, helped bring about this mid-1960s birth of academic programs. Their future growth and development face many uncertainties and the infant mortality rate may be high.

Several factors contribute to the problems of survival of educational programs throughout the country. Many of today's new programs born in the 1960s and early 1970s benefited from the educational boom in which many people felt, despite reports to the contrary (Mayhew, 1970), that higher education could expand indefinitely. Increasing faculty size, turning out more Ph.D.s, and continuing growth were seen as inevitable. Labor-force reports such as those by the Carnegie Commission and by professional societies all seemed to be ignored until we turned the corner on 1970 and, indeed, even until a little later when the country began to experience the combined effects of recession and inflation. Educational institutions suddenly moved into a period of retrenchment. This change is generally observable across the country; all programs are being systematically examined by a variety of means of evaluation and measures of accountability to determine which ones should be provided where, or whether they should be provided at all. In the last five years of growth, with expansion in areas of service delivery, research, and teaching, programs have been sharply curtailed by economic realities.

In view of this upward surge in the 1960s and retrenchment in the 1970s, the role of the federal government is interesting and complex in that its capacity or desire for leadership in the field of gerontology seems to have diminished. The early promise was for continuing funding and for the development of an academic discipline that was new and that offered something to a neglected segment of our population. That promise now seems to have become diffused by lower federal priorities that have resulted in a retreat into the issuing of uncertain guidelines and into decreasing allocations for training, research, and demonstration throughout the states. Although the

National Institute of Aging (NIA) may rectify this situation through increased research funds, present federal policies, though not clear enough to be criticized adequately, appear to lead gerontology futher into uncertainty by continuing to give priority to seeding new programs all over the country at undergraduate and graduate levels and in a variety of training settings. At a time when there is such fierce competition for dollars from established disciplines within universities and colleges, th:s dilution of programs can only lead to further confusion and disorganization in the field. In sum, it appears that federal policy is based on seeding new programs, which, in effect, create an ever-widening pool of underfunded programs. New programs cannot properly be staffed in many settings, and short-term training, although useful for professionals who have some related background, will never supplant the need for more fully trained workers in all areas of gerontology.

I have set out to provide the rationale for evaluation in the policy area in gerontology. It is true that we have sufficient professional and disciplinary demands for evaluation for quality education and perhaps this should be enough. For a fledging discipline, however, fathered by serious advocates of the field of gerontology (Tibbitts and others) and now caught in its middle childhood between the whimsical parenting of uncertain leadership in Washington and the stern disciplinarian of academic retrenchment, we are potentially in crisis. The strength in the field of gerontology is presently in the disciplines associated with it. The methodology of those disciplines and the gerontological content are sufficient, if marshaled together, for a careful development of the field, keeping national educational priorities (not synonymous with federal priorities) in mind. Funding priorities indirectly set the program objectives that are necessary for evaluation.

In this chapter, I make recommendations that will allow those who agree to build upon them and those who disagree to provide better alternatives. The issues must be faced and the answers that are arrived at by concerned persons in the field will ultimately be useful to all. In my review of the potential for evaluation that now exists, the following areas are discussed:

Background issues related to evaluation processes
The development of a national consultative body
Utilization of a case history approach
A measurable objectives approach
Job analysis and worker development studies
Follow-up evaluation of graduates
Consumer studies: quality of service and satisfaction

Considering the age of the field, it is certainly premature to attempt to impose stringent accountability requirements on the variety of new programs inasmuch as they are usually still developing their objectives or goals, staffing, population to be reached, or functions of the students. We do need, however, to provide specific and formal guidelines useful to academic administrators in budget-minded university and college settings throughout the country in developing new programs. Evaluation should provide a basis for decision making, for program monitoring through feedback, and finally, for assessing the impact of training on the consumer.

BACKGROUND ISSUES
IN GERONTOLOGY

Despite the problems, in many ways the growth of education in gerontology has been phenomenal in recent years. Several landmark publications document this growth and the issues of concern to the field. A brief backward look at where the field has been may help illuminate the issues of today. In 1967, a committee of the section on psychological and social sciences of the Gerontological Society published their report, *Graduate Education in Aging within the Social Sciences*. Its issues are still with us, paraphrased from Kushner and Webber (1967) as follows:

1. Gerontological training as single discipline, multidiscipline, or both
2. Workforce needs present and projected to solve problems of the aged
3. Issues on breadth or specialization of training
4. An emphasis on incorporating social gerontology as an area of specialization within the established social science disciplines
5. Consideration of training in social gerontology as an independent discipline
6. Specialized training for professional services
7. Kinds of research facilities
8. A review of current status of education in social gerontology, with models examined

In each issue, questions yet to be answered are raised: How to train whom for what about what in which setting to serve whom?

The next major review of the state of the art in education and training was the 1971 White House Conference on Aging statement *Training— Background and Issues,* by Birren, Gribbin, and Woodruff (1971). They noted that, while compared to the 1960s, growth has been rapid, "from evidence presented in this report that in relation to surveyed and demonstrated need, the amount of training and education activities in the field is astonishingly low" (p. 1). Thus we see an apparent, rapid growth in training far outdistanced by current and projected increases in the proportion of older people in our society.

The issues emerging from this background paper (Birren, Gribbin, & Woodruff, 1971) were:

1. *Given, that manpower development in aging is lagging seriously behind the proven need, should responsibility for the development of a more vigorous national plan and continuing surveillance of training be lodged in a single Federal agency created for the purpose? Or, should funds be made available to several Federal agencies for the support of manpower training in accordance with their individual perceptions of needs, as at present?*

2. *Should policy formation and planning for manpower training in aging be the sole responsibility of government agencies having statutory responsibility for programs and services for older people? Or should these functions be shared with nongovernmental groups such as scientific and professional organization and organizations of older and retired persons?*

3. *Should the major focus and priority be placed on doctoral-level training for teaching and research? Or, should equal or greater priority be placed on short- and long-term training of professional and semiprofessional personnel for planning and delivery of services to the older population?*

4. *Should there be developed regional university-based multidisciplinary training centers in gerontology? Or, should research and training be fostered in a wide range of colleges and universities in individual departments or multidisciplinary programs in gerontology?*

5. *Is the need for personnel especially trained for serving the older population and for teaching and research critical enough to call for continued or increased Federal and State government financial support? Or, should educational institutions at all levels build training for work in aging into their programs and look to their established sources (State appropriations, tutition, gifts, and foundations) for support?*

6. *In allocating funds for support and recruitment of personnel to be trained in aging, should priority be given to young persons yet to make a career commitment? Or, should the major focus be on providing knowledge and skills in aging to persons who have had work experience in other areas or who may have retired? (pp. 73–78)*

Many of these issues are similar to the ones cited earlier. The major new ingredient is the concern about locus of responsibility for planning and development, government or nongovernment support, and sources of support.

By 1974, the White House conference issues remained unresolved and the new ones had risen. The 1974 *Gerontologist* devoted part of one issue to "The Real World and the Ivory Tower: Dialectics of Professional Training, Education, and Delivery of Services to Elderly Persons." Beattie (1974) introduced a set of propositions with implications for evaluation. The propositions are offered as suggestive for those who wish to develop programs in gerontology. They are:

1. *That the development of gerontological programs for research, education and training, and practice must be carried out within the context of the changes occurring within higher education itself and the societal forces which impinge on higher education.*

2. *That the status of gerontology in higher education is similar to the status of older persons in the society—low in visibility, low in prestige, and low in recognition and rewards.*

3. *That gerontology is related, with varying degrees of identity and intensity, to all disciplines—scientific and humanistic—and professions.*

4. *That a conceptual-philosophical framework is essential for determining administrative and curricula goals and strategies and for the clarification of research, teaching, and service responsibilities and priorities.*

5. *That administrative strategies and understandings in regard to a multidisciplinary setting for interdisciplinary linkages and disciplinary depth are essential if we are to move beyond isolated unidimensional course offerings to substantial commitments of resources—faculty, facilities, and fiscal—for the development of gerontological programs relevant to academic and societal needs.*

6. *That one or two faculty committed and working in the area of gerontology does not constitute a gerontological program. Rather, the goal should be to work toward a critical mass of faculty within and among academic units.*

7. *That there is need for all students, regardless of career goal— research, education and training, or service (and these goals are not dichotomous)—to have, in addition to the class-laboratory cognitive learning of the campus, affective learning with older persons in a variety of community settings. The goal is for students to know, relate to, and learn from and with the "well" aged, as well as the "impaired" aged.*

8. *That the elderly have important contributions to make on the campus and in the classroom and should: (1) be envisioned as colleagues and contributors; (2) have access to the resources of higher education—students, faculty, administration, and facilities—to meet their own needs and identities in pursuit of lifetime learning, new careers, and in the formulation of life goals; and, (3) contribute to academic programs as mentors, tutors, and educators in their own right.*

9. *That students of all ages have a participatory role and contributions to make to the design of their learning and the institutional curricula arrangements vis-a-vis gerontology.*

10. *That academic institutions offering work in gerontology must be willing to invest and give of themselves in affecting the well-being and lives of older persons in the larger society.*[1]

From three perspectives, Kushner and Bunch (1967), Birren, Gribbin, and Woodruff (1971), Beattie (1974), I have drawn issues that share great commonalities and suggest questions for evaluation. Where possible, the common issues are dealt with in the body of this chapter in the context of suggestions for approaches to evaluation. A common theme of several basic unanswered questions is found in all three documents reviewed; it has been put in the form of questions common to the documents and combined and summarized as follows.

Who Should Do the Planning and Set Priorities for Program Development in Gerontology?

A critical mass of personnel and resources in gerontology exists in higher education and should be mobilized to do definitive planning and set priorities for the field. An input system from active programs should be developed so that the widest possible range of information is available for decision making and disseminating such decisions. Moreover, the decision-making power of active programs should be greatly enlarged. It was appalling to me as a professional gerontologist to sit at a recent meeting of the Association for Gerontology in Higher Education and speculate with a group of other training-program directors concerning the potential directions in which a federal agency might point us in the coming year. At the same time, a meeting was going on to tell us in the business of education, training, and research in the social and behavioral sciences, which directions and priorities would be set by another agency. The fact that higher education gave up its initiative for the sake of money some years ago does not mean that we could not become leaders rather than followers in the search for new ideas and new programs.

If a unit in a higher education system asked whether it should have a program in gerontology, we should be available to help answer that question. Not all would ask and not all would care to hear the answer, but the fact that professional guidance and counsel is available would be appreciated by many. This would contrast sharply with the present approach, which is largely that of meeting the guidlines for a new contract from the Administration on Aging, guidelines set by unknown faces and reviewed by the same unknown faces.

What Are the Workforce Needs and Who Determines Them?

Some years ago the regional Office on Aging in Atlanta conducted a workforce study and found that there was indeed a need for knowledge and training in the field of aging (Smyth & Cole, 1963). We must keep in mind, however, that if such a study had been done ten years ago and had asked how many people were seeking a master's in gerontology, we would never have started any programming because the answer would have been zero. We are in a position of creating a workforce need, to provide services that have never been provided, from an educated base that has never existed. There are enough graduates from a variety of training programs in gerontology presently working in the field so that more sophisticated job analysis and workforce studies could be conducted today. We need better job analysis of the kinds of functions being served by the graduates of our programs and appropriate change in programming where necessary.

Barriers to employment still exist in the field of gerontology, and many major agencies such as the Veterans Administration do not recognize a master's degree in gerontology. Many state merit systems or civil service systems have not incorporated training and education in gerontology into jobs that are related to the field of aging, although some accept them in lieu of, perhaps, a master of social work. These barriers need to be an active target in every state and in the federal government. The Administration on Aging, the very agency that has funded most of the training, has never made any real effort, to my knowledge, to require that their programs be operated by people trained in the field of aging.

What Kinds of Academic Structures Should Be Supported?

A quick tally of my own information and a look at the Association for Gerontology in Higher Education (AGHE) *National Directory of Education Programs in Gerontology* reveal something over 35 different names under which gerontology programs are being offered. This diversity probably leads to considerable confusion among students who wish to get training in gerontology and encounter everything from an elderly services program to an all-university gerontology center to an institute to a human life center.

The continuous review and updating of the status of available programs throughout the nation would be most useful as a planning device. At present, based on the AGHE catalog, the structure appears to be something like the following:

1. Single-course offerings, either in gerontology or within disciplines that assist students with the following goals:
   a. Understanding the life cycle
   b. Changing attitudes concerning aging

    c. Acquiring elective credit in general education
    d. Developing career interest

2. Core concentration of courses, wherein several courses relating to gerontology are found grouped together, usually called "gerontology," that assist
students with the following goals:
    a. Understanding the life cycle
    b. Changing attitudes
    c. Acquiring elective credits or fulfilling minors
    d. Developing career interests and getting work-related training, such as an
        associate of arts program for nurses' aids, community aids, or recrea-
        tion workers

3. Bachelor of arts in gerontology; assists students with the same goals as
listed above and, in addition, with:
    a. Providing a career entry level for jobs
    b. Serving as a ladder for further graduate study

4. Master of arts in gerontology or in other disciplines such as sociology,
psychology, economics, or political science with provision for doctoral level
study

5. M.A. in gerontology—considered a terminal service degree

6. Ph.D. in a discipline, with gerontology or developmental specialty

7. Other college or community programs that are primarily service

As the field matures a more functional classification system will emerge. The
listing provided, however, is illustrative of the present state of development.

    At this point, the word *center* seems to be the key, and almost every
college has its own center of gerontology. The centers range from well-
developed and structured programs to one person who has named herself or
himself a center. They range from centers resembling the partial vacuum
found in the center of a tornado; to centers that gather together all
age-related activities on a campus, list them in a brochure, and call the result a
center; to those performing multidisciplinary and multifaceted roles both
within the university community and the community at large. There are
enough different kinds of institutional structures existing now so that we
could make some professional comparisons of their strengths and weaknesses
in terms of general program objectives.

Where Should the Emphasis
Be Placed in the Career Ladder?

    All of the steps on the academic career ladder, from the associate of arts
to the bachelor of arts to the masters of arts to the Ph.D, and also
intermediate steps with certificates and specialty degrees, are developing. The
issue is whether or how we encourage and assist, and in what ways, the
development of this career ladder. Many students begin with an associate of

arts degree, are trained as nursing aides, home health care technicians, mental health service technicians, or a whole range of other titles, and may or may not work actively in the field. What will their next step be, to the bachelor of arts or to a master's or PhD? Some programs clearly should be assisted in helping develop training programs appropriate for serving their own areas or regions. Others may have the resources and ability to train workers who might be useful or employable anywhere in the nation and at a different career-ladder level.

What Are the Relative Merits of Short-term and Long-term Training?

Research on the impact on knowledge, attitude, and practice of short-term and long-term training would greatly assist in providing data to answer the question. Meanwhile we probably will continue to train and educate on the basis of individual biases. To some, short-term training is a way of widening the pool of undertrained workers, and to others, long-term training is a way of making junior academicians who do not understand practice in the field. Neither view needs to be correct. We can clearly question, however, whether the limited federal dollars should be split down the middle for short-term and long-term training. The priority may actually be misplaced because long-term training is needed to produce people with bachelors' and masters' degrees in gerontology to staff programs in agencies for the aging. Given a base or background in gerontology to start with, short-term training in agency management, budgeting, grant preparation, public relations, and many of the other tasks that are necessary in the field becomes meaningful. On the other hand, using short-term training (and it's usually very short and on someone else's terms) to effectively bring about knowledge, attitude, and practice changes in someone who is not trained at all in the field is probably a waste of time and money, although it looks good on paper.

What Should Be the Relative Contributions of Teaching, Research, and Service from Academic Settings?

We often separate these three categories for the sake of faculty evaluation and sometimes for the sake of requesting outside funds to help operate a program. In fact, as most people in the academic world know, they are mutually complementary and virtually inseparable. Universities differ greatly in their capacity to do basic research and often, because of their location, to do service. Guidelines and advice from other institutions involved in the multifaceted roles could be helpful in getting institutions to set priorities. The choices are sometimes simple yet difficult in that the question may be Should I spend the time to teach one more course in introductory gerontology, or take the same time to develop an evaluation plan for a community aging program, or make some other direct service contribution?

What are the Advantages and Disadvantages of the Trend of Role Reversal Whereby the Federal Establishment Asks the Questions and Universities Scramble to Find Answers?

My phrasing of the question reveals my bias. Meeting short deadlines for short-range answers drains creative thought about the real issues in aging. Some of the government's contracts, model projects, and request for proposals may result in better utilization of current knowledge, but the new knowledge gap widens.

RECOMMENDATIONS

Develop a National, Consultative Body

If this is to be accomplished, some changes in the current approach to programming must take place in gerontology. First, a separation of academic status from Washington is necessary. Budgeting, priority setting, research direction, and planning have been done without adequate representation of the concerned publics—us. How is this to be accomplished? The most obvious vehicle is the Association for Gerontology in Higher Education in association with the Gerontological Society and other groups such as the First National Congress on Education in Gerontology; together, they might carry out the development and implementation of an adequate evaluation model.

If this proposal were accepted and the Association for Gerontology in Higher Education or some other body of scholars developed an interest in carrying out these objectives, what would they do in relation to program planning and evaluation in gerontology? I would suggest the following:

1. Establish a planning committee to project population change and its implications for workforce needs and social policy over the next 20 years, on a national, regional, and local basis.
2. Provide consultation, at cost only, to the wide range of institutions contemplating gerontology programs to help them analyze resources within area needs, national needs, staffing needs, and development of clear program goals. This would be consultative and not restrictive.
3. Provide consultation to existing programs on the direction for future growth and development.
4. Develop a curriculum-exchange center so that the best possible teaching materials would be available.

5. Establish relationships with foundations and other private sources of funds.
6. Provide input to AOA; NIA; National Institute of Mental Health; and regional, state, and area offices on aging.

Use a Case History Approach

In addition to developing a consultative body to provide the myriad kinds of inputs that would be helpful to a program, it could be of great value to develop case histories of existing programs sampled from the various types found around the country. A format should be developed that would include kind of sanction provided for a program at what levels in the university and system, kind of administrative structure, nature and sources of funding, and a year-by-year accounting of progress. Although such a case history would follow a general outline, it would also allow for the idiosyncratic differences that exist in programs to be shared and so provide many answers to problems presented daily by people attempting to begin programs.

The issues go further than those listed above in that the relationship of the university structure with the outside community should be explored. The use, composition, and function of advisory or policy-making bodies is of continuing interest in this area. Case histories could be useful here, too.

The determination and development of new curricula based on program goals and objectives and how they are accomplished need to be shared. Many of the inquiries received concerning program development say simply, "We are starting a new program in gerontology and need materials. Can you help us?" From a collection of perhaps 20 case histories, many of the kinds of questions and answers posed by people considering starting programs could be answered, many of the pitfalls could be avoided, and a sharing could take place that would be healthy and useful for a young discipline trying to set its own directions and goals.

Take a Measurable Objectives Approach

All programs should, with some guidance, be able to set measurable objectives in concrete terms. These can range from reaching certain kinds of students to offering certain numbers of courses to certain numbers of graduates in long-term training programs. At the same time, short-term training programs would offer more immediate feedback both on change in direct, day-to-day working skills and in evaluations of further need for training.

A number of models for program evaluation exist, although few have worked effectively in the field of education. In the area of nonformal education, which has received considerable interest in the last few years, the knowledge, attitude, practice, and effectiveness (KAPE) model seems to be one worthy of discussion in the total process of evaluation of educational programs in social gerontology. By utilizing this model, a simple, skeleton outline can be developed so that first levels of knowledge and expected change based on the kind of input being provided are identified. Next, levels of attitude and expected change based on the kind of input being provided are identified. Then, an attempt is made to identify behavior changes, again based on the kind of knowledge and attitude data provided. Last, effectiveness measures are provided to demonstrate whether the practices that are observed are truly more effective and more useful than those seen before.

Provide Funds for Job Analysis

To determine the nature and quality of training in aging that is required to fill jobs in public and private agencies, and then to convert these findings into programmatic changes, job analysis is needed. Planning should be based on projections of changes in workforce needs for the aging population over the next 20 years and should not rely only on current problems. The need for continual planning for dealing with today's problems and for projecting needs for future service-delivery systems is critical.

Systematically Follow Up Graduates

Students who have graduated from an associate of arts, bachelor's, or graduate program should be followed up nationally to find out if they are filling places in the job market as needed. Studies of their concerns and interests and the services they provide should be conducted. Such feedback would help develop a reliable bank of workforce information and, in addition, expand the boundaries of work inasmuch as many students show initiative and innovativeness in ways far beyond program aspirations and fit their training into new settings and new services. As long as we remember that the students are likely to know more than we have taught them and therefore to utilize this information in effective ways, we have a reliable source of new data. Yearly follow-up of graduates in gerontology at the University of South Florida, for example, reveals high employment in age-related positions as well as suggestions for program revision.

Plan Consumer-Service-and-Satisfaction Follow-ups

Working with agencies, again public and private, to determine levels of consumer service and satisfaction would be useful for providing feedback in a formal way. A study of graduates with training in aging, with level of training controlled, to determine how they are employed should be carried out in relation to quality of service.

Measuring consumer satisfaction from older clients would be a useful index of services provided. The only danger here is that all resources cannot be devoted to dealing with today's problems; many must instead be devoted to program-planning and prevention aspects so that better services will be developed for people not yet in the older age category. It might well be that proper reconsideration of priorities would place emphasis on prevention services to people in the middle years at least equal to the emphasis on services to people in the older years, where most resources have been concentrated.

SUMMARY

In this chapter, I have examined and reviewed some of the paper issues that have influenced the development of gerontology over the past decade. I have treated the growth of the field of gerontology from the perspective of social policy, from the views of members of the profession of gerontology, and by consideration of the special conditions placed on the field by its emergence at a time of national and academic retrenchment. The development and application of evaluation procedures in gerontological education and training is necessary for its continued growth and development. The rigor of the evaluation required reflects a time of accountability in our society. Other, more established disciplines are just now beginning to be questioned, and new ones must meet the standards of proof of need.

In setting educationally and socially appropriate goals for education in gerontology, we provide the basis for the measurement of effectiveness and in turn a justification for the existence of the field. In this world of finite resources, priorities will, I hope, be set based on the data that we provide and not on historical precedent or whims of the federal or educational bureaucracy.

Although the technology of evaluation may be viewed as both in its infancy and in a state of disorder, there are evaluation approaches that can be applied to many of the pressing problems concerning the field. In this chapter, I have suggested six different approaches; and they provide different ways of appraising programs, from the use of outside, consultative bodies to the development of meaningful measures of goals, objectives, and products of the program. None of the approaches requires great expenditures of dollars, and all could be applied immediately to most areas of programming in gerontology. Certainly, more clear-cut communication links between guideline makers, funding sources, program planners, and program operators could be established with minimum funding and modest goodwill. The very process of evaluation becomes less disorderly if it is applied to the stage appropriate to the field. We are still gathering data and need interchange of descriptive information about current programs.

In today's growth and confusion in the field, there is the real opportunity for advancement to a discipline of gerontology. All of the evaluation approaches discussed have considerable potential for adding information about where we are and should be going in the field. If we apply ourselves to the problem of evaluation of the developing gerontological programs of education, research, and service; we will have more knowledge about the impact of gerontological programs on this nation than that available to any other educational program.

REFERENCES

Association for Gerontology in Higher Education. *National directory of education programs in education.* Draft Edition, University of Wisconsin, Madison, 1976.

Baker, E. L., & Popham, W. J. *Expanding dimensions of instructional objectives.* Englewood Cliffs: Prentice-Hall, 1973.

Beattie, W. M., Jr. Gerontology curricula: Multidisciplinary frameworks, interdisciplinary structures, and disciplinary depth. *The Gerontologist,* 1974, *14,* 545–548.

Birren, J. E., Gribbin, K., & Woodruff, D. S. *Training–Background and issues.* Washington, D.C.: White House Conference on Aging, 1971.

Blummon, P. D. *Behavioral objectives: Teachers success through student performance.* Chicago: Science Research, 1971.

Elias, M. F. Symposium—The real world and the ivory tower: Dialectics of professional training, education and delivery of services to older persons. *The Gerontologist,* 1974, *14,* 525–553.

Kushner, R. E., & Bunch, M. (Eds.). *Graduate education in aging within the social sciences.* Ann Arbor: University of Michigan, 1967.

Kushner, R. E. and Webber, I. L. Summary. In R. E. Kushner and M. Bunch (Eds.) *Graduate education in aging within the social sciences.* Ann Arbor: University of Michigan, 1967, pp. 110–112.

Mayhew, L. B. *Graduate and professional education, 1980.* New York: McGraw-Hill, 1970.

Perloff, R., Perloff, E., & Sussna, E. Program evaluation. In M. Rosenzweig & L. Porter (Eds.), *Annual Review of Psychology,* 1976, *27,* 569–590.

Pfeiffer, E. Translating aging research into training: Getting the job done systematically. *Training needs for services to the elderly.* Atlanta: Southern Regional Education Board, 1972, pp. 1–18.

Phi Delta Kappa National Study Committee on Evaluation. *Educational evaluation/decision making.* Itasca, Ill.: F. E. Peacock, 1971.

Popham, W. J., & Baker, E. L. *Planning an instructional sequence.* Englewood Cliffs: Prentice-Hall, 1970.

Smyth, V. M., & Cole, W. E. A regional assessment of personnel and training needs. In J. C. Dixon (Ed.), *Continuing education in the late years.* Gainesville, Fla.: University of Florida Press, 1963.

Yeager, J. L., & Robertson, E. A. Academic planning in higher education. *Management Forum,* 1974, *3*(7), 1–4.

9

CAREER EDUCATION FOR THE PREPARATION OF PRACTITIONERS IN GERONTOLOGY, WITH SPECIAL REFERENCE TO ADULT EDUCATORS

MARGARET E. HARTFORD

University of Southern California

The inclusion of content on aging in the curricula of career education in the human services becomes increasingly imperative, if we accept the premise, based on a demographic prediction of population trends, that practically all workers being educated today for the human services will spend some part of their careers in practice with or in behalf of older adults. An increasing proportion of workers will specialize in the field of aging, in developing or working in new service areas directly related to older adults. Career education in this chapter refers to the preparation of nurses, adult educators, primary and secondary teachers, medical doctors, dentists, public administrators, librarians, social workers, lawyers, occupational therapists, recreation workers, clergy, planners and architects, public health administrators, business administrators, and others who work directly for or in behalf of the human services.

Consideration is given in this chapter to some of the rationale, educational design, and curricular aspects of content on aging for all students in the human services and for those students specializing in services particular to the field of aging. Note is taken of career education at the community college level, the baccalaureate level, and the master's level of professional education. The students in professional education today show no age boundaries. They may be young adults in the late teens or 20s, in their initial educational preparation; second-career people in their 30s to their 50s; and third-career or retired people from their mid-50s to their 70s, preparing for professional work with their peers. It is not the intent in this chapter to neglect doctoral studies, in which much of the basic research on gerontology takes place, but rather to focus more sharply on professional education, which in most of the human services is centered at the undergraduate and first-graduate levels.

With the decreasing birth rate, lower mortality rates, and newer methods of prolonging human vigor and productivity both through disease control and through greater understanding of the circulatory, respiratory, digestive and endocrine systems, a new, more vigorous, and potentially more involved older population is emerging. It is a population that may spend almost as long out of the work force in retirement as it spent working, if present employment practices and attitudes continue. The implications for economics, social relationships, life-styles, health services, housing, and for various other education, welfare, and health programs begin to open up new horizons.

Siegal and O'Leary (1973) predict that the population of the United States will become stationary very early in the twenty-first century. Once the population has stabilized, it will rapidly begin to get proportionately older, provided the birth rate stays the same and the mortality rate decreases. When the young students of today reach the prime of their careers in 15 or 20 years, it may be predicted that a vast proportion of their practice will be with or about older adults and their families, in social policy and planning, in individual care, education, support, and counseling. The aged will no longer be the exception or the recipients of marginal services but will become central to many services. It is imperative that such a predictable population shift and consequent need for services be anticipated today with a preventive, epidemiological approach. Planning, development, and program design should be undertaken now and in the immediate years ahead to establish the necessary approaches, programs, and services. Today's students should be as well prepared as possible with knowledge about aging, should develop skill in working with and in behalf of older adults, and should develop a philosophy and an attitudinal set that encourages enlightened engagement in appropriate practice. They must also develop skills in divergent thinking in order to find new solutions to both old and newly emergent problems.

The thesis put forth by the futurists, including Alvin Toffler in his book *The Eco-spasm Report* (1975), is that the society must seek new approaches to the social changes that are occurring: in occupations, where white-collar jobs have outnumbered blue-collar jobs; in family life-styles, in which old patterns no longer serve the needs of much of the population, particularly those of older adults; and in geographic and social changes and the mobility of a highly transient society in which people must make or break old relationships and build new ones with things, places, people, and organizations at an ever more rapid pace. Preparing students in the human services for work with and in behalf of older adults and for the creation of new programs and services as yet undreamed of is, without a doubt, part of the wave of the future. Not only do the demographic predictions for the years ahead suggest changes in types of services, but the social changes in the economy, in family life-styles, in employment patterns, in retirement and leisure patterns, in population transiency and mobility, and in the rapid obsolescence of things, customs, problem solutions, and relationships—all these social changes combine to shake the very core of our culture, our socialization process, and the ways we have learned to cope with life about us. Our generation is affected, as are those who came before and come after us. Although we hold onto the fundamentals of our foundations, our beliefs, our knowledge, and the science that has emerged from our cultural heritage; we may at the same time find ourselves at the epicenter of so much cultural and social shaking that, if we do not have the flexibility to bounce and rock with the tremors, we may crumble because of a rigid tenacity that does not permit response to change. For students to be not just prepared for the present, but to be responsive to, even be leaders of the future, career education must take into account the rapidly changing future and the population trends and accompanying social needs of a society that is growing older.

The demand for flexibility may lead us to look at newer modes of curriculum development, new styles of teaching, and new arrangements of available knowledge. The intent is that graduates who become professional workers in the human services will have in-depth mastery of the content of an array of social problems as well as the mastery of technical skills in several modes of intervention in individual and group approaches to education, therapy, and growth of individuals, families, and other small groups. Students should also learn some administration and management, some planning and program development, some coordination and collaboration of services, and some community organization and change. Graduates in the human services specializing in gerontology may need both administrative skills and the capacity to work directly with older adults.

It is evident that professional practitioners—especially educators, health practitioners, social workers, and others who are used to working directly with individuals and families—must learn to find the sources of support not only for funding but also for the organization of citizen support, for the formation of boards and councils, for the preparation of proposals for the development of programs and the location of funds, for determining the nature of policy issues, and for seeking out the laws and regulations supporting certain types of programs. This administrative knowledge and skill must accompany the capacity for program design, curriculum development, and teaching or practitioner skill.

Some educators in professions have been concerned that students in their brief, professional education programs might not be able to master all of these skills nor the necessary range of knowledge of the many kinds of social problems. True, in no field do students master a professional practice in an educational program; rather, they are exposed to options; and they are given an opportunity to try their skills; and they may develop a beginning competence in assessing situations, making judgments, and acting deliberately in a variety of modalities. Real mastery, however, comes with time. Students should be exposed to the potential for growth in many areas of approach. Mastery, in the futurists terms, may be a capacity for the flexibility needed to transfer knowledge and technical skill from one situation to another. Professional education sets the frame of reference, develops the attitudes, teaches the basic skills, provides, we hope, the base on which the graduates grow and develop their own styles and capacities. This is the framework within which the following educational designs in curriculum development and the models for preparing human-services practitioners to work with and in behalf of older adults have been developed.

THE CHANGING FUTURE

As we seek new ways to work with the issues in gerontology that are emerging in our society and as we find new ways to view life with a new focus, we will prepare students for these changes and for a flexibility in the face of future conditions. Toffler (1975) predicts, for instance, that full employment most probably will never mean the return to highly industrialized labor force; rather it will take place through an expanding development of new service jobs, especially those involved in providing more adequately for the elderly. New kinds of jobs in new types of programs will be emerging, as the nature of the social problems associated with an increased older population becomes clear. Thus we may find a larger and somewhat different group of students seeking professional or career education. They will not only need to be educated for providing the services now available, but they will also need to be stimulated to create new and imaginative approaches toward the newly emerging aging population, which has experienced a different history and has a different set of social and educational needs from the aging population that preceded it.

For example, in viewing the trend toward age segregation that has characterized retirement homes, public housing for seniors, and nursing homes for the elderly, Margaret Mead (*Los Angeles Times,* May 4, 1975) suggests that we need to find a way to have a mixed society in which grandparents live down the block—not in the house, but a short distance away—and therefore can provide a place for the teenager to run away to for 24 hours. Fifty years go, when there was less mobility and transience, and when fewer of our grandparents lived into their 80s, 90s, and 100s, some of us had the opportunity to live with or near our grandparents. Today, in most of the country, the grandparents are either back in the community from which the family moved, or in Florida or Arizona, or in a retirement community, senior apartment complex, or nursing home where they cannot have overnight guests. They may be on the other side of town, but they are probably on the other side of the country. If we could have mixed communities, as Mead suggests,

"Grandma could come over and house sit for the plumber for the several days it may take him to arrive." To carry the idea a little further, in the mixed society, the son or the daughter or the in-laws can take grandparents who can no longer drive shopping, to the doctor, to the bank, or to the club, without either generation having to give up their privacy or their independence.

How Human Services Education Must Adapt

From where we are today, however, such a society will necessitate a different approach to social problem analysis, program planning, and service delivery. It would also have to emerge from a different set of social values than are present today, either about aging or in the self-fulling prophecy that has captured the older adults themselves—the work ethic, role definition by productivity, the youth culture, the nuclear-family life-style, or the obsolescence of the old. Professional education in the human services will have to preface its skills training with some value modification in students to parallel that which must come in society. Social planners and social philosophers may need to work on encouraging and facilitating age-integrated communities and family life-styles as well as age-integrated classrooms and activities. We may, in fact, need busing of older adults to educational programs so that they may be integrated within the classes and programs.

Professional education for the human services, therefore, must have a heavy component on philosophy, values, and value changes related to aging and agism. Not only should there be curriculum content and educational experiences designed to affect the students' attitudes, but students also need to be prepared with the methodological approaches with which to change attitudes about age in individuals and in the society as a whole. They will need to be prepared to help older adults to avoid being caught up in the self-fulling prophecy that has caused some of them to believe in the stereotypes about aging and to thus behave in such a way as to further perpetuate these false ideas. Mixing age groups in the classroom is one helpful way to work on this matter.

Two examples of the programatic aspects that future adult educators must be able to consider are: (1) senior-adult educational programs in which social relationships, finding new peers, and gaining a sense of adequacy are *as* important as learning the subject matter, and (2) assistance and preparation for new careers after 60 and developing competency in them. Adult educators will also begin developing educational programs for residents of nursing homes whose bodies may be limited but whose minds can respond to education and learning; who may suffer physical limitations from strokes, Parkinson's, or other disabilities, but who also have the potential to keep learning and enjoying the life about them. Activity of this type has only begun in very limited amounts and holds a tremendous potential.

Shifting Composition
of Student Bodies

If we follow the predictions of the futurists and again look at population trends, we may see a shift in the composition of the student bodies of professional schools. People seeking career education, especially in work with and in behalf of older adults, may have somewhat different characteristics than in the past. Already we see signs of this shift in the young people who want to vocationalize their college education at the community college or baccalaureate level. They want a solid academic education, but they want occupational or job-related content and experience also. Some of these students are attracted to the field of practice with older adults because they have found a challenge in conditions they have observed in nursing homes or old, residential hotels in the central city, crowded with lonely and isolated old people; they have visited grandparents in segregated, retirement communities with plush surroundings and equipment and have seen the overeager participants frantically trying to find things to do to keep busy; or they have worked in senior centers where there is need for some organization and direction for self-developed activities. Young people with these experiences are seeking professional education to enhance their skill to work in these kinds of positions and to facilitate the development of social relationships in people who have lost mates, peers, occupations, or meaningful connections. Adult educational programs are a way for older people to achieve new social relationships and new roles as well as preventing their disengagement, isolation, and obsolescence in the rapidly changing society.

A second segment of students who indicate interest in the practice of social gerontology are middle-aged adults, in their 30s to their 50s seeking second careers. They are frequently people with some life experiences that equip them for service careers. They are seeking professional education at all three levels: community college, baccalaureate, and master's. Some of them are disenchanted with their business dealings. Others have become obsolete in aerospace, industry, automotive manufacturing, insurance, real estate, public education, or the military. Some are homemakers whose families are old enough to allow them to be away from home all day or who wish to define themselves with a service type of vocational activity. These second-career students see in the field of aging an opportunity for a new professional activity, and they know they are needed. Many of these people have also experienced the responsibility for an older relative, at home, in a nursing home, or in another part of the country, and are convinced that society has not come up with adequate services. They are seeking new education to prepare themselves for employment opportunities in the field of aging.

As educators, we are discovering that the motivation, interest, learning capacity, demands, and expectations of second-career students are somewhat different from those of young adults just preparing for their first work experience. Education designed for second-career students must make use of what they already know, must rearrange knowledge and values, must teach new skills, and may have a heavy component of attitude change. It must also take into account the threatening nature of midstream shifts and the consequent possibility of expressions of anxiety, but it will also be rewarded by the rapid acceleration toward learning once middle-aged students have pulled themselves together and found new direction.

The third category of students is older people themselves. Some who have been retired for several years wish to prepare themselves to work professionaly with their own peers, not only on a volunteer basis, but within the workforce, providing services for older adults, in health, welfare, education, or social services; in recreation, volunteerism, nutrition, nursing care, housing, or social relationships.

In light of the evidence regarding job placement and career opportunities for people in their later years, if we accept these students, we may also need to accept some responsibility for placing them or at least, once they have completed their work, for getting them in contact with potential employers. We need to be more innovative in developing career education opportunities to prepare older adults to become human-services workers—gerontologists themselves—who design programs, develop services, administer organizations, and teach courses for their peers, not only on a volunteer basis but on a regular, professional level.

There are many examples of older people who have gained or retained leadership in the arts, in professions, and in politics; we also see leadership emerging among the older adults in the field of aging. We need only look at the Senior Community Service Project program, administered by the Department of Labor via several of the organizations for older adults, including the American Association of Retired Persons/National Retired Teachers Association (AARP/NRTA) and the National Council on Aging (NCOA), in which retired professsionals are employed to design, develop, and expand a program to find employment opportunities for people over 55. Most of the administrative staff of this program were employed after retirement from full careers in other professions. Consider Ethel Percy Andrus who designed and launched the NRTA and later the AARP after she retired as a school principal. She founded an organization that pioneered in obtaining benefits for older adults in insurance, housing, travel, recreation, education, and legislation. Consider Maggie Kuhn who organized the Gray Panthers, a major advocacy organization, after her retirement from traditional human services; Ollie Randall of the NCOA who continues to fly about the country speaking brilliantly to conferences and conventions; or Arthur Flemming who continued as commissioner on aging in his later years. Look at the many highly paid executive consultants and workshop leaders in agencies for the aged who have retired from the YMCA, welfare councils, or community chests. Many people now retiring, early or later, have indicated an interest and have enrolled in formal educational preparation for turning to new careers in social gerontology, social services in aging, and adult education geared to older students.

Surely in education for the professions, where we understand engagement, mastery, independence, and the importance of a personal contribution to the welfare of others as a means of keeping involved; we should be the first to engage people in an educational process to work in their own behalf and that of their peers. We should lead the way in dropping age barriers to education, employment, and program development and in recognizing the contributions to their peers of people over 60. This may mean modification both in age criteria for admission to professional schools and in tuition requirements. It also means access to scholarships and student loans that now have age cutoff points. There is enough evidence now from research on brain cells, on memory, on continued learning capacity, and on motivation to counteract the old stereotypes about the ability of people to continue to learn throughout life, provided there is motivation and the opportunity to do so. Content and curriculum on aging is an ideal and natural spot in human-services education for those older adults who are interested, are motivated, and have the capacity to engage in the rigors of study. What we know about andragogy (the education of adults), which makes use of peer teaching of each other based on the knowledge acquired through life experience and previous study, is particularly applicable to second- and third-career students. Perhaps we need to develop a new class of education called *geragogy*, "education of and by the old." Geragogy, if such should exist, would consist of education that includes a high component of self-pacesetting, social interaction and relationships, activity to maximize involvement, use of the talents of each individual, and continuous learning.

Objectives

From the rationale for career education that includes gerontology and an exploration of the types of students and their motivation to enter careers in gerontology, the educational objectives begin to emerge:

1. To provide *all* students in education for the human services with some exposure to course content related to gerontology and some practical field experience in working with or in behalf of older adults
2. To provide *some* students with expertise, or a specialization, in working with and in behalf of older students
3. On the basis of the predictions of the future regarding the social, health, and educational needs of older adults, to include philosophical and attitudinal content regarding the meaning of aging and its implications for older adults in the society
4. To integrate content on the specific needs of older adults with content on children; adolescents; early adulthood; and special social

problem areas such as delinquency, drugs, education, housing, mental retardation, race and ethnicity, family relationships, alcoholism, mental health, health care, and recreation inasmuch as all of these areas touch upon one or another apsect of the problems of the older population

5. To establish a teaching style that leads students to a flexibility in their approach to practice that will make it possible for all practitioners to transfer knowledge and practice skills from one modality and content area to another and to provide a potential for more future practice with and in behalf of older adults

CURRICULUM DESIGN FOR THE FUTURE

In considering curricular design, each department, program, or school generates for itself the general component parts of knowledge, skill, and value that are peculiar to its context, region, or particular leadership and educational approach. There continues to be debate about:

Life span approaches to human behavior versus a systems approach
Developmental versus behaviorist theory of human functioning
Social problems versus intervention modality approaches to teaching practice or methods
Historical versus existential approaches to social policy
Theoretical versus experiential teaching of knowledge

It is more appropriate here to consider more specifically the content that students need to know and what they need to be able to do to work with older adults.

Content

Social Policy All human-services practitioners should know (1) the provisions of the Social Security Act and its amendments; (2) the Older Americans Act, the services provided through each of its titles, and the local services of any given geographical area that have been funded as a result of the act; and (3) the Medicare provisions and the procedures for taking advantage of them. Students should know how to go about discovering and locating all of the services for older adults that exist in any given community. They should be familiar with state licensing of nursing homes and other institutional facilities. They should know the educational provisions for older adults within their areas; for example, community colleges, boards of education, universities and colleges, community centers, and private clubs and forums. They should understand the working of probate court as it relates to the elderly. They need some grounding in legal procedures and the resources for legal protection of the elderly. They should know about the senior volunteer programs, the employment programs for senior adults, and the various adult educational programs geared to retired adults. They need to be aware of special consumer affairs and citizen protection programs that serve as resources for older people.

Specialists in gerontology may need a great deal more knowledge on public social policy and may want a good grasp of the history of services for the elderly and some grasp of the economic and demographic factors that affect them. Specialists also need to be able to analyze existing laws and regulations and to begin to develop some know-how about changing inadequate laws and regulations. Whether this content is taught in a general social policy course or in an age-specific course will depend on the context, the resources, and the total program.

Human Behavior and Social Environment Whereas knowledge of the biology and physiology of aging, the psychology of aging, and the sociology of aging are important theoretical bases, especially at the undergraduate level, even more important are the relationships between health and nutrition; e.g., the effect of diet on digestion, circulation, and respiration, and the relationship of all of these to mood, mental health, thinking, and problem-solving capacity. Knowledge of the relationship of exercise to depression, relaxation, sleep, nutrition, and the capacity for gratifying interpersonal relationships is important. All of these factors are also interrelated with isolation, alienation, social relationships, self-image, territoriality, and social functioning.

Curriculum content in aging should have meaning in the career education program at the applied level, as research findings are translated from understanding of concepts into program development, service design and delivery, legislative provisions, and economic support. The scientific knowledge is preliminary; the applied biopsychosocial sciences are at another level that would constitute the real heart of career education. Such teaching may require a new kind of teacher in career education who can develop the *theories of the middle range,* that is, applied theories for practice.

From the generalized knowledge about aging to be integrated with practice, there can be taken specific knowledge applicable to populations in double jeopardy; e.g., the aged poor, aged blacks, aged Chicanos, aged Asian people, who face double discrimination and double liability. The healthy elderly, who face certain role changes and economic, status, and place losses, comprise a different segment of society from the frail or ill elderly. Part of the educational aspect of the human-behavior and social-environment content should be an understanding of the various subsections of the aged population, by age, health, and sex differentials; by socioeconomic, racial and ethnic, generational, and regional differences; and by historical experiences.

Practice Skills Graduates who will work specifically in the field of aging will need to be taught a mixture of intervention modalities, or practice skills. Whereas they need to be able to use individual and group methods for working with older adults and their relatives, they also need skill in program planning, development, and administration. Experts in social gerontology will discover that the demands for new and innovative services to meet the emerging needs of older adults will require the most imaginative use of knowledge and skills for developing services and programs. Students, therefore, must have some theory and experience in practice that will provide them with alternative modes of problem solving to use once they have assessed the given conditions. In fact, social gerontologists should be able to engage many potential clients in their own assessment and design of programs and plans for themselves.

As practitioners who use the findings of social and biological research in designing programs and delivery services, they may realize, for instance, that many programs discriminate against racial and ethnic minorities. Consider the emerging facts that the average life expectancy for black men is 60 and for black women is 62; yet all blacks who are employed pay into a Social Security plan from which less than 50% of them will benefit (Jackson, 1974)). Consider the fact that, at any one moment, no more than approximately one million, or 5-10%, of the aged are in any kind of institutions for health care; yet the health-care service provisions of Medicare, for instance, are available only for hospital services or attendance of a doctor. Ethal Shanus (Shanus & Sussman, 1976) has estimated that about two million people over 70 are confined to their homes by health problems, but never have the services of a doctor, hence never benefiting from Medicare. Provisions for home health care, home medical attention, and home nursing care are lacking in many areas and not given programmatic support (Shanus & Sussman, 1976). These kinds of factors become policy issues of concern to human-services workers in their planning as well as in their work with older adults and their families. The students should be helped to recognize findings of research such as those that show effects on larger numbers of older adults; and they should learn how to find ways to translate the findings into services. Some political sophistication is also essential for workers as they recognize the need for new laws, bills, regulations, court orders, and licensing, and as they gain access to lawmakers. Human-service workers specializing in gerontology should gain credibility and influence through their practice in the real world of specific problems of older adults and their relatives and through the application of their analyses of social and biological research.

Thus all workers in gerontology need some knowledge of individual and group methods for working with individuals, families, and unrelated groups; and in program development, design, administration, planning, community development and organization, and social and environmental planning. Workers whose emphasis may be on individual work will nonetheless find that they need some social and community skills. Workers whose emphasis is on legislative action, community organization, or work with systems will also need some firsthand knowledge and skill in working with individual old people and their relatives. Thus, all workers' education should include knowledge and practice at the micro and macro levels of programs and service delivery.

Philosophy and Beliefs Human-services students must confront their own attitudes that are products of a culture that rewards youth and productive work. They may be *agist* without realizing it, so subtle is the tendency to patronize, sentimentalize, or reject old people. They must also acknowledge some responsibility for changing the attitudes of those about them, none the least of whom may be older adults themselves who have come to believe stereotypes about themselves as a self-fulfilling prophecy. They must come to terms with the meaning of life and of death and learn to help others with these values and realities. They must view the aged person as one with a life to live, with the capacity to function even with pervasive illness and disease, with a thrust toward physical and mental health despite some deterioration. When death is inevitable, they must be able to help the person and the family to face and handle their emotions, their beliefs, and the reality of death. They must deal with the tendency to sentimentalize and be overprotective of older adults; they must not encourage dependency where independence may be important; yet they must support dependency where it is indicated. These attitudes, this philosophy, and these capacities come, not just through books, lectures, and discussions, but also through interaction with people who are experiencing these crises. Thus a good emphasis on gerontology in career education means some direct contact with older people within the services that are being studied.

Research Workers in gerontology must be knowledgeable consumers of research. They need their own beginning mastery of research methodology and statistics, scientific method, problem analysis and research design, and the appropriate types of research methodology for the study of social problems and the evaluation of programs. Most particularly, they need enough knowledge to read and to make use of authoritative research in gerontology in order to translate the findings into programmatic development. They need to be able to see researchable questions and problems in their practice in order to suggest studies for the scientists, even if they are not in a position to do research themselves.

Levels

So how does all of this translate into curriculum at the various levels of education, and with various models of learning and teaching? Surely the students at all levels need the fundamental knowledge of the aging person and the interrelatedness of the bio–psycho–social developments and dysfunctions. In fact, a time may come soon when a course in gerontology, a multidisciplinary, multiprofessional approach to understanding the aging, may appear as an elective or a requirement in primary, secondary, and higher education programs for general public consumption; right along with basic English, languages, social studies or sociology, psychology, biology, chemistry, physics, and math. The content of this course will prove crucial to the understanding of life and living. At the community college level, this fundamental knowledge may be in the form of an overview with preparation to practice as an associate, as a paraprofessional aide, or as a health or social assistant. At the baccalaureate level, it may be descriptive and provide a sound academic knowledge as preparation either for further graduate study, or for entry jobs in practice of recreation, adult education, health care, technical assistance, or social services. For all students at the master's level, there should be (1) considerable searching out of primary data from research; (2) the integration of the data into some comprehensive view of aging and its effects on the people, and, in the process, (3) the acquisition of the ability to transfer knowledge from one situation to another. Those who would specialize in aging would go into greater depth with some of the major studies, their findings, and the implications for work with older adults and their families.

Summary

All students, from community college to master's level, should have basic knowledge of the Social Security Act and its amendments, the Medicare provisions, and the Older Americans Act. The specialists will need to know how to process applications for Social Security and Medicare, a special skill in itself. They will also need knowledge both of ways of acquiring funds for programs and of the existence of local programs developed from the Older Americans Act. The specialists will also need familiarity with state laws covering nursing homes, institutions, and health plans. The undergraduates need familiarty; the graduates need experience in conceptualizing such provisions into services and programs.

Some of the content on values, philosophy, and beliefs; on specific skills translated for work with older adults and their relatives; on knowledge of the basic legal provisions for older adults; and on biopsychosocial development should be in curricula for all human-services workers. Some examples of research related to aging should permeate all of professional education. The specialists in gerontology need additional, elective courses to go into depth in human behavior theory as it relates to aging, services for aging, working with older adults, and programs and social policy related to the elderly. The undergraduate programs should have basic knowledge and some practice with older adults. Master's-level students should have knowledge and research integrated with some practice with older adults and their families and some practice at the administrative and planning levels of practice in programs for older adults.

THE FUTURE BEGINS NOW

As we look to the future, then, we can anticipate that in the human services of health, welfare, and education, more attention will need to be paid to education for designing programs, establishing services, and working directly with older adults. The demographers and the futurists give us the message. If we look around us now, however, we will see that already there is a large population of unserved, or inadequately or inappropriately served, older men and women. Responsibility for the preparation for careers in the development of innovative and imaginative services rests to a large degree with the educators at both the undergraduate and graduate levels. Somehow we must spark our students to become excited about developing the new frontier of social gerontology.

REFERENCES

Eisele, F. (Ed.). Political consequences of aging. *The Annals,* September 1974.
Harris, L., & Associates. *The myth and reality of aging in America.* Washington, D.C.: National Council on the Aging, 1975.
Jackson, J. J. NCBA, black aged and politics. *The Annals,* September 1974, p. 415.
Shanus, E., & Sussman, M. B. *The elderly, the family and bureaucracy.* Durham: Duke University Press, 1976.
Siegal, J. & O'Leary, W. Some demographic aspects of aging in the United States. In *Current Population Reports* (Special Reports, Series P. 23, No. 43). Washington, D.C.: Government Printing Office, 1973, p. 6.
Toffler, A. *The eco-spasm report.* New York: Bantam, 1975.
Woodruff, D. S., & Birren, J. E. (Eds.). *Aging: Scientific perspectives and social issues.* New York: D. Van Nostrand, 1975.

10

AFFIRMATIVE ACTION AGAINST EMPLOYMENT AGE BIAS: A CHALLENGE FOR EDUCATORS

ELIZABETH L. MEIER
Portland State University

One of the great challenges facing the field of educational gerontology and society as a whole is the need to create the opportunity for everyone to have, not only a long life, but a socially useful and productive long life. Life expectancy in the United States has been extended, by a decade for men and more for women, but it cannot be said that the opportunity for full participation in our society has been similarly extended. This is particularly true for participation in economic activity. In many businesses and professions, emphasis on the youthful image and on youthful aggressiveness and stamina is paramount. It is even prevalent in the agencies that are providing services to the elderly, for few older workers are to be found on the staffs of federal, state, and area agencies concerned with aging programs. The indeed pervasive bias against older people in employment and some suggestions for overcoming that bias with educational programs are the substance of this chapter.

RETREAT FROM THE LABOR FORCE

Over the past several decades, the time span for economic productivity has steadily been shrinking. Not only has retirement at the age of 65 become increasingly institutionalized, but the numbers of people who retire before that age are growing, and more and more people retire not only from a given job, but from the work force. This trend becomes most apparent by an examination of labor-force participation rates published by the U.S. Department of Labor. These figures show that the proportion of men and women who are in the labor force, either working or looking for work, starts to decline after age 55 and drops precipitously after age 65. This is a relatively new phenomenon, particularly for men.

In 1947, about 10% of men age 55 to 64 were *not* in the labor force. By 1975, this percentage had more than doubled, to 24%. For men 65 or over, the increase in nonparticipation was even more dramatic. Almost half of the men in this group were in the labor force in 1947. By 1975, 22%, or only about a fifth, of those 65 or over either had jobs or were looking for jobs. Older women, who had been showing a countertrend of increased work participation, now appear to be experiencing a similar trend toward withdrawal. As can be seen in Table 1, between 1970 and 1975, rates decreased for those 55 to 64 from 43% to 41%; for those age 65 and over, from 10% to 8%. Nonwhite women had higher rates of participation than white women, both at the beginning of the period and at the end, but their rates in 1975 were closer to those of white women because of slightly larger decreases. Nonwhite males, on the other hand, had lower participation rates than white men in 1970, and this difference was more pronounced in 1975. Nonwhite males 60 to 64 had the sharpest drop of any cohort group over the period.

Discouragement

Some reasons for declining labor-force participation are not hard to find. They include poor health, the desire for leisure, and the increasing adequacy and availability of retirement income. There are also other job-related reasons that are often ignored that have accelerated the trend toward retirement at earlier ages. One of these factors is long periods of unemployment, for it is a documented fact that older workers undergo longer terms of unemployment than younger workers. During 1975, government figures show that the average length of unemployment for those age 35 to 54 was almost 16 weeks. For those 55 to 64, it increased to almost 18 weeks, and for workers 65 and older, the average duration was 24.5 weeks, or about six months. At the same time, the length of teenage unemployment was 9 weeks (U.S. Bureau of Labor Statistics, 1976, p. 144).

After a long and futile job search, older workers tend to withdraw from an active search for jobs because of discouragement about ever finding a job. A study of discouraged workers by age found that "older workers 55 and over have the largest proportion of persons discouraged for job market reasons of any age group. In addition, there is an indication that more older people are taking themselves out of the labor market completely for other than personal reasons." (Rosenblum, 1975, p. 22).

Employer Age Bias

Many older people become discouraged workers because of employer age bias, as was shown by a nationwide survey conducted recently by Louis Harris and Associates (1975) for the National Council on the Aging (NCOA). Representative members of the total public (age 18 and over) were asked if

TABLE 1 Labor-force Participation Rates

Sex, age, color	Annual averages (total labor force)					
	1970	1971	1972	1973	1974	1975
Males:						
55–64	83.0	82.2	80.5	78.3	77.4	75.8
55–59	89.5	88.8	87.4	86.2	85.7	84.4
60–64	75.0	74.1	72.5	69.1	67.9	65.7
65 and over	26.8	25.5	24.4	22.8	22.4	21.7
White:						
55–64	83.3	82.6	81.2	79.0	78.1	76.5
55–59	90.1	89.2	88.1	87.0	86.5	85.2
60–64	75.2	74.6	73.2	69.7	68.5	66.4
65 and over	26.7	25.6	24.4	22.8	22.5	21.8
All other races:						
55–64	79.2	77.8	73.6	70.7	70.2	68.7
55–59	83.5	84.8	80.8	78.3	77.4	76.9
60–64	73.6	68.9	65.5	62.3	62.4	59.3
65 and over	27.4	24.5	23.6	22.6	21.7	20.9
Females:						
55–64	43.0	42.9	42.1	41.1	40.7	41.0
55–59	49.0	48.5	48.2	47.4	47.4	47.9
60–64	36.1	36.4	35.4	34.2	33.4	33.3
65 and over	9.7	9.5	9.3	8.9	8.2	8.3
White:						
55–64	42.6	42.5	42.0	40.8	40.4	40.7
55–59	48.5	48.0	48.0	47.1	47.0	47.5
60–64	35.8	36.1	35.2	33.8	33.2	33.2
65 and over	9.5	9.3	9.0	8.7	8.0	8.0
All other races:						
55–64	47.1	47.1	43.9	44.7	43.5	43.8
55–59	53.4	53.1	49.9	50.3	51.3	52.1
60–64	39.0	39.3	37.2	38.3	35.2	34.6
65 and over	12.2	11.5	12.8	11.1	10.0	10.5

Note. From U.S. Bureau of Labor Statistics, *Employment and earnings,* January 1972, 1974, 1976 (Household data, annual averages).

they agreed that "most employers discriminate against older people and make it difficult for them to find jobs" (p. 8). Fourth-fifths of those surveyed either agreed strongly or agreed somewhat with that statement, and there was not much difference in this perception among young people, the middle-aged, and the elderly. The proportion that disagreed strongly with the statement ranged only from 2% to 4% among the various age groups. Furthermore, the survey also showed that 87% of the people who identified themselves as responsible for hiring and firing employees agreed that employers discriminate

(Meier, 1976) This is brutal confirmation of the perception by the total public of job discrimination against older people.

The attitude toward age in private industry was well stated by one of the participants in an NCOA seminar who was a former vice-president of industrial relations for Pan American Airways. As he pointed out:

> *No one ever said racial discrimination was a good idea. No one ever said religious discrimination was a good idea. But how many times have you seen a manager praised and promoted because he headed an organization that was filled with young tigers; old lions just don't seem to boost you up the corporate ladder.*
>
> *How many annual reports proudly state that the average age in the top management has come down from, say 58 to 46. I don't think I have ever seen an annual report that proudly proclaims a boost in the average age of management.*
>
> *What we are doing, and what we have done, is to create an environment where in fact young is better than old and represents an underlying corporate value (U.S. Congress, 1973, p. 5).*

Negative attitudes toward older people as employees are not limited to employers. One aerospace company with an average age of 54 was criticized by the U.S. Air Force at a congressional hearing with "How can you build the bomber we need with such an old age force?" (Boren, Terry & McCally, 1976, p. 95).

EMPLOYMENT SERVICES
FOR OLDER WORKERS

In the U.S. Department of Labor, there is an "older worker" category that is defined as those 45 or over. Older workers are regarded as a disadvantaged group in the employment market; yet older workers can also be regarded as a disadvantaged group in the employment and training programs operated by the Department of Labor in conjunction with state and local governments.

Comprehensive Employment
and Training Act

The Comprehensive Employment and Training Act (CETA) provides for grants to local and state prime sponsors and for services to the unemployed, the underemployed, and the economically disadvantaged. CETA grants under Title I provide an almost limitless variety of employment services, such as vocational training, counseling, and work experience programs. Approximately 1.5 million people were expected to receive employment services under Title I in fiscal 1976, but in the first half of the fiscal year, less than 2% of those served were 55 or over and less than 1% were 65 or over. A report from the Department of Labor for the first three quarters of fiscal 1976 states, "The typical enrollee was white, male, in prime working age of 22–44, a high school graduate and unemployed." Fiscal 1976 statistics also indicate that 30,000 jobs are being subsidized under Public Service Employment grants. Most of the participants are in the 22-to-44 age range with only 14% 45 or over (Federal Efforts, 1976, p. 91).

U.S. Employment Service

Each state operates an employment service, aided by federal funds, that provides placement and other job services. These agencies should ideally serve as centers of employment assistance for older people thrown out of jobs or wishing to reenter the work force. Yet, as with CETA, the figures show small proportions of services to older people.

In the past several years, the NCOA has made, through analysis of data from the Employment Security Automated Reporting System, two statistical studies of the services, such as job referrals and placements, given by the U.S. Employment Service to applicants. Both studies found that, with few exceptions, the proportion of an age group receiving a particular service declines as age increases. Thus, those applicants under the age of 22 received the largest proportion of services and those 65 or over the least. For example, in fiscal year 1974, only a fourth of employment-service applicants aged 55 to 64 received any services at all compared to more than a half of those under 22. Only 10% were placed in jobs compared to 25% of those under 22, as is shown in Table 2.

Senior Community
Service Project

The Senior Community Service Project (SCSP) provides low-income people 55 or over with work experience and training in subsidized, part-time, human-service jobs. It is authorized by Title IX of the Older Americans Act and is administered by the Department of Labor through five national contractors: the National Council on the Aging, the National Farmers Union, the National Council of Senior Citizens, the National Retired Teachers Asssociation/American Association of Retired Persons, and the U.S. Department of Agriculture Forest Service. Through the SCSP, eligible applicants are given experience and training in public service jobs that are usually unrelated to their previous experience, which ranges from professional to laborer. A majority are over age 65 and a majority are women.

Many of the enrollees are employed in jobs that involve services to older people, such as homemaker service, escort or visitor service, and information referral. Some are also employed in community health and nutrition services. All of them are performing useful work and are, at the same time, earning

TABLE 2 Employment Service Applicants and Those Receiving Services by Age, Fiscal Year 1974

Services	Total		Age—Percentage Distribution					
	Number	Per-cent	Under 22	22–39	40–44	45–54	55–64	65 and over
Total	17,723,647	100.0	31.2	46.5	5.7	9.6	5.4	1.6
Receiving services	7,651,555	43.2	51.5	43.1	37.0	33.5	25.2	21.2
Counseled	981,516	5.5	6.7	5.7	4.7	3.9	2.6	2.3
Tested	853,521	4.8	6.8	4.8	3.1	2.3	1.1	0.7
Enrolled in training	348,601	2.0	3.2	1.7	1.3	0.8	0.4	0.5
Job development contacts	937,411	5.3	5.0	5.9	5.3	4.7	3.7	2.9
Referred								
Non-agricultural	6,024,514	34.0	41.1	34.1	27.2	25.3	19.7	16.7
Agricultural	300,660	1.7	2.2	1.4	1.6	1.6	1.2	1.2
Placed	3,333,702	18.8	25.1	17.5	14.6	13.3	10.3	10.0

Note. From E. M. Heidbreder & M. D. Batten. *ESARS II, a comparative view of services to age groups as reported in the Employment Security Automated Reporting System.* Washington, D.C.: National Council on the Aging, 1974, p. 2.

money and learning new skills. They are also given the opportunity to participate in group training sessions and to receive individual counseling.

The Title IX program is the only employment program operated with government funds specifically for older people. In fiscal 1976, 12,400 part-time job positions were allocated under this program, a much smaller number than the 330,000 jobs under the CETA Public Service Employment referred to earlier. Also, although the SCSP programs are an admitted success and have far more applicants than job slots, funding is in question from one year to another, primarily because of the emphasis on decategorization of government employment and training programs.

AGE DISCRIMINATION
IN EMPLOYMENT ACT

Older people are increasingly being squeezed out of jobs and the job market. They are also underrepresented and underserviced in major, governmental, employment and training programs. In addition, the only federal law that is designed to fight age bias in employment, the Age Discrimination in Employment Act (ADEA), is underenforced and less than complete in its coverage. Congress enacted ADEA in 1967 after studies by the secretary of labor had proved extensive age bias in employment. ADEA sought to end age discrimination by employers in hiring, firing, and other terms and conditons of employment and by the employment agencies and labor unions who refer job seekers to employers. Help-wanted advertisements are not to use such terms as *boy, girl, young* or to designate a specific age group, such as 25 to 35.

The scope of the law is, however, incomplete, as it protects workers from age 40 only through age 64. Older workers 65 or over are not protected and attempts to extend the law to this age group have not as yet succeeded.[1] Smaller businesses are also not included in the law. Employers with less than 20 employees and the employment agencies and labor unions that refer workers to these employers are not covered.

A major omission from the enforcement of the law is the lack of affirmative action in employment. Unlike the requirements for such action on behalf of minorities and women, no positive action is required. Furthermore, enforcement by the Department of Labor has been slow and difficult, and the budget for such activities has been low. The staff time available to enforce the law across the nation approximates about 70 to 80 man- or woman-years. The Wage and Hour Division, which is assigned responsibility for enforcing ADEA, also administers the minimum-wage, equal-pay, overtime-pay, and child-labor provisions of the Fair Labor Standards Act (FLSA), among other things. The result is small priority given to the enforcement of ADEA by compliance officers.

Recent testimony given before the Pennsylvania Senate Committee on Aging and Youth illustrates the enforcement problem:

> *Lack of resources to adequately staff the administrative agencies is frustrating to both those whose responsibility it is to enforce the law and those who come forward seeking to redress violations of the law. Unable to put the proper energy and effort into resolving individual complaints, the agency representative feels that he or she is letting down the public. The public in turns views the agency as not living up to its charge and fosters a sense of futility about using the law to redress grievances. For instance, in over a dozen cases of age discrimination which we have filed with the Pennsylvania Human Relations Commission and the United States Department of Labor, our clients received a letter or call from agencies' representatives that they were unable to substantiate the charges in the complaints. The clients were never provided with any explanation of the agencies' findings and the clients were never offered the opportunity to refute contentions advanced by the employer or union. As a result, our clients are more frustrated after having filed a complaint than if they never came forward in the first place. The complainant feels that unless he or she presents the agencies with a signed confession from the employer or union, all is wasted. (Ezra & Raggio, 1976)*

[1] The U.S. Congress passed legislation in 1977 which would extend coverage to age 70.

Enforcement efforts have recently been increased but the impact is still not great. In fiscal 1976, investigation disclosed monetary violations amounting to $8.6 million involving 1,908 individuals; $3.5 million was returned to 742 workers. This shows some increase compared to previous years, for: in 1975, there were monetary violations of $6.5 million and 2,400 individuals; in 1974, violations of $6.3 million involving 1,650 workers; and in 1973, findings of $2 million involving 1,000 workers. Yet when the monetary violations are compared to some other laws enforced by Wage and Hour, the relatively small impact can be seen. During fiscal year 1976, $17.9 million was found owing to 24,610 people under the Equal Pay Act of 1963 (Section 6, Part D of the FLSA); $7.8 million was restored to 16,728 people. In the same year, monetary violations in the amount of $37.9 million involving 296,324 individuals were disclosed under the minimum-wage provisions of the FLSA, and over $51 million was found owing to 261,892 persons under its overtime provisions (U.S. Bureau of Labor Statistics).

The cases investigated under ADEA reflect the attitude of employers and society to older workers. The following are some examples:

- In October 1975, the U.S. Court of Appeals for the Fourth Circuit broadly sustained the Department of Labor's position that such terms as *recent grads, career girls,* and *those unable to continue in college* are age discriminatory and ordered the district court to grant a requested injunction against Approved Personnel Service, Inc., of Greensboro, North Carolina, to prevent publishing of such ads.
- An investigation of a coal company disclosed a failure of the firm to hire applicants over age 40 for jobs as *red hats* ("no experience") for underground mining. More than 80 individuals were identified as over-40 applicants; the firm agreed to offer employment to all of them. Some months later, there were 28 on the company's payroll with earnings of $311,200 per year. The firm is also preparing "damage" checks totaling $25,000 and is self-auditing other mines to take affirmative steps to correct their hiring practices.
- An ADEA conciliation with a producer of Kentucky bourbon whiskey was recently completed. A 61-year-old sales representative was terminated after 13 years with the firm due to "unsatisfactory performance." The terminated sales representative was given a choice: apply for early retirement, available at the option of the employee, or be fired. He elected to exercise his option and applied for early retirement. At the same time, he exercised another option—he contacted the Wage and Hour Division. As a result of the conciliation, he is still on early retirement but obtained $35,966 in an additional settlement.
- A 44-year-old man complained that he was effectively barred from officiating at high school football games because the State Football

Officials' Association, which controls such jobs, refused to take in new members over the age of 40. The association's argument was that men over 40 were not spry enough to keep up with fast, young, running backs. Starting with the fact that many association members, regularly assigned to games, were officiating at ages 50 to 60, the compliance officer persuaded the association to drop the age-40 limit.

- In April 1976, Phillips Petroleum Company was charged with discriminating against some 400 sales and marketing division employees. In a suit filed in the U.S. District Court in Joplin, Missouri, the government charged that the employees, located at Phillips' facilities nationwide, were victims of forced early retirement or discriminatory job reclassifications during a personnel reduction begun by the company in 1971. The suit seeks to recover lost pay and damages as well as reinstatement and other benefits. The requested back-wage recovery amounts to several million dollars. (Peavy, 1976)

As can be noted in the above examples, some of the more successful actions resulting from ADEA have come from noncourt activity. In another instance, forced retirement of New York City municipal employees 55 or older during the city's financial crisis was averted when the city was advised by the Department of Labor that the contemplated action could be in violation of the law. In this case, city officials were "educated" as to the probable effects of their proposed course of action. Much more education of this kind needs to be done, not only through increased enforcement efforts by the Department of Labor, but by gerontologists, by aging organizations, and by older people themselves, who must fight for their employment rights.

MANDATORY RETIREMENT

According to the NCOA/Harris survey (Harris & Associates, 1975), a large majority of Americans feel that "nobody should be forced to retire because of age" (p. 216), and a smaller majority agree that "most older people can continue to perform as well on the job as they did when they were younger (p. 216). Yet, in mid-1974, 37% of those who were retired said they did not retire by choice. As can be seen in Table 3, more men than women and more blacks than whites had been forced to retire. Those with low incomes and with less than a high school education had larger proportions of forced retirements than those with higher incomes and more education.

In the younger age cohorts, there were larger proportions of retirees who had been forced to retire than in the upper age cohorts. Two-thirds of those in the 40 to 54 age category were forced to retire as compared to 40% of those 55 to 64 and 37% of those 65 or over. This indicates that those below age 65 are less likely to retire voluntarily than those 65 or over and

TABLE 3 Retirement Choice by Sex, Income, Race and Education, Percentage Distribution*

Group	Retired by choice (%)	Forced to retire (%)	Not sure (%)
Sex			
Men	58	41	1
Women	66	32	2
Income			
Under $3,000	53	46	1
$3,000–$6,999	62	36	2
$7,000–$14,999	68	30	2
$15,000 and over	65	35	–
Race			
White	63	36	1
Black	43	50	7
Education			
Some high school or less	58	41	1
High school graduate, some college	67	30	3
College graduate	70	30	–
Total	61	37	2

Note. From "Implications for Employment" by Elizabeth L. Meier. In *Aging in America* (No. 7 in a series based on the NCOA/Louis Harris study "The Myth and Reality of Aging in America"), 1976, p. 10. Copyright 1976 by The National Council on the Aging, Inc., Washington, D.C. Reprinted by permission.

Base: 63 percent of public 65 or over who are retired.

that they may have had an occupation such as police officer that required early mandatory retirement. The Supreme Court recently upheld the right of the state of Massachusetts to retire a policeman at age 50 even though he was admittedly in excellent health.

Mandatory retirement is a twentieth-century phenomenon, and its recent expansion in the United States has paralleled the increase in coverage and benefits of social security and private pension plans. During the past two decades, mandatory retirement has been the predominant issue in discussion of older-worker retirement policies. Although advocates on behalf of the elderly have been almost unanimous in calling for an end to (or at least flexibility in) mandatory age policies, there has been no observable decline in the existence of such provisions. Furthermore, individuals have been almost entirely unsuccessful in claiming in court that employers' retirement polices violate the equal protection clause of the Fourteenth Amendment; the courts have turned down such claims time and time again.

A recent arbitration agreement has also held that an employer can force an employee to retire at "normal" retirement age of 65 even if the collective bargaining agreement does not make it mandatory (*BNA Pension Reporter*, 1976).

The grievant argued that his forced retirement was the result of age discrimination, and that it violated his seniority rights. He also argued that retirement at age 65 is not mandatory and that the company has retained a number of employees beyond that age.

The arbitrator says the company's action was "not arbitrary, capricious, or discriminatory" and he rejects the age discrimination charge on the grounds that neither the collective bargaining agreement nor the Age Discrimination in Employment Act of 1967 prohibits the company from retiring an employee at age 65. The act does not apply to individuals over 65 and the contract reflects the intent of the parties to "treat employees differently" when they reach retirement age. . . . (p. A9)

Mandatory retirement policies tend to put an upper age limit on many employment opportunities for older people, most often at the usual retirement age of 65. Thus, for example, participants in the SCSP age 65 or over have found the existence of a mandatory retirement age a barrier to permanent employment in the agencies in which they have had successful, employment-training experience. Mandatory retirement also limits opportunities for people in their late 50s and early 60s because employers feel that their years of employment would be limited.

Inasmuch as courts have not been sympathetic to overturning mandatory retirement rules, more could probably be accomplished through education. Difficulties in adopting flexible retirement ages have been overemphasized and too readily accepted. In the NCOA/Harris survey (Harris & Associates, 1975), only 37% of those 18 to 64 with responsibility for hiring and firing (as compared to about half of the general public) felt that it makes sense to have a fixed retirement age for everyone, and these are the very people who could be expected to be proportionately more in favor of fixed retirement ages because of the administrative simplicity.

Furthermore, a majority of workers voluntarily retire either before or at the age of 65 because of personal preference. The numbers of those who wish to work after age 65 would probably no more than offset the number of those who wish to retire in their 50s and early 60s and thus would not greatly expand the labor force if mandatory retirement policies were to be dropped and flexible policies adopted. A longer period of work for some would also help to offset the cost to social security and pension systems of those who retire early.

NEW EDUCATIONAL APPROACHES NEEDED

As it has been evolving, the field of gerontology has had multi-disciplinary dimensions, but much of it has focused on a medical-treatment model for service organization and delivery. The emphasis has been on dysfunction rather than function of the aged. The well and functioning aged have been relatively ignored. Further, the study of aging has concentrated on the population age of 65 or over. Little attention has been paid to those in their 40s, 50s, or early 60s who may be encountering significant economic and social problems as society already begins to label them too old for full participation, particularly in the world of work, and such problems of people approaching normal retirement age may significantly affect their adjustment to old age. Involuntary early retirement, for example, could affect, not only retirement income, but physical well-being in later years, just as the trauma of forced retirement could affect mental and physical health. The American Medical Association (1972) sees the relationship between unemployment and health as follows:

> *There is ample clinical evidence that physical and emotional problems can be precipitated or exacerbated by denial of employment opportunities. Few physicians deny that a direct relationship exists between enforced idleness and poor health. The practitioner with a patient load comprised largely of older persons is convinced that the physical and emotional ailments of many . . . are a result of inactivity imposed by denial of work. Physicians generally agree that chronic complaints develop more frequently when a person is inactive and without basic interests. It is easy for the unemployed, unoccupied person to over-concern himself with his own normal physiological functions, and to exaggerate minor physical or emotional symptoms. (p. 2)*

About the only current educational programs specifically for those of preretirement age are preretirement counseling or planning courses being developed in schools of gerontology, community colleges, and elsewhere. Such courses are aimed at easing the transition from work to retirement for those who are ready for retirement. Largely neglected, however, are the needs of those who are not ready for retirement at 50 or 55, or 62, or 65 or 70, or whenever. There is also the danger that the emphasis on preretirement courses without also emphasizing the productive capacities of older employees can reinforce employer's and employees' negative images of aging and the early-retirement syndrome.

In his article on educational gerontology and the state of the art, David Peterson (1976) defines three interrelated components concerned with successful aging:

1. Educational endeavors designed for people who are middle-aged or older
2. Educational endeavors for a general or specific public about aging or older people

3. Educational preparation of people who are working, or intend to be employed, in serving older people in professional or paraprofessional capacities

Each of these aspects is important for the elimination of age bias in employment through affirmative action.

Education for the Middle-Aged or Older

First, more educational programs should be designed to allow middle-aged and older people to update their job skills or start second careers, for it is apparent that many more people desire such training than are participating in such programs. The NCOA/Harris survey (Harris & Associates, 1975) asked the total public if they were "interested in learning new skills or participating in job training programs in order to take on a different kind of job" (p. 93). Almost half (47%) of those age 40 to 54 were either very interested or somewhat interested. In the age groups 55 to 64, 37% registered interest. Although interest dropped in the 65-or-over group, there were still 21% of those 65 to 69 and 13% of those 70 to 79 who were interested. Considering the barriers to employment that exist for this age group, it is surprising that even this many were interested.

These figures are certainly much higher than the proportion in these age categories involved in CETA government employment and training programs, and they are also much higher than those enrolled in nongovernment programs. Although figures are not available as to how many older adults are receiving employment-related education and training, the numbers we do have show that only a small percentage of older people are receiving adult education of *any* kind. U.S. Office of Education figures show that, in 1972, only 15% of those 45 to 54, 6% of those 55 to 64, and 2% of those 65 or over were in adult education.[2]

From these figures, it is obvious that there is a great gap between the desire older people have for renewing and extending their job skills and the filling of this need. Older people's needs are diverse too. Some middle-aged women will be seeking training in order to reenter the job market after dropping out for family reasons. Other women and men will be seeking more meaningful and rewarding jobs in second and third careers, even though presently employed. Still others are looking for job training after early retirement from the military, from police and fire-fighting forces, and from other government jobs. Those who retire later may need help in acquiring new job skills for part- or full-time or intermittent work in order to supplement retirement income and develop new interests.

Williard Wirtz (1975) has suggested that the need for work opportunity

---

[2] From *Never Too Old to Learn*, 1974, p. 11. Copyright 1974 by the Academy for Educational Development. Reprinted by permission.

for older people may require the devising of *senior careers* for those who want them and arranging for "the education and training some of these careers will require if they are to be meaningful—with the recognition that learning is itself one such type of career (p. 144). One possible approach, he goes on to say, is "to make a year's free public education available to everybody after he or she reaches age sixty, as an organized series of educational and training opportunities thoughtfully and carefully designed to meet this situation . . . " (p. 145). This "could change materially people's attitudes about themselves and their place in society—at a time in life when there is particular question about whether there is a place at all" (p. 145).

Wirtz's approach would go far beyond the usual preretirement courses or sundry adult education courses and would not be appropriate for everyone, just as extended work is not for every older person; but it would create the *opportunity* for older people to continue to participate fully. This is, however, only one possible approach. Considering the differing training needs of middle-aged and older workers, it is apparent that the educational programs to fill these needs must be varied and plentiful, and they should be available at the community level for maximum access.

Education about Aging or Older People

Second, special endeavors need to be made by educational gerontologists to acquaint both government and business policy makers with older-worker employment problems and retirement-income problems. With few exceptions, policy issues with regard to older-worker employment problems and employment-related, income-maintenance problems have been virtually ignored in the educational and gerontological world. Although a good deal of attention has been paid to increasing social security benefits and social security financing problems, little attention has been paid to employment as an alternative to ever-increasing demands on the social security system. Early retirement also needs to be reevaluated in light of the growing experiences of social security, and private and governmental pension plans due to inflation and workers' increased expectations for higher benefits. Mandatory retirement policies need to be reexamined, not only for their cost, but for their human toll on those who want and need to work.

The relationship between low social security benefits and a poor work record in the years before retirement has been studied by the Social Security Administration. One study found that early social security retirees are much more likely to have had sporadic work histories or unemployment in the years preceding entitlement. In 1966, men taking reduced benefits at age 62 earned about $2,700 in their last year of employment—$1,300 less than the average for those taking full benefits at age 65 (Bixby & Rings, 1969, p. 9). Because of the relationship between workers' work records and their social security benefits, the answer to improving retirement income may be to increase employment opportunities for people in their 50s and 60s rather than to rely on across-the-board increases after retirement to improve retirement income, particularly for those with low benefits, because those who enter retirement with low benefits will always have relatively low benefits.

Many of those with low social security benefits are women, and the economic problems of older women is a subject that assumes particular importance in the field of aging. Older women are a majority in the aged population and constitute a large majority of the aged poor. Their poverty can often be traced to such factors as low wages, lack of survivor pension benefits, and sex and age discrimination in employment. Widows and divorced women in their 40s, 50s, or 60s are now one of the groups most in need of employment and counseling services and of aid in combating age discrimination in employment, which is added to sex discrimination. Only if their preretirement employment needs are solved will it be possible to prevent additional numbers from being added every year to the numbers of aged women in poverty. The economic problems of older women should be of major importance to gerontologists and policy makers.

Education for Gerontologists

Third, educational programs for future gerontologists and other students who intend to work with older people should include information on their productive capacities and economic contributions, as well as on their economic problems. Thus, it is important for students who are going to work in fields such as counseling to realize the importance of work to older people, both in the past and present. The NCOA/Harris survey (Meier, 1976, p. 12) asked the employed public about the things they would miss if they stopped work. Money was the most important thing, followed by the people at work, and then by the feeling of being useful. The feeling of being useful was the *most important thing* to employed women over 65.

A more specific need is the need to develop specialists in aging in the field of career and employment counseling to work with older people. Now, most such counselors are trained to work with those under age 25. Prior to enrolling in job-training or vocational education programs, many older job seekers and second careerists need counseling, guidance, and testing in order to evaluate their skills and experience in terms not only of personal goals, but of the labor market. Placement specialists are also needed to help unemployed older people find jobs by successfully selling their skills to employers.

Administrators of services for the aging and those who work in the field of legal aid should receive training, not only in the policies, programs, and laws of long-term care but of employment as well. Students should be made aware of the provisions of the federal and state age discrimination in employment acts and the CETA legislation. They should be aware of the controversies centering around mandatory retirement and the court cases that have resulted. Gerontologists, particularly administrators and other policy makers, can be key advocates in eliminating age bias in employment.

Role of Educational Gerontology

In summary, educators in the field of gerontology can do much to help overcome age bias in employment, which is shown in declining labor-force participation, in lack of training opportunities, in mandatory retirement policies, and in employer attitudes. More educational programs need to be designed to allow middle-aged and older people to update their job skills. Education about aging and older people should include information about older worker employment problems and employment-related income problems in order to change attitudes and policies. This same type of information, as well as specialized employment-counseling training for older people, should be included in gerontology curriculums. These actions would do much toward not only creating an awareness of the age bias in employment, but developing affirmative programs to solve this pervasive problem.

REFERENCES

Academy for Educational Development. *Never too old to learn.* New York: Author, 1974.

American Medical Association. *Retirement: A medical philosophy and approach.* Chicago: Author, 1972.

Bixby, L. E., & Rings, E. E. Work experience of men claiming retirement benefits, 1966. Social Security Bulletin, August 1969, pp. 3–14.

BNA Pension Reporter, No. 100, August 27, 1976. Washington, D.C.: Bureau of National Affairs, 1976.

Boren, N., Terry, K. M. Y., & McCally, M. Second careers: An integrated learning experience in career change for older persons. *Industrial Gerontology,* Spring 1976, pp. 75–103.

Ezra, I. B., & Raggio, J. J. Strengthening enforcement of the age discrimination and pension reform statutes and expanding protection under the laws. Testimony before the Senate Committee on Aging and Youth, Philadelphia, Pennsylvania, September 1, 1976.

Federal efforts in developing and protecting employment opportunities for older workers (a panel). *Industrial Gerontology,* Spring 1976, pp. 91–95.

Harris, L., & Associates. *The myth and reality of aging in America.* Washington, D.C.: National Council on the Aging, 1975.

Meier, E. L. Implications for employment. In *Aging in America* (No. 7), in a series based on the NCOA/Louis Harris study "The Myth and Reality of Aging in America." Washington, D.C.: The National Council on the Aging, 1976.

Peavy, N. C. ADEA: Age Discrimination in Employment Act; recent decisions, settlements and pending cases. *Industrial Gerontology,* Summer 1976, pp. 198–203.

Peterson, D. A. Educational gerontology, the state of the art. *Educational Gerontology,* 1976, *1,* 61–73.

Rosenblum, M. The last push, from discouraged worker to involuntary retirement. *Industrial Gerontology,* Winter 1975, pp. 14–22.

U.S. Bureau of Labor Statistics. *Employment and earnings*. Washington, D.C.: U.S. Government Printing Office, January 1976.

U.S. Congress, Senate Special Committee on Aging. *Improving the age discrimination law* (Committee Print). Washington, D.C.: U.S. Government Printing Office, 1973.

Wirtz, W. *The boundless resource, a prospectus for an education-work policy.* Washington, D.C.: The National Manpower Institute, 1975.

11

FUTURE TRENDS IN EDUCATION FOR OLDER ADULTS

JAMES A. THORSON

University of Nebraska at Omaha

Diagnosing present trends and projecting the future is often an imprecise business. Even the casual observer may note that most prophecy takes something of a shotgun approach and that direct hits are rare. One may now find articles in old issues of popular magazines such as *Look* and *Life* (journals that were unsuccessful at seeing their own future) that provide examples of how widely those who would look into the future have missed their marks. Articles with themes such as What will life be like in 1970? illustrate now-comical visions of people being shot from place to place via pneumatic tubes and of interplanetary travel for the masses. Just a few short years ago, it seemed to many educators that many educational services would be provided through computer hookups and electronic teaching machines in the home. Even in a society that readily adapts to change and exerts considerable pressure for the adoption of the newest innovations, one must often be content with gradual evolution and realize that in some areas we are only beginning to make progress. Such is the case in education for the aged.

Peterson (1976) points out that, among 15 programs providing educational services to older adults surveyed by Donahue in 1955, the passage of over 20 years has shown little in the way of development:

> *Although programs have continued to expand, little has changed since that time. Activities continue to be reactive, responding to discrete, perceived needs on an* ad hoc *basis rather than being based on a comprehensive, philosophical framework designed to facilitate life long growth experiences. (Peterson, 1976, p. 62)*

Although many may be impatient for immediate change, the field of education for older people has been a largely neglected one until very recently, and progress will probably be perceived as being frustratingly slow for some time to come.

Despite these and other problems of seeing where we really are, much less where we are going, there are many new things on the horizon to be viewed by those who will only lift up their eyes and see. The world will of course be very different for everyone in the year 2000, and the world of education for the aged will have changed remarkably.

Despite a declining birth rate and projected zero population growth, the population of the elderly will continue to grow through at least the first half of the next century. An accurate projection can be made, because these are people who are already born, and, assuming no change in current mortality rates, there will be a significantly larger population of older people in the United States in future years. Whereas the proportion of older people relative to younger people will not change dramatically from current levels until the postwar babies become postwar senior citizens in the year 2011, the observer at the end of this century will see a significant increase in absolute numbers of older people and a gradual increase in the median age of the overall population. Over the course of the twentieth century, the proportion of the population over age 65 in the United States will have changed from 4% to about 12% or 13%. The total number of older people alive in the year 2000, as compared to 1974 levels, will have increased from 30% to 40%. According to Fowles (1975), by the end of this century, there will be a total of 40,590,000 people who are age 60 or above and 30.6 million who are age 65 or above. For comparison purposes, there were, in 1974, 31,020,000 people in the United States who were age 60 or more and a total of 21,815,000 who were 65 or above.

The older adult will, of course, be a very different person in the year 2000, in terms of educational attainment, nutrition and health status over the life-span, material resources, expectations, and years of useful life remaining. Gerontologists are now beginning to realize that there are two different populations of the elderly: the *young old,* those who are age 65 to 75, and the *old old,* those who are over the age of 75. The young old comprise about two-thirds of the total over-65 age group and, for the most part, exhibit few of the decrements that are popularly associated with old age. They are relatively healthy, mobile, prosperous, alert, and active. Most of the young old have little need for supportive services and are living life with considerable satisfaction. One of the few things that differentiates them from the cohort of people age 55 to 64 is that many of the young old have had leisure inflicted upon them by mandatory retirement. It might be expected that this time of useful and self-actualizing life will expand in years to come, particularly if progress in research against chronic illness parallels in any way the great strides that have been made in the conquest of communicable disease (Havighurst, 1969).

Life expectancy at age 65 is presently about 15 years. We can expect this figure to rise significantly if cancer, stroke, heart disease, and major cardiovascular renal disease are significantly controlled or eliminated. If major break-throughs do occur in these areas, we can anticipate an increase in average life expectancy of 16 years over and above the present 15. In other words, average life expectancy at age 65 might be 31 years. (p. 5)

Even if progress against these leading causes of death in old age is slower than was the discovery of the cure and prevention of many of the communicable diseases, older people of the future may expect more of their remaining years of life to be of a high quality in terms of health status. They will be a generation that has experienced fewer physical traumas from infectious disease, a better level of medical care over the life-span generally, a better diet, and better public health services than many in the current generation of older people.

It has been well established that people who have a high level of educational attainment are more likely to participate in adult and continuing education programs than those who have had fewer years of education, and that years of education among older people will increase in years to come. According to Riley and Foner (1968), the age cohort (males and females) that will be from ages 65 to 69 in the year 2000 will have an average of 12.3 years of education, whereas the group that is from age 65 to 69 in 1976 has a median number of years of education of 9.4 for males and 10.1 for females. One definition of functional illiteracy is having fewer than four years of schooling, and in 1976, this is the case for 7.6% of those age 65 to 69, 10.4% for those in the age group 70 to 74, 13.3% for those who are 75 to 79, and 18.2% for those people 80 years old or above. In the year 2000, only 2.9% of all people over 65 will have had fewer than four years of formal education. The same trend can be seen for the immediate future. During the 15-year-period ending in 1985, the percentage of people over age 65 who have not completed eight years of school will have dropped from 60.6% to 39.0%. During the same period, the proportion of those 65 or over who have completed one or more years of college will have increased from 11% to 16%.

It is known that the rate of participation in continuing education among people who have completed high school is about twice as high as that among those who have completed only elementary school (Johnstone & Rivera, 1965). Experience with adult education activities also has an influence on the likelihood of future participation. Johnstone and Rivera's (1965) study of adult education participation reveals that, in 1962, 35% of people age 60 or above had had some prior experience with formal continuing education activities. At the same time, 57% of those in the 30-to-39–year age group had experience with some form of adult education. As this group of heavier users of continuing education services becomes elderly, the rate of participation of older people in adult education activities will also increase. If the present trend toward earlier retirement continues, this healthier, better educated group of people who will be retired in the year 2000 will have even more years of life in which they will have leisure time to devote to educational pursuits.

Changes in attitude are as important as the demographic changes in the population. The present group of elderly people has what some would consider to be a disappointing rate of participation in educational activities. In 1972, only 2.4% of all older people were current participants in adult education programs, and only 6.3% of the age group 55 to 64 had participated in adult education programs during the prior year (Academy for Educational Development, 1974). Reasons for this low level of participation include cost, inconvenience, transportation problems, attitudes toward self and toward educational institutions, and anxiety over negative attitudes of faculty and other students. The fact is that the current generation of older adults has not been well served by our traditional educational institutions, many of which remain exclusively oriented toward youth. This youth orientation in society can be seen in governmental programs as well as in our educational institutions. Many programs have excluded the elderly either overtly or subtly. Many older adults have quite perceptively felt unwelcome.

Attitudes of older people toward the services that they might receive from educational institutions may well change with their increasing level of education. Attitudes and actions of educators may be undergoing a process of change as well (see especially chap. 9 and 10 in this book). More and more programmers in continuing education are gaining exposure to elements of gerontology during their professional training, and this trend will be growing in years to come. This can be seen by the recent growth of educational services for the elderly discussed in a later section of this chapter. Self-confidence of older people will also improve with their educational level. Research by this author has shown that attitudes toward the elderly are significantly better among people with more years of education (Thorson, 1975a, 1975b).

Demands from the elderly for educational services will also have an influence on programming. The people who are now older grew up expecting relatively little from government and have perhaps had a relatively passive attitude toward public institutions. The emergence of activist groups such as the Gray Panthers is an indication of a changing level of expectation. When the group of young people who learned participatory democracy during the civil rights and antiwar movements of the 1960s becomes elderly, a much greater level of responsiveness on the part of educational institutions can be anticipated.

Adult educators have, over the past decade, become increasingly aware of the continuing abilities of older adults to be effective learners. Various researchers (Baltes & Labouvie, 1973; Birren & Woodruff, 1973; Eisdorfer, 1969; Granick & Friedman, 1973; Labouvie-Vief, 1976; Labouvie-Vief & Gonda, 1976; Schaie, 1975) have demonstrated that intelligence and learning ability do not necessarily decline with age as was once supposed. Rather, many older people maintain a high level of intellectual functioning into very old age, and older people seem to demonstrate a kind of plasticity in learning ability, being able to respond well to challenges. Much earlier research had been complicated by factors such as timing, competition, distance from formal education, an unequal number of years of education, physical decrements, and problems of self-concept that reflected badly on older subjects' test scores. Eisdorfer (1969) explains that many older people did not score as highly as younger subjects on achievement tests because of their test-taking behavior; that is, the explanation for much of the differential in scores on intelligence tests in cross-sectional comparisons between generational groups might be the demonstrated reluctance of older people to engage in risk-taking behavior: "The possibility that 'fear of failure' replaces 'need to achieve' as a motivating force in older individuals cannot be ignored" (p. 246).

It can be seen that improved knowledge about older people on the part of adult educators, more active demands from older people for educational services, improving attitudes toward education and toward their own abilities on the part of older individuals, and the increasing rate of experience with adult education that older people of the future will have had will combine with the factors of higher levels of education and greater absolute numbers of older adults to greatly increase the numbers and percentages of older people participating in continuing education activities in years to come. Other factors, such as a desire for knowledge about one's self and an acceptance of a life-span philosophy of education, will also increase the numbers of older participants in educational programs. In the next section, some theoretical considerations are examined that may have an influence on the kinds of educational services that this new generation of older learners will require.

MOTIVATIONS FOR PARTICIPATION

Why older adults participate in adult education activities, or what they seek from their participation ought to be of prime importance to adult educators of the future as they seek to serve this growing audience. To a large degree, the motivation behind participation in educational activities might be viewed by looking at the type of activity in which the participant engages. Theoretic constructs proposed by Havighurst (1963/1964) and elaborated by Londoner (1971; see also chapter 4) and Hiemstra (1972, 1973), and another system proposed by Houle (1963) help to put motivation into perspective.

Briefly, Havighurst (1963) differentiated types of adult education into two categories, *instrumental* and *expressive:*

> *Instrumental education means education for a goal which lies outside and beyond the act of education. In this form, education is an instrument for changing the learner's situation. Instrumental education is thus a kind of investment of time and energy in the expectation of future gain.*

Expressive education means education for a goal which lies within the act of learning, or is so closely related to it that the act of learning appears to be the goal. Expressive education is a kind of consumption of time and energy for present gain. (pp. 17, 18)

To oversimplify, instrumental education for older adults might thus be seen as something in which the participants engage because it is good for them; they will derive some knowledge from the educational experience that will improve the quality of life. Courses in preretirement planning, investments, or consumer protection are examples of instrumental education. Expressive learning experiences, on the other hand, are engaged in because they are fun. Ballroom dancing, contract bridge, or watercolor painting are examples of expressive educational activities. Of course, the reasons people have for taking a course might influence one's thinking of what types of activities should be considered to be instrumental and what activities should be defined as expressive. One might, for example, take a crafts course because one plans to sell one's products and earn extra money in retirement. In that case, one's view of the course might be seen as being instrumental. The reader may quickly see that both categories might well apply in a number of situations.

Londoner (1971) argues that the kinds of educational activities usually provided for older learners have not really been of service in equiping them with the survival skills that will be needed in the future. Scarce resources ought to be applied to helping older people cope with a complex variety of problems in our changing society. We should shun the expenditure of our time and dollars on activities that merely entertain and pacify older participants. In a very real sense, it is patronizing to think that older people have nothing better to do with their time than to make pot holders or ceramic ashtrays.

Londoner's viewpoint is becoming widely accepted among the people who provide educational services for older adults. In the next section of this chapter, some emerging trends are examined that provide hope for the future in instrumental program development. It should be added, however, that the participants might well wish to express a view as to what programs are offered in the future, and all of the future participants in educational activities that are designed for older people may not, in fact, turn out to be puritans.

Whatley (1974) sought to determine whether instrumental or expressive types of educational experiences would be preferred by a sample of older adults. She also surveyed sample groups of adult educators and gerontologists for their perceptions as to what types of courses they thought older adults might like to take. Allowing older adult respondents to check any courses that they might like to take and having the adult educators and gerontologists check any they thought older people would like to take, Whatley found that the older people made about two-thirds of their choices from among the instrumental courses and the remaining third from expressive topics, whereas both the gerontologists and the adult educators thought that older people would select significantly more instrumental activities than they actually did choose. No expressive versus instrumental preference trends were found among the older respondents on the basis of their age, sex, or level of education. There are two ways to interpret Whatley's data. Perhaps the professionals, the gerontologists and adult educators, have gone overboard in projecting their own values onto what they thought older participants ought to be taking for their own good, reasoning that education, after all, is a serious business and that people should not be wasting their time by having a good time. Another view is that the older respondents had been subjected to a barrage of pottery and finger-painting courses and were seeking some blessed relief by making the majority of their choices from among more serious subjects. In the words of a 74-year-old friend of the author, when asked why she did not attend a local senior citizens program, "I hope I never have to make another goddamn pot holder as long as I live!"

There is no doubt of the value of or the need for offering serious survival and adjustment skills to the older learners of the future. Researchers often, however, are guilty of mixing concepts of what older people want with why they participate. Houle (1963) reported on a survey of what might be called, in today's language, a sample of adult education groupies. He sought to find out why heavy users of adult education services participated and what differentiated people who had what he called an "inquiring mind" from others.

Houle (1963) was able to describe those he studied according to three categories of motivation; they were either: *goal oriented, activity oriented,* or *learning oriented.* The goal-oriented were often participating in adult education activities for vocational improvement. More than vocational gains, though, they sought self-improvement generally.

> *The goal-oriented are all alike in their confident acceptance of adult education as a way to solve problems or to pursue particular interests. They describe themselves as seekers after goals, they attribute similar motives to other learners, and the history of their continuing education shows clearly that they have always taken courses or engaged in other forms of activity chiefly because they will be helped thereby. (p. 35)*

The activity-oriented seek socialization. They might take a course in real estate or in contract bridge as a vehicle for meeting interesting people; they "Face frankly the fact that they are engaged in continuing education for some reason other than the knowledge it provides" (Houle, 1963, p. 36). Course work for them is a social outlet. The learning-oriented, on the other hand, have almost a preoccupation with learning. They have a love of learning that often is indiscriminant, and they will frequently read anything that they can get their hands on. The learning-oriented respondents often described learning as their way of having fun.

Allen Tough's (1971) research has shown that many adults display these motivations at one time or another but that many learners gain needed information outside of the classroom. A person need not sign up for an adult education course at the community college or take part in the seminars held at the senior center in order to be an effective adult learner. Tough says, in fact, that most adult learning is self-planned and self-initiated and takes place outside of the formal, educational structures that we commonly identify.

> *Almost everyone undertakes at least one or two major learning efforts a year, and some individuals undertake as many as 15 or 20. The median is eight learning projects a year, involving eight distinct areas of knowledge and skill.*
>
> *A learning project is simply a major, highly deliberate effort to gain certain knowledge and skill (or to change in some other way). Some learning projects are efforts to gain new knowledge, insight, or understanding. Others are attempts to improve one's skill or performance, or to change one's attitudes or emotional reactions. Others involve efforts to change one's overt behavior or to break a habit. (p. 1)*

Tough maintains that people seek knowledge from a variety of sources, including books and magazines and knowledgeable friends. Many, of course, take courses, but many also undertake and execute learning projects independently. Most seek either informal or formal learning planners to assist them. Tough argues that one goal of the educational system ought to be to make students more competent and efficient at developing these learning episodes.

Another perspective on motivation has been provided by Birren and Woodruff (1973). They cite three goals of education for older adults: *alleviation, enrichment,* and *prevention.* Alleviation is finding a remedy, through educational programs such as adult basic education, for a lack of knowledge that learners see as vital to their lives. Enrichment is a combination of motivations for entertainment, socialization, self-improvement, and love of learning. Prevention is of particular interest to the educational gerontologist; it is a kind of educational intervention to prevent decrements that might befall an individual with the coming of age. Educational intervention strategies are examined more fully after the next section, in which some harbingers of change in programming for older adults are examined and integrated with the various theories that have been presented.

SOME TRENDS IN PROGRAMMING

In a sense, the entire philosophy of public educational institutions during the past 100 years has been that education is, in itself, beneficial and that learning is so important that legal requirements will be placed on some segments of the population to make them engage in it—or at least attend school in body if not in mind. This point of view is, fortunately, not at all successful in adult education. Potential adult learners vote with their feet; they can disassociate themselves from unpleasant or unrewarding educational environments. Many people have had enough negative experiences with public schools to keep them away from schools for a lifetime. The lack of response, historically, of educational institutions to the needs of adults has been largely responsible for older people finding alternative means for satisfying their educational goals. A survey conducted by the Academy for Educational Development (1974) revealed that, of people over the age of 65 who participated in some form of adult education, only 21% were being served by a public or private school, and only 5% were having their educational needs met by a college or university. The largest group of older participants in adult education, 42%, was being served by some kind of community organization.

The emergence of community organizations, such as senior centers, as educational institutions for older adults might be seen as a trend that will continue in years to come. A National Council on the Aging survey of 4,870 senior centers in the United States indicates that 63% of those programs responding to a mailed questionnaire indicated program offerings of an educational nature, including classes, lectures, and discussion groups (Leanse & Wagner, 1975, p. 29). The responding programs indicated an average of 154 participants at each center and an average of 22 hours per month of educational activities, as compared to 22 hours per month of "active recreation" and 61 hours per month of "sedentary recreation." An example of the kinds of learning activities offered can be seen in the weekday schedule for the Celeste Campbell Senior Community Center, which is sponsored by the Parks and Recreation Department of Eugene, Oregon:

MONDAY

Creative writing	9:30–11:30
Knitting	10:00–noon
Ceramics	10:00– 2:00
Women's pool	all day
Advanced French	10:00–noon
Lip reading	3:30– 4:30
Shop	10:00– 4:00

TUESDAY

Pinochle instruction	10:00–noon
Intro. to conversational Spanish II	10:00–noon
Intro. to conversational German	10:00–noon
Senior swim	11:15–12:15
Pool	all day
Advanced Spanish	1:00– 3:00
Beginning oil painting	1:00– 4:00
Figure drawing	9:00–noon
Lip reading	3:30– 4:30
Shop	10:00– 4:00

WEDNESDAY

Pinochle	10:00– 2:00
Sewing and quilt tying	10:00– 2:00
China painting	10:00– 2:00
Beginning Spanish	10:00–noon
Copper tooling	10:00–noon
Picture framing	10:00–noon
Pool	all day
Beginning French	2:30– 4:00
Bingo (4th Weds. only)	2:00– 3:30
Wives' coffee	2:30– 3:30
Lip reading	3:30– 4:30
Watercolor	7:00– 8:30
Shop	10:00– 4:00

THURSDAY

Friendship	10:00– 1:30
Advanced drawing	2:00– 4:30
Pool	1:30– 4:30
Campbell Center Singers	2:00– 4:00
Tile painting	10:00–12:30
Sewing	9:00–noon
Hand-building pottery	1:00– 4:00
Lip reading	3:30– 4:30
Shop	10:00– 4:00

FRIDAY

Intro. to oil painting	9:00–noon
Beginning bridge	10:00–noon
Bridge	10:00–noon
Intro. to conversational Spanish I	10:00–noon
Jewelry	10:00– 4:00
Beginning conversational Spanish	1:00– 3:00
Advanced painting	1:00– 4:00
Lip reading	2:30– 3:30
Men's pool	all day
Shop	10:00– 4:00

There are no fees or dues charged for these activities, and over 200 older people are regular participants. Evidently, a wide variety of expressive activities are popular with a senior audience in this setting, and these kinds of options ought to be open to adults who want to enjoy themselves while they learn. This growth of senior centers and their response to needs of older adults has been remarkable over the past 30 years, and this trend will no doubt continue. The addition of instrumental learning experiences, lip reading in this sample, will also grow as the programs of senior centers develop.

Traditional educational institutions are starting to respond to needs of the elderly. Howard McClusky (1973) has cited the growth of community schools and community colleges as trends for the future in providing relevant institutional responses to the educational needs of the elderly. Many community colleges have developed large and creative programs of involvement for older learners. An example is Palomar College in San Marcos, California. Their Pacesetter College program is offered to older people without charge, and services are provided in a variety of community settings as well as on the campus. Learning experiences include a lecture series, held in a senior center, with topics focused on instrumental concerns of the elderly such as preparation for retirement, estate planning, the law as it applies to seniors, medical considerations for older adults, widows and widowers living alone, positive thinking, and death with dignity. Satellite classes include creative writing, experimental arts and mixed media, nature-outdoor classroom, physical conditioning, ways of coping and growing, basic office skills for seniors, a retirement living series, a course entitled "Be Alive as Long as You Live," and a series of six gerontology courses open to both practitioners and older adults. Other cultural and enrichment activities of the college are also open to the older students.

Many colleges and universities are responding to needs of older adults by providing free and reduced tuition programs. Usually, these seek to integrate older learners into the regular instructional program of the institution. Many programs allow older students to register for courses free on a space-available basis and thus at no real cost to the institution. A 1974 survey of institutional members of the National University Extension Association (Rawlings, 1974) revealed that 28 out of the 158 respondents to a mailed questionnaire had some program of free or reduced charges for older students. An early leader in this effort was the University of Kentucky's Donovan scholars program, which began as an administrative waiver of tuition charges and now receives $20,000 annually from university appropriations for support of the program. Another successful program was pioneered by Fairleigh Dickinson University at Madison, New Jersey. There, people 65 or over may register for any course, on a space-available basis, either for credit or on a noncredit basis. Most educational prerequisites, including a high school diploma, are waived. By early 1973, 57 people were taking advantage of the program. The reported popularity of the program has grown to such an extent that it is now being opened to any parent, regardless of age, of a regular, full-time Fairleigh Dickinson student.

Success of free and reduced tuition plans depends principally on their implementation. If barriers are taken down and older people are made to feel welcome on the college campus, they will be enthusiastic participants and boosters of the institution. Free tuition alone, however, does not guarantee participation. One vice-president of a major state university reports that their free tuition plan for people 65 or over has never been promoted and thus has minimal participation. On the other hand, an administrator at the state university in a nearby state reports good success in assigning a staff member to counsel older applicants, to walk them through the bewildering registration process, and if necessary, to get them to their first classes. This program is highly popular and has few dropouts. Institutions that have such programs report that benefits are received, as well, by their younger students, who have an opportunity to interact with people who have a different perspective on life than do most younger people.

Another way institutions are removing barriers is through the use of television. Educational institutions are beginning to expand their offerings broadcast over educational television to include content of special interest to older adults. Younger and middle-aged people currently see television as a more important source of information, and printed newspapers and magazines as a less important source, than do older people (Schramm, 1969). As these younger people age, television will be seen as a more important medium for providing educational services for the elderly. Davis (1975) emphasizes the potential that television has for development of educational programs for older learners. He cites a project at Cosumnes River Community College in Sacramento, California, where 24 video cassette programs, each one-half hour in length, have been developed for use in cable and closed-circuit television systems. Topics have been developed around instrumental themes:

The New Social Security and You
Medicare, Medicaid, and Medi-Cal
A Place to Live
A Place of Care
Tax Benefits for Senior Adults
You Have the Right
Legislation for Senior Adults
Estate Planning—Wills and Inheritance Taxes
Estate Planning—Trusts and Inheritance Taxes
The Bunko Boys
Consumer Beware
Nobody's Victim
Quackery—The False Profit
Community Resources and Services
A Distant Drum
To Work or Not
What is Old? Myths and Realities of Growing Older
What is Old? Part II
What Is Old? Part III
Fit as a Fiddle
Hobbies for Fun
Hobbies for Profit
Older Americans—A Natural Resource
Living the Life

Another example of television programming that has been adapted to meet the needs of older people is a project that the University of Georgia's Center for Continuing Education has recently completed in preretirement education (Thorson, 1976). Funded by the Administration on Aging, the project was titled "New Wrinkles on Retirement." It consisted of a three-phase program in the development of curriculum materials, training of instructors, and the implementation of community-based preretirement planning seminars throughout the state of Georgia. Half-hour television programs on eight different topics that the person planning for retirement will confront were developed during the first phase of the project. Topics were designed to influence the quality of life that the retired person will lead:

Facing Inflation. How to start financial planning for retirement in an inflationary economy

Vigor Regained. How to maintain physical health and vigor in the retirement years

A Time to Learn and a Time to Play. How to plan for effective use of leisure time

Marriage and Love in the Middle Years. An examination of conflicts that husbands and wives may have when the children leave the home

Confronting Loss. Managing stress and coping with the loss of a spouse

Your Heritage. Avoiding legal problems through proper planning

Avoiding Quacks and Frauds. How to keep from being the victim of crime

Maintaining Happiness. Keeping one's mental health and adjusting to the transition of retirement

Phase two of the project consisted of training instructors from a variety of junior and senior colleges on how to lead a community seminar series on retirement planning. The implementation phase of the project came when the programs were broadcast over the state's educational television network, one program each week for eight weeks. Seminars at the colleges met at the same time as the broadcasts; participants viewed the half-hour of content as it came over the air and then joined in a discussion, led by one of the trained instructors, of the concepts that they felt were relevant to them. Participants were also provided with an easy-to-read text (Collins, 1970) and a program guide (Wray & Thorson, 1975) that was written to bridge the gap between issues raised in the television shows and in the text. The combination of educational television, discussion, and supplementary reading made for a successful and popular series. Demand was such that the programs were later rebroadcast and more seminars were organized. By the end of the project period, a total of 18 eight-week community programs had been held, involving 718 participants. The series has since been broadcast by educational stations in New York, New Hampshire, and Missouri, and service agencies and retirement communities have ordered the shows on video cassettes.

Many institutions of higher education have followed the lead of the University of Michigan (Hunter, 1973) in the development of preretirement planning programs. For example, the University of Nebraska at Omaha has developed a multimedia program called, "Planning and the Third Age," that involves the use of slides, audio tape cassettes, and reading materials for groups of up to 25 people meeting in a series of 10 two-hour sessions. The program emphasizes human growth activities, content components, and integrating activities. Training of a group facilitator is included in the cost of the program package.

Although a former secretary of Health, Education, and Welfare has called for the development of a national program of preretirement counseling that individuals would begin at age 50 (Cohen, 1974), governmental and industry response has not kept pace with that of the educational institutions. Despite the demonstrated benefits of such programs for industrial workers (Glamser & DeJong, 1975), few United States corporations have developed retirement planning programs for their employees, and fewer still have developed them to the level of sophistication that is common in Western Europe. In 1969, for example, the Bekaert Steel Company of Zwevegem, Belgium, began the first cycle of what has developed into a 5-year program of preretirement preparation for its workers. Employees begin participation at age 60 for several hours weekly, with program contacts increasing to the equivalent of eight full working days at age 61, 12 days at age 62, a total of 48 half days at age 63, and another 48 half days for those age 64. Clinical medical examinations following each person's 60th, 62nd, and 64th years are a part of the routine. In groups of 15, professionals and factory workers together—with spouses participating in many cases—take part in a curriculum that includes conceptual information, cultural activities, and physical exercise. Participants learn of pension benefits and of insurance and tax matters, receive advice concerning family budgeting and housing, and learn to deal with problems of adjustment. Participants are responsible in most cases for planning their own group's activities. They have entered into the program with enthusiasm; the current rate of nonparticipation is 2%. Few companies in the United States have such comprehensive programs.

Educational institutions are now beginning to offer a variety of learning experiences for older people that may be seen as trends for the future. Special institutes for senior learners, at which older people live on campus for several days and participate in many enrichment activities, are being offered at institutions such as Clemson University, Georgia Southern College, and the University of Nebraska. Popular topics, again, revolve around instrumental themes such as development in later life, everyday law, assertiveness training, the role of the older woman, the legislative process, financial planning, nutrition, and coping with the energy crisis.

Other interesting trends involve successful, institutionalized programs that use older people as a teaching resource. Oakland University has a program in peer-group counseling that can definitely be seen as a forerunner of the kind of programs other institutions will be developing. Their Continuum Center trains older adults to be paraprofessional group leaders in a self-exploration program that is offered through community centers in the Detroit area (Waters, Fink, & White, 1976). Emeritus College in California is another example of an educational program that draws on the resources that older people can provide. Over 3,000 older people now take part in the classes and activities that are offered there. The prototype for this kind of institution is the New School for Social Research's Institute for Retired Professionals. Founded in 1962, the institute has a volunteer faculty of retired professors and professionals, and it offers older adults over 60 different courses at any one time. Topics range from current affairs and the social sciences to languages, literature, and the arts. Over 600 people regularly participate in the institute's courses. Programs such as these, that emphasize the usefulness and wisdom of older adults, ought to be seen as models for the program developers of the future. A variety of motivations and expectations are being met by these innovative programs. Learning tasks that may be vital for the older person of the next century are the subject of the next section.

SOME NEW LEARNING TASKS

In 1948, Havighurst (1974) proposed a series of developmental tasks of later maturity that have provided much of the focus for our thinking on development in the later decades of life. Briefly listed, they include:

1. Adjusting to decreasing physical strength and health
2. Adjusting to retirement and reduced income
3. Adjusting to death of spouse
4. Establishing an explicit affiliation with one's age group
5. Adopting and adapting social roles in a flexible way
6. Establishing satisfactory physical living arrangements (pp. 108-116)

Havighurst (1964) has also cited a series of dominant concerns, relating to particular decades of life, that govern a person's behavior. The dominant concerns listed for the decades from 60 to 70 and from 70 to 80 are, respectively, "deciding whether to disengage and how" and "making the most of disengagement" (p. 25). Older people of the future may well confront a different social situation than the current older generation but will, nonetheless, need to confront these tasks and concerns as they age. In fact, it can be seen that many of the educational programs described in the preceding section were designed to address one or more of these tasks or concerns.

There are, in addition, several other, interrelated *learning tasks* that will confront older people in years to come.

Adapting to Change

Much of adult, or any, learning is devoted to the acquisition of skills that will allow the learner to cope with the environment, adjust to reality, and learn how to adapt to change. A problem, of course, is the danger of accepting the wrong reality. Eisdorfer (1972) describes the problems of mental patients and dying patients adapting—through surprisingly effective learning behaviors—to situations imposed upon them by institutional environments rather than to the actual reality of their particular situations (pp. 47–49). Much learning behavior is adapting to change and adjusting to reality.

There is no reason to think that the older people of the future will be confronted with anything less than an increasingly accelerated rate of change in our society. As Toffler (1970) develops this concept in *Future Shock,* changes will come with increasing rapidity in future years; he maintains that those not able to cope with accelerated change will become what might be thought of as psychological dropouts, the truly disengaged people of society. The person who currently is 75, though, was born in the preflight era and now functions in the space age, giving us a marvelous example of the adaptability of the human species. Considering the great amount of change older people have successfully confronted, one might think of dismissing the concept of adaptation to change from a list of learning tasks and survival skills.

Holmes and Rahe (1967), however, have laid out a systematic method of looking at the real stress of adjusting to change as it is compounded in everyday life. Their observation has been that, whenever a large number of changes, or a number of large changes, occur in one's life, one becomes a prime candidate for a number of dysfunctions. These dysfunctions may be manifested as mental or physical illness, or as an increased susceptibility to things such as alcoholism, accidents, or suicide. Holmes and Rahe have developed a scale of stressful life events, assigning a point value to different incidents. The list starts with death of spouse (100 points) and includes divorce (73), marital separation (65), a jail term (63), and other stressful events on down to minor violations of the law (11). Everyone, of course, has a different breaking point, but Holmes and Rahe maintain that the general danger level is an accumulation of 200 or more points on the stress scale in any one 12-month period. Their theory would provide a rationale for the well-documented increases in mortality rates during the year following institutionalization as well as during the year following death of a spouse (Payne & Thorson, 1976). The point, of course, is that all people who live until old age go through stressful periods of development. Changes in life patterns that commonly occur late in life include retirement, loss of income, perhaps changes in physical health, loss of role and status, changes in the schedule of daily activities, perhaps children leaving the home, perhaps change in residence, change in recreation and social activities, and generally a host of small changes in living conditions and personal habits. The older person who has to confront one of the major stresses in life, such as the death of a spouse, would be well advised to sensibly manage or postpone other life changes for a period of time. Widows who sell their houses and move to other communities shortly after their husbands die are courting serious problems with the management of stress. As societal changes in the future accelerate, people, such as the elderly, who are at vulnerable transition points in life, will need education and counseling in the management of stress and in coping with change.

Continuing to Grow

It is now known that all older people do not necessarily disengage (Busse, 1969, pp. 27–28); longitudinal studies have shown little evidence to support the disengagement theory. There is a difference, however, between not disengaging and not becoming stagnated. Some older people cease to learn and to grow. For a variety of reasons, many older people have lost confidence in their own ability to learn and have accepted the stereotype that they can no longer be effective learners. Society conspires with this acceptance of a negative self-image by excluding older people from situations, such as work, that act as continuing stimuli for growth. To be able to gain the skills necessary for survival in the twenty-first century, older people will have to reject the forces that seek to disengage them from society, and they will have to seek new opportunities for growth.

Many scientists are now saying that a lack of educational opportunities has contributed to stagnation among older people. Baltes and Labouvie (1973) have said that

A concerted program of intervention will allow us to control large segments of intellectual aging to a greater degree than is commonly supposed. (p. 205)

and that

It seems justifiable to conclude that research has yielded a strong case for the essential plasticity of intellectual ontogeny during late adulthood and old age. In fact, the recognition that (a) intellectual aging is modifiable and (b) a significant portion of the gerontological ontogeny in intelligence reflects societal expectations and associated environmental settings allocates a major responsibility for innovation and change to society as a whole. (p. 202)

The lack of stimulus imposed by forces of society can be associated with mandatory retirement, barriers to participation erected by some educational institutions, and the youth orientation of public and private service programs. Such barriers to growth must be broken down. Older people who desire further development will benefit intellectually from the stimulation that increased interaction with the society will provide. Schaie (1975, p. 121) and Granick and Friedman (1973, p. 63) come to the same conclusion: people who live in a rich, stimulating environment will continue to grow; they will best maintain—and expand—their capabilities. Those who live in a static environment will decline. The failure to use intellectual capabilities will lead to intellectual atrophy and deterioration. Much like people who are raised in institutions, older people who are cut off from stimulation will show mental deficits. Pollack, Goldfarb, and Kahn (1962) see the situation, however, as hopeful: "The general increase in educational level, as well as improvements in medical care, would also seem to forecast a decrease in the proportionate degree of mental impairment to be found in our aged population of the future" (p. 613). Baltes and Labouvie (1973), as well as Birren and Woodruff (1973), have called for lifelong education as an intervention mechanism to insure that older people have adequate opportunities for continued growth.

Perpetuating the Culture, Putting One's Life into Perspective, and Finding Self-acceptance

These three learning tasks might be grouped together because they relate to the process of life review. Robert Butler (1963) and Butler and Lewis (1973) have said that the life review is a universal process that is normal and that is undertaken by all people as they age. They describe it as a progressive return to consciousness of past experiences and unresolved conflicts. A life review is often brought on by the realization of approaching death. If it is successful, the life review can give new meaning to life and reduce fear and anxiety (Butler & Lewis, 1973, p. 43).

Adult educators will note that introspective people may undergo several life reviews over the course of a life-span. Examples of this can readily be observed in people who return to the university in mid-life because of changes in their life plans or career goals. Butler says, however, that reminiscence and life reviewing provide a particular function among older people by helping them to put their lives in order.

A particularly interesting form of emerging adult education that relates to the three learning tasks listed and the concept of the life review is the writing by older adults of autobiographies or life histories. A retired educator, Leone Noble Western, has developed an organized system for recording significant life events, either on cards or tape recordings, and organizing the events into comprehensive life histories. Originally used at Fairhaven College in Bellingham, Washington, more than 4,000 older people across the state of Washington have now used Western's system. Writing one's autobiography might be seen as tantamount to going through the therapeutic process of a life review. It is an organized way of passing on the culture to family members who may live hundreds of miles away. It is good education, good recreation, good therapy—and good history. Many of the values and qualities of life in an earlier age are not transmitted to younger generations living in an increasingly complex society. People in the United States, many of whom move every couple of years, have been criticized as having no roots, and many of us do not know who we really are. A vital link to the past has been broken with the dissolution of the three-generation family. Many of us do not really know where our families came from and suffer from a lack of order and sense of place. Memoirs of one's grandparents would not only provide interesting family history, but would also help to establish generational continuity.

Passing on oral or written reminiscences is a way of perpetuating the culture, and it also helps people to put their life into perspective, to see who they really are, and to find self-acceptance. Butler (1963) points out the difficulty that younger people may have with patiently listening to this nostalgia, but he also refers to it as a natural healing process (Butler & Lewis, 1973, p. 44) that is necessary and healthy for the older person. He also points out its benefits for those fortunate enough to be able to listen to their elders review their lives (Butler, 1963):

> *In the course of the life review, the older person may reveal to his wife, children, and other intimates, unknown qualities of his character and unstated actions of his past; in return, they may reveal heretofore undisclosed or unknown truths. Hidden themes of great vintage may emerge, changing the quality of a lifelong relationship. Revelations of the past may forge a new intimacy, render a deceit honest; they may sever peculiar bonds and free tongues; or they may sculpture terrifying hatreds out of fluid, fitful antagonisms. (p. 75)*

Reviewing one's life, then, satisfies the learning tasks of perpetuating the culture, putting one's life into perspective, and finding order and self-acceptance in life. Butler says that it is such an important function that we might think in the future of employing paraprofessional listeners to assist older people in reviewing their lives. Such educational projects as life-history writing classes would serve a valuable function in encouraging this process.

Remaining Integrated in Society

Eisdorfer (1972) has said that people who suffer from mental illness in later life frequently are not the "loners" as much as the "aloners." Older people living alone have much higher rates of mental illness, alcoholism, suicide, and mortality than people of the same age who are not alone. Lowenthal (1964; Lowenthal & Haven, 1968) has documented the fact that isolation is a correlate, and perhaps a cause, of mental illness during old age.

Remaining integrated in society would seem to be not only a learning task, but almost a prerequisite for survival as well.

Because of the fact that most older people live alone, it is even more vital that they maintain contact with other individuals. Lacking the constant contact of a significant other, people who live alone need to make an extra effort to interact with and be stimulated by other people. It would seem that people who disengage do not pull themselves out of the social fabric so much as they are pushed out. Lowenthal & Haven (1968) show that maintenance of a close, personal relationship with at least one other person—a confidant—helps the older person to retain social and mental stability and avoid the negative effects of isolation. "The presence of an intimate relationship serves as a buffer both against gradual social losses in role and interaction and against the more traumatic losses accompanying widowhood and retirement" (p. 20). Although helping to foster confidant relationships among isolated, older people might seem to be more the role of the social worker than the adult educator, maintenance of contact with society is nonetheless an important learning task for older adults. With the increasing urbanization and depersonalization of the society of the future, educational programs for older adults can be seen to be important mechanisms that provide the setting for vital socialization opportunities.

Maintaining Control and Avoiding Helplessness

Too frequently, adult educators have seen their role in gerontology as providing educational opportunities for the young old, the active and alert people who can get out on their own and get to programs. Often, programs are merely serving the population that is easiest to reach. Few adult educators have realized that what they have to offer can actually be a kind of therapy for people who are really suffering from the decrements of old age. Labouvie-Vief (1976) has called for research on how intervention can assist older people to maintain control in the difficult situations that may be imposed upon them:

> It may be postulated that intervention-oriented research be directed not only to ameliorating possible cognitive deficits, but also to closing the competence-performance gap by modifying such noncognitive variables as self-confidence on labeling of self as competent or incompetent, and by encouraging a view of the self as effective and able to exert control. (p. 86)

A familiar phenomenon seen by health care personnel who work with the elderly is that, shortly after admission to a nursing home or other long-term care facility, a relatively large number seem to give up hope and die. Wershow (1976) has documented that 44% of the deaths that occur in the nursing homes in one metropolitan area take place during the first month after admission. It was observed during World War II that those prisoners of war who died in the camps seemed to be not necessarily the sickest or the most malnourished, but those who had given up control of their daily activities, become passive, and lain down and died. Richter (1959) has provided experimental data to document the fact that the giving up hope causes almost immediate death among laboratory animals. It has also been observed that nursing-home patients who stay in touch with their environment tend to have a better chance of survival. Seligman (1975) and Hooker (1976) have detailed the concept that *learned helplessness*—especially among those who are institutionalized—is a cause of disengagement and death. Helplessness comes as a learning experience to those who observe that there are no prospects for escape from an unacceptable environment. Under such circumstances, people cease to interact, lose the will to live, and literally give up the ghost.

Many of the current older generation grew up at a time when the county poor farm or rest home was the last stop in life for the elderly person who had no resources. They learned that people went to nursing homes to die, and, expectation being a predictor of behavior, many still make this association between institutionalization and death into a self-fulfilling prophecy. They exhibit an acceptance of the wrong reality and do not realize that many modern nursing homes rehabilitate people and return them to the community. The people who know that maintaining control over their lives is the surest route to regained health will be those who survive the institutionalization experience. Health care for the elderly of the future will of course improve from present levels of care, and more and more older people should look on the long-term care facility not as a place to die but as a place to get well. The educational gerontologist has a new role here of devising intervention strategies with institutionalized populations to teach them ways of maintaining control and avoiding helplessness.

CONCLUSIONS

Education for older people is a broad field. It ranges from providing social outlets with expressive learning activities in senior centers to instrumental education to equip older people with survival skills. All of these kinds of programs have their roles and serve functions. There will be an even greater diversity of programs in future years. Programming for older adults has emerged from being a small field in which token programs have occasionally been offered for a few older people to become a large and growing branch of adult education.

There will be many more older students in years to come. They will be healthier, wealthier, better educated, and more likely to demand a role in designing programs. They will also be more likely themselves to be educational resources. As self-images change, older adults will participate to a greater extent in adult learning, both in independent learning projects that are self-initiated, and in structured programs sponsored by educational institutions and community organizations. As barriers continue to fall, older people will more readily become integrated into educational programs that have, up to now, been designed primarily for younger people. As more people opt for early retirement, an increasing number of people will add vocational goals to the socialization and love-of-learning motivations.

Programmers must be cautious when designing programs not to fall into the trap of providing only what they think is good for older learners. Often, merely providing the setting for adults to interact is providing a needed service and therapy. Survival needs, of course, should be high on the list of necessary topics in the curriculum. It must be remembered, though, that older people should not be categorized. Not all senior adults are in need of services or need instruction in survival skills. A large number of the present and future participants in educational programs are, and will be, people who have mastery of their environment and have coped well with outside forces over the course of a life-span. Older people of the future will be a capable population; they will seek to accomplish their learning goals with energy and vitality. The role of the adult educator of the future will be to provide a wide variety of outlets and learning experiences and to involve the older people themselves in the design and accomplishment of their learning projects.

REFERENCES

Academy for Educational Development. *Never too old to learn.* New York: Author, 1974.

Baltes, P. B., & Labouvie, G. V. Adult development of intellectual performance: Description, explanation, and modification. In C. Eisdorfer & M. P. Lawton (Eds.), *The psychology of adult development and aging.* Washington, D.C.: American Psychological Association, 1973.

Birren, J. E., & Woodruff, D. S. Human development over the life span through education. In P. Baltes & W. Schaie (Eds.), *Life span developmental psychology.* New York: Academic, 1973.

Busse, E. W. Theories of aging. In E. Busse & E. Pfeiffer (Eds.), *Behavior and adaptation in late life.* Boston: Little, Brown, 1969.

Butler, R. N. The life review: An interpretation of reminiscence in the aged. *Psychiatry,* 1963, *26,* 65–76.

Butler, R. N., & Lewis, M. I. *Aging and mental health—Positive psychosocial approaches.* St. Louis: Mosby, 1973.

Cohen, W. Political implications of education for aging. In S. M. Grabowski & W. D. Mason (Eds.), *Learning for aging.* Washington, D.C.: Adult Education Association of the U.S.A., 1974.

Collins, T. *The complete guide to retirement.* Englewood Cliffs: Prentice-Hall, 1970.

Davis, R. H. Television communication and the elderly. In D. S. Woodruff & J. Birren (Eds.), *Aging—Scientific Perspectives and social issues.* New York: D. Van Nostrand, 1975.

Eisdorfer, C. Intellectual and cognitive changes in the aged. In Busse & Pfeiffer (Eds.), *Behavior and adaptation in late life.* Boston: Little, Brown, 1969.

Eisdorfer, C. The impact of scientific advances on independent living. In Thorson (Ed.), *Action now for older Americans toward independent living.* Athens: University of Georgia Center for Continuing Education, 1972.

Fowles, D. G., *Estimates of the size and characteristics of the older population in 1974 and projections to the year 2000* (U.S. Department of Health, Education and Welfare Statistical Memo No. 31) Washington, D.C.: U.S. Government Printing Office, 1975.

Glamser, F. D., & DeJong, G. F. The efficacy of preretirement preparation programs for industrial workers. *Journal of Gerontology,* 1975, *30,* 595–600.

Granick, S., & Friedman, A. S. Educational experiences and the maintenance of intellectual functioning by the aged: An overview. In L. Jarvik, C. Eisdorfer, & J. C. Blum (Eds.), *Intellectual functioning in adults.* New York: Springer, 1973.

Havighurst, R. J. Changing status and roles during the adult life cycle: Significance for adult education. In H. W. Burns (Ed.), *Sociological backgrounds of adult education.* Syracuse, N.Y.: Publications in Continuing Education of Syracuse University, 1964. (Originally published, 1963.)

Havighurst, R. J. The status of research in applied social gerontology. *The Gerontologist,* 1969, *9,* 5.

Havighurst, R. J. *Developmental tasks and education.* New York: David McKay, 1974.

Hiemstra, R. P. Continuing education for the aged: A survey of needs and interests of older people. *Adult Education,* February 1972, pp. 100–109.

Hiemstra, R. P. Educational planning for older adults: A survey of "expressive" vs. "instrumental" preferences. *International Journal of Aging and Human Development,* 1973, *4,* 147–156.

Holmes, T. H., & Rahe, R. H. The social readjustment rating scale. *Journal of Psychosomatic Research,* 1967, *11,* 213–218.

Hooker, C. E. Learned helplessness. *Social Work,* 1976, *21,* 194–198.

Houle, C. O. *The inquiring mind.* Madison: University of Wisconsin Press, 1963.

Hunter, W. W. *Preparation for retirement.* Ann Arbor: University of Michigan Institute of Gerontology, 1973.

Johnstone, J. W. C., & Rivera, R. J. *Volunteers for learning.* Chicago: Adline, 1965.

Labouvie-Vief, G. Toward optimizing cognitive competence in later life. *Educational Gerontology,* 1976, *1,* 75–92.

Labouvie-Vief, G., & Gonda, J. N. Cognitive strategy training and intellectual performance in the elderly. *Journal of Gerontology,* 1976, *31,* 327–332.

Leanse, J., & Wagner, S. B. *Senior centers: Report on senior group programs in America.* Washington, D.C.: National Council on the Aging, 1975.

Londoner, C. A. Survival needs of the aged: Implications for program planning. *International Journal of Aging and Human Development,* 1971, *2,* 113–117.

Lowenthal, M. F. Social isolation and mental illness in old age. *American Sociological Review,* 1964, *29,* 54–70.

Lowenthal, M. F., & Haven, C. Interaction and adaptation: Intimacy as a critical variable. *American Sociological Review,* 1968, *33,* 20–30.

McClusky, H. Y. Education and aging. In A. Hendrickson (Ed.), *A manual on planning educational programs for older adults.* Tallahassee: Florida State University, Department of Adult Education, 1973.

Payne, B. P., & Thorson, J. A. Death and mental health. In R. Kronley (Ed.), *Exploring mental health parameters* (Vol. II). Atlanta: Paje Publishing Co., 1976.

Peterson, D. A. Educational gerontology: The state of the art. *Educational Gerontology,* 1976, *1,* 61–73.

Pollack, M., Goldfarb, A. I., & Kahn, R. L. Social factors and mental illness in the institutionalized aged person: Role of education. In C. Tibbitts and W. T. Donahue (Eds.), *Social and psychological aspects of aging.* New York: Columbia University Press, 1962.

Rawlings, J. *Reduced fees for older adults.* A report to the University Senate of Ball State University, Muncie, Ind., March 28, 1974.

Rhyne, D. C. Variations on a theme by Thorndike. *Adult Education,* 1962, *12,* 91–97.

Richter, C. P. The phenomenon of unexplained sudden death in animals and man. In Feifel (Ed.), *The meaning of death.* New York: McGraw-Hill, 1959.

Riley, M. W., & Foner, A. *Aging and society (Vol. I: An inventory of research findings).* New York: Russell Sage Foundation, 1968.

Schaie, K. W. Age changes in adult intelligence. In D. S. Woodruff & J. E. Birren (Eds.), *Aging—Scientific perspectives and social issues.* New York: D. Van Nostrand, 1975.

Schramm, W. Aging and mass communication. In M. W. Riley, J. W. Riley, & M. E. Johnson (Eds.), *Aging and society (Vol. II: Aging and the professions).* New York: Russell Sage Foundation, 1969.

Seligman, M. E. P. *Helplessness.* San Francisco: W. H. Freeman, 1975.

Thorson, J. A. Attitudes toward the aged as a function of race and social class. *The Gerontologist,* 1975, *15,* 343–344. (a)

Thorson, J. A. *Variations in attitudes toward the aged held by selected groups in the southern United States.* A paper presented at the 10th International Congress of Gerontology, Jerusalem, Israel, June 27, 1975. (b)

Thorson, J. A. A media approach to pre-retirement education. *Adult Leadership,* 1976, *24,* 344–346.

Toffler, A. *Future shock.* New York: Random House, 1970.

Tough, A. *The adult's learning projects: A fresh approach to theory and practice in adult learning.* Toronto: Ontario Institute for Studies in Education, 1971.

Waters, E., Fink, S., & White, B. Peer group counseling for older people. *Educational Gerontology*, 1976, *1*, 157–170.

Wershow, H. J. The four percent fallacy—Some further evidence and policy implications. *The Gerontologist*, 1976, *16*, 52–55.

Whatley, L. F. *Expressive and instrumental educational interests of older adults as perceived by adult educators, gerontologists, and older adults.* Unpublished master's thesis, University of Georgia, 1974.

Wray, R. P., & Thorson, J. A. *New wrinkles on retirement.* Athens, Ga.: University of Georgia Center for Continuing Education, 1975.

12

MODELS OF COGNITIVE FUNCTIONING IN THE OLDER ADULT: RESEARCH NEEDS IN EDUCATIONAL GERONTOLOGY

GISELA LABOUVIE-VIEF

Wayne State University

Recent demands for extending educational opportunities to the later phases of the life cycle have created new and unprecedented needs for educators, who are consequently searching for data and theory to answer their questions as they attempt to design sound, specialized programs for older learners. It is my purpose in this chapter to explore some possible answers from my perspective as a psychologist interested in life-span developmental processes. On the one hand, given the interdisciplinary nature of the problem, my perspective may well be somewhat limited; on the other hand, such a life-span view may also serve to broaden our understanding of the problem. A primary focus on processes of development may force us to examine any answers, not merely from the vantage point of how currently available research can be translated into classroom applications, but also with the superordinate goal in mind of understanding all those interactions of elderly people with each other, with other strata of society, and even with researchers, and of understanding as well the ways in which those interactions may serve to enhance or dampen cognitive competence in later life.

The main thesis of this chapter may at first sound overly pessimistic, but I hope it may help to delineate more sharply the research needs in learning, intelligence, and cognitive processes in later life. According to this thesis, the emerging emphasis on growth, change, and education in later life has caught the theoretician as much by surprise as it did the practitioner. Both have been socialized into an outlook on late adulthood that has its roots in a static conceptualization of the needs and capabilities of the older adult. Both have come to expect adulthood to be the achievement of a static level of maturity and the endpoint, rather than the continuation, of education. As a result, we are now observing a curious mismatch between theory and social reality: whereas much of our theory appears to document the frailties and limitations of old age, this picture is already being denied by many elderly who are searching for avenues toward continued growth.

The rapid changes in our society, of which this mismatch is but one indication, have created, among theorists concerned with the developmental capacities of adults, a growing disenchantment with the available body of theoretical constructs, research methodologies, and even content issues, all of which appear better suited to the past than to the present, let alone the future. As a result, the time-worn and comfortable assumptions that we have held about the abilities of the older individual are eroding, and we are beginning to expose a new view of adult development that is opening up new interpretations, new avenues of research, and new goals as they relate to education in later life.

In this chapter, therefore, I am not attempting to derive prescriptive statements about the education of older people from what at present appears to be an accepted body of knowledge about the intellectual and cognitive capabilities of the aging individual. Toffler (1974) has recently argued that goals and policies relating to education must spring from images about the future. To search for answers in the past is merely to adopt a timeless view of development in which yesterday predicts today and in which tomorrow is only more of today. Such a view is bound to yield obsolete research findings, for phenomena are changing at a faster rate than researchers are able to provide useful data about them. In line with this position, I am less concerned with clear answers than with raising questions, less with knowledge as a static goal than with knowledge as a process and a potentiality.

IDEALISM IN ADULT
DEVELOPMENTAL THEORY

At first sight, the problem of isolating those issues and questions that are particularly deserving of research attention in the future may appear simple enough; we might elect simply to survey issues on the basis of some assessment of empirical needs. The problem is not quite so straightforward, however. This is so because, for those trained in a particular discipline, interesting research problems are not defined merely by current needs (e.g., the educational needs of older populations); rather, many of those research problems appear to involve a time dimension that is more easily grasped from a historic perspective. Any scientific discipline tends to evolve a specialized language, a certain way of looking at reality, that may often appear to be somewhat removed from real-life applications. Indeed, it is often this language system that not only reformulates important real-life issues, but also generates new corollary issues that, although they may be highly challenging to the community of scientists, are often rather removed from any immediate, practical import.

The point just raised is of some importance because, contrary to widespread popular opinion, the activity of researchers does not merely amount to constructing a faithful copy of "things as they are." Rather, it is our own ways of conceptualizing, interpreting, and looking at things that determine the way they appear in the first place. This is why merely recording currently known findings in the area of adult cognitive functioning may not be particularly useful in elucidating what we need to know. Instead, we need to go one step further here and consider why, in the past, certain questions have been deemed more worthwhile of research attention than others, why certain interpretations have been favored, and why, as a result, many current views of adulthood are slanted toward a picture that is not necessarily complete, convincing, or valid.

Idealistic Views of Development

The traditional view of how our knowledge of certain empirical givens originates has been to assert that this knowledge derives from a careful recording of reality. Knowledge, in this view, is not seen to be potentially contaminated by more pragmatic considerations such as its usefulness or its compatibility with a certain ideological position, but is thought, rather, to be somehow defined, independent of human existence, in an a priori sense. This view is expressed in Plato's theory of innate ideas, which has exerted a powerful influence on Western philosophy of science and serves as a model for many current ways of conceptualizing the process of development. It was Plato's assertion that the concepts, truths, and laws known to humans were not merely a somewhat whimsical construction by human minds, but rather reflected a system of laws and truths inherent in the universe. Development from birth to maturity could thus in many ways be likened to a "rediscovery" of those innate ideas, and the most mature level of development—the age of reason—would therefore be the time in a persons's life-span at which these universal truths could be understood with a relatively high degree of faithfulness. Thus, the end of development is thought to be fixed a priori by some ideal conception of maturity, and as a result, views of development deriving from the Platonic system may be called *idealistic* (Labouvie-Vief & Chandler, 1978; Riegel, 1975).

To be sure, the particular basis, according to which the ideal outcome of development was fixed, has varied throughout the course of the centuries (*see*, for example, Muuss, 1975). Thus, in medieval systems, maturity was a state of knowledge of principles revealed to humans from God, whereas more recent theories have opted for a more evolutionary view according to which "mature" criteria represent the highest evolutionary accomplishment of which humans are capable. Whatever the basis, however, the resulting views of development all fit one general pattern. As development is thought to be realized in some fixed goal or end state, it is thought to be teleologically oriented toward this final stage of maturity. Just as this mature state is given a priori, so also is the route along which individuals move as they mature: growth is thought to proceed in a unilinear fashion, moving through a series of imperfect, preliminary stages until the ultimate, ideal stage is realized. As development is thus conceptualized in terms of ideal end states that are realized via a universal development pathway, the ensuing notion of development acquires prescriptive overtones; that is, it serves as a standard against which to judge variations in the rate of progression and final achievements of development. What is "normal" in development, consequently, is judged, not by pragmatic criteria, but by idealistic standards.

Although still popular in development psychology, similar idealistic notions have largely been abandoned in contemporary philosophy. The danger inherent in idealistic positions, as pointed out by several writers (e.g., Barrett, 1962; Habermas, 1971), is that they may easily confuse descriptive and normative aspects of a science. Thus, recording and observing the course of development often becomes equivalent to theorizing about it: The resulting patterns of development are assumed to be indicative of one, universal, organic process of development that is not substantially altered if examined from other perspectives, for example, from those of other subcultural groups, other cultures, or other periods of history. Such a position easily entails the danger of ruling diversity in development out of court. More recent views, in fact, have emphasized that what appears to be a relatively firm objective truth from the perspective of idealism, often may be contaminated by particular biases, interests, and time-bound conceptions that are not objective by any means.

The position that research findings and accepted "truths" of a science are only relative to particular ideological contexts from which they emerge has quite profound implications for our current evaluation of what is known about adult development. In line with others (e.g., Buss, 1975; Gergen, 1973; Giorgi, 1971), I maintain that much of what is currently accepted about the capacities of older people must be taken with a bit of caution, as it is likely to reflect not inevitable psychological processes, but cultural norms that need to be reexamined on the basis of their particular historical-ideological context.

Prevalent Conceptualizations of Adult Intelligence

Before discussing more specifically some of the pitfalls that idealistic notions of development may entail, it may be useful to present a brief synopsis of current conceptualizations of adult intelligence, together with a discussion of how their idealistic slant may have resulted in a somewhat prejudicial account of what older people can do. As argued previously (e.g., Baltes & Labouvie, 1973; Labouvie-Vief & Chandler, 1978), the notion underlying much of life-span cognitive theory is one that has proven to be a useful working assumption primarily when discussing development from infancy to adolescence. According to this notion, intellectual development displays distinctive features of growth (e.g., Flavell, 1970): it is thought to be relatively momentous, universal, and irreversible. This uniform, normal growth pattern is usually attributed to the constraining principles of biological-maturational growth; it does not discount the role of experience in intellectual development, however. Experience is thought to operate in concert with the constraining process of biological growth. Thus, although experience may introduce a source of variation, uniformity of growth is nevertheless virtually guaranteed, and the resulting deviations from an idealistically conceived developmental path are attributed to differential tempos of development.

The conviction that childhood development follows highly universal pathways and is characterized by rather dramatic transformations from stage to stage may have created a bias in theoreticians of adult development to primarily attend to similar, eye-catching phenomena in late life. Thus, much of current theorizing about life-span cognition can be seen as an effort to isolate what one might call "true," "normal," and universal components of aging, which are contrasted with those processes of development not held to be intrinsic to aging. This dualistic system of normal and extrinsic factors of aging has provided a framework for what, in reality, is a highly diverse pattern of both improvements and deterioration in tasks of intellectual competence throughout adulthood and old age.

The empirical data on intellectual change after maturity have been extensively summarized elsewhere (e.g., Baltes & Labouvie, 1973; Botwinick, 1967, 1973; Horn, 1976; Jarvik & Cohen, 1973), and a brief summary will suffice at this point. Those functions that appear to be least sensitive to the passage of time are, in general, those thought to reflect the effects of lifelong learning. Thus, cognitive tests that assess an individual's accumulation of verbal skills and general information, or tasks of learning, memory, and problem solving that are well embedded in a matrix of meaning, are those typically found to improve throughout adulthood and well into old age. On the other hand, tests relating to the perception of relationships among abstract symbols (e.g., geometric shapes), to the integration of new and complex material, or to the effective use of information under conditions of time restriction and in highly abstract contexts are the kinds of tests on which older adults tend to do much more poorly than their younger counterparts.

On an empirical level, this differential pattern of growth and decline has been substantiated across literally hundreds of research studies, and it must therefore be accepted as a rather sound finding of the geropsychological literature. What is less convincing, however, is the theoretical interpretation it has received. It has often been thought that the abstract, more *age-sensitive* (Botwinick, 1967) measures are particularly telling of a presumed, primary universal component of aging. Specifically, it has been proposed that these more abstract performances are particularly well integrated with biological-maturational processes and that their decline is tied to "loss and degeneration of the psychological (particularly neurological) substratum, as produced either by (or both by) catabolic maturational changes or (and) irreversible damage brought on by illness and injuries" (Horn, 1976, p. 463). In contrast, the cognitive, *age-insensitive*, functions were usually thought to be less telling of such sweeping and universal aging processes. Rather, they are usually said to reflect the effects of lifelong information accumulation and the overlearning of well-established habits and, therefore, have not been of as much interest to many developmental psychologists because they are viewed as distractions from the truly dramatic effects of advanced age on cognitive functioning.

Thus, we see that the rather dramatic picture of childhood cognitive changes is, in essence, continued throughout the rest of the life-span. Aging processes, like earlier developmental changes, are thought to display the characteristics of universality and irreversibility; although, unlike growth processes, they are regressive rather than progressive. But we also see that this continuity of theoretical interpretation along the age continuum is bought at a certain expense: "True" aging no longer is universally expressed across the total range of behaviors. In fact, it appears only if one becomes rather selective in the definition of what are valid criteria of true aging. Whether or not one is willing to underwrite traditional interpretations of adult cognitive functioning, as a consequence, depends upon whether one feels this selectivity is an asset or a fateful limitation of one's view.

The latter opinion has been expressed in a number of recent writings that despite the rather overwhelming case against cognitive competence in later life, have opted for a more positive view by questioning the heavy decremental emphasis in traditional theories of intellectual aging. Decrement, according to these interpretations, is not necessarily a reality of adult cognitive functioning; it may result from the fact that current models of life-span intellectual functioning contain a number of unquestioned and untested assumptions and from the fact that the interpretations, as a consequence, may be based upon biased methodologies and unduly narrow measures of cognitive performance.

At the crux of the emerging, competing interpretations is the recognition that generalizations from empirical data often tend to confuse descriptive and normative aspects. That there *is* a relationship between increasing age and decreasing competence on tests of speeded, abstract performance certainly is descriptively accurate. What is less certain, however, is that this empirical fact can be construed to represent a theoretical law, or the prescriptive, idealistic conclusion that such a relationship *ought* to exist. This questionable "is" to "ought" (Kohlberg, 1971) reference, in fact, has formed the basis for several equally fateful assumptions, which are discussed more fully throughout the remainder of this chapter.

The first of these assumptions relates to the presumptive organizing principles of development, which are seen to reflect the epigenetic unfolding of biological-maturational capacities. This maturational bias has not only resulted in a tendency to biologize the aging process on the basis of quite inadequate evidence, but—with its corollary assumption of the irreversibility of such changes—has also led to a too-ready acceptance of the view that whatever apparent decrement was demonstrated reflected the result of a universal, irreversible process of deterioration. A second assumption is that development is universal and therefore transcends boundaries of history, culture, and locale; as a consequence, the potential transitoriness of what appeared to be relatively inevitable aging changes has not been sufficiently subjected to critical test. A third assumption, recently reevaluated, relates to the presumed teleological end goal of development. Although it is probably true that any developmental analysis ought to presuppose a rather thorough conceptualization of its end point, it is also true, however, that most theories of cognitive development may have located this "final" stage at a rather early point in the life-span. As a result, the achievements of adults and older people are rarely assessed against age-appropriate standards, but more often against those of adolescents and youth who may be involved in wrapping up the final stages of their formal education. By this comparison standard, the achievements of adults and elderly individuals often have appeared static at best, amateurish at worst. Finally, as it was believed that all of behavior is ultimately governed by the same set of universal, maturational principles, there has been an implicit tendency to think that the particular behavior under study did not really matter. In contrast, I think that this assumption, rather than guaranteeing truly universal insights about the learning of the elderly, has encouraged criterion measures of learning and cognition that may be best suited to the relatively lifeless, meaningless context of a laboratory and at least suited to the concrete, day-to-day demands adults encounter.

PSYCHOBIOLOGICAL MATURATION AND COGNITION IN THE ELDERLY

Although the notion that cognitive development grows and declines under the control of physical maturation carries much intuitive appeal, this assumption is, in actuality, supported by a minimum of empirical evidence. It is, rather, most usually an explanatory hypothesis thought to subsume two major sets of observations. First, as already pointed out, developmental changes, at least those from childhood to adulthood, often appear to be both universal and dramatic: "Cognitive changes during childhood have a specific set of 'morpho genetic' properties that presumably stem from the biological-maturational growth process underlying these changes: Thus, childhood cognitive modifications are largely inevitable, momentous, directional, uniform, and irreversible" (Flavell, 1970, p. 247). Second, this organismic maturational hypothesis appeared to provide an adequate explanatory framework for the large body of empirical data on the decline of abstract cognitive functioning alluded to in the previous section.

What evidence, then, is there for the supposition that the same kind of organismic maturational control applies to postmaturational development? As Baltes and Labouvie (1973; *see also* Labouvie-Vief, 1976) have pointed out, the presumed causal connectedness between maturational changes and certain cognitive functions has rarely been subject to any rigorous empirical tests. Often, for instance, studies that have claimed to support an association between symptoms of biological and psychological deterioration have actually inferred both from behavioral data such as tests of intellectual and memory functions; thus, they merely attest to the fact that cognitive decline on one set of psychological measures is often predictive of decline on others. Also, many studies have merely conjectured that cognitive decline must be caused by biological decline, supporting their arguments by pointing to the many instances in which aging and biological deterioration are correlated. To find evidence of psychological decline in one sample of elderly people and to find indexes of biological deterioration in other, independent samples does not really permit a causal connection of the two sets of syndromes to be made. Even if both were found to be correlated across the same set of subjects, one cannot infer causal dependencies, as it is not clear which set of changes causes which.

In most cases, therefore, the notion of psychobiological maturation is used as a hypothesis that in actuality, refers to a host of unspecified processes presumed to be organic and biological (Baltes & Labouvie, 1973; Denney & Wright, 1975). It is important, as a consequence, to clearly differentiate between the changes for which there are unmistakable organic antecedents, and those changes that show considerable covariation with other factors (i.e., environmental and sociological factors).

Biological Antecedents

If examined from a more stringent perspective, in fact, the notion that biological decline inevitably brings about cognitive decrement in later life appears to have rather restricted validity. Much recent evidence, for instance, points to the conclusion that neither decline in cognitive functions nor biological decrement are normally distributed within the population of the elderly but are instead indicators of conditions of pathology, poor health, and/or nearness to death (Birren, 1970). Thus, strong relationships between biological indicators and cognitive performance are usually found only in those elderly subjects who may already show signs of failing health, such as people with elevated blood pressure (Eisdorfer & Wilkie, 1973) or institutionalized elderly subjects who suffer from various neuropsychiatric disorders (Obrist, Busse, Eisdorfer, & Kleemeier, 1962; Wang, 1973). In contrast, two major studies observed no such correlation. In one of these, (Birren, Butler, Greenhouse, Sokoloff, & Yarrow, 1963), a sample of exceptionally healthy elderly men was subjected to a variety of medical and psychological assessments, and the number of significant biobehavior relationships in this sample proved to be negligible. In a second, more representative study, Hertzog, Gribbin, and Schaie (1975) in a 14-year longitudinal study sought to isolate physical health antecedents of cognitive declines. Although there were indexes of such health problems as hypertension and arteriosclerotic disease, none of these were correlated with the declines that appeared in some subjects. Hence, it now appears that no significant portion of variance in intellectual behavior may be accounted for by readily demonstrated maturational change *as long as* subjects are in reasonably good health and/or living in the community.

Conversely, where cognitive and biological changes occur together, they may both be indicative of major health changes that eventually lead to natural death. Thus, several researchers have conducted large-scale, longitudinal studies in which it was possible, as subjects died out of the research population, to retrospectively examine cognitive changes, not as a function of chronological age, but of distance from death (Eisdorfer & Wilkie, 1973; Jarvik, 1973; Palmore & Cleveland, 1976; Riegel & Riegel, 1972). Once the reference point was changed in this way, most of the elderly appeared to exhibit, throughout their adult life-spans, a remarkably stable level of intellectual functioning; it was only in the few years preceding death that major cognitive declines became apparent, which usually were accompanied by arteriovascular and cerebrovascular disease. Thus again, the conclusion is suggested that cognitive impairment is not so much a universal concomitant of advancing age as of impending death. This conclusion would suggest, of course, that great care must be taken in the selection of these samples of elderly subjects from which one wishes to draw generalizations concerning a "normal" aging process—a precaution that has not been observed by many researchers who, under the pressures of time and economic restrictions, may have relied on captive populations of elderly subjects who tend to represent the lower, more frail spectrum of the total population of the elderly.

In light of the difficulty in establishing powerful biocognitive relationships in relatively healthy, normal samples of elderly subjects, the frequent explanation of adult cognitive decrement in terms of progressive neural impairment is being challenged for a major portion of the adult life-span. Birren (1963), in this context, has argued for the possibility of a discontinuous relationship between physiological indexes and cognitive behavior. According to this *discontinuity* hypothesis, physiological factors account for variability in behavior only if they reach critical abnormal ranges, as they will in individuals suffering pathology or approaching death. As long as they stay within a normal range, physiological conditions provide a necessary basis for behavior, but they become determining and sufficient causes only when healthy limits are exceeded. If they are not, there appears to be little evidence to point to the notion of universal biologically based cognitive declines; thus, the assumption of unidirectional (biology ⟩ behavior) cause–effect sequences may be a highly problematic one and should be rejected in favor of more complex, interactive models (*see also* Flavell, 1970; Reese, 1973; Woodruff, 1973, 1975).

If health may not constitute such a powerful explanatory variable—at least as long as health is measured by such relatively crude parameters as the absence or presence of pathology—what, then, may be the causes of cognitive decline in later life? Many such causes, I think may lie in defeating life-styles and environmental conditions that may be detrimental to high-level cognitive functioning. This is not to say, however, that such causes may not have a biological component or concomitant. Some researchers, for instance, have conjectured that such life-style factors as physical exercise habits—rather than aging, per se—may be predictive of cognitive declines. Botwinick and Thompson (1971) have suggested that age differences in psychomotor speed may be related to poor exercise habits rather than to age. Lack of physical exercise has similarly been implicated in the decline of measures of abstract intelligence (Barry, Steinmetz, Page, & Rodahl, 1966; Powell & Pohndorf, 1971). In another study (Woodruff, 1973, 1975), it was suggested that slow behavior in the elderly, together with its biological mediator (brain-wave slowing), might be a result of certain learning experiences rather than an inevitable consequence of advanced age.

It is important to stress that the above arguments and data are not to be construed as a rejection of the role of biological factors in the cognitive performance of older subjects. To do so, in fact, would be shortsighted and violate the intuitive conviction of most behavioral scientists that behavioral expressions must in some way have a physical counterpart. They do suggest, however, that the role of biology in much of past research on the aging process has been conceptualized in altogether too simplistic a fashion, in that often biological decrement was accepted as an a priori given out of which behavioral decrement would, in some automatic and inevitable sense, naturally follow. What is more likely, instead, is that both biological and psychological changes may often be a result of certain conditions of life, and in this sense, are more intricately and interactively related (Woodruff, 1975). What these conditions are, of course, remains to be shown by future research. I can, however, suggest some that may be particularly fruitful candidates for research attention. I have already alluded to the role of habits of physical exercise. Other important sets of factors might relate to nutritional and dietary practices, to preventive health practices, and, as I argue later, to even more "psychological" habits geared toward the maintenance of effective coping styles.

Behavioral Plasticity

If one opts for a less inevitable relationship between advancing age and cognitive performance, it is also natural to pose the question of whether cognitive declines, in those cases where they do occur, are really a sign of some irreversible, deteriorative process. In the past, many studies suggested this interpretation; more recently, however, considerable interest has mounted in examining whether it has been premature to conceive of the elderly individual's cognitive performance as something beyond adaptive control. To examine this issue, a number of researchers have introduced systematic variations into the conditions under which cognitive performance was assessed and then observed the effects of such treatments on subsequent cognitive performance.

I have already remarked on interventions that may take place on a more biological level, and several authors have indeed reported positive results on indicators of cognitive functioning as a function of either physical exercise (Barry et al., 1966; Powell, 1974) or biofeedback training (Woodruff, 1975). What is of particular significance about these studies is that they have utilized measures of abstract reasoning or speeded performance—those indexes that have, in the past, been linked with "normal," age-related, biological deterioration. Similarly, comparable measures were found to respond quite favorably to more psychological interventions as well. In one study (Hoyer, Labouvie, & Baltes, 1973), for instance, it was hypothesized that the often-reported low levels of functioning on highly speeded tests might reflect the elderly person's lack of experience with such tasks. Consequently, a sample of elderly women received some training on three tests of psychomotor speed. Despite the brevity of the training program, which consisted of two 30-minute sessions, subjects were found to significantly improve their speeds.

In another study (Labouvie-Vief & Gonda, 1976), elderly subjects received training in the particular strategies that are helpful in solving abstract cognitive problems. It was believed that, as a function of either lack of experience or heightened apprehension, older people might engage in a variety of behaviors that are irrelevant and even detrimental to the solutions of such tasks (e.g., not systematically scanning all components of an item or repeatedly asserting that one is not "clever" enough to figure an item out). More helpful behaviors were modeled for the subjects, who subsequently improved their performances, not only on the same tasks, but also on related ones. Moreover, this positive training effect could still be demonstrated two weeks after initial training—an unlikely result if one favors a simple biological-decrement interpretation. Similar results have also been reported in a series of other studies (Denney, 1974; Hornblum & Overton, 1976; Ismael & Labouvie-Vief, 1976; Mergler & Hoyer, 1975; Panicucci & Labouvie-Vief, 1975; Plemons, Willis, & Baltes, 1975), and further research has suggested that poor cognitive performance may be the result of the older person's greater susceptibility to fatigue (Furry & Baltes, 1973), raised anxiety level (Eisdorfer, Nowlin, & Wilkie, 1971), or reluctance to merely guess when not sure (Birkhill & Schaie, 1975)—a strategy automatically adopted by any younger person who knows the advantage of guessing in such tasks.

What are the implications of these studies for future research? In a sense, it is easiest to state the implications at a very general level. I believe that, despite all the evidence that might cause the case for a severe cognitive deficit to appear open and shut, more recent studies would suggest that the case deserves serious reevaluation. Often, relatively fateful conclusions concerning the older adult's adaptability have been resolved on the basis of fairly superficial examination, usually relying on single-occasion, one-shot assessments. The ready tendency of older people to respond favorably to a variety of helpful interventions, however, suggests that this weighty conclusion is a most unfortunate one. It often seems, indeed, that what older people do at first in tasks of learning and cognition is a rather invalid indicator of what they *can* do, given the right kinds of supports and conditions. At present, of course, we know little about what exactly those conditions are, although some of them are discussed more fully in a later section. To discover the various factors that might aid in the optimization of cognitive adaptability and continued learning, therefore, presents a tremendous challenge to future generations of researchers.

SOCIOHISTORICAL CONTEXT AND ADULT INTELLIGENCE

Much of the evidence reviewed in the previous section certainly is difficult to reconcile with the assumption that cognitive behavior in adults and older people is bound to decline as a function of some species-specific, epigenetic developmental program. Whatever this program might be, we find evidence to suggest that the resulting trajectories are not so inevitably fixed, but may be significantly altered under the influence of certain external and situational indexes. Indeed, it is my conviction that more situational variables are of much greater importance than has traditionally been conceded; and, as I demonstrate in this section, this likelihood has a tremendous number of exciting implications for further research on the education of older people.

Historical Time

I have argued that much of the somewhat negative and fatalistic outlook on adult intelligence may have been a result of a view of development that was relatively static and fixed and that this bias appears to have caused a certain degree of methodological oblivion on the part of many researchers concerned with the intellectual competence of older adults. This same oblivion is also reflected in the use of the very paradigm that developmental psychologists have long deemed appropriate to the study of ontogenetic change. As such research is usually carved out of a cross-section of subjects of varying ages obtained at one particular historical date, the assumption that the resulting age-group differences reflect nothing but the effects of development on behavior carries with it the implicit conviction that neither the particular historical point at which a study was done, nor the widely different historical strata in which different subjects were born and raised, must really be a matter of deep concern to theoreticians of development and aging.

As originally pointed out by Kuhlen (1963), Schaie (1965), and Baltes (1968), however, the idealistic notion that development can be assessed with the use of what Proshansky (1976) has called "time-less" cross-sectional designs contains serious difficulties. Their argument is perhaps most intuitively grasped by citing evidence, not from the area of intellectual development, but of age-related changes in physical development. Although this aspect of development is truly universal in the sense that adolescents of all cultures and historical times pass through the growth acceleration accompanying puberty, it is also known that this pattern varies somewhat across cultural groups and historical times (Tanner, 1972). Thus, the final, adult height achieved at the end of pubescence, over the course of the last two decades or so, has increased at the rate of about one inch per generation. As a consequence, if one were to take a cross-section of adults originating from different generations, one would observe an age-related decrease in height; a decrease that does not reflect developmental *change* over one's adult life-span, however, but results from generation-related growth acceleration that has differentially affected each of the generations in the study population.

Similarly, as in any cross-sectional study in which subjects differ, not only in age, but in their birth years as well, the resulting "age" differences may actually reflect either developmental or historical change, or they may be a compound of both. This argument, almost self-evident if such behaviors as sex-role conceptualizations or political attitudes are under consideration, still has, for many, an almost heretical ring when applied to something as immutable as intelligence. Yet, if appropriate designs are implemented (Nesselroade, Schaie, & Baltes, 1972; Schaie, Labouvie, & Buech, 1973), it is invariably found that intraindividual, longitudinal changes in people of the same age (originating from the same cohort) are minor as each cohort maintains a stable performance level through periods as long as 14 years. Thus, the sharp drops so typically found in cross-sectional gradients are an artifact. They do not assess age change at all, but rather, pronounced differences in the performance levels of successive cohorts. Consequently, it is not in relation to their own younger days that the aged can be described as deficient, but only in relation to younger, better educated populations.

Thus, as Nesselroade and Baltes (1974) have argued, we see that a quite distorted picture of the process of development may be the result of the use of designs based upon an essentially ahistoric idea of ontogenesis that ultimately is rooted in the idea of idealistically predetermined developmental outcomes. Instead, the existence of generation-related differences in behavior forces one's attention to the fact that development does not merely unfold in a cultural-historical vacuum; it is inextricably interwoven with a particular sociohistorical context.

Intelligence and
the Social Context of Aging

We conclude, then, that what is "normal" and presumably universal in development may often be a relative matter in that is rather futile to talk about development without consideration of the influence of a particular sociocultural milieu. As a result, it is also more compelling to look at the often-reported, age-related ups and downs of cognitive development not so much as an inevitable, preprogrammed course of cognitive growth and decline, but as something that is fashioned by the particular growth-generating or growth-attenuating experiences that adult and aging individuals are encountering. This conclusion restates, in fact, the proposition cited earlier that throughout adulthood—and in the view of other authors (e.g., Baer, 1973; Gewirtz, 1969; Nesselroade & Baltes, 1974), throughout the total *process* of development—it may be variables related to one's social context rather than to one's age that account for the particular developmental gradients obtained. Rather than relying on quasi-biological arguments, such a viewpoint suggests that one consider a variety of change-producing experiences throughout adult life. Whether they be called societal "prods and brakes" (Neugarten and Datan, 1973), "changing reinforcement systems" (Labouvie-Vief, Hoyer, Baltes, & Baltes, 1974; Lindsley, 1964), or "normative life crises" (Datan & Ginsberg, 1975), such experiences, then, ought to be viewed as the catalysts that activate cognitive change.

Such an interpretation has extremely important implications for theory and research on adult and elderly populations. Consider, first, the now-accepted finding that throughout most of adulthood intellectual development is characterized by stability rather than by change. On the one hand, one might take this as a somewhat uninteresting, though encouraging, indication of the fact that most of adulthood is a rather static period. On the other hand, one might wish to doubt this apparent peacefulness and argue that what appears to be stability is merely a somewhat artifactual result of the likely fact that most, significant, adult experiences (e.g., establishment of a career, marriage, parenthood) are rather poorly ordered along an age continuum, so that the stable picture might just be the result of the smoothing out, by averaging, of individual developmental pathways that actually display considerable warps. If this were true, it would be much more fruitful to examine adulthood changes in cognition, not as a function of chronological age, but as a function of the temporal distance from one or another of these life crises. As similar research based on younger populations has suggested (*see* Bayley, 1970; Bloom, 1964), the apparent placidity of adult intellectual change might easily break up into a fascinating pattern of highs and lows if research subjects were grouped according to shared life experiences rather than according to age.

This same interpretation may also shed new light on what does appear to be rather universal developmental progression. If universality is sought, not in age, but in certain invariant context-behavior relationships, then apparent universality in developmental progression may be seen to reflect the fact that a particular context, or change in context, is the function of certain social policies. Such policies (e.g., entrance into school, college, or retirement) may be age graded due to particular economic and political conditions, but may not really reflect any inherent developmental capacities that are often presumed to be the primary cause of social policy decisions based on chronological age.

On a concrete level, therefore, it is rather interesting to observe that probably the only adult life crisis that is highly correlated with chronological age is that of retirement; and it is indeed entirely possible that retirement, not aging, is a major cause of the ubiquitous decline in cognitive functioning found after the age of 60 years. Indeed, this hypothesis has been suggested by a number of recent reinterpretations drawing on social-ecological models for cognitive decrement in later life (Baltes & Labouvie, 1973; Labouvie-Vief et al., 1974). Thus, as many authors believe that the present social context of retirement creates many problems of personal and social adjustment, so many also believe that the particular social climate in which many, perhaps a majority, of elderly people live is one that discourages those competence-related behaviors that are relevant to effective intellectual functioning (Labouvie-Vief et al., 1974; Lindsley, 1964).

At present, there is little research that directly examines such a sociocultural hypothesis of declining cognitive competence in old age. I am not aware of any research that—as in the domain of social adjustment and levels of social activity (e.g., Bengtson, 1973; Maas & Kuypers, 1974)—follows people into retirement in temporal sequence and examines their cognitive behavior as they establish their different patterns of adjustment to retirement. There are, however, more indirect indications of the fact that such a hypothesis is, indeed, a highly fruitful one.

I have already summarized studies that suggest that cognitive "deficit" in the elderly may be a rather transitory and situation-bound phenomenon that responds readily to a variety of situation-related manipulations and interventions. This fact itself suggests that cognitive behavior is not so inevitably linked to biological deficit, but may result from the particular scheduling of rewards and reinforcements that elderly people experience (e.g., Labouvie-Vief et al., 1974). But in what ways could it be said that changing reward contingencies produce, as it were, cognitive incompetence? Several authors have remarked on this issue and pointed out possible mechanisms.

First, old age appears to be the target of a variety of negative stereotypes. If compared to other periods of the life cycle, old age is often viewed as a time of dependency, frailty, and decrement (e.g., Bennett & Eckman, 1973; Nardi, 1973). Indeed, few positive labels appear to be associated with the process of aging in either the lay or scientific communities. Thus, the elderly may often be unjustifiably treated as "sick." They may be discouraged from exercising their skills because to do so may either create problems within the current economic structure or interfere with efficient (if not to the same degree humanistically oriented) institutional administration. The detrimental consequences of expectations rooted in the sick role of the elderly were dramatically demonstrated in a study by MacDonald and Butler

(1974), who found institutionalized elderly subjects who were wheelchair bound but showed no organic deficit to proscribe their walking. When encouraged to walk and attended to while walking, these patients showed immediate "recovery," and their walking or not walking appeared to depend entirely on whether or not they were encouraged to do so. In a similar vein, it is also likely that many older people are conveniently pushed into a social niche in which they are deprived of their independence and of decision making, and in which, as a consequence, their competence is either not reinforced or negatively reinforced (Labouvie-Vief et al., 1974).

Second, in addition to relatively active discouragement of intellectual competence, the life situation of many older people further exacerbates their sense of being unable to cope effectively. What little anticipatory socialization toward old age does exist in our society appears to encourage older people to have the negative expectations surrounding aging well internalized. Thus, their self-concepts are often unduly poor, as was demonstrated in a study by Ismael and Labouvie-Vief (1976) in which elderly women and men significantly improved their cognitive performances after receiving a "social support" treatment aimed at rectifying some of the negative stereotypes concerning cognition in old age.

Third, there are also many personal crises older people may encounter that may corrode their sense of efficacy, such as crises related to failing health, loss of loved ones, social isolation, and similar personal traumata. On a somewhat suggestive level, Seligman (1975) has argued that both of these factors—i.e., the more cognitive aspect of labeling oneself as ineffective, and the more direct one of being overwhelmed with personal and social losses without simultaneous social supports—may precipitate a state in older people that is characterized by an intense sense of loss of control and helplessness and that strongly interferes with their ability to function effectively in a variety of cognitive situations. Indeed, in a 14-year longitudinal study by Schaie and Gribbin (1975), it was found that social isolation was the life-style indicator most strongly predictive of intellectual losses.

CRITERIA OF DEVELOPMENT AND MATURITY

Despite the more optimistic posture contained in the previous sections, however, our idealistic dilemma would be only incompletely resolved if we were to stop at this point. We might wish to rush and examine all imaginable context effects, whether "natural" or of human origin, on the cognitive functioning of the older individual. To do so effectively, however, we need to face a particularly tricky problem dormant in idealistic conceptions of development: how to measure the criterion behavior of adult cognition in the first place.

Adult-appropriate versus
Youth-centered Criteria

As already noted earlier in this chapter, one's view of what constitute acceptable criteria of cognitively "mature" behavior is intricately interwoven with one's particular theory of development in general. With very few exceptions, current theories of cognitive development culminate in a concept of maturity that not only is rather context free, but also tends to be located in that period of one's life-span in which one is extensively involved in the process of formal education. Thus, those measures of learning, cognition, and intelligence available to us tend to be derived from theories that speak to adolescent and young-adult subjects and/or are specifically constructed for the purpose of evaluating and predicting academic achievement in young people. If evaluated against such youth-centered criteria, adult behavior often appears to be a rather amateurish attempt to behave like the young. It may be questioned, however, if such a pejorative view is really necessary and inevitable.

The contention that adulthood should not be evaluated against now-prevalent criteria of cognitive growth may seem farfetched at first sight. It certainly appears to violate all the evidence that points to the conclusions that (1) development is directed toward the perfection of exactly those kinds of performances I have mentioned thus far in this chapter, and (2) the progression toward this goal so readily appears to conform to and to occur with such universal regularity as to preclude any doubt that these acquisitions might not be of utmost, universal significance. Nevertheless, as Hamlyn (1971) has argued, the peacefulness of this unilinear view is, ultimately, more a result of the conceptual selectivity of scientists than of the existence of clear, inevitable laws. What appears as a universal teleology (and thus as self-evident and inevitable) is ultimately based upon an a priori selected, to-be-explained, mature form of behavior, and specific theories are constructed to teleogically explain exactly that behavior. In so doing, many other possible goals and behaviors are deselected from the realm of theoretically interesting phenomena. Indeed, Hamlyn argues, if one were to examine cognitive development from a less idealistic, more empirical perspective, one could point to many instances in which the course of cognitive growth defies any unilinear view and in which inconsistencies, detours, and blind alleys, discarded for the sake of a more elegant view, are exposed. Such inconsistency is a relative matter, however, and may become much more meaningful if examined from a somewhat different perspective.

The question of what is to constitute an acceptable end point of development—and thus what is to define an appropriate criterion of mature, adult behavior—has been discussed much more in the literature on cognitive anthropology (e.g., Cole & Scribner, 1974) than in that on adult development.

A number of recent writings in cognitive anthropology have suggested that the ways in which we have come to conceptualize development and maturity are not necessarily universal; rather, what appears universal to the Western thinker may actually reflect the particular value system and cultural pace to which Western societies are accustomed (Berger & Luckmann, 1966). That is, forms of behavior that appear intuitively necessary and important from a narrow cultural perspective, may not be of similar importance from the vantage point of other cultures. Hence, it may be inappropriate to examine any cultural (or age) group through the narrow experiential framework derived within another cultural (or age) group (e.g., Buck-Morss, 1975; Cole & Scribner, 1974). In other words, according to this rationale, one must entertain the possibility that individuals who appear deficient according to the measurement criteria that are applied to them are deficient only in *relation to those standards* but might perform much more adequately if more appropriate standards were applied.

How plausible is it to apply the same argument to the elderly? At present, to be sure, firm evidence is rather lacking, and I wish to raise possibilities for future research rather than to defend a posture that is to be understood as a "fact." With this caution in mind, I nevertheless point to a few research results that may suggest that the hypothesis that older adults are put at an undue disadvantage by established research procedures is, at least, not an unreasonable one.

It has often been argued, for instance, that the cognitive behavior of children shows striking similarities to that of elderly subjects (e.g., Denney, 1974; Papalia, 1972), a fact that has been taken to mean that the elderly person is "childlike," "primitive," "unsophisticated," or otherwise deficient in her or his approach to cognitive tasks. Such an interpretation is sometimes based, however, on rather superficial similarities. In research on the classification of behavior in subjects of widely varying age levels, for instance, it has been reported that young children and older adults tend to group on the basis of complementariness rather than conventional class relations (e.g., Denney, 1974; Denney & Wright, 1975). As Kogan (1974) has pointed out, however, there are also striking differences between the performance of each of these age groups. In his research, elderly individuals also produced categories that were more inclusive and hence might be called more abstract. Thus, the first criterion (basis of classification) might suggest "deficit" in the elderly, whereas the second (inclusiveness of categories) would lead one to conclude the opposite. Certainly, such a state of affairs suggests that the diverse differences between younger and older subjects are not always captured by a decremental hypothesis, and, as a consequence, it would be of value to take a more careful, less biased look at many ways in which performance differences between young and old subjects may arise.

Indeed, other authors have gone even further and argued that current conceptualizations of "mature" cognition may in actuality describe forms of cognitive behavior that are but a preliminary stage. Riegel (1973), for instance, has proposed that the stage of formal operational cognition quite inconsistently captures the cognitive activity of mature adults, which he believes is directed at the creation and tolerant coexistence of inconsistency rather than at its removal. Arlin (1975) has similarly provided suggestive results in support of the hypothesis that currently available theories of cognitive development do not properly concern themselves with the creative, problem-generating activities of adults. Thus, it is certainly fair to state that too little research has been directed at spelling out the possible strengths of the older learner. In contrast, I believe that the imposition of youth-centered standards on older adults will often automatically yield results in line with a deficit view of cognitive functioning—a deficit that may, however, sometimes have its root in a certain degree of egocentric interpretation of research data rather than in the research subjects themselves.

Ecologically Valid Criteria

A final problem inherent in idealistic models of adult cognitive functioning is related to the one just discussed and similarly may form a potential starting point for future research into the education of the elderly. It is an implicit conviction of idealistically oriented theories that ultimately all development follows the same path, although this path may be most easily recognized if one focuses on a few selected instances that are particularly telling. As already discussed, the measures thought particularly revealing have tended to be those of abstract cognitive functioning, that is, of the ability to manipulate abstract symbols and material of low meaning. The point to be considered here is that this conviction, in actuality, may have created a widening gap between what are considered important theoretical concepts and what are the realities of day-to-day cognitive performance.

The last decade or so has witnessed a proliferation of writings (e.g., Buss, 1975; McClelland, 1973; Proshansky, 1970, 1976) reassessing psychological theory in the light of what Proshansky (1970) has called "phenomenon legitimacy," that is, the ability of theories to generate predictions about real-life outcomes. In this view, many theories may have sacrificed scope and relevance for internal consistency and promoted criteria of cognition and intelligence that are relatively overspecialized, tautological, and validated by their fit to theory rather than to reality.

Despite the widespread use of intelligence tests and related cognitive measures in life-span research, for instance, the notion that such tests predict important life outcomes within a life-span framework has rarely been subjected to any critical tests. To be sure, the correlation, mentioned earlier, of cognitive measures with social status, education, health, age, and mortality has connoted to many (e.g., Kohlberg, LaCrosse, & Ricks, 1970; Jensen, 1973) that such tests indeed measure what they are to measure: a person's ability to adapt to life's demands. Such an interpretation is not so inevitable, however, as pointed out by McClelland (1973). As long as these tests are based on individuals from widely divergent social strata, such correlations may be a rather tautological consequence in a society in which opportunities are stratified along class and age lines. If the association is examined within more homogeneous groups, measures of intelligence often fail to predict life outcomes (McClelland, 1973). Nevertheless, such indexes have attained the rather autonomous status of some ultimate criterion, as exemplified in Borings's famous tautology that "intelligence is what intelligence tests measure." Indeed the assumed superiority of cognitive measures over relevant behavioral samples is so widespread a phenomenon that, to this date, there is no research available examining the ecological validity of measures of cognitive functioning from a life-span perspective.

The question of ecological validity is not merely of importance from the perspective of whether or not cognitive research can be applied outside of highly controlled laboratory settings (Botwinick, 1973; Jenkins, 1974); it may also throw a new light on what are "good" measures as judged by other criteria. Because the validity of cognitive measures tends to be evaluated primarily on the basis of measurement and theoretical considerations, most current cognitive indexes tend to encourage samples of achievement of extreme specialization. Insensitivity to situational variability tends to be required, both from psychometric (McClelland, 1973) and developmental-theoretical considerations (Kohlberg, 1971; Wohlwill, 1973). In contrast to this view, McClelland (1973) has argued that situational *sensitivity* should be made the sine qua non of validity considerations; that is, tests should be constructed in such a way that scores *change* as a person grows in experience, wisdom, and the ability to successfully cope with life's problems.

From this perspective, the consistent finding that age differences are augmented on tasks of high abstractness and low meaning—far from attesting to their validity as indicators of powerful developmental dimensions—rather raises doubts concerning their validity. In the absence of clearly demonstrated real-world correlates, statements about levels of cognitive-structural complexity may be quite misleading. On the contrary, age functions may change in a most decisive manner if tasks are devised that are high on both meaning and abstractness (Arenberg, 1968; Fozard & Poon, 1976).

Thus, there is a need to attempt to redefine what are important cognitive skills related to life outcomes in the elderly. Whereas research on "abstract" cognitive skills abounds, for instance, there is almost no available documentation of such important outcomes as communication skills, response delay, ego development, and the abstraction of meaning from verbal and written communication. Research in this area, I believe, has been too widely guided by a priori assumptions; a healthy pendulum swing in the opposite direction is needed, with careful naturalistic and ethological mapping of relevant cognitive skills.

CONCLUSION

In sum, I have argued that much of what we now know about the educability of older adults is in need of revision. Research in this area has tended to derive its assumptions, predictions, and interpretations, via deduction, from idealistic, maturational, youth-centered models of cognitive functioning. It is, as a result, excessively biased in favor of decremental interpretations that tend to foster doubt about the feasibility and value of education in later life.

In contrast, my position is that many pessimistic interpretations of the past are far from inevitable and necessary and that the intellectual potential of the older person is, to this date, essentially unexplored. To some, this might be a position lacking in objectivity, particularly as it is at variance with a vast body of research on the cognitive abilities of older adults. It must be reiterated, however, that it is the opinion of many philosophers and scientists (e.g., Buss, 1975; Habermas, 1971) that the role of objectivity in science may have been somewhat misunderstood in the past. Thus, objectivity in the conduct of research and in the gathering and interpretation of data is a sine qua non of scientific activity; it does not, however, render objective those prescientific assumptions that have suggested the phenomena to be studied and the hypotheses about their conduct in the first place. Objectivity of this latter kind is achieved, rather, by attempting to broaden one's viewpoints. Therefore, I have intended this chapter to serve as a heuristic and to generate alternate viewpoints that are intended, not as the erection of a new dogma, but rather as guidelines for research that I deem particularly important in counteracting a context of hopelessness about the elderly individual's cognitive status.

I suggest that researchers direct their attention to the investigation of variables that are unique and representative of aging behavior, thus concentrating efforts on the potentially progressive aspects of adult cognitive development (Labouvie-Vief & Chandler, 1978; Schaie, 1976). For example, wisdom (Alpaugh, Renner, & Birren, 1976), personal control and mid-life crises (Brim, 1974a, 1974b), and adult coping with professional inter- and intrapersonal stress (Coelho, Hamburg, & Adams, 1974; Lowenthal & Chiriboga, 1973) are all representative of research efforts aimed at issues particularly relevant to adulthood and late maturity. Accordingly, a stronger emphasis on contextual and experiential factors in the explication of aging behavior is needed.

REFERENCES

Alpaugh, P. K., Renner, V. J., & Birren, J. W. Age and creativity: Implications for education and teachers. *Educational Gerontology*, 1976, *1*, 17–40.

Arenberg, D. Concept problem solving in young and old adults. *Journal of Gerontology*, 1968, *23*, 279–282.

Arlin, P. K. Cognitive development in adulthood: A fifth stage? *Developmental Psychology,* 1975, *11,* 602–606.

Baer, D. M. The control of the developmental process: Why wait? In J. R. Nesselroade & H. W. Reese (Eds.), *Life-span developmental psychology: Methodological issues.* New York: Academic, 1973.

Baltes, P. B. Longitudinal and cross-sectional sequences in the study of age and generation effects. *Human Development,* 1968, *11,* 145–171.

Baltes, P. B., & Labouvie, G. V. Adult development of intellectual performance: Description, explanation, and modification. In C. Eisdorfer & M. P. Lawton (Eds.), *The psychology of adult development and aging.* Washington, D.C.: American Psychological Association, 1973.

Baltes, P. B., & Willis, S. L. Toward psychological theories of aging. In J. E. Birren & K. W. Schaie (Eds.), *Handbook on psychology of aging.* New York: Van Nostrand-Reinhold, 1976.

Barrett, W. The twentieth century in its philosophy. In W. Barrett & H. D. Aiken (Eds.), *Philosophy in the twentieth century.* New York: Harper, 1962.

Barry, A. J., Steinmetz, J. R., Page, H. F., & Rodahl, K. The effects of physical conditioning on older individuals: II. Motor performance and cognitive function. *Journal of Gerontology,* 1966, *21,* 182–191.

Bayley, N. Development of mental abilities. In P. H. Mussen (Ed.), *Carmichael's manual of child psychology.* New York: Wiley, 1970.

Bengston, V. L. *The social psychology of aging.* Indianapolis: Bobbs-Merrill, 1973.

Bennett, R., & Eckman, J. Attitudes toward aging. In C. Eisdorfer & M. P. Lawton (Eds.), *The psychology of adult development and aging.* Washington, D.C.: American Psychological Association, 1973.

Berger, P. L., & Luckmann, T. *The social construction of reality.* Garden City, N.Y.: Doubleday, 1966.

Birkhill, W. R., & Schaie, K. W. The effect of differential reinforcement of cautiousness in intellectual performance among the elderly. *Journal of Gerontology,* 1975, *30,* 578–583.

Birren, J. E. Psychophysiological relations. In J. E. Birren, R. N. Butler, S. W. Greenhouse, L. Sokoloff, & M. R. Yarrow (Eds.), *Human aging: A biological and behavioral study.* Washington, D.C.: U.S. Government Printing Office, 1963.

Birren, J. E. Toward an experimental psychology of aging. *American Psychologist,* 1970, *25,* 124–135.

Birren, J. E., Butler, R. W., Greenhouse, S. W., Sokoloff, L., & Yarrow, M. R. (Eds.), *Human aging: A biological and behavioral study.* Washington, D.C.: U.S. Government Printing Office, 1963.

Bloom, B. S. *Stability and change in human characteristics.* New York: Wiley, 1964.

Botwinick, J. *Cognitive processes in maturity and old age.* New York: Springer, 1967.

Botwinick, J. *Aging and behavior.* New York: Springer, 1973.

Botwinick, J., & Thompson, L. W. Cardiac functioning and reaction time in relation to age. *Journal of Genetic Psychology,* 1971, *119,* 127–132.

Brim, O. G., Jr. *The sense of personal control over one's life.* Unpublished manuscript, Foundation of Child Development, New York, 1974. (a)

Brim, O. G., Jr. *Selected theories of the male mid-life crisis: A comparative analysis.* Unpublished manuscript, Foundation of Child Development, New York, 1974. (b)

Buck-Morss, S. Socio-economic bias in Piaget's theory and its implications for cross-cultural studies. *Human Development,* 1975, *18,* 35–49.

Buss, A. R. The emerging field of the sociology of psychological knowledge. *American Psychologist,* 1975, *30,* 988–1002.

Coelho, G. V., Hamburg, D. A., & Adams, J. E. (Eds.) *Coping and adaptation.* New York: Basic Books, 1974.

Cole, M., & Scribner, S. *Culture and thought: A psychological introduction.* New York: Wiley, 1974.

Datan, N., & Ginsberg, L. H. (Eds.) *Life-span developmental psychology: Normative life crises.* New York: Academic, 1975.

Denney, N. W. Classification abilities in the elderly. *Journal of Gerontology,* 1974, *29,* 309–314.

Denney, N. W., & Wright, J. C. *Cognitive changes during the adult years: Implications for developmental theory and research.* Paper presented at the biannual meeting of the Society for Research in Child Development, Denver, Colorado, April, 1975.

Dohrenwend, B. S., & Dohrenwend, B. P. (Eds.) *Stressful life events.* New York: Wiley, 1974.

Eisdorfer, C., Nowlin, J., & Wilkie, F. Improvement of learning by modification of autonomous nervous system activity. *Science,* 1971, *170,* 1327–1328.

Eisdorfer, C., & Wilkie, F. Intellectual changes with advancing age. In L. F. Jarvik, C. Eisdorfer, & J. C. Blum (Eds.), *Intellectual functioning in adults.* New York: Springer, 1973.

Flavell, J. H. Cognitive changes in adulthood. In P. B. Baltes & L. R. Goulet (Eds.), *Life-span developmental psychology,* New York: Academic, 1970.

Fozard, J. L., & Poon, L. W. *Age-related differences in long-term memory for pictures.* Paper presented at the annual meeting of the Gerontological Society, New York, October, 1976.

Furry, C. A., & Baltes, P. B. The effect of age differences in ability-extraneous variables on the assessment of intelligence in children, adults and the elderly. *Journal of Gerontology,* 1973, *28,* 73–80.

Gergen, K. J. Social psychology as history. *Journal of Personality and Social Psychology,* 1973, *26,* 309–320.

Gewirtz, J. L. Mechanisms of social learning: Some roles of stimulation and behavior in early human development. In D. A. Goslin (Ed.), *Handbook of socialization theory and research.* Chicago: Rand McNally, 1969.

Giorgi, A. Phenomenology and experimental psychology. In A. Giorgi, W. F. Fischer, & R. Von Eckartsberg (Eds.), *Duquesne studies in phenomenological psychology* (Vol. 1). Pittsburgh: Duquesne University Press, 1971.

Habermas, J. *Knowledge and human interests.* Boston: Beacon, 1971.

Hamlyn, D. W. Epistemology and conceptual development. In T. Mischel (Ed.), *Cognitive development and epistemology*. New York: Academic, 1971.

Hertzog, C., Gribbin, K., & Schaie, K. W. *The influence of cardiovascular disease and hypertension on intellectual stability*. Paper presented at the annual meeting of the Gerontological Society, Louisville, Kentucky, October, 1975.

Horn, J. L. Human abilities: A review of research and theory in the early 1970's. *Annual Review of Psychology*, 1976, *27*, 437–485.

Hornblum, J. N., & Overton, W. F. Area and volume conservation among the elderly: Assessment and training. *Developmental Psychology*, 1976, *12*, 68–74.

Hoyer, W. J., Labouvie, G. V., & Baltes, P. B. Modification of response speed deficits and intellectual performance in the elderly. *Human Development*, 1973, *16*, 233–242.

Ismael, M., & Labouvie-Vief, G. *Self-concept and intellectual performance in the elderly*. Unpublished manuscript, University of Wisconsin, Madison, 1976.

Jarvik, L. F. Discussion: Patterns of intellectual functioning in the later years. In L. F. Jarvik, C. Eisdorfer, & J. C. Blum (Eds.), *Intellectual functioning in adults*. New York: Springer, 1973.

Jarvik, L. F., & Cohen, D. A biobehavioral approach to intellectual changes with aging. In C. Eisdorfer & M. P. Lawton (Eds.), *The psychology of adult development and aging*. Washington, D.C.: American Psychological Association, 1973.

Jenkins, J. J. Remember the old theory of memory? Well forget it! *American Psychologist*, 1974, *29*, 789–795.

Jensen, A. R. *Educability and group differences*. New York: Harper, 1973.

Kogan, N. Categorizing and conceptualizing styles in younger and older adults. *Human Development*, 1974, *17*, 218–230.

Kohlberg, L. From is to ought: How to commit the naturalistic fallacy and get away with it in the study of moral development. In T. Mischel (Ed.), *Cognitive development and epistemology*. New York: Academic, 1971.

Kohlberg, L., LaCrosse, J., & Ricks, D. The predictability of adult mental health from childhood behavior. In B. Wolman (Ed.), *Handbook of child psychopathology*. New York: McGraw-Hill, 1970.

Kuhlen, R. G. Age and intelligence: The significance of cultural change in longitudinal vs. cross-sectional findings. *Vita Humana*, 1963, *6*, 113–124.

Labouvie-Vief, G. Towards optimizing cognitive competence in older adults. *Educational Gerontology*, 1976, *1*, 75–92.

Labouvie-Vief, G., & Chandler, M. J. Cognitive development and life-span developmental theory: Idealistic vs. contextual perspectives. In P. B. Baltes (Ed.), *Life-span development and behavior*. New York: Academic, 1978, in press.

Labouvie-Vief, G., & Gonda, J. N. Cognitive strategy training and intellectual performance in the elderly. *Journal of Gerontology*, 1976, *31*, 327–332.

Labouvie-Vief, G., Hoyer, W. J., Baltes, M. M., & Baltes, P. B. Operant analysis of intellectual behavior in old age. *Human Development*, 1974, *17*, 259–272.

Lindsley, O. R. Geriatric behavioral prosthetics. In R. Kastenbaum (Ed.), *New thoughts on old age.* New York: Springer, 1964.

Lowenthal, M. R., & Chiriboga, D. Social stress and adaptation. In C. Eisdorfer & M. P. Lawton (Eds.), *The psychology of adult development and aging.* Washington, D.C.: American Psychological Association, 1973.

Maas, H. S., & Kuypers, J. A. *From thirty to seventy.* San Francisco: Jossey-Bass, 1974.

MacDonald, M. L., & Butler, A. K. Reversal of helplessness: Producing walking behavior in wheel chair residents using behavior modification procedures. *Journal of Gerontology,* 1974, *29,* 97–101.

McClelland, D. C. Testing for competence rather than for "intelligence." *American Psychologist,* 1973, *28,* 1–14.

Mergler, N. L., & Hoyer, W. J. *Cognitive performance of elderly adults as a function of strategy training and non-contingent social praise.* Paper presented at the annual meeting of the gerontological society, Louisville, Kentucky, October, 1975.

Muuss, R. E. *Theories of adolescence* (3rd ed.). New York: Random House, 1975.

Nardi, A. H. Person-perception research and the perception of life-span development. In P. B. Baltes & K. W. Schaie (Eds.), *Life-span developmental psychology: Personality and socialization.* New York: Academic, 1973.

Nesselroade, J. R., & Baltes, P. B. Adolescent personality development and historical change: 1970–1972. *Monographs of the Society for Research in Child Development,* 1974, *39* (1).

Nesselroade, J. R., Schaie, K. W., & Baltes, P. B. Ontogenetic and generational components of structural and quantitative change in adult cognitive behavior. *Journal of Gerontology,* 1972, *27,* 222–228.

Neugarten, B. L., & Datan, N. Sociological perspectives on the life cycle. In P. B. Baltes & K. W. Schaie (Eds.), *Life-span developmental psychology: Personality and socialization.* New York: Academic, 1973.

Obrist, W. D., Busse, E. W., Eisdorfer, C., & Kleemeier, R. W. Relation of the electroencephalogram to intellectual function in senescence. *Journal of Gerontology,* 1962, *17,* 197–206.

Palmore, E., & Cleveland, W. Aging, terminal decline, and terminal drop. *Journal of Gerontology,* 1976, *31,* 76–81.

Panicucci, C., & Labouvie-Vief, G. *Effect of training on inductive reasoning behavior.* Paper presented at the annual meeting of the Gerontological Society, Louisville, Kentucky, October, 1975.

Papalia, D. The status of several conservation abilities across the life-span. *Human Development,* 1972, *15,* 229–243.

Plemons, J. K., Willis, S. L., & Baltes, P. B. *Challenging the theory of fluid intelligence: A training approach.* Paper presented at the annual meeting of the Gerontological Society, Louisville, Kentucky, October, 1973.

Powell, R. R. Psychological effects of exercise therapy upon institutionalized geriatric mental patients. *Journal of Gerontology,* 1974, *29,* 157–161.

Powell, R. R., & Pohndorf, R. H. Comparison of adult exercisers and nonexercisers on fluid intelligence and selected physiological variables. *Research Quarterly,* 1971, *42,* 70–77.

Proshansky, H. M. Methodology in environmental psychology: Problems and issues. *Human Factors*, 1970, *14*, 451–460.

Proshansky, H. M. Environmental psychology and the real world. *American Psychologist*, 1976, *31*, 303–310.

Reese, H. W. Life-span models of memory. *Gerontologist*, 1973, *13*, 472–478.

Riegel, K. F. Dialectic operations: The final period of cognitive development. *Human Development*, 1973, *16*, 346–370.

Riegel, K. F. From traits and equilibrium towards developmental dialectics. In W. Arnold (Ed.), *Nebraska Symposium on Motivation*. Lincoln: University of Nebraska Press, 1975.

Riegel, K. F., & Riegel, R. M. Development, drop, and death. *Developmental Psychology*, 1972, *6*, 306–319.

Schaie, K. W. A general model for the study of developmental problems. *Psychological Bulletin*, 1965, *64*, 92–107.

Schaie, K. W. Toward a stage theory of adult development. *International Journal of Aging and Adult Development*. 1977, in press.

Schaie, K. W., & Gribbin, K. *The impact of environmental complexity upon adult cognitive development.* Paper presented at the 3rd biennial conference of the International Society for the Study of Behavioral Development, Guildford, England, July 13–17, 1975.

Schaie, K. W., Labouvie, G. V., & Buech, B. U. Generational vs. cohort-specific differences in adult cognitive functioning: A fourteen-year study of independent samples. *Developmental Psychology*, 1973, *9*, 151–166.

Seligman, M. E. P. *Helplessness.* San Francisco: W. H. Freeman, 1975.

Tanner, J. M. Sequence, tempo, and individual variation in growth and development of boys and girls aged twelve to sixteen. In J. Kagan & R. Coles (Eds.), *Twelve to sixteen: Early adolescence.* New York: W. W. Norton & Company, 1972.

Toffler, A. (Ed.). *Learning for tomorrow.* New York: Random House, 1974.

Wang, H. S. Cerebral correlates of intellectual functioning in senescence. In L. F. Jarvik, C. Eisdorfer, & J. C. Blum (Eds.), *Intellectual functioning in adults.* New York: Springer, 1973.

Wohlwill, J. F. *The study of behavioral development.* New York: Academic, 1973.

Woodruff, D. S. The usefulness of the life-span approach for the psychophysiology of aging. *Gerontologist*, 1973, *13*, 467, 472.

Woodruff, D. S. A physiological perspective on the psychology of aging. In J. E. Birren & D. S. Woodruff (Eds.), *Aging: Scientific perspectives and social issues.* New York: D. Van Nostrand, 1975.

13

LEADERSHIP TRAINING FOR RETIREMENT EDUCATION

As Lore Adjustment
Excellent

CARL I. BRAHCE
WOODROW W. HUNTER
University of Michigan

Like aging itself, retirement may be studied as a complex process having multiple meanings for the individual. Viewed most simply as a change over time from a working role to a nonworking role, retirement seems to have a noticeable impact upon all other positions held by retirees as well as upon all of their relationships with others (Sussman, 1972). This phenomenon is usually associated, in our industrialized society, with negative connotations that are primarily due to the preoccupation in the United States with the work role. "Retirement is a demotion in the work system. For most individuals it means a sharp reduction in income. Less income may result in inability to meet behavioral expectations in a group or organization. The consequence is a change in status."[1]

Although the factors relating to the retirement process are complex, research studies indicate the importance of economic and health variables. Research on social-psychological factors shows that both men and women who tend to work longer have higher income levels, higher positions in the occupational structure, and higher education attainments. It also shows that, in our work-oriented society, the older person who works is, over time, more likely to feel useful than the person who retires (Streib & Schneider, 1971, p. 159).

Research findings raise theoretical questions about the process of retirement and its impact on the individual. These questions, in turn, present considerations and choices for the retirement educator. Glamser (1976) investigated the factors relating to a positive attitude toward retirement among older, male, industrial workers and concluded that:

[1] Reprinted from Gordon F. Streib and Clement J. Schneider, S.J.: *Retirement in American Society*, p. 159. © Copyright 1971 by Cornell University. Used by permission of Cornell University Press.

Workers who can realistically expect a positive retirement experience in terms of finances, friends, social activity, and level of preparedness were likely to have a positive attitude toward retirement . . . . The worker's appraisal of his present situation and the kind of experience he expects to encounter in retirement was much more important than the meaning of work per se. (p. 107)

In the Scripps Foundation studies in retirement, Atchley (1971) found that although retirement did result in loss of a sense of involvement, this was not related to the other self-concept variables of optimism and autonomy. Differences in adjustment to retirement were found according to occupational status, with upper white-collar jobs oriented around symbols, middle-status jobs oriented around people, and semiskilled jobs oriented around things. He concluded that there is no concrete evidence that retirement per se has a negative influence on the quality of one's life. Atchley (1971) suggests that as retirement becomes more an expected part of the life cycle, work may be seen as a temporary phase of life rather than as the dominant life function for many people.

Usefulness has a significant effect on the individual's ability to adjust to the changing impact of retirement during the time intervals—usually 10 to 20 years—before death. The years after retirement, for both the individual and the spouse, are marked by continuing changes. Roles in later maturity would ideally involve anticipatory socialization, inasmuch as workers often know the exact time at which they will retire. Many older people, however, delay in making plans. Traditionally, educational institutions are not as concerned about socialization for new roles in later life as in earlier periods of the life cycle (Streib & Schneider, 1971).

Learning to be retired is an unusual kind of adult socialization because it exposes individuals to a kind of double jeopardy. Not only do older people have to learn roles that are new to them, but the roles themselves are new, and consequently not well defined in the social repertory of most industrial societies. The increasingly long period between the loss of a social maturity that is derived from a work world and the physical decline of old age has created a new retired state in the social life cycle. Without the help of specialized agents to teach them about these changing social roles of retirement, older people frequently seek informal ways to clarify roles with their peers (Ross, 1974).

The French author, Simone de Beauvoir (1972), derides the societal treatment of the retired in our culture: "The worker is condemned to idleness much earlier than he was formerly . . . . The idleness forced upon the aged is not something that necessarily happens in the course of nature, but it is the consequence of a deliberate social choice" (pp. 223, 232).

In their transcultural study, Doris and David Jonas (1973, p. 107) learned that only in a few roles, such as the papacy, heads of other religions, and senates of the world, do the elderly still hold positions of leadership. In the practice of medicine, many prefer younger physicians, and teaching is succumbing to youth and technology. The old yield to compulsory retirement to assure the vigor of new blood in the conduct of offices and to permit the promotion of younger aspirants for power and influence. In all other areas of daily life, our elders have become, or are rapidly becoming, functionless.

Researchers of the Cornell retirement study (Streib & Schneider, 1971) observed that it is not enough to view retirement in terms of new roles in a changing industrial society. Not only is the retirement process something with negative or positive impact on the individual, but it also may have favorable or unfavorable consequences for the operation of organizations, institutional structures like the economy, and the society itself. An important conclusion of the Cornell study has implications for the retirement educator as well as the sociologist: the higher the individual's educational and professional status, the more positive attitudes and the more resources that individual has available in coping with the changing circumstances of retirement. The unskilled and uneducated are the least prepared and have the least personal, economic, and social resources with which to meet life's challenges upon retirement.

The increasing body of knowledge about the retirement process has implications for the education of retired people, and correspondingly, for the training of professionals who would be engaged in planning and carrying out education programs. First, both psychological and social factors can be critical in how well men and women adjust to aging. The ingredients of satisfactory old age are: a stable relationship with the immediate and extended family, purposeful activity, and a sense of one's own value. These qualities are aptly illustrated by Esther Hunt More of Hickory, North Carolina. An elementary school teacher for 40 years, she was named Mother of the Year in 1970, and she was the first black woman to register and vote in her county. After her children were graduated from college, she studied at Columbia University, earned her master's degree at the age of 64, and went on to teach mentally retarded children (Jonas & Jonas, 1973).

Second, there is a questioning of the very basis of the whole concept of retirement. To date, the attempts of governmental agencies and those who are responsible for formulating policies to improve the lot of the elderly have been concentrating on improving the conditions that now exist. Such actions promote, rather than decrease, dependency, and they do nothing to help retirees fill their time constructively. "It is ironic that those members of such panels who themselves are elderly, whether they are physicians, sociologists, or politicians, advocate such things—and forget that the reason for their own well-being and physical fitness is precisely that they are active and purposeful."[2]

[2] From *Young till We Die* by Doris Jonas and David Jonas. New York: Coward, McCann & Geoghegan, 1973, p. 164. Copyright 1973 by David Orr. Reprinted by permission.

Third, some earlier assumptions about work and retirement require careful analysis and new theoretical applications. In a study of older men and women to learn about social and psychological differences between men and women in later life, Atchley (1976) controlled for age, marital status, education, and income adequacy. His findings contradict some earlier assumptions that work is not a primary role for women who work. Women in his sample reported difficulty in getting used to retirement more often than did men. Whereas men often responded to aging in terms of how it affected their relation to the social system, women neither accepted social aging nor tried to fend it off by continued engagement; instead, they responded to aging with high levels of psychological stress. Atchley notes that it is possible that differences observed in his study may *not* be the same for upcoming cohorts of older people.

Fourth, the impact of retirement is a continuing, complicated process, affecting older people in different ways and with varying degrees of force. It is not likely to diminish in importance as industrialized societies like our own confront the increasing growth of technology. Retirement education has concerned itself primarily with helping individuals and their spouses understand and adjust to the changes retirement brings to their normal workaday worlds. Gerontologists need not only to be concerned with preparation for retirement, but even more urgently, to determine the educational needs of men and women throughout the later years following retirement. A major question for the retirement educator is: What can the system of education do to train professionals to provide meaningful and helpful education programs for the elderly during the extensive postretirement years?

To place this discussion of retirement in perspective requires an overview of the past and current roles of institutions in retirement education.

HISTORIC DEVELOPMENTS
IN EDUCATION FOR THE ELDERLY

The first major development was the historic enactment of the Older Americans Act of 1965, which established the Administration on Aging and provided for funding for training and research. Although total appropriations to carry out community programs to provide services to older Americans totaled only $7.5 million during 1966, the action to provide services in the field of aging in recognition of diverse needs of older men and women was consequential. The act recognized the need for training and research by giving universities and colleges the funding to begin what has become a significant new direction in higher education in the United States, not only serving older people, but also extending educational gerontology, workforce training, and multidisciplinary graduate programs, as well as research, both empirical and applied, crossing many fronts.

Appropriations increased steadily in subsequent years, with the 1972 total being $101.7 million. More than one million older people were served by over 1,500 community projects funded under Title III, the services including those for independent living, group and home-delivered meals, community programs involving older volunteers, transportation, and health and health-related services (United States Senate, 1973). The 93rd Congress enacted the Older Americans Comprehensive Services Amendments of 1973 to strengthen and improve the Older Americans Act. The Administration on Aging was reorganized within the U.S. Department of Health, Education, and Welfare; the Federal Council on the Aging was created, as well as a National Information and Resource Clearinghouse for the Aging. The commissioner on aging was authorized to make grants to the states for special library and education programs for the elderly, to conduct research in the field of aging, and to make grants and contracts for training personnel for programs for the aging, including the establishment of multidisciplinary centers of gerontology (United States Senate, 1973).

The second major development was the creation of a new dimension—community service—to the two-year junior college. During the 1960s, as the states determined to meet an unprecedented demand to educate youth, community colleges were established to extend post-secondary education to every citizen. During the accelerated movement in education, 500 community colleges were created. Junior colleges became community centered, i.e., within commuting distance for most people (Gleazer, 1974). At the same time, the social turbulence of the 1960s brought about the development of community services departments in these two-year institutions. Aided by the catalyst of federal funds, these emerging departments began to serve special community groups—including senior citizens—and their identified needs. It was a fortunate circumstance for the elderly, who were suddenly recognized in the public sectors as neglected citizens requiring support services.

Those 65 or older were also identified as target populations most in need of education following the enactment of the Older Americans Act in the middle of the decade. Colleges, which were filled with young people, began offering a variety of educational programs to specific community groups including the aged. A variety of formats, or delivery systems, emerged under the community services structure: short courses, seminars, lectures, short-term workforce-training programs, recreational programs, extension center courses, social-action programs, and community development institutes (Myron, Huber, & Sweeney, 1971). The position of continuing education director was reshaped into the role of dean of community services charged with the responsibility for making college resources available to all groups and citizens in the college community district.

A third significant development was the 1971 White House Conference on Aging. Delegates, who represented public and private institutions and whose interests spanned many fields of study and endeavor, developed and recommended policies that, in many cases, led to important improvements in the quality of life of older people (*Toward a National Policy*, 1973, pp. 1–8). In his address to education section delegates, Howard Y. McClusky (1973) observed that education should be regarded as a program category to which all other aspects of living in the later years should be related. He said education for older people is an investment by society in resource development, that older people have experience and special assets that the society needs for the cultivation of its health and well-being. He singled out the community colleges and community schools for promise of "superior achievement in education for aging" (McClusky, 1973, pp. 5–6).

A fourth development provided timely leadership and stimulation to community and two-year college administrators just at the time that they were recognizing an educational imperative to serve their older constituents. The Administration on Aging, in 1971, awarded a two-year grant to the American Association of Community and Junior Colleges (AACJC). This grant provided funds to AACJS to work with the nation's 1,100 community and junior colleges as well as with technical institutes. The objective was to develop an awareness of the needs of older Americans and to explore ways in which these community-oriented institutions might contribute to an improvement in the quality of life of the nation's elderly population.

The timing also was significant in another way. As Arthur S. Flemming, commissioner on aging, noted:

> *It is gratifying that community college recognition of this new field of social action as an opportunity for extending its services parallels a basic objective of the Administration on Aging, namely, that of fostering the establishment of a network of state and area agencies on aging charged with planning, conducting, and expanding services for older people throughout the country. (p. 3)*

The 1971 White House Conference on Aging underscores the directions taken by Andrew S. Korim, director of the AACJC aging project, in rallying colleges throughout the nation to extend learning opportunities to older people, to seek cooperative development of programs with area agencies on aging and community organizations, and to improve workforce training for the field of aging.

A fifth development occurred when community service and continuing education programs at several community colleges specifically sought out the older learner under such federal funding as Title I of the Higher Education Act of 1965 and Title III of the Older Americans Act of 1965. These grants greatly accelerated program development by providing for a coordinator or part-time program director to design and implement courses for older men and women. New community colleges, already expanding their education programs to adults through community service departments, recognized the potentials of a new student population—the older American. College programmers did not believe that society should declare statutory senility upon the 20 million Americans 65 or older.

Community services directors found that retirees were responsive to a variety of offerings. At North Hennepin Community College, Brooklyn Park, Minnesota, most of the programs were in the area of self-development or direct services to senior citizens. Popular classes included trimnastics, psychology, dancing, painting, public speaking, creative writing, films, rap sessions with students, defensive driving, and senior power (Bauer, 1973).

Innovative programs involved not only community agencies, but also local television stations, as colleges extended their resources and sought answers to problems of the elderly in their districts. Vincennes University, Indiana, first organized a 13-week television series with experts discussing community issues including problems of the elderly. Following this, senior citizens were encouraged to enroll for credit courses with tuition discounts and permitted to attend academic classes by paying low audit fees. The institution then obtained a Title III grant from the Indiana Commission on Aging and Aged to conduct a six-county project called Community Development for the Aged. Later, the university became designated as an area agency on aging and received a state grant to become the training and resource agency for southwestern Indiana for the staffs of area agencies on aging in that quarter of the state (Bottenfield, 1974).

Kirkwood Community College in Cedar Rapids, Iowa, developed an extensive program for the elderly that utilized elderly volunteers and specialists to provide a variety of services to older people: a speakers bureau of senior citizens, instructor aides, student tutors and advisors, recreational and leisure-time activities involving college students and staff, extensive preretirement programs, a resource library, and a seven-county-area senior citizen monthly newspaper with a 40,000 circulation (Feller, 1973).

Other community colleges were able to begin programming for senior adults under state grants for developing community services. For example, Schoolcraft Community College, Livonia, Michigan, in 1971, became the first institution in that state to provide a full-time coordinator of programs for older people.

These historic developments led to an unparalleled acceleration of educational efforts on behalf of the nation's older population. Not since the millions of returning World War II veterans took advantage of the GI bill and swept into colleges and universities had these institutions faced the challenge of a new constituency.

THE ROLE OF INSTITUTIONS

Colleges Recognize Need for Training

It is not surprising that many of the two-year colleges suddenly found that they were unprepared to extend their programs to the elderly. Most of the community services directors and coordinators of adult education programs had no training in gerontology. The Institute of Gerontology, affiliated with the University of Michigan and Wayne State University, became the first to recognize the developing thrust of community college programming and services to older constituents. This recognition followed earlier programs under the leadership of Wilma T. Donahue to meet the workforce shortage in the field of aging. In 1967, 29 adults, including community college faculty, were graduated from a crash-implemented training program, which served as a model for training professional and technical personnel, under a grant from the U.S. Administration on Aging. Under AOA Title V funding to train specialists in aging, the Institute of Gerontology began, in 1972, to develop a comprehensive program of in-service training for community service directors of community colleges, and to effect a statewide effort at education programming for older people. The Institute staff provided several kinds of consultation:

1. on conducting community surveys
2. on discovering community leaders among older people
3. on assessing existing programs and services for the elderly
4. on writing proposals and designing programs or working with college faculty in the disciplines of nursing, sociology, psychology, and other social sciences
5. on introducing gerontological content in existing courses
6. on designing new curricula in aging

Consortium projects were developed in cooperation with the Michigan Community College Community Services Association.

The Institute of Gerontology offered a summer institute program to extend its training facilities to personnel of colleges and other institutions serving the elderly. A course in community college teaching and programming in aging was developed. Participants attended from various institutions representing many states, and resource leaders from colleges responded eagerly from as far away as Hawaii.

Training Roles of the University

Retirement education began in this country in the spring of 1948 when Clark Tibbitts offered the first course for older people at the University of Michigan. Shortly thereafter, Wilma T. Donahue and Woodrow W. Hunter adapted Tibbitt's course for older people *before* retirement (Tibbitts, 1948).

Today, the emphasis of most universities in gerontology education is on graduate instruction or career training rather than on the training of professionals who are in a position to develop pre- and postretirement education programs for older people. Starting with the Older Americans Act of 1965 (and continuing with the Older Americans Comprehensive Services

Amendments of 1973), grants have been made to help initiate, expand, or strengthen research and instructional programs with a primary emphasis on social, economic, and professional services. Seven career and job areas of training were identified: national, state, and community planning; personnel for retirement housing; senior-center personnel; specialists in aging; faculty institutes on aging; semiprofessional and technical personnel; and volunteer leaders (Donahue, 1967, p. 85).

Most of these areas fall in the purview of university instruction. In March 1966, the Administration on Aging awarded a grant under Title V to the University of Georgia for a one-year project designed to equip university and college faculties throughout the seven-state region with the information and knowledge needed to provide gerontological instruction. The timing was fortuitous; universities were ready to respond to the need for a large number of qualified professional personnel and the availability of training moneys. Within 13 months after the first grant was awarded, programs at 16 more universities were funded (Donahue, 1967, p. 86). These included the University of Michigan, which became the base along with Wayne State University, for the first institute of gerontology in a university setting created by state statute.

The university may be said to have both direct and indirect roles in leadership training for retirement education. Although some overlap may occur, direct responsibilities include: the planning and offering of short-term courses, seminars, workshops, and institutes to education personnel, including administrators, program coordinators, and faculty; research in the design of new curricula for the aged; research on the problem areas of aging that relate to program development and service to the elderly; and graduate instruction to train professionals in the areas of education, administration, and service delivery to older people.

The university's indirect training roles encompass consultative services to professional people who are actively engaged in programming for the elderly or in community organization work, mostly at the community colleges; collaborative efforts to establish consortia with other universities, community and junior colleges, and private institutions in the interest of cooperative programming or improving educational opportunities; and resource development including the preparation of bibliographies, instructional materials, and teaching aids.

The variety of subjects and target participants suggests that leadership training in retirement education is multidisciplinary and, at the same time, broad enough in curriculum content to interest professional workers in many service areas. Tibbitts (1967) identified four categories of professional personnel that would be required to create the environment and provide the services needed by the older population: (1) direct providers of services; (2) planners, administrators, and program directors; (3) researchers; and (4) teaching faculty (p. 58).

The increasing scope of training to serve gerontology's rapidly accelerating service area as the needs of the elderly become the focus of education and service bears out Tibbitt's (1967) statement: "Again, there are no estimates of the numbers of faculty personnel required for teaching gerontology either to those who will prepare for work in the professions or in research or to those who are to train these teachers" (p. 58).

University-College Linkage

In his work, *Older Americans and Community Colleges: A Guide for Program Implementation,* AACJC aging project director Andrew Korim (1974) suggests that colleges take the initiative in establishing links with universities in order to obtain needed services and to influence programming development: "University centers of gerontology are a valuable resource regarding research on aging and the needs of the elderly, and centers can assist the two-year institutions by providing personnel and graduate student internships" (p. 101).

Centers that have been of value to community colleges include those at the University of California, Duke University, the University of Nebraska, the University of Oregon, Pennsylvania State University, and Syracuse University, as well as at the University of Michigan. Korim expects college-university relationships to expand in the future as two-year colleges increase their services in the field of aging. Two examples may be cited to illustrate how expanding university pursuits in research and education can stimulate 2-year institutions to offer programs for retired people. The first concerns an Institute of Gerontology research project on older drivers, which began in 1974. Under joint sponsorship of the NRTA/AARP Andrus Foundation, the Michigan Office of Highway Safety Planning, and the National Highway Traffic Safety Administration of the U.S. Department of Transportation, this research resulted in the development of an older driver refresher course. Age-related changes likely to affect driving behavior of older people were studied and incorporated in the training program, which will be tested at various community colleges. The ultimate application to curriculum will involve the training of college administrators and driver education teachers as well as the older people themselves.

In the second example, in cooperation with four community colleges in the Detroit metropolitan area, a 2-year research project, titled "Development of Post-Retirement Education Models with a Community College Consortium on Aging," was launched by the Institute of Gerontology on July 1, 1974. The objective was to design, implement, and evaluate, drawing upon resources of the four colleges, postretirement education programs that would be directed to poor, ethnic, single, and institutionalized populations of retired people. This project was one of 11 community service and continuing education projects funded under Title I of the Higher Education Act. A series of instructional videotape and tape-slide presentations was developed to provide information to administrators and faculty of 2-year institutions interested in assisting the elderly constituents in their districts to successfully meet the changes occurring in their lives. The presentations include: the rationale and importance of education for retirees, methodologies and strategies in teaching older adults, and administrative processes in designing and offering programs to retirees. Faculty who were participating in the project supplied the answers and cross-fertilization of ideas that were obtained in response to the university-sponsored workshops. The data were then analyzed and corroborated with field research before being translated into instructional materials. Throughout the project, a teamwork approach proved beneficial in bringing the university and college staffs together to address problems.

The implications are clear: (1) the university's role in research is crucial to the design and implementation of programs offered by colleges directly to retired people; (2) knowledge obtained from research, both theoretical and practical, can and should be utilized for training educators and providing them with the theoretical as well as the applied systems; (3) the growth of knowledge through university research efforts can be effectively translated into programmatic actions, and this is possible only with the cooperative understanding and involvement of faculty and administrative staff of other institutions, in this case, 2-year colleges.

Communication Exchange

In a growing, changing field like gerontology, it is essential to keep the communication lines open between universities and colleges and the other community agencies involved in programming for retired people. As personnel in the field experience different situations imposed by social and institutional changes, these can be communicated to university faculty who are responsive to these patterns. Therefore, faculty should be involved in research and program development projects whenever possible. In addition, community agencies and civic groups may occasionally call upon faculty for assistance in providing new information or interpreting advances in scientific theory and knowledge for the practitioner and citizen.

TRAINING RETIREMENT EDUCATORS
Identifying the Needs

It is perhaps axiomatic that the first requirement in training educators to program for the retirement years is to help them understand the needs of the retired people themselves. Among the needs identified by gerontologists are income, health and nutrition, housing, transportation, consumer protection, employment, retirement roles and activities, education, and spiritual well-being (Myran, Huber, & Sweeney, 1971, pp. 4-9).

McClusky (1975) has also identified five categories of educational needs with programmatic relevance. The first are *coping* needs. They must be satisfied in order for adequate social adjustment, psychological health, and physical well-being to continue. They take priority over all other needs and may be termed survival needs. They are most urgent for the aged poor and the isolated ethnic populations living in deteriorating cities or in isolated rural environments. Education responses have been short-term sessions providing knowledgeable resource persons to give the elderly useful information that can be important for survival itself. Community police officers, for example, can provide useful hints about self-protection, or social security personnel can interpret the latest policies.

The second category is *expressive* needs, the needs for involvement in activities for the sake of the pleasure the activity gives. Educational responses could be providing courses in personal interest areas such as genealogy, current affairs, or improving skills in a hobby.

The third category is *contributive* needs, the needs of older people to give. They desire to contribute something acceptable to others and to the community. These needs can be easily met through volunteer programs such as foster grandparent or retired senior volunteers. Older people can also satisfy this kind of need by working as volunteers in a college, aiding teachers or administrators. McClusky believes older people represent a reservoir of wisdom and experience that society needs but has not yet learned to exploit.

The fourth need category is *influence.* As we get older, we have a need to exert greater influence on the circumstances of our community, our society, and the world around us. According to McClusky, this kind of need is actually the need to affect the direction and quality of life. Educational programs that are intellectual and that open new dimensions of service in political activity and community leadership may meet these needs.

The need for *transcendence* is the fifth category and is manifested during the later years by the need to become something better than one has been, to achieve a sense of fulfillment in the later years. This kind of need may well be satisfied as a by-product of the gratification of another need. It has to do with ego satisfaction and is an introspective attainment that can be reached only in the mature years of life (pp. 330–338).

Defining the Task

The second requirement in training educators is to translate the real, life-directed needs into educational programs that can answer those needs in a positive way. Underlying any theory of the education of older people is the fact that people change as they become older and their relations with others change. In the important work compiled by Donahue, *Education for Later Maturity,* John E. Anderson (1955) makes the point that an educational program for older people should be broadly conceived, and, as with youth, the very process of development presents unique problems concerning when to present content in relation to the emergence of a need.

The first purpose of education, notes Anderson, is to give older people an understanding of the changes that are taking place and an awareness that they are facing problems in common with other people. The second purpose centers on the imparting of knowledge and skills that will maintain health, retain or increase mental capacity, and enable people to use their own resources more effectively and thus make the most of the facilities available in the environment. The third purpose recognizes the fact that learning, of itself, can be interesting and stimulating. The fourth purpose concerns the richer social experience and better understanding of the world that a longer life gives. Education and guidance provide a real opportunity to build constructively upon the interests that older people show in daydreaming or thinking about the meaning and purpose of life.

Approaches to Preretirement Education

Since the first education course was offered to older people by Tibbitts 25 years ago, there has been a proliferation of such programs, taking place not only in university and college settings, but also in industry, labor unions, public schools, libraries, YW-YMCAs, churches, religious communities, university centers, senior housing projects, multipurpose senior centers, government agencies, and the armed forces. The key to carrying on this unprecedented growth of programs is the preparation of leaders to offer quality programs. Basic aspects of leadership training for preretirement education include objectives, content, and method of training; resources for training; and program evaluation. In training preretirement educators, it is important first to help students develop a frame of reference focused on aging and the *retirement process.* This difficult objective may be met by exposing students to the psychology and sociology of aging; the economic status of older people including social security, Medicare and Medicaid, and other health insurance programs; the health status of older people; housing; income planning; leisure; and community planning and organization for aging. This aspect of the training course should not only provide students with knowledge about the process of aging, but also encourage them to develop a positive philosophy of aging.

A second need is to give students experience in planning, conducting, and evaluating educational programs designed to facilitate the transition of older people from a work to a retirement way of life. Here the emphases are on helping students plan and develop program sessions as well as on providing opportunities to practice what they have learned. Students also acquire skill in identifying and assessing community resources to which older people can turn in an attempt to manage problems of everyday living.

Potential leaders in preretirement education ought to know not only the specific content areas for program development, but also something about effective promotion, community involvement including the use of resources, and evaluation. Sponsorship is directly related to effective promotion of a preretirement education program. Groups of hourly-rated workers sometimes are more likely to participate if their labor unions are involved in conducting the program. Other employees show a preference for programs that are sponsored by management; still others show more inclination to participate when sponsorship includes both union and management support. Delegates to the 1971 White House Conference on Aging endorsed the idea that public education should encourage the support and cooperation of as many interested groups in the community as possible. Preretirement education councils have been highly successful in Great Britain. Membership includes public education, industries and labor organizations, and groups providing services and programs to the elderly, such as committees on the aging, libraries, social agency councils, YM-YWCAs, public housing departments, churches, legal aid, recreation, and so forth. Leaders from such groups may be asked to serve as resource persons in preretirement education programs; others may offer organizational facilities for programs. Leadership qualities should include the abilities to: establish a positive philosophy of aging as a basis for promoting the program, create a congenial atmosphere to help older people overcome their fears and concerns about facing retirement issues and to encourage them to ask questions and to participate in discussion, and make clear that the program is intended to reflect the concerns and interests of participants rather than sponsors.

The training of program leaders includes the skills to conduct group discussion sessions; the breadth of information to assure they can lead and encourage discussion of a variety of solutions to retirement programs; and the need to be informed about community resources available to retired people. Discussion leaders are encouraged to take an inventory of community resources and to interview a sample of people who represent the same occupational, economic, and social characteristics as those with whom they will be working.

The shortage of professionally trained personnel has prompted educators at the University of Michigan and other institutions to train discussion leaders from among personnel directors, union leaders, recreation workers, librarians, and others. Older people themselves may be encouraged to serve as resource persons familiar with their communities. In such roles they can be valuable aides in helping other retirees obtain information about local resources and policies, changing tax benefits; and legislation in such areas as drug prescriptions, legal rights, and consumer information.

Credit courses for graduate students in preretirement education principles and practices are offered at some university centers with gerontology programs. A major training center directing programs to personnel staffs from industry is the University of Chicago Industrial Relations Center. Roosevelt University in Chicago has emphasized training programs for labor leaders. One of the most active centers is the Drake University Pre-Retirement Planning Center, which offers five-day workshops. An AOA model project grant has been awarded to the University of Michigan Institute of Gerontology to train preretirement educators in six midwestern states comprising region V, U.S. Department of Health, Education, and Welfare.

Approaches to Postretirement Education

Another need in the training of leaders is to help them understand that learning should not terminate upon retirement, but should continue throughout life. Problems of living and adjustment do not stop with the cessation of employment. Indeed, if anything, the mature years are a critical time for adjusting to changes in individual and social status, relationships to others, health and well-being, as well as often adverse economic circumstances. In addition, mental health and mental activity are seen to be correlated with successful adjustment to the aging process. To this end, adult educators must themselves assume responsibility for responding to the changing educational needs of retired individuals and their spouses by offering a variety of education programs. Educators may exercise their greatest creativity in program planning in this challenging endeavor, realizing that variety in course format, design, and content, may be as varied as the institutions involved in this growing activity.

National surveys[3] of education for aging indicate an increased awareness among educators of the need to program for, and the potential to serve, older adults. In a survey conducted for the National Council on the Aging, Harris (Harris & Associates, 1975) found that educated older people appeared to have more positive self-images in both mental and physical activities than the less educated. Although this is impressive, the data reveal that research is needed to substantiate findings, to investigate problems, and to study implications for all systems of public education.

Needs assessment is a critical area in programming for older adults, and the literature suggests several strategies, from community surveys to the nominal group process (McElreath, 1976). Hunter (1975) found, in a community survey done in collaboration with Schoolcraft Community College, that older people expressed interest in obtaining information about social security, Medicare, aspects of the law, retirement housing, social services, selecting a place to live, making good use of leisure time, volunteer activity, making the most of retirement income, and ways to maintain health during retirement. Respondents in sizable numbers also expressed interest in participating in cultural events and in being of service to the community. Schools for retirement set up at the college were basically organized to supply information about aspects of aging and to teach retirees skills in solving problems of everyday living.

[3]*National Inventory of Learning Opportunities for Older Adults* by Roger DeCrow for the Adult Education Association of the U.S.A.; *National Survey of Education and Training for Older Persons* by Norman Auburn for the Academy for Educational Development, Inc.; *Older Americans and Community Colleges* by Andrew Korim for the American Association of Community and Junior Colleges.

Programs developed in Detroit-area colleges supported the need for many elderly, particularly urban residents with low educational attainment, to acquire information to help them survive in a hostile, changing environment (Brahce, 1976). A preretirement education program organized in the city of Ann Arbor by the Institute of Gerontology in cooperation with the Kiwanis Club and the Ann Arbor Public Schools Continuing Education Department also supported the continuing need of retired people for basic information that is traditionally regarded as preretirement content. Retired participants indicated a strong desire for information to help them in their struggles with diminishing income, health, and other problems such as how to spend their time. These programs suggest that older adults require specific information at different stages in post-retirement living, in addition to their need to explore new cultural outlets and leisure pursuits. Useful information for retirees may touch on volunteer roles as well as job opportunities. A program that has proved beneficial to retirees, including nursing-home residents, in all socioeconomic and age categories is an intergenerational project to utilize older people as teacher support staff in the Ann Arbor Public Schools (Brahce, 1975).

Program content is limited only by imagination and creative insight of the planner in meeting the requirements of older adults. It was found that courses, such as legal affairs in later life, home nursing, physical fitness after 50, senior adult forum on social security and income, and medical and health services, that deal with practical informational and functional-support needs are most urgently needed by many older people. At the same time, educators at Schoolcraft Community College and Henry Ford Community College (Dearborn, Michigan) determined that courses could also be designed to solve life-change and adapting problems, like "Living Alone and Liking It" for the widowed or the "Know Thyself" offering in self-awareness.

College programmers have discovered that it is essential to provide short sessions or to have frequent breaks in longer periods. Several colleges have successfully designed the minicourse format, which also is useful in giving prospective older adults some ready insights into new offerings. A project in rural, sparsely populated Upper Michigan supports the idea of short offerings with considerable variety. Traveling short sessions were organized at 15 different sites in a health-and-heritage educational adult delivery system organized by administrators at Suomi College under funding from Title I of the Higher Education Act of 1965. A total of 3,919 senior citizens participated in 143 learning sessions, receiving instruction from a combination of college faculty and community residents, including senior adults. Local people or senior scholars coordinated the sessions in such subjects as: social security measures, understanding grief, weaving skills, first aid techniques, protecting valuables, psychology of aging, physical fitness and exercise, nutrition and diet, Finnish heritage, recollections of a bush pilot in Canada, wild flowers, creative retirement, student folk music, recreational dancing, and the metric system (Puotinen, 1976).

In the Institute of Gerontology Consortium Project, teachers of older adults placed strong emphasis on methodology. They stressed the desirability of group discussion and of maximum involvement of the older adult while relaxing the pace of the delivery of new information and of the time required for completing tasks. More individual attention and personal support was encouraged in classes that were designed specifically for older adults.

Educators, then, are advised to keep up-to-date on research in the field of gerontology. Universities share a responsibility to disseminate findings of research and to interpret significant data for professionals working in the field.

The positive affirmation of the powerful force education can exert on changing the lives of elderly has been demonstrated in the Wayne County Consortium on Aging Project. Through the use of videotape evalution, university researchers learned that college programs designed to help older people improve their self-perceptions and to understand such traumatic changes in their lives as death of the spouse or retirement can be valuable in giving the retirees greater self-confidence, independence, and dignity and a feeling of usefulness in their later years.

As Peterson points out:

The challenge that faces adult educators is to re-orient their thinking in such a way that they acknowledge the educational needs of older people and accept the tenet that individuals of all ages have the potential for development and continued growth. This will place educators in a unique position in relation to other professionals providing services to the older population. Other professionals tend to emphasize the decline that accompanies old age . . . . (Peterson, 1975, p. 50)

The importance of motivation in older adult learning is recognized by gerontologists as being very important for the teacher of older adults and the program planner. As Anderson (1955) noted, older people easily drop into a routine and become complacent about life. Because they have met and solved most of their life problems, there is no great pressure for vocational or personal success. These attitudes are obstacles to learning. The instructor's problem is to change these attitudes by showing older people, through activities that appeal directly to immediate needs, that they can learn.

LEARNING PROGRESSION
IN LATER YEARS

Evaluation of the Post-retirement Education Model Project courses at Detroit metropolitan-area colleges revealed that senior adults often seek the challenge of more advanced education stimuli, regardless of their levels of educational attainment. Once they have overcome their hesitancy to enter the college classroom (attributed to a fear-of-failure mind-set and often accentuated by being out of school for many years), older people become self-motivated to pursue more difficult, complex courses of study or skill. This is evident for people with only a few years of schooling as well as for those older adults who have done some college work earlier in their careers. After successfully taking classes, some retirees also realize they have sufficient talent to teach classes. This occurrence, in both men and women, is termed the *learning progression phenomenon* (Brahce, 1976, p. 57).

This acceptance of the next challenge apparently follows the educative needs suggested by McClusky (1974). Those adults with limited (elementary level) educational experience who entered the learning setting at the coping scale of course instruction were seen to aspire to enrollment in courses offering them greater intellectual challenges. Many of the retired people who first participated in quiltmaking or leathercraft courses in which they overcame their fears of failure, shyness with the instructor, and general feelings of inadequacy, went on to take a course in art and music appreciation. Others who signed up for a senior adult forum giving basic information about social security were later sufficiently motivated to enroll in a course in Bible literature. Some students who had never touched a musical instrument learned to distinguish artists' works and to play simple tunes on the piano. Retirees who first enrolled in survival courses to help them understand about social and consumer protection services went on to enroll in mini-courses dealing with politics and letter writing at Highland Park Community College and cultural appreciation at Wayne Community College. Retirees who were participating in a senior aid course in conjunction with a part-time work program made definite improvements in cognitive, emotional, and social growth after program evaluation. When a pilot group of senior adults were given a course in drama, however, many dropped out. This was attributed either to being motivated to move too rapidly (in some cases it was believed that they could not feel comfortable enough about their reading skills to read dramatic parts) or to not being given sufficient encouragement by the teacher. Older people who were at the other end of the scale of educational achievement, having completed some high school or college work, displayed a similar desire to pursue more challenging courses after first enrolling in college programs. These men and women decided to try academic (degree) courses after mastering course material designed for people who had been out of school a long time. Here, self-confidence resulted in older people moving without difficulty from age-segregated settings to age-integrated ones.

Max R. Raines (1974), one of the early teachers of community-college community-leadership functions, has developed a theory of *life-centered education*. Its central thesis is that the equitable and humane society has a moral obligation to provide its members with developmental assistance in acquiring those transactional competencies necessary for (1) reconciling personal needs with societal expectations, and (2) discovering meaning in their lives through their essential life roles. Senior citizens head the list of potential target groups for Raine's life-centered education.

PROGRAMMING

Retirement educators face a three-fold task: (1) they must understand the potentiality of education as a life-centered enterprise of profound consequences for older people; (2) they must determine the resources of their colleges or institutions to answer the continuing needs of their older constituents; and (3) they have to rally those resources effectively within their communities to effect a significant educational response.

University courses directed at community service deans and directors of adult education programs have been constructed with this multiple purpose. An effective instructional methodology, as colleges develop interest, financial support, and commitment, has been to invite educators with experience in program design and implementation to share their knowledge and firsthand information with seminar or workshop participants. The university acts as a catalyst for resource and information dissemination, at the same time providing theoretical knowledge about the developing field of gerontology. Gerontology centers also are able to demonstrate training methodologies, such as milieu therapy, that have proved beneficial to people employed in various institutional settings.

Consortia in Programming

Although community college consortia have not been conducive to progressive developments in some academic areas, examples may be cited of innovative programming and the creation of beneficial educational opportunities for older adults through consortia in aging. A series of bibliographies of short stories, poems, novels, essays, and other works of literature were produced through the Southeastern Michigan Consortium on Gerontology and the Humanities. A variety of intergenerational programs and creative works by seniors were prepared through the project, involving Eastern Michigan University and five community colleges, and funded by the National Endowment for the Humanities. Six colleges in Michigan were funded for the second year to produce programs for older adults in the Consortium for Aging and Retirement Education, one of 11 special community service and continuing education projects funded by the Department of Health, Education, and Welfare, under Title I of the Higher Education Act. Informative newsletters, workshops, and conferences have helped disseminate information to participating and other institutions. As a result of the two-year Post-retirement Education Model Project involving the four colleges in the Detroit area and the Institute of Gerontology, instructional materials have been developed to assist faculty and administrators at two-year institutions in program development and teaching strategies. The Michigan Community College Community Services Association has stimulated both research and program development. A massive program-development project was undertaken by the colleges and universities of the state of Wisconsin, resulting in statewide programs in consort with community agencies. In California, regional educational organizations have given attention to interinstitutional coordination of programs. The Northeastern Council for Higher Education, made up of representatives of six community colleges, California State University at Chico, and the University of California at Davis, has established a task force on older Americans. A planning group, the Regional Association of East Bay Colleges and Universities, has prepared a report on the older citizens of East Bay. The San Francisco Consortium of Institutions of Higher Education is reported to be developing a plan so that people over 65 could take courses at reduced fees on member campuses (California Higher Education Study for the Aging, 1975).

Another approach is a program developed by retirees themselves with the help and encouragement of the New School for Social Research in New York City. It is the Institute for Retired Professionals, and it recognizes that "the vast pool of experience and talents in the retired population must somehow be used constructively in retirement for the benefit of retirees as well as society" (Kauffman & Luby, 1975, p. 143). The institute offers an opportunity for many highly trained, retired professionals to renew their educations at the university level without the usual course procedures. Using their experience and talents in a retiree's self-directed program represents a new approach in adult education.

Directed by Leroy E. Hixson, the Institutes for Lifetime Learning seek to eliminate any discomfort a retiree might feel upon returning to a learning setting. The institutes, an activity of the National Retired Teachers Association and its public unit, the American Association of Retired Persons, offer noncredit courses of shorter duration than the average college semester, usually an eight-week semester with one 90-minute class per week (Kauffman & Luby, 1975).

Media Approaches

The electronic media, powerful forces for public opinion and instant communications, are playing a fast-developing market that reaches to the older adult. Educational awareness through public broadcasting is reaching into production capabilities for educational television, cable television, and the audiovisual outlets as well. Videotape series of programs, *Elderview,* are produced as a joint project of the New England Gerontology Center and the Harbor Institute of the University of Massachusetts, Boston. Funds are provided to the New England Center for Continuing Education by the Administration on Aging. Programs are produced through a grant from AOA. The productions are for groups of individuals, classes, or home viewing via cable television. The Georgia Center for Continuing Education, similarly funded by AOA, has produced a series of films titled *New Wrinkles on Retirement.* They consist of eight half-hour programs dealing with issues confronting the retired person or the person who is planning for retirement. The series has been introduced over originating station WFTV Athens/Atlanta and over the statewide Georgia educational television network. The first national television series ever to deal with the subject of aging premiered January 21, 1976, on the Public Broadcasting Service. Eight one-hour programs, *Images of Aging,* were produced by WITF, Hershey, Pennsylvania, with a grant from the Corporation for Public Broadcasting.

In a new media and aging section of the Gerontological Society, the important role of the mass media was depicted and discussed, including analysis of current programming and research needs, at the national annual meeting in New York, October 14–17, 1976. A commission on media and aging was proposed to develop and promote policy, coordinate research, and study media production and distribution.

Colleges like Jackson Community College in Jackson, Michigan, have extended special offerings to senior adults in cooperation with the local cable television outlet. Videotape is being studied as both a training tool and an evaluation method in training and program design in aging at the Institute of Gerontology.

TRENDS

Expanding forces now operating in retirement education have predictable consequences for training in the field. Several may be singled out:

- As adults reach retirement age in the next decade or so, many of them will have been among the waves of returning GI's who took advantage of educational opportunities. Future retirees therefore will have a higher educational attainment than those now becoming separated from work. Also, the trend toward earlier retirement may be softened with more phased-out retirement. Both events will increase the likelihood of future retirees responding to lifelong educational opportunities.
- More and more women are now working at full- or part-time jobs. Future retirement education will have to make a considerable shift in understanding of spouse relationships, family relationships, and income planning, as more women will be experiencing retirement from work. The whole dimension of sharing years of leisure roles and pursuits will be much different from now on. New educational materials will need to be produced.
- Both men and women will be more interested in obtaining degrees in different fields, or in career change, as the late middle years approach.

- Responsibility for providing retirees not only with pensions, but with lifelong learning aids, will be shared by both labor and industry.
- As legislation to provide lifelong learning options becomes enacted, state and federal education bodies will finally recognize the magnitude of adult learning as a lifelong continuum for people of all socioeconomic groups. More support for education in the later years will be the result.
- Educational institutions, public as well as private colleges and universities, will give credence to the idea of life-centered education. Multidisciplinary programs will become much more common in the field of gerontology, and professional schools will recognize the need for gerontological content in their specialized fields, from law and political science, to nursing and medical training and including psychiatry.
- Institutions will be under pressure to regard graduates as entitled to lifelong certificates of eligibility instead of terminal degrees.
- Research in many disciplines will accelerate the need for gerontology-center coordination and distribution of information and training materials, including multimedia programs.
- The field of postretirement education will assume more significance and importance as the older population increases and institutions recognize the potential of service to this target population of expanding resource value.

REFERENCES

Anderson, J. E. Teaching and learning. In W. T. Donahue (Ed.), *Education for later maturity.* New York: Whiteside 1955.

Atchley, R. C. Retirement and leisure participation: Continuity or crisis. *The Gerontologist,* Spring 1971, pt. 1, pp. 13–17.

Atchley, R. C. Selected social and psychological differences between men and women in later life. *Journal of Gerontology,* 1976, *31*(2), 204–211.

Bauer, B. *A "new" clientele for a "new" community college.* Paper presented at the Summer Institute on Social Gerontology, University of Michigan, Ann Arbor, July/August 1973.

Bottenfield, J. L. *What a community college with limited resources can do in the field of aging.* Paper presented at the Summer Institute in Gerontology, University of Michigan, Ann Arbor, July 1974.

Brahce, C. I. Art bridges the age gap. *Innovator,* 1975, 7(2), pp. 1; 3–5.

Brahce, C. I. *Development of postretirement education models with a community college consortium on aging* (Final report). Ann Arbor: University of Michigan, 1976.

California Higher Education Study for the Aging. *Summary Report.* Sacramento: Author, 1975.

de Beauvoir, S. *The coming of age.* New York: Putnam's, 1972.

Donahue, W. T. Development and current status of university instruction in social gerontology. In R. E. Kushner & M. E. Bunch (Eds.), *Graduate education in aging within the social sciencies.* Ann Arbor: University of Michigan, 1967.

Feller, R. A. *Education for the elderly: Part of a comprehensive service program.* Paper presented at the Summer Institute on Social Gerontology, University of Michigan, Ann Arbor, 1973.

Glamser, F. D. Determinants of a positive attitude toward retirement. *Journal of Gerontology,* 1976, *31,* 104–107.

Gleazer, E. J., Jr. After the boom . . . what NOW for the community colleges. *Community and Junior College Journal,* December/January 1974, pp. 6–11.

Harris, L., & Associates. *The myths and reality of aging in America.* Washington, D.C.: National Council on the Aging, 1975.

Hunter, W. W. Preretirement education and planning. In *Education for the Aging.* S. M. Grabowski & W. D. Mason (Eds.), *Learning for aging.* Washington, D.C.: Adult Education Association of the U.S.A., 1975; Syracuse: ERIC Clearinghouse on Adult Education.

Jonas, D., & Jonas, D. *Young till we die.* New York: Coward, 1973.

Kauffman, E., & Luby, P. Non-traditional education: Some new approaches to a dynamic culture. In S. M. Grabowski & W. D. Mason (Eds.), *Learning for aging.* Washington, D.C.: Adult Education Association of the U.S.A., 1975; Syracuse: ERIC Clearinghouse on Adult Education.

Korim, A. S. *Older Americans and community colleges: A guide for program implementation.* Washington, D.C.: American Association of Community and Junior Colleges, 1974.

McClusky, H. Y. Section on Aging. In *Toward a national policy on aging: Final report of the 1971 White House Conference on Aging* (Vol. 11). Washington, D.C.: U.S. Government Printing Office, 1973, pp. 1–10.

McClusky, H. Y. Education for aging: The scope of the field and perspectives for the future. In S. M. Grabowski & W. D. Mason (Eds.), *Learning for aging.* Washington, D.C.: Adult Education Association of the U.S.A., 1975; Syracuse: ERIC Clearinghouse on Adult Education.

McElreath, M. P. How to figure out what adults want to know. *Adult Leadership,* March 1976, 232–235.

Myran, G. A., Huber, R., & Sweeney, S. M. *Senior citizens services in community colleges* (Research and Report Series, No. 5). East Lansing: Michigan State University, 1971.

Peterson, D. A. The role of gerontology in adult education. In S. M. Grabowski & W. D. Mason (Eds.), *Learning for aging.* Washington, D.C.: Adult Education Association of the U.S.A., 1975; Syracuse: ERIC Clearinghouse on Adult Education.

Puotinen, A. E. *Heads up—Health and Heritage Educational Adult Delivery System: Upper Peninsula.* Hancock, Mich.: Suomi College, 1976.

Raines, M. R. *Life-centered education.* (Research and Report Series, No. 6). East Lansing: Michigan State University, 1974.

Ross, J. K. Learning to be retired: Socialization into a French retirement residence. *Journal of Gerontology*, 1974, *29*(2), 211–223.

Streib, G. F., & Schneider, C. J. *Retirement in American society: Impact and process.* Ithaca: Cornell University Press, 1971.

Sussman, M. B. An analytic model for the sociological study of retirement. In F. M. Carp (Ed.), *Retirement.* New York: Behavioral Publications, 1972.

Tibbits, C. Aging and living: A report of the first course offered to assist people in making adjustments to old age. *Adult Education Bulletin*, 1948, *13*, 204–211.

Tibbits, C. Social gerontology in education for the professions. In R. E. Kushner & M. E. Bunch (Eds.), *Graduate education in aging within the social sciences.* Ann Arbor: University of Michigan, 1967.

Toward a national policy on aging: Final report of the 1971 White House Conference on Aging (Vol. 11). Washington, D.C.: U.S. Government Printing Office, 1973.

United States Senate, Special Committee on Aging. *Older Americans comprehensive services amendments of 1973.* Washington, D.C.: U.S. Government Printing Office, 1973.

14

DYING AS THE FINAL STAGE OF GROWTH: ISSUES AND CHALLENGES

HANNELORE WASS

University of Florida

Throughout history, human beings have struggled to understand the meaning of their existence. Different cultures and civilizations have produced different ideas about life and death. Marcuse (1959) gives us a glance into the wide variety of theories about death formulated just in the course of Western thought alone when he states: "The interpretation of death has run the gamut from the notion of a mere natural fact, pertaining to man as organic matter, to the idea of death as the *telos* of life, the distinguishing feature of human existence" (p. 64). Every life-death theory, whether it is formulated in the context of a religious belief system or in a system of philosophic thought, is, in the final analysis, an attempt to derive a sense of order and comfort in the face of one's mortality. Each individual, regardless of his or her commitment to, negation of, or indifference to institutionalized religious thinking or the cultural Zeitgeist or milieu, has to conceptualize and confront his or her own death and derive his or her own personal meaning. Herman Feifel (1959), the famous psychiatrist, a philosopher and pioneer in the field of death and dying, has suggested in the introduction to his book *The Meaning of Death* that the critical existential question "is not the sham dichotomy of life and death but rather how each of us relates to the knowledge that death is certain" (p. xi). Unfortunately, avoidance of such personal confrontation is common in modern Western civilizations. Herman Feifel (1959), the late British historian Arnold Toynbee (1968), the British anthropologist Geoffrey Gorer (1965), and many other contemporary social scientists have made this observation, but it is the psychologists and psychiatrists who most impress upon us that we can ill afford to indulge ourselves with such avoidance. As Feifel (1959) points out, this escapism can result in severe psychological illness because it affects the very core of our being. According to Feifel (pp. xi–xii) and many existential philosophers as well, our identity as unique individuals becomes meaningful only as we realize that we are finite. It is the recognition of this fact that makes life precious. Erikson (1959, 1963), in his theory of human development and particularly in his formulations about the final stage of man (discussed later), comes to similar conclusions.

Perhaps this is the fundamental factor in the human tragedy: On the one hand, we grow to learn the pride of achievement and of our ability to look back into the past and transcend our present to envision the future; thus we are able to escape our bodies with soaring dreams and imagination and are able to develop our sense of power and uniqueness. On the other hand, we are continually frustrated and humiliated by our ultimate finiteness and our impotence in the face of death, and we are possessed by a deep anxiety over our eventual fate. To come to accept this fate in the twentieth-century Western world is no mean task, and its accomplishment is a great victory. Erikson (1959, 1963) has developed a theory about the obstacles that have to be overcome to achieve this victory.

THE FINAL STAGE OF LIFE: INTEGRITY VERSUS DESPAIR

Erik Erikson's (1950, 1959, 1963) theory of human development asserts that there are eight stages through which a person has to pass in moving through the life cycle from infancy to old age. Each stage in the development presents a crisis in one's understanding of oneself, of one's purposes, and of one's relationships with others. One may not be consciously aware of these crises, as in the early stages, but they exist nevertheless. The developmental task at each stage is to resolve the crisis successfully; only then can the person progress to the next stage of maturity. Erikson (1959, pp. 55–100) identified the eight stages and crises as follows: (1) infancy; trust versus mistrust, (2) early childhood: autonomy versus shame and doubt, (3) play age: initiative versus guilt, (4) school age: industry versus inferiority, (5) adolescence: identity versus identity diffusion, (6) young adulthood: intimacy versus isolation, (7) adulthood: generativity versus self-absorption, and (8) senescence: integrity versus despair. Although this discussion is concerned with the last stage in the development, it is important to note that, according to Erikson, a person must have been successful, at least to some degree, in solving the seven crises that come before in order to be able to resolve the crisis of the final stage. It is also important to recognize that senescence is the final stage and, unlike the others, is not a stepping stone to a more mature level of development. Erikson (1963) states: "Each individual, to become a mature adult, must to a sufficient degree develop all .the ego qualities of the previous stages, so that a wise Indian, a true gentleman, and a mature peasant share and recognize in one another the final stage of integrity" (p. 268).

The task of the final stage of life is to achieve integrity. By Erikson's own admission, integrity has no clear definition. What he means by integrity is the achievement of a state of mind at the end of life that is a conviction that one's life has meaning and purpose, that having lived has made a difference. It is an understanding that—despite the struggles and defeats one has experienced in growing up and as a parent, mate, friend, or co-worker—one's life, in its culminating phase, is positive, and one's humanity has been fulfilled. More than that, one comes to comprehend that one's life is a link between past and future generations and has its place in the flow of history (Erikson, 1950). Other psychologists have formulated similar concepts, such as Abraham Maslow's (1968) *self-actualization,* Gordon Allport's (1961) *self-objectification,* James Birren's (1964) *reconciliation,* and Robert Peck's (1956) *ego-transcendence.*

This mental state is illustrated in a religious context by Paul when he writes about his understanding of the meaning of his life, in a letter from his final imprisonment in Rome to his young apprentice Timothy: "As for me already my life is being poured out on the altar, and the hour for my departure is upon me. I have run the great race, I have finished the course, I have kept faith" (2 Tim. 4:7). In the last eight lines of his poem "Terminus," Ralph Waldo Emerson expresses a similar attitude and the view that the termination of life is exultant:

> *As the bird trims her to the gale,*
> *I trim myself to the storm of time,*
> *I man the rudder, reef the sail,*
>
> *Obey the voice at eve obeyed at prime:*
> *"Lowly faithful, banish fear,*
> *Right onward drive unharmed;*
> *The port, well worth the cruise, is near,*
> *And every wave is charmed."*

A similar expression is found in the form of a sculpture that stands in front of the Faculty of Medicine at the University of Madrid. A young man on horseback, poised to take off on a race, reaches back to take a scroll extended by an aged man almost prostrate on the ground. The expression on the old man's face is one of serenity, as if in his final moments he sees himself as an effective, meaningful link in the continuing human chain. As Erikson (1963) puts it: "He knows that for him all human integrity stands and falls with the one style of integrity of which he partakes. The style of integrity developed by his culture or civilization then becomes the 'patrimony of the soul,' the seal of his moral paternity of himself. In such final consolidation, death loses its sting" (p. 140). An excellent illustration of this attitude is the statements made by the 63-year-old Reverend Bryant in the moving film documentary *Dying* (Roemer, 1976). After the physician told Reverent Bryant that he had cancer of the liver and there was nothing that could be done, he replied: "Well, I've never had it told to me before, but it's all right; we're going on forward," and in a later scene, he said: "I can say right now that I'm living some of the greatest moments in life.... The doctors told me that I don't have much longer to live, but I'm not upset. I want to live as long as I can, but I'm not going to die on account of death."

But pity the person who does not attain this final integrity. According to Erikson, she or he experiences a deep fear of death and cannot accept the one and only life cycle as the ultimate life. Despair is overwhelming at the realization that time is short, too short to start another life, to find alternate ways of living and achieving integrity. Such despair, in Erikson's view, is difficult to overcome. It is the final identity crisis and the final loss of one's sense of worth. Erikson's views are very pessimistic, however. There are many instances in which an old, dying person—although not accepting life—may come to accept death, particularly when the person either is deeply religious or is given understanding and love in his or her final moments. As Charles Mayo, (Thanatology, 1964), retired surgeon of the Mayo Clinic, put it: "I hope that when I die, it will be quick. But if there is some delay, then I hope I'll have somebody I love with me—somebody to hold my hand" (p. 95). Mayo's wish is probably shared by most, but when deep faith is absent and no loved ones are around, help may still be rendered. Lawrence Roose (1969) of the Department of Psychiatry at Mount Sinai Hospital in New York, in his article "To Die Alone," pleads with eloquence that hospitals make psychological and psychiatric service available to help nonpsychiatric physicians better understand and help dying patients, particularly those who are desperate, terrified, and alone.

THE LIFE REVIEW

Erikson discusses the crisis at the final stage and gives us a good understanding of the mental state of integrity versus despair, but he does not discuss how one reaches this state. An answer is found in the process by which an old person redefines his or her life to obtain a new and more mature meaning, a process that is accomplished by the *life review*, a concept advanced by R. N. Butler (1963). Although Butler never related his notions to Erikson's, it is apparent that the two are in close harmony. Whereas Erikson outlines the substance of the crisis at the final stage of development and its consequences of solution and failure, Butler postulates the process necessary to resolve the crisis. Butler, however, goes beyond merely asserting the life review as a natural and universal process characteristic of old people; he also postulates a purpose. According to Butler, the life review is triggered by the realization that one has reached the end of life and that death is near. The life review serves to prepare a person for dying, and it may decrease the fear of death.

Old people are known to reminisce a great deal and are often accused of living in the past. Frequently they try the patience of the listener, who tends to view this reminiscing as excessive or even as a psychological disorder. According to Butler, however, such reminiscing has an important function; it is nothing less than the attempt to revive past experiences, reevaluate them, sum them up, and integrate them into a new understanding. Obviously, this task can be helped or hindered by those around the old people. Because self-esteem is centrally involved, and reviewing of the past reaches into the present, the attitudes and behavior of old people's relatives, friends, or care givers can affect their success or failure in accepting their deaths. Nurturing and empathic people can help the aged a great deal. A chilling example of a hostile environment and its effect is found in Simone de Beauvoir's (1973b) book *A Very Easy Death*, in which she describes, with moving frankness and self-analysis, her own inability to give emotional support to her dying mother and the incredible indifference and coldness of the hospital staff.

Regardless of the environment, however, the life review, according to Butler, does not always lead to well-integrated serenity. When unresolved conflicts arise from the past, and unrealized ambitions and missed opportunities come crowding into the mind at a time when it is too late to do anything about it, a deep depression often sets in which may lead to disturbance or even suicide. Even if the life review process leads in the end to an acceptance of death, the process may involve anguish, terror, and despair. An outstanding example is the experience of Ivan Ilych in Leo Tolstoy's (1960) classic short story "The Death of Ivan Ilych." Ivan Ilych knew with certainty that he was dying, even though his physician and his family pretended that it was not so. Ivan began his internal dialogue and traveled back through his life:

> He began to recall the best moments of his pleasant life. But strange to say none of those best moments of his pleasant life now seemed at all what they had seemed—none of them except the first recollections of childhood. There, in childhood, there had been something pleasant with which it would be possible to live if it could return. But the child who had experienced that happiness existed no longer, it was a reminiscence of somebody else. As soon as the period began which had produced the present Ivan Ilych, all that had then seemed joys now melted before his sight and turned into something trivial and often nasty. And the further he departed from childhood and the nearer he came to the present the more worthless and doubtful were the joys. (p. 147)

As Ivan Ilych reminisced about his career as a government official, about his marriage and early disenchantment, his hypocrisy and the emptiness of his life, he said to himself: "Maybe I did not live as I ought to have done" (p. 148). Over the next two weeks, he suffered the agonies of physical pain from his cancer and the even greater agonies of mental pain over the loss of his life, and he suffered the anguish and the urgent need to understand what life was all about. Then the question began to torment him: "What if my whole life has really been wrong?" (p. 152). It was after Ivan Ilych admitted having lived with falsehood and deception, hiding life and death, that he began to scream, and his screaming continued for three days. He became quiet two hours before his death with the realization that "it was not right . . . but that's no matter. . . . " Then Ivan caught sight of the life, "and it was revealed to him that though his life had been wrong, it could still be rectified. . . . And he felt sorry for his son and for his wife. His fear of death vanished. In its place he felt there was light. "So that's what it is,' he suddenly exclaimed. 'What joy!' " (pp. 155–156). Ivan Ilych found his meaning very late but not too late. It was his final understanding that made his dying dignified, serene, and even joyful.

A good many people are spared such agonies and are deprived of such opportunities for grasping their final truths, because they die in accidents, in their sleep, under heavy sedation, or in a comatose state. Others who die with conscious awareness do not achieve or strive for the state of serenity and peace that Ivan Ilych did. Many people die screaming and fighting to their last breaths, and that may be the best they can do; and in terms of who they were in life, that may be appropriate and even dignified. But in United States culture and the Judeo-Christian tradition, the ideal is that dying be accomplished in reconciliation, peace, and serenity. The American poet William Cullen Bryant expresses this in the final lines of his poem "Thanatopsis."

> So live, that when thy summons comes to join
> The innumerable caravan, which moves
> To that mysterious realm, where each shall take
> His chamber in the silent halls of death,
> Thou go not, like a quarry-slave at night,
> Scourged to his dungeon, but, sustained and soothed
> By an unfaltering trust approach thy grave,
> Like one who wraps the drapery of his couch
> About him, and lies down to pleasant dreams.

Yet, although this is the ideal, the attitudes and practices of the culture make it a very difficult one to achieve.

YOUTH CULT AND DEATH TABOO

Growing old in the United States is difficult to accomplish, painful to experience. Members of this society worship youth and trim, firm bodies. It is made particularly hard for women to accept their aging. Somehow, in this society, physical attractiveness and sexual attractiveness are made synonymous, and sociologists tell women they lose their sex appeal around the age of 35. This perception is not confined to the United States; Simone de Beauvoir (1973a) has harshly criticized European societies as well for their negative attitudes toward the mature and older woman.

The United States cosmetics industry makes millions of dollars annually from promoting a frantic need to appear young. Television commercials tell the viewer, at least implicitly, that young is "beautiful" and old is "ugly." Using the "right" brand of detergent will make a mother's hands look just like her daughter's; soaps have the power to wash away the wrinkles and make the female skin velvety smooth. Encouraging such self-deception is not helpful for the aging person. This author has traveled in other countries and found no society in which so many women copy the fashions of the young, wear bright colors, and go miniskirted and bikinied, with hair bleached, cheeks rouged, and faces surgically lifted. It is sad to observe such futile attempts at hiding the facts of aging; nothing is quite so pathetic as an old person trying to look young. Physical aging is less of a problem for men because, with the double standard still much in practice, an older man, graying at the temples, dressed expensively in the carefully designed casualness of the tailored leisure suit, is often found quite attractive in a variety of ways by women of all ages. But men are also prone to adopting the trappings of the youth cult, manifested in dyed hair, toupees, and so forth.

It is said that "beauty is in the eyes of the beholder," but it is equally true that concepts of beauty are adopted wholesale from the mass media and the film industry. It takes time, open minds and hearts, and some guidance to learn to appreciate the beauty of old age. Old faces have, nonetheless, excited painters and sculptors for centuries. There can be much beauty in an old face where the wrinkles tell the story of a rich life filled with hardships, successes, sorrows, and joys. There is beauty in a face that shows wisdom and serenity. Appreciation of old age is an attitude that is learned. It needs to be learned from childhood on. It needs to be learned by the aged themselves.

In a country where youth is worshipped as much as in the United States, there is little room for death. It is a forbidden topic. Fortunately, however, the taboo on death is being lifted. Rapidly the subject is becoming more acceptable for open discussion and as subject matter for education. The movement has been swift, for it it has only been a decade or less since the renowned British anthropologist Geoffrey Gorer (1965) observed that death is treated as if it were pornography; since the famous historian the late Arnold Toynbee (1968) charged that Americans consider death un-American—a violation of their right to life, liberty, and the pursuit of happiness; since the well-known French writer-sociologist Philippe Ariès (1974) wrote about "forbidden death"; since Avery Weisman (1972) wrote his important analytic work *On Dying and Denying*; since Ernest Becker (1973) wrote his incisive book *The Denial of Death*; and since the journalist David Hendin (1973) told us, with the title of his book, to see *Death as a Fact of Life*. So, we have rediscovered death. The general public is coming increasingly in contact with death through the mass media, notably through the extensive national press coverage of the Karen Ann Quinlan case, and particularly through television films, documentaries, and special programs. In 1976, for example, the viewer could see such films as *Death Be not Proud* by John Gunther, *Brian Piccolo* by Jeannie Morris, *Eric* by Doris Lund, the documentary *Dying* produced by Michael Roemer (1976), and several interviews with Elizabeth Kübler-Ross, as well as a number of other films and programs on death and dying. This new awareness of death, of our own personal finiteness in particular, is a laudable development, and it is to be hoped that it will not come to be viewed as just another fad or temporary fascination.

In spite of open discussion of death and dying in many college classrooms and in the public media, the subject is still largely avoided in the presence of children, terminal patients, and old people. It is amazing that there is such reluctance to talk about death with old people. They are nearing the end of the life cycle and presumably are closest to death, not only with respect to time, but with respect to psychological orientation as well. There is speculation among scientists as to why talk of death is avoided with the elderly. Some believe that younger adults avoid the topic because it reminds them too chillingly of their own eventual demise. Others believe the subject is avoided so as not to upset an old person unduly and cause additional anxiety.

Even old people sometimes adopt such death-denying attitudes. Muriel Spark (1959) has brilliantly illustrated this death denial in her novel *Momento Mori*. She writes:

> *Dame Lettie telephoned to the Assistant Inspector as she had been requested to do. "It has occurred again," she said.*
>
> *"I see. Did you notice the time?"*
>
> *"It was only a moment ago."*
>
> *"The same thing?"*
>
> *"Yes," she said, "the same. Surely you have some means of tracing—"*
>
> *"Yes, Dame Lettie, we will get him of course."*
>
> *A few moments later Dame Lettie telephoned to her brother Godfrey. "Godfrey, it has happened again!"*
>
> *"I'll come and fetch you, Lettie," he said. "You must spend the night with us."*
>
> *"Nonsense. There is no danger. It is merely a disturbance."*
>
> *"What did he say?"*
>
> *"The same thing. And quite matter-of-fact, not really threatening. Of course the man's mad. I don't know what the police are thinking of, they must be sleeping. It's been going on for six weeks now."*

"Just those words?"

"Just the same words 'Remember you must die'—nothing more."

"He must be a maniac," said Godfrey.[1]

OLD PEOPLE'S ATTITUDES ABOUT DEATH

How pervasive is death denial among the elderly? Do they indeed become more anxious and upset when death is talked about? Do they indeed avoid talking about it among themselves and with younger people? Answers are found in a number of studies.

Old People Talk about Death

Riley (1968), surveying a national sample of 1,500 adults, reported that the majority of older people think about death and say openly that it is an important issue. The author (Wass, 1976, 1977; Wass & Sisler, 1978) has asked nearly 300 old people, either by interview or through questionnaire, a number of personal questions about death and found almost all of her subjects willing to answer, many of them eager to do so and only a very small fraction to be reluctant or actually upset. Robert Kastenbaum (1963) found that people close to death in a geriatric hospital made more positive than negative or neutral references to death. The ratio was 7 to 1 in favor of positive statements. On the other hand, Roberts, Kimsey, Logan, and Shaw (1970) reported in their study that 35% of nursing-home residents said they almost never think about death, whereas 23% think about death often, and Kimsey, Roberts, and Logan (1972) reported that 50% of nursing-home residents avoided talking about death. But then Matse (1975) asked nursing-home staff whether or not death was talked about among the residents. His findings indicated that it was a frequently talked about topic among the residents. It should be noted here that it is practically impossible for the staff of a nursing home to provide an accurate record of all statements made by residents. In addition, as Kastenbaum (1967) has pointed out, there are many possible ways of referring to death indirectly, and it is quite likely that more subtle references are not recognized by nursing-home staff.

It appears that whether or not old people talk about death depends to a large extent on the kind of environment they find themselves in. Environments can be restrictive with an unwritten rule "No talk of death here," or they can be open and honest. (Restrictive and permissive environments are discussed in more detail later.) If the reader still needs to be convinced of the willingness of old people to talk about death, an article by Saul and Saul

---

[1] From *Momento Mori* by Muriel Spark. Copyright © 1959 by Muriel Spark. Reprinted by permission of J. B. Lippincott Company.

(1973), "Old People Talk about Death," should remove the doubt. Except for a brief introduction and summary, this paper consists entirely of transcripts of taped discussions between a therapist and a group of elderly residents in a nursing home in the Bronx.

Fear of Death among Old People

Psychologists agree that facing up to death or denying it is closely related to one's fear of death. The general consensus among experts is that it is the fear of death that brings about the death denial in the first place. Reviewing a number of studies in which aging people's fear of death was investigated should help with an understanding of the causes of the fear.

First it must be stressed that the aged are by no means a homogeneous group. Old people have certain characteristics in common, most important among them the facts that they are in the final phase of their lives and that death is imminent. There is variation, however, in the manner in which old people cope with these facts, and there is variation in the environmental circumstances in which old people exist. This variability becomes particularly apparent when studying the fear of death. There is no uniformity concerning the fear of death among old people as there is no single, common attitude toward death.

James Birren (1964) categorized the aging into five groups according to their attitudes toward death: death-welcomers, death-accepters, death-postponers, death-disdainers, and death-fearers (p. 274). A less elaborate but similar classification is offered by Swenson (1961): His subjects wrote essays that fell into three categories: positive or optimistic, evasive or apprehensive, and fearful. A study by Jeffers, Nichols, and Eisdorfer (1961) showed only 10% of the elderly expressing fear, and the "no fear" responses were associated with religiosity and fewer feelings of rejection and depression. Similarly, Swenson (1961) found higher death acceptance among old people with fundamental religious conviction and habits and among those who lived with family or friends. Wass and Sisler (1978) surveyed elderly people living in the community and found that rural, poor elderly people with little formal education are more fearful of death than urban, financially independent or well-off, highly educated elderly people. Those living with their families show less death anxiety than those living alone, and men are less afraid of death than women. Studies by Rhudick and Dibner (1961) and by Richardson and Freeman (1968) showed fear of death among old people is associated with poor physical and mental health, and Wolff (1970) and Templer (1971) have shown that fear of death is more prevalent among old people with severe emotional disturbances and personality disorders.

In a number of studies, the fears of aged, institutionalized people were examined or their fears were compared with those of elderly people living in the community. Kimsey, Roberts, and Logan (1972) discovered that 50% of the elderly in nursing homes show death denial whereas only 16% of the noninstitutionalized elderly do. Shrut (1958) compared the fears of death of aged, female residents in the apartment section of a home for aged and infirm Hebrews with those who lived in the more institutionalized Central House of the same home. He discovered that those living in the apartments show less fear than those in the more institutionalized setting. In a study by Lieberman and Coplan, (1969) it is reported that elderly people who are near death and living in the community are less anxious than dying, aged people waiting to be admitted to a nursing home or those who have recently been admitted.

The picture that emerges from these various findings is that old people's fear of death is affected by numerous factors, physical, psychological, and social. We see that physical health affects the fear of death and so does psychological health, religiosity, and the degree of social distance in the community. We see that old people's fear of death is less for those living with family than for those living alone, and, more powerfully, is less for those living in the community than for those who are institutionalized.

Marshall (1975) has stated that the elderly may not fear death as much as they fear the process of dying; that is, they are more concerned about the expected pain, or about isolation and abandonment, physical or emotional, than about death itself. This observation is borne out by the studies mentioned above. Most of the studies cited here do not make distinctions like Marshall does. There may, in fact, be other kinds of fear in addition to the ones Marshall names, for example, the fear of losing one's consciousness and mental faculties or the fear of total dependence upon others, either family or hospital or nursing-home staff. There may be a closer relation between these fears and the issue of euthanasia than is apparent at first glance.

EUTHANASIA OR THE RIGHT TO DIE

How often is an old person "sentenced to life," or, as Cicely Saunders (1969) puts it, how often are we, in our medical care, "prolonging dying," rather than living (p. 52)? The question of euthanasia is highly complex. It is a social, ethical, moral, religious, legal, and personal issue, and answers are difficult to find. Debate on the pros and cons of euthanasia is currently in full swing and will probably continue for some time to come. Clergymen, physicians, lawyers, ethicists, sociologists, psychologists, and "consumers" are involved in the debate. The terms *euthanasia, death with dignity, dignity,* and even *death* still mean different things to different people. The word *euthanasia* is derived from the Greek and literally means "good death." Distinctions, such as "active" and "passive" euthanasia, are made. A doctor giving an overdose of morphine or ordering the plugs pulled on machines that keep life systems functioning artificially are examples of active euthanasia, also called "mercy killing." A doctor withholding a life-prolonging drug, treatment, or technical device would be an example of passive euthanasia, which has generally been more acceptable than active. Even active euthanasia may be becoming more acceptable now, the high courts having recently ruled in the Karen Ann Quinlan case that a team of physicians, with permission of the family, could take Karen off the machine that was artifically supporting her life. In practice, the distinction between active and passive euthanasia is often blurred. One pediatric nurse, during a panel discussion at a meeting of critical-care nurses, pleaded for active euthanasia. She told of cases in which defective infants with no chance for survival and normal development are left to die at the hospital where she is employed; that is, she is ordered not to feed the infants. It takes about a week and sometimes longer before such infants die.

The key issue, particularly when considering the dying old person, is whether or not to use mechanical devices to keep cardiac or respiratory systems functioning in cases in which there is no reasonable hope for recovery. The issue is complex. Physicians are bound by the Hippocratic oath to cure illness and save lives; this is the essence of their profession. In addition, the legality or illegality of practicing euthanasia is still unclear. But what is the person's right? Surprisingly perhaps, United States citizens have no constitutional rights to die; they do have a constitutional right to live, however. Even so, the Euthanasia Educational Council of New York has formulated and makes available a living will. In it, any adult, while well and fully competent, can express the wish not to be maintained by artificial means in the event of serious illness with no reasonable hope of recovery. Although such a document is not legally binding, in most states it may be morally binding to family and physician, and apparently, even in the Quinlan case, would have made it easier for the courts to make their rulings. A living will would certainly help the families of aged people and their physicians in making the difficult decision about prolonging or shortening life when dying people are confused or comatose. This would lessen considerably the mental anguish associated with such decisions.

In the recent past, the demand for accountability of physicians and hospitals has been forcefully voiced in the United States. As a result, patients' rights have become of considerable concern to health professionals and hospital administrators. A list of patients' rights was developed by the American Hospital Association in 1973. Also in 1973, the American Medical Association produced a list of principles of medical ethics. Interesting for review with respect to the issues of death with dignity is the set of guidelines adopted by the general assembly of the World Medical Association at Geneva, Switzerland, in 1948. These lists are too extensive to reproduce here but can be found in Dr. Heifetz's book *The Right to Die* (1975, pp. 174–184). In the same book can also be found the very widely discussed report by an ad hoc committee of the Harvard Medical School concerning an up-to-date medical definition of death. It may be disturbing to the reader, but there is no universally agreed-upon medical definition of death at the present time, other than what is now known as "brain death." The Harvard report, which basically consists of technical guidelines to determine death has, however, become the standard for the United States (for the complete report, *see* Heifetz, 1975, pp. 184-199).

Two critical questions in connection with a medical definition of death and with the issue of euthanasia are: What do we mean by life? and What is the quality, as compared to the quantity, of life? Is it not surprising that old people should want to be allowed to die when they have lived full lives, are either weak and suffering much pain or sedated and conscious only part of the time, and are totally helpless and dependent upon those who care for them. It may be humane to let such people die.

It is impossible in these pages to give a full account of the complex issues involved in euthanasia, death with dignity, and the right to die. The reader is referred to the following works for excellent discussions and further information: Edwin Shneidman (1976), *Death: Current Perspectives,* Chapter 8; Orville Brim, H. E. Freeman, S. Levine, and N. A. Scotch (1970), *The Dying Patient,* part III; Milton Heifetz (1975), *The Right to Die*; Marya Mannes (1974), *Last Rights*; and Cicely Saunders's (1969, 1972, 1976) articles about her work at St. Christopher's Hospice in England.

Before leaving the subject, it is important, however, to report briefly on studies about what old people themselves have to say about euthanasia, death with dignity, and the right to die. In a survey of 171 rural and urban elderly people in Florida conducted by the author (Wass, 1977), an adaptation of Edwin Shneidman's (1976) death questionnaire was used to determine the views and opinions of old people concerning death. Two of the questions dealt with the timing of death. To the question If your physician knew that you had a terminal disease and a limited time to live, would you want him to tell you? 87% of the elderly responded yes. To the question What efforts do you believe ought to be made to keep the seriously ill person alive? 73% responded that a person ought to be permitted to die a natural death, and none felt that a person should be kept alive by artificial means. Similar results have been reported by Mathieu and Peterson (1970) in a survey of 183 elderly people in California. Of their respondents, 80% said they would want their physicians to tell them if they were terminally ill, and only 4% were in favor of keeping a person alive at all cost.

Feifel (1961) commented that the temporal nearness or distance of death is an important factor in determining one's attitude toward death. Could it be, then, that attitudes of aging people toward euthanasia change as death becomes imminent? This question has been answered. There is today enough evidence from clinical studies with aging, terminal patients to show that their attitudes are the same as those of people not in the terminal stage. Kübler-Ross (1969), Weisman (1972), Hinton (1966, 1967), and Saunders (1969, 1972) have all found that most terminally ill geriatric patients quietly accept their death and often wait for or actually look forward to dying. Many nurses and physicians have told the author how old patients time and again plead with the doctor or with God: "Please let me go," or "How much longer will it be? I am waiting." As can be seen, old people have strong convictions with regard to the timing of death. Other death-related views held by old people are discussed next.

ATTITUDES TOWARD FUNERAL PRACTICES

The French writer-sociologist Ariès (1974) has observed an interesting difference between Europe and the United States in twentieth-century attitudes toward and practices of funeral rites and body disposal. He considers the American attitudes a strange compromise between opposing trends. On the one hand, certain traditional rituals have survived in the United States, such as the wake, which has been largely abandoned in modern, industrialized Europe, especially among the middle classes, but has survived in the United States in the form of lying in state in an open casket. Viewing the body publicly is unthinkable in England or Germany. This custom has created, in the United States, the practice of embalming and dressing up the body, a practice that most contemporary Europeans find appalling and which has provided the material for Evelyn Waugh's (1948) biting satire *The Loved One*. On the other hand, although Europe has broken with the tradition of the wake and although cremation is a much more common form of body disposal than in the United States, Europeans are not willing to admit their disregard for elaborate funeral ritual. They would be shocked at the United States funeral industry's open promotion of quick, convenient services, for example, advertising of easy access and the number of parking spaces, or even of the new convenience of the drive-in funeral home (Hendin, 1973) where people can view the body through a window while remaining in the car, just like in window banking.

Ariès believes that Americans are satisfied with their funeral customs. This may have been true a few decades ago, but it is no longer true today. American attitudes toward funeral practices are changing. For some time now, the American funeral industry has come under severe scrutiny by federal agencies and citizens groups, mostly for the high prices of caskets and the high prices for the packaging of services. Jessica Mitford (1963), with her national bestseller *The American Way of Death,* probably deserves much, if not most, of the credit for the recent public interest and concern about the funeral industry. Along with this general concern, American attitudes toward funeral practices are changing. Shneidman (1971) in a survey of readers of the journal *Psychology Today,* received 30,000 responses to his death questions. Among other findings, he discovered that 70% of the respondents disapproved or strongly disapproved of lying in state and 80% considered funerals in the United States much overpriced. Shneidman concluded, from his analysis of the responses of his predominantly young and highly educated national sample, that this may be "a critical minority which may reveal where the rest of society is heading" (1971).

Indeed, using Shneidman's questionnaire, a survey (Wass, Milton, Myers, & Murphey, in press) of 171 elderly people with various educational and social backgrounds from three locales showed that almost the same percentage, 78%, considered funeral prices too high. Of lying in state, 48% of the elderly disapproved or strongly disapproved, whereas 40% did not care one way or the other. Another survey (Wass, 1976) of 366 people, ranging in age from 15 to 76 years, revealed that almost 50% of both the youngest age group (15 to 18) and the oldest age group (65 years or older) reported they disapproved or strongly disapproved of lying in state, and 70% of the age group 22 to 45 years of age indicated such disapproval. The majority in all age groups considered funeral prices to be much too high. The range of this response was from 60% to 76% across the various age groups. These findings make clear that attitudes toward funeral practices are changing and that this change can be found at all the different age levels from adolescence to old age.

THE PROCESS OF DYING

No one really knows what it is like to die. Dying is as mysterious as being born. Although dying is a most significant and universal human event, observing and reporting it is at best incomplete and at worst impossible. Nevertheless, attempts have been made and continue to be made to come as close as possible to describing the experience of dying and, at least, to determine how dying people cope with impending death and adjust and prepare for this inevitable event.

Elizabeth Kübler-Ross (1969), the famous psychiatrist and missionary for humanizing the dying process, identified five psychological stages of dying or ways of coping with one's impending death. Her formulations are based on interviews with terminal patients at a Chicago hospital. The five stages are as follows:

1. *Denial.* At this stage, the person refuses to believe. Kübler-Ross also calls it the "not me" stage. She describes how various individuals express denial. Some insist that X-rays or laboratory tests have gotten mixed up; others declare their doctors to be incompetent. This total denial as the initial reaction to the devastating realization of one's own death is thought to serve as a buffer allowing for time to absorb the shock of the news. According to Kübler-Ross, only very few patients deny to the very end. Most move on to the other states.

2. *Rage.* Now the message has been received and has registered, and the response is anger and fury. "Why me? What have I done to deserve

such misfortune? Why am I punished this way?" As Kübler-Ross points out, anybody near the patient can become the target of the patient's rage—physician, nurse, family, or friends.

3. *Bargaining*. The bargaining stage sets in when rage has exhausted the patient. Now the bartering begins. The patient may try to bargain with God: "Lord, just let me live long enough to celebrate my twentieth wedding anniversary, please." Or the patient may attempt to bargain with the physician, or the nurse. Kübler-Ross states that attempts at bargaining are often very subtle, but they are short-lived. When their futility is realized, the patient progresses to the next stage.

4. *Depression*. This stage has also been termed the stage of "anticipatory," or "preparatory," grief. The patient expresses sorrow for all that she he is about to lose—loved ones, experiences, self, possessions, the world. Kübler-Ross describes this as the silent stage. She believes that being able to experience depression will facilitate the final step.

5. *Acceptance*. Now the dying person has worked through the negative stages of denial, rage, bargaining, and depression and arrives at a point where he or she can "contemplate his coming end with a certain degree of quiet expectation" (p. 112). According to Kübler-Ross, this is also the time when the dying person may accept dying far better than the family does.

Kübler-Ross stresses over and over that medical personnel, members of the family, and friends can do much to help the dying person as she or he goes through the stages of dying, from denial to acceptance. Medical personnel should be honest and open with the patient, as should the family. They should all be sensitive to the dying person's frame of mind and try to understand the dynamics of the various stages the person goes through to cope with dying. For example, when the dying person at the stage of rage throws flowers and vases into the corner, rejecting the signs of goodwill, friends and family should not turn away hurt nor feel resentful but should bear with the person, recognizing that such behavior is "normal" for someone who is dying. Similarly, when the dying person at the stage of deep depression turns her or his back on loved ones and refuses to communicate, they should stay with the person and patiently wait till she or he comes around to the final stage of acceptance.

A number of thanatologists, also with much experience with terminal patients, have come up with descriptions that are at variance with the five-stage formulation by Kübler-Ross. One expert, the noted thanatologist Edwin Shneidman (1976), has raised the issue of the linear progression of the dying stages, wondering how a dying person makes the psychological leap from the four negative stages—denial, rage, bargaining, and depression—to the final, positive stage of acceptance. On the basis of his extensive work with terminal patients, Shneidman finds that, whereas dying people go through states of bargaining, depression, acceptance, and denial, these are not necessarily clearly definable stages of the dying process, nor do they necessarily occur in the order asserted by Kübler-Ross, or in any kind of order at all. Shneidman states:

> What I do see is a complicated clustering of intellectual and affective states, some fleeting, lasting for a moment or a day or a week, set . . . against the backdrop of that person's total personality, his philosophy of life. . . . There seems to be a constant coming and going. The emotional stages seem to include a constant interplay between disbelief and hope, a waxing and waning of anguish, taunting and daring and even yearning for death—all these in the context of bewilderment and pain. (pp. 446–447)

This position is supported by another authority in the field of death and dying, Avery Weisman (1972), who, in his book *On Dying and Denying*, discusses the complexities of the psychological states we term *acceptance* and *denial*. Weisman points out that there are degrees of denial, and that these degrees vary with the people with whom the terminal patient communicates. He also stresses that denial is so closely linked with a person's value system and self-esteem that when they are threatened, a person will immediately call upon denial to defend himself or herself and thus cope with the threat. On the other hand, Weisman points out that acceptance of one's own death does happen and is quite common among aged people, a phenomenon that is difficult for young people to understand. The possibility that one may not only accept death, but actually yearn and pray for death to come because one is tired of living, one's physical strength and vital energies have been depleted, one wishes to be released from pain, or simply, one's life has been fully lived and one is fulfilled is not readily comprehended by younger people, but there is much evidence to attest to the fact that many old, seriously ill, and even not too seriously ill people have such feelings.

DYING IN INSTITUTIONS

It has been established that most dying people want to die at home, but regardless of the dying person's wishes, in most instances, dying occurs in an institution rather than at home. In 1963, according to Robert Fulton (1964), 53% of all deaths in the United States occurred in hospitals and many more in nursing homes. A more recent estimate is that as many as 75% of Americans today die in a dying place, either a medical institution or a nursing home. Even though Kübler-Ross and others remember with nostalgia earlier times when most people died at home in their familiar environments with their loved ones around them, medical progress has advanced to a stage at which medical treatment and technical care can most efficiently be provided only in a hospital.

Dying in a Hospital

For this efficiency, patient and family pay a heavy price. In hospitals, families are typically subjected to restricted visiting regulations; these are most severely restricted when the patient has been admitted to an intensive care unit. Frequently, this means that terminal patients are lonely and family members are not with the loved one at the moment of death. At regional, metropolitan, or geriatric hospitals, according to Glaser and Strauss (1965), family visits are minimal even during visiting hours, either because family members live too far away or because they have already abandoned the patient (p. 157). Particularly when the patient is elderly and the process of dying is prolonged, relatives may spend little time at the bedside (p. 152).

Feifel, Kastenbaum, Glaser and Strauss, Kübler-Ross, and many other thanatologists have observed that, typically, physicians are reluctant to tell the patients they are terminal and open discussion between physicians and patients are infrequent. Various explanations have been offered for this omission. One explanation is that the information may disturb the patient. Another is that the patient may disturb other patients and disrupt hospital routine. Still another explanation given is that physicians often have difficulty accepting the fact that one of their patients is dying, viewing this as a professional failure. Yet another explanation is that physicians cannot cope with the reality of their own deaths and are therefore unable to talk to their dying patients. Whatever the reasons, the fact is that many patients are kept uninformed of their impending deaths. What happens frequently is what Glaser and Strauss (1965) have termed "the ritual drama of mutual pretense;" that is, physicians, nurses, patient, and family all know the patient is dying but keep up a facade of hope and confidence.

The *conspiracy of silence* occurs when medical staff and family have an implicit or explicit understanding to keep the patient uninformed, but the strategy all too often fails. As Kübler-Ross and other thanatologists have pointed out, most dying patients know at some point that they are dying. They find out in different ways. They check for external cues—a subtle difference in the nurse's behavior, a change in care activities, fewer and shorter visits from the physician, a move to a different room, or a curtain drawn around the bed. A number of patients apparently also experience internal signs; Kübler-Ross and others have reported cases in which dying people predicted the time of their dying with amazing accuracy. But some patients keep guessing, seeing a sign for hope one day, a contrary sign the next.

Many psychologists and psychiatrists view this as unfortunate and believe that honest and open discussion of a patient's prognosis with few exceptions helps rather than harms. For one thing, dying people may have some unfinished business to take care of, but more important, they need to be able to share their grief, dread, or fears with others so they can find the emotional support that will make their dying easier. Kübler-Ross is best known for her forceful support for openness with terminal patients.

Glaser and Strauss (1965, 1968) have done a most incisive piece of work in their structural and functional analysis of the hospital as a medical and social institution, and they have sharply pointed out how the organization affects the individual patient. David Sudnow (1970), in his article "Dying in a Public Hospital," gives a most disturbing account with appalling illustrations of how one particular county hospital copes with dying patients. One can only hope that there are not many such hospitals in operation. Levine and Scotch (1970), in an article "Dying as an Emerging Social Problem," further point at the dilemma presented by the bureaucratization and routinization of events in the hospital and how they lead to the dehumanization of dying. Apparently this is particularly true when the dying people are elderly. Robert Kastenbaum (1964) asked nurses to list priorities for saving lives when time and energy were limited, giving as choices as 21-year-old patient, an 80-year-old patient, and a pet dog. He discovered that the ratio of importance of the 21-year-old to the 80-year-old was greater than that of the 80-year-old to the dog.

Glaser and Strauss (1968) have noted that family visits to elderly, dying patients are minimal, and the deaths of elderly people do not create any fuss on the ward. Richard Kalish (1969) lists a number of factors that contribute to this lack of concern: The elderly people are no longer breadwinners, and are not valued as decision makers or advice givers; their activities and affiliations with their churches often diminish although their religiosity tends to become intensified. All this further underlines the negative attitude toward aging in our society, and the desperate need for change in attitude is obvious.

The Hospice

There are medical institutions, however, in which death is openly discussed. Called *hospices*, they are famous for their openness in dealing with death. The hospice movement began with St. Christopher's Hospice in London, England, founded in 1948 by Cicely Saunders. The term *hospice* dates back to the Middle Ages, when it was a place where hungry and tired pilgrims traveling in Europe were welcomed. Later, hospices expanded and became places for the elderly, for the poor, and for foundlings.

St. Christopher's Hospice welcomes not only the sick and poor, young and old, but specifically those who are dying. It is a place where dying people go to live out their final days, weeks, or months and receive *comfort care*, inasmuch as they are beyond curative treatment. It is also a place where families are assisted in learning to accept their loved one's dying and how to provide comfort care at home. In either case, the fact of dying is confronted and faced squarely by staff, families, and patients alike; and death is talked about by the dying people whenever they feel the need to talk about it. According to a number of acquaintances of the author who have visited this hospice, and according to Cicely Saunders's own description, St. Christopher's is a cheerful place, often noisy with playing children, often happy and joyful, with a climate of love, warmth, and caring. The motto is "death with dignity," and as Cicely Saunders stated at a recent conference at Yale University, St. Christopher's has no problem with machines that keep people alive artificially—they do not have any such devices. In addition, careful drug treatment for pain is given that avoids the necessity for sedation of patients. Often such ordinary things as beer, wine, or liquor are used as pain relievers. The interested reader will find a more detailed description of hospice philosophy, goals, and practices in Cicely Saunders's (1976) article "St. Christopher's Hospice" in Schneidman's (1976) book *Death: Current Perspectives* (pp. 516–523). The hospice movement has spread to the United States, where a hospice has been operating in New Haven, Connecticut, for several years; others are in various stages of development.

Nursing Homes

Unfortunately, the gentle and humane attitudes of the hospice movement are not characteristic of most of the institutions in which elderly people die. Certainly, this is the case with most nursing homes. The typical nursing home in the United States deserves neither the label "home" nor the label "nursing," for it is less homelike than many other institutions, and there is commonly no nurse at the home." Unfortunately, most state health agencies have minimal standards for licensing, inadequate supervision, and little control. In Florida, as in other states, probes into the nursing-home situation are conducted periodically. The reports usually contain long lists of deficiencies, severe reprimands by the investigation committee, and a list of urgent recommendations to the state health officials for alleviating the deficiencies. The press usually publicizes these reports, telling the public about the stench of urine, the filth, the disarray of medication, the poor food, the untrained staff of inadequate size, and the physical abuse of residents. The public is upset for a while, but nothing happens, and the typical nursing home stays about the same. It must be recognized that, in the United States, nursing homes are private business enterprises. In an inflationary economy, to make a good profit from their customers (usually with modest incomes) or from Medicare or Medicaid assistance from the state, owners have to curtail the quality of the services to the residents. Thus, the conditions in the typical nursing home are deplorable. For too many elderly, the last years or weeks of life are filled with terror. The reader interested in a detailed description of conditions in nursing homes is referred to the book by Garvin and Burger (1968), *Where They Go to Die: The Tragedy of America's Aged.*

In addition to being in such an environment, many patients are not visited by their families. In one of the nursing homes in which the author has worked, 90% of the residents have literally been abandoned by their families; that is, their families never visit, never write, and never make any inquiries to the nursing-home staff as to the health status and general well-being of their aged relatives. Fortunately, there are many dedicated volunteers, church or civic groups and college students, who visit these abandoned people at the nursing home and alleviate some of their loneliness and sadness. Fortunate also is the fact that only a small percentage of our elderly population lives in nursing homes; most are able to avoid it.

The U.S. Department of Health, Education, and Welfare has published a booklet titled *Nursing Home Care* (available from Consumer Product Information, Pueblo, CO 80119). A list of questions developed from this booklet has been published in *McCall's,* May 1974. These questions constitute a set of criteria for good nursing-home care and may be valuable in assisting those who need to select a nursing home for themselves or for an aged relative. An abbreviated list of these questions follows.

1. Are halls, rooms, beds, and kitchens neat and clean?
2. Are there offensive odors in the home?
3. Is the atmosphere friendly?
4. Do ambulatory patients have enough to do? Are there crafts, games, television, movies, books? Do they get enough exercise? Do they get outside enough? Is there an organized activities program?
5. Is a bedridden patient turned at least every two hours to prevent bedsores?
6. Does each bed have a nurse-call system? Do staff members respond quickly to calls for assistance? Are staff members neat in dress and cheerful with patients?
7. Are patients neat in appearance, with nails clipped and hair cut? Do they have fresh water at their bedsides? Do they dine together, communicate with one another?
8. Are licenses, membership certificates and diplomas posted? A home with no license, or an expired one, should not be considered.
9. Is a plan for evacuation in case of fire or other emergency posted? Are the floors nonskid? Are there handrails in the hallways and grab bars in bathtubs, showers, and near toilets?
10. Are meals nutritious and attractive? Does the home have a dietician or trained food-service supervisor?
11. Does the home have an entrance contract requiring patients to sign over their possessions to the home? If you sign such a contract, make sure there is a provision for return of property after care has ended.
12. Is there a staff physician? May a patient have his or her own physician? Are patients seen by a doctor at least once a month? Does a patient get a physical examination within 48 hours of

admission? Are medical charts maintained on all patients? Is emergency medical care available? Are there rehabilitation and physical-therapy programs? Does the home have arrangements with one or more general hospitals for care of its patients?

To grow old in the United States is often, as we have seen, an emotional experience of pain brought about by the loss of social prestige and the personal loss of attractiveness to others, which frequently result in a negative self-concept and a low sense of worth. But to be old *and* poor in the United States is sheer misery. There are of course excellent nursing homes in this country, but their waiting lists are long or their prices high, so that many old people with modest retirement incomes cannot afford such homes. It can be seen here, as in the discussion of hospitals, that changes need to be made so that all old people have an opportunity to live out their lives and die in dignity.

IMPLICATIONS FOR DEATH EDUCATION

One inevitable conclusion from the foregoing discussion is that people in this country must become more knowledgeable, and hence change their attitudes, about death and dying. This presents a major challenge to education. About two million people die each year in the United States, and it is high time that the general public take notice, but merely taking notice is not enough. We must become informed about the facts of death and must learn to recognize and accept our own finiteness. To change the perceptions, misperceptions, and denial mechanisms of an entire society is no simple matter. It will take time, concerted effort, and a long-range view on the part of educators and educational institutions and agencies. Fortunately, this country has knowledgeable, articulate, and dedicated leaders in thanatology and death education. Their efforts have led to encouraging beginnings. It is obvious that in order to bring about a change in society's attitude toward death and to offer scientific information about death and dying, death education must occur at various levels of society and through a variety of means. The clients for death education should be children and youth, parents, teachers, administrators, health care professionals, scientists, clergy, counselors, and, last but not least, old people.

Discussing Death with Old People

Over the last decade or two, the issues of aging in the United States have been brought to the foreground, and—through concerted efforts of government and private funding agencies and senior citizens organizations—health, nutrition, social, recreational, and educational programs for old people have sprung up throughout the country. This development is most encouraging. It offers old people basic care as well as opportunities to stay active and involved. Educational programs span a wide range from defensive driving to ceramics. Along with these activity programs, catchy slogans have come into being, such as "the Golden Oldies," "On Top of the World," "You are not getting older; you are getting better," and "Add years to your life and life to your years." New concepts such as *recycling* and *career retraining* for senior citizens have added an air of respectability to many programs, and so has the rediscovered concept of *lifelong learning.*

Despite the wealth of programs now in full swing, the author has not found one that deals with the subject of death and dying. It seems there is a light-headed triviality about many of these programs and a false innocence and pretense that actually promote the denial of death with old people. Therefore, in addition to basic health, nutrition, and other educational programs, and in addition to shuffleboard and sing-alongs, there should be opportunities for serious discussions about death and dying conducted by qualified people. From findings reported on the previous pages, the effect of such discussions would, in most instances, not lead to depression, as is generally believed. On the contrary, by allowing for open expression of the thoughts and feelings old people experience near the ends of their lives, and by fostering the sharing of feelings, fear and dread concerning death will actually be reduced. Open and honest talk sessions about death would put other activities in proper perspective. The author is convinced that it would make daily living more meaningful for old people.

To bring about such open discussion we need to first convince the experts on aging to accept the fact of death. In a recent survey by the author (Wass & Scott, 1977) it was shown that of 48 scientific and textual books on aging written by nationally and internationally known authorities in the area of gerontology, 65% of the books devote less than 1% of their space to discussion of death and dying, 90% devote less than 5% to the topic. It is as if the writers pretended that there is aging without death.

There are many possible approaches to death education, and methods, materials, and techniques will vary depending on the specific nature of the clients. Regardless of obvious variabilities, however, the following broad, fundamental objectives for death education in all levels are suggested:

1. Learning the basic facts of death and dying
2. Coming to terms with the reality of death
3. Learning to live with the fact of death
4. Being able to care for and help the dying

These objectives in no way interfere with any religious orientations a person may have. They are long-range objectives that cannot be expected to be attained in one discussion session on death. They deal with both knowledge and feelings, and they cannot all be "taught" in the traditional sense of the word. All objectives, if achieved, have positive consequences that would prevent most if not all of the unhappy experiences and conditions described earlier.

REFERENCES

Allport, G. W. *Pattern and growth in personality*. New York: Holt, 1961.
Ariès, P. *Western attitudes toward death*. Baltimore: Johns Hopkins University Press, 1974.
Becker, E. *The denial of death*. New York: Free Press, 1973.
Birren, J. E. *The psychology of aging*. Englewood Cliffs: Prentice-Hall, 1964.
Brim, O., Freeman, H. E., Levine, S., & Scotch, N. A. (Eds.). *The dying patient*. New York: Russell Sage Foundation, 1970.
Butler, R. N. The life review: An interpreation of reminiscence in the aged. *Psychiatry*, 1963, *26*(1), 65–76.
de Beauvoir, S. *The coming of age*. New York: Warner, 1973. (a)
de Beauvoir, S. *A very easy death*. New York: Warner, 1973. (b)
Erikson, E. H. *Growth and crises of the healthy personality*. In *Symposium on the Healthy Personality*. New York: Josiah Macy, Jr., Foundation, 1950.
Erikson, E. H. Identity and the life cycle: Selected papers. *Psychological Issues*, 59, *1*, 1–171.
Erikson, E. H. *Childhood and society*, (2nd ed.). New York: Norton, 1963.
Euthanasia Educational Council. Personal communication, June 8, 1976.
Feifel, H. Attitudes toward death in older persons: A symposium. *Journal of Gerontology*, 1961, *16*, 64–66.
Feifel, H. (Ed.). *The meaning of death*. New York: McGraw-Hill, 1959.
Fulton, R. Death and self. *Journal of Religion and Health*, 1964, *3*, 364.
Gavin, R. M., & Burger, R. E. *Where they go to die: The tragedy of America's aged*. New York: Delacorte, 1968.
Glaser, B. G., & Strauss, A. L. *Awareness of dying*. Chicago, Aldine, 1965.
Glaser, B. G., & Strauss, A. L. *Time for dying*. Chicago: Aldine, 1968.
Gorer, G. *Death, grief, and mourning*. New York: Anchor, 1965.
Heifetz, M. D., with Mangel, C. *The right to die*. New York: Berkley, 1975.
Hendin, D. *Death as a fact of life*. New York: Norton, 1973.
Hinton, J. M. Facing death. *Journal of Psychosomatic Research*, 1966, *10*, 22–28.
Hinton, J. M. *Dying*. Baltimore: Penguin, 1967.
Jeffers, F., Nichols, C., & Eisdorfer, C. Attitudes of older persons toward death. *Journal of Gerontology*, 1961, *16*(1), 53.
Kalish, R. A. The effects of death upon the family. In L. Learson (Ed.), *Death and dying: Current issues in the treatment of the dying person*. Cleveland: The Press of Case Western Reserve University, 1969, pp. 79–107.
Kastenbaum, R. Cognitive and personal futurity in later life. *Journal of Individual Psychology*, 1963, *19*(2), 216–222.
Kastenbaum, R. *The interpersonal context of death in geriatric institutions*.

Paper presented at the 17th annual meeting of the Gerontological Society, Minneapolis, October 29–31, 1964.

Kastenbaum, R. The mental life of dying geriatric patients. *The Gerontologist,* June 1967, Pt. 1, 97–100.

Kimsey, L., Roberts, J. L., & Logan, D. L. Death, dying, and denial in the aged. *American Journal of Psychiatry,* 1972, *129*(2), 161–166.

Kübler-Ross, E. *On death and dying.* New York: Macmillan, 1969.

Levine, S., & Scotch, N. A. Dying as an emerging social problem. In O. G. Brim, H. E. Freeman, S. Levine, & N. A. Scotch (Eds.), *The dying patient.* New York: Russell Sage Foundation, 1970, pp. 211–224.

Lieberman, M. A., & Coplan, A. S. Distance from death as a variable in the study of aging. *Developmental Psychology,* 1969, *2*(1), 71–84.

Mannes, M. *Last rights—A case for the good death.* New York: Morrow, 1974.

Marcuse, H. The ideology of death. In H. Feifel (Ed.), *The meaning of death.* New York: McGraw-Hill, 1959.

Marshall, J. R. The geriatric patient's fears about death. *Postgraduate Medicine,* 1975, *57*(4), 144–149.

Maslow, A. H. *Toward a psychology of being,* (2nd ed.). New York: D. Van Nostrand, 1968.

Mathieu, J., & Peterson, J. A. *Some psychological dimensions of aging.* Paper presented at the 23rd Annual Meeting of the Gerontological Society, Ontario, October 21–24, 1970.

Matse, J. Reactions to death in residential homes for the aged. *Omega,* 1975, *6*(1), 21–32.

Mitford, J. *The American way of death,* Greenwich, Conn.: Fawcett, 1963.

Peck, R., Psychological development in the second half of life. In J. E. Anderson (Ed.), *Psychological aspects of aging.* Washington, D.C.: American Psychological Association, 1956.

Rhudick, P. J., & Dibner, A. S. Age, personality, and health correlates of death concern in normal aged individuals. *Journal of Gerontology* 1961, *16*(11), 44–49.

Richardson, A. H., & Freeman, H. E., Attitudes toward death. In M. W. Riley & A. Foner (Eds.), *Aging and society (Vol. 1: An inventory of research findings).* New York: Russell Sage Foundation, 1968.

Riley, J. W. Attitudes toward death. In M. W. Riley & A. Foner (Eds.), *Aging and society, (Vol. 1: An inventory of research findings).* New York: Russell Sage Foundation, 1968.

Roberts, J. L., Kimsey, L., Logan, D. L., & Shaw, G. How aged in nursing homes view death and dying. *Geriatrics,* April 1970, *25*, 115–119.

Roemer, M. (Producer). *Dying* (documentary film). Boston: WGBH, aired by PBS-TV, May 1976.

Roose, L. J. To die alone. *Mental Hygiene,* 1969, *53*(3), 321–326.

Saul, S. R., & Saul, S., Old people talk about death. *Omega* 1973, *4*(1), 27–35.

Saunders, C. The moment of truth: Care of the dying person. In L. Pearson (Ed.), *Death and dying. Current issues in the treatment of the dying person.* Cleveland: The Press of Case Western Reserve University, 1969, 49–78.

Saunders, C. St. Christopher's Hospice. In E. Shneidman (Ed.). *Death: Current perspectives.* Palo Alto: Mayfield, 1976, pp. 516–523.

Saunders, C. The last stages of life. In M. H. Browning and E. P. Lewis (Eds.), *The dying patient: A nursing perspective.* New York: The American Journal of Nursing, 1972, pp. 247–256.

Shneidman, E. S. You and death. *Psychology Today,* June 1971, pp. 43ff.

Shneidman, E. S. (Ed.), *Death: Current perspectives.* Palo Alto: Mayfield, 1976.

Shrut, S. D. Attitudes toward old age and death. *Mental Hygiene,* 1958, *42,* 259–266.

Spark, M. *Momento mori.* New York: Avon, 1959.

Sudnow, D. Dying in a public hospital. In O. G. Brim, H. E. Freeman, S. Levine, & N. A. Scotch (Eds.), *The dying patient.* New York: Russell Sage Foundation, 1970, pp. 191–208.

Swenson, W. M. Attitudes toward death in an aged population. *Journal of Gerontology,* 1961, *16*(1), 49–52.

Templer, D., Death anxiety as related to depression and health of retired persons. *Journal of Gerontology,* 1971, *26*(4), 521–523.

Thanatology. *Time Magazine,* November 20, 1964, p. 95.

Tolstoy, L. *The death of Ivan Ilych and other stories.* New York: New American Library, 1960.

Toynbee, A. (Ed.). *Man's concern with death.* New York: McGraw-Hill, 1968.

Wass, H. Public opinion concerning funeral practices. *Florida Funeral Director,* 1976, *42*(3), 5–6; 16.

Wass, H. Views and opinions of elderly persons concerning death. *Educational Gerontology,* 1977, *2*(1), 15–26.

Wass, H., Milton, C., Myers, J., & Murphey, M. Similarities and dissimilarities in attitudes toward death in a population of older persons. *Omega,* in press.

Wass, H., & Scott, M. Aging without death? *The Gerontologist,* 1977, *17*(4), 377–380.

Wass, H. & Sisler, H. Death concern and views on various aspects of dying among elderly persons. Paper presented at the International Symposium on the Dying Human, Tel Aviv, Israel, January 15–20, 1978.

Waugh E., *The loved one.* New York: Dell, 1948.

Weisman, A., *On dying and denying.* New York: Behavioral Publications, 1972.

Wolff, K. The problem of death and dying in the geriatric patient. *Journal of the American Geriatrics Society,* 1970, *18*(02), 954–961.

INDEX